The Routledge Reader on Writing Centers and New Media

This collection of essays appears on the wave of digital media tutoring developments in university and college writing centers in the United States and around the world. It provides students and scholars of literacy, new media, and communication as well as writing center practitioners with a valuable new tool for understanding the progress and direction of new media debates at the intersection of writing, technology, and communication.

Comprised of nineteen essays by leading scholars in media, communication, composition, and writing center studies, *The Routledge Reader on Writing Centers and New Media* is a major new reader that provides rich cross-disciplinary scholarship. As a resource for students and scholars, and as a sourcebook for writing center practitioners, this collection fills a critical gap in writing center scholarship that is essential and significant for the emerging practice of new media tutoring and for future developments in writing center studies.

Sohui Lee is the former Associate Director of the Hume Writing Center and the founder of its Digital Media Program. She teaches in the Program in Writing and Rhetoric at Stanford University and publishes in visual and digital communication, writing pedagogy, and writing center issues.

Russell Carpenter is the Director of the Noel Studio for Academic Creativity and Assistant Professor of English at Eastern Kentucky University. He has published widely on the use of technology in writing centers.

D0923780

The Routledge Reader on Writing Centers and New Media

EDITED BY
Sohui Lee and Russell Carpenter

NEW YORK AND LONDON

First published 2014
by Routledge
711 Third Avenue, New York, NY 10017

Simultaneously published in the UK
by Routledge
2 Park Square, Milton Park, Abingdon, Oxon OX14 4RN

Routledge is an imprint of the Taylor & Francis Group, an informa business

Library of Congress Cataloging in Publication Data
The Routledge reader on writing centers and new media / edited by Sohui Lee, Russell G. Carpenter.
    pages cm
    1. English language—Rhetoric—Study and teaching—United States—Computer network resources.
    2. English language—Rhetoric—Computer-assisted instruction. 3. Mass media and education.
    4. Writing centers—Automation. 5. Media programs (Education) I. Lee, Sohui.
    II. Carpenter, Russell G., 1979–
    PE1408.R755 2013
    808'.0427—dc23
    2013023320

ISBN: 978–0–415–63445–8 (hbk)
ISBN: 978–0–415–63446–5 (pbk)

Typeset in Minion Pro
by Swales & Willis Ltd, Exeter, Devon

Printed and bound in the United States of America by
Edwards Brothers, Inc. Lillington, North Carolina

To James, Iain, and Auden. –SL

To Barbie, Kendall, and Baxter. –RC

Contents

List of Figures

Acknowledgements

We are grateful to our institutions, Stanford University and Eastern Kentucky University, for their support of a project of this size and scope. We are particularly indebted to Stanford University's Program in Writing and Rhetoric for the Research Award, which helped to fund the research for this collection, as well as to Andrea Lunsford for writing the Foreword.

We are also thankful to the following publishers and journals for their permission to reprint their chapters and articles in this edition: University of Chicago Press, MIT Press, Harvard Educational Review, *Writing Center Journal*, Oxford University Press, Cambridge University Press, National Council of Teachers of English (NCTE), Penguin, *Writing Lab Newsletter*, and Hampton Press. Our thanks are extended to Georgette Enriquez and the Routledge editorial staff for their support in launching this book.

S. Lee & R. Carpenter

Foreword

Andrea A. Lunsford

Late in the fall of 2000, I got a phone call every WPA dreams of: it was the Vice Provost's office, asking if I could meet to talk about "that writing center idea you had." Stanford didn't have a writing center, a fact I had bemoaned when I accepted the invitation to join the faculty earlier that year, but I hadn't expected an opportunity to appear so very quickly. But luck was on our side, and several drafts of a proposal later, we had a document ready to present to the Vice Provost and George and Leslie Hume, the prospective donors for whom our Center is now named. I recall the coming months vividly: Marvin Diogenes had joined our Program in the summer, and we began planning in earnest. A space miraculously appeared (an old science lab, full of sinks and stools nailed to the floor—in the basement of our building but available) and so we set to work to transform it into our own vision of a center. Corinne Arraez, our Academic Technology Specialist, played a key role in design. With a strong sense of our needs and a flair for style and design, she turned that musty old lab into what we thought of at the time as a state of the art writing center, complete with individual tutorial carrels, space for group tutorials and meetings, "soft" furniture for students to lounge about on while working, a small but useable performance space, bookcases to hold our small library, and brand new computers that ringed two weight-bearing and otherwise useless columns in the center of the center's space, and smart panel, projector, and screen. Corinne and Marvin and I (and lots of others) worked feverishly through the summer months to ready our center for opening in fall, 2001.

That was the fall of 9/11, of course, and in the wake of that devastation the university had made plans to begin school later than usual in case students weren't able to get there for our late September opening. Eventually we opened on time, and we rallied to welcome the class of 2005, many of whom arrived still in states of shock. During parents' weekend in February of 2002, the mother of one student who was to become closely associated with the Center, read a letter she had written a few days after 9/11 as she was driving her daughter through the Caldecott tunnel toward Stanford, wondering if they would make it and experiencing more than usual the pangs of leaving a beloved daughter at a new and unfamiliar school.

So the atmosphere on campus that fall was charged—with anxiety as well as exhilaration, with the pain of loss as well as the hope of possibility. In that atmosphere, we launched our Center on October 30, 2011, with our President, Provost, Vice Provost, and all Deans in attendance. Each spoke briefly but memorably about the role of writing in their lives—and we were off! The first week we advertised a workshop for 25: 55 appeared, a sign that, yes, if you build it, they will come. And come they have: when we celebrated the Hume Writing Center's 10th anniversary, we could report on a decade that saw number of tutorials grow from 700 in those first two quarters to 7000 this last year. We have done hundreds upon hundreds of workshops, held countless performances and special events, and worked as hard as possible to build and sustain a culture of writing at our university.

But we have not been satisfied. The work of our center (and yours) has paralleled a vast sea change in writing, what I think of as the biggest literacy revolution the world has ever seen. Writing is now no longer (if it ever truly was) words on paper or screen. Rather, writing now is literally electrified, encompassing all manner and modes of communication, mixing and remixing genres and bringing in the aural/oral as well as the visual at every turn. Thus we began, after some years of ongoing growth, to realize that what once seemed state of the art seemed much less so now. We spoke of taking our center to "the next level" and wished for more space and more resources. We began to offer services to students working to transform written essays into oral performances, and from there we began to train ourselves and our tutors to offer help with multimedia and/or new media projects as well. This work has proceeded, as my grandmother used to say, slowly … but slowly. But just recently we learned that the our center will move into more centrally located and slightly larger quarters sometime before too long, and we have formed a partnership with our outstanding Oral Communication Tutorial program. We see pretty clearly where we want to go … now we have to find a way to get there.

Our vision of what the "next level" of writing center work can be has been shaped by Eastern Kentucky's Noel Studio for Academic Creativity, which houses a "center for invention" along with a presentation Center, a research center (with real live librarians), and a discovery seminar room. This is a center with big ambitions, as its expanded title and services indicate. It marks the way, in my mind, for the direction writing centers need to move, with all deliberate speed, if we are to meet the needs of today's college students. We have also had other models to learn from: Texas Christian has a New Media Writing Studio to complement its writing center; Iowa State's Writing and Media Help Center works with their Written, Oral, Visual, and Electronic Communication Program (WOVE); Michigan State's Writing Center advertises services including one-to-one consulting; creative writing consulting; digital media consulting; workshops; writing groups; multimedia productions; Agnes Scott's center focuses on speaking as well as writing; as does the outstanding center at Mount Holyoke, and Clemson not only has a writing center housed in the English Department but the very successful Pearce Center for Professional Communication and its associated Class of 1941 Studio for Student Communication. These centers—and their new ways of naming themselves and identifying the work they do—mark a key moment in writing center history, as writing becomes multimodal, multimedia, multilingual, and multivocal and as writing centers move to adapt to students' shifting communicative needs.

The editors of this volume, who have been instrumental in shaping and building the centers at Stanford and Eastern Kentucky, help to capture this key moment and point the way to the future as they outline the role writing centers can play in an age of new media along with what a state of the art center can look like well into the second decade of the twenty-first century. In doing so, they have drawn on and learned from the group of significant landmark essays presented here. Beginning with Dick Lanham's prescient "Digital Rhetoric and the Digital Arts," a chapter in his 1993 *The Electronic Word,* and proceeding through a who's who of writers on new media, Lee and Carpenter begin very broadly before homing in on writing centers and multimodal, new media connections. The last three essays in the volume focus specifically on the shifting role of tutors and tutoring in the late age of print, on creating a broad-based center for communicative design, and on "multiliteracy consulting." This volume thus speaks to the needs of writing centers across the country and, increasingly, around the world that are struggling to reconsider their missions, to expand their services, and to support student writers whose compositions are increasingly digital and multimodal. These essays will also speak to every director of such a center as well as to those who staff the centers and, perhaps more to the point, those who fund them.

It's been highly instructive and pleasurable to read these essays in chronological order, to follow the path they carve out along the exciting and often frustrating route from print to digital literacies. Lee and Carpenter have shaped a set of essays that ably map that terrain. Readers can now join the fun and the fray.

May 21, 2012. Stanford, CA.

Introduction

Navigating Literacies in Multimodal Spaces

Sohui Lee and Russell Carpenter

In 1993, the World Wide Web was made public and graphically accessible for the first time. It was also the year Richard A. Lanham published *The Electronic Word*. For Lanham, digitization of writing was not only about the electronic mode of writing through the computer. It introduced a radically new and expressive rhetoric, whose "motival structure ... differ[s] from that of print" (84). This rhetoric was "new" in the way that it shaped our style of writing, changing the ratio of icon and alphabetic text. Moreover, it was new in the "interactive" possibilities that reshape reading and writing behavior. Today, the concepts that Lanham introduced are pivotal for scholars of digital media and composition. Lanham's work is one of many landmark essays that contribute to our understanding of digital composition theory and literacies. The writing, reading, and sharing of digital and multimodal texts is, as Cooper (2007) writes, "inescapable" (181); and digital literacies are being included in student learning outcome goals in a growing number of university courses across the nation.

This shift toward digital literacies is registered not only in the composition classroom but also in a growing number of writing centers. For convenience, we use the term "writing centers" to identify traditional writing centers as well as communication centers and studios that offer their center as a campus resource for oral, visual, and multimodal communication across the curriculum. As a new media reader for writing center administrators and scholars, this book stands as a testimony to the critical role of new media in transforming and, in some ways, reviving the importance of writing centers in colleges and universities. *The Routledge Reader on Writing Centers and New Media* attempts to generate new and timely conversation that occurs within writing centers, taking into account a variety of social, cultural, and political factors that shape how we write and communicate today. Our book adds rhetorical, technological, and multidisciplinary perspectives from the past like Lanham's to the existing body of literature in writing centers. In creating this collection, we hope to encourage new directions for future writing center practice as well as support the growing academic interest in multimodal composition that are central to writing and communicating in our digital age.

For years, scholars and practitioners in the writing center field have debated the role of technology, and now new media, within our spaces and the work we do. Many of our concepts and theories are built on scholarly work in composition but also fields such as media studies, communication, and cognitive science. We have assembled writing center literature alongside key readings in new media and placed them in relation to one another so that readers can read historically or thematically in order to identify intersections, overlaps, gaps, and opportunities.

In fact, this book emerged out of intersections and opportunities. In 2010, the International Writing Centers Association (IWCA) held its conference in Baltimore with a theme that invited participants to reflect on writing centers as a harbor, a place of shelter but also a place of opportunity to explore writing. Indeed, for us, the theme proved powerful, not only in terms of how students take "shelter" in our spaces and discover through writing centers, but also how the institution itself might explore digital and multimodal writing in tutor training and practices. Andrea Lunsford set the tone for the IWCA conference during her keynote address, by declaring that we are living in a historical moment—marking a critical time of change for writing but also a key moment in writing center history. Meeting over dinner with Andrea following her speech, we were excited by her vision of new media in writing centers, and our conversations developed into the idea for this book. While a few centers like the Sweetland Center for Writing at the University of Michigan supported students working on digital media compositions for many years, most writing and learning centers are only recently considering how they will offer tutorials for students creating multimodal arguments. We both felt that writing center scholars and practitioners needed a shared reference point of scholarship to help them improve their understanding of new media writing and launch new media tutoring initiatives at their centers.

This collection acknowledges the many years of excellent writing center scholarship but also foregrounds the need for connecting our research with other fields that have explored how new media shapes communication. In that way, this book extends existing scholarship while creating space for emerging conversations. Moreover, we owe this collection to the ways in which students create and communicate in the 21st century. Thus, we see this move to new media as a necessary one, driven by the students we tutor.

Finally, this book helps readers explore whether (and to what degree) tutoring new media is new. In fact, there are and will be many similarities with tutoring old media and well as some fundamental differences. However, as the essays in this collection may reveal, digital communication asks us to rethink our traditional conceptions of writing, authorship, and audiences. We encourage readers to explore these essential developments in writing center theory through the chapters that follow. At the same time, we encourage readers to join us in reflecting on the important ways that language is experienced in a multimodal or digital environment.

Objectives of this Book

This collection is shaped by three major interrelated objectives, each of which aims to significantly enrich the theoretical foundations for understanding new media to further multimodal practices in writing centers.

An Interdisciplinary Lens: While readings in our collection primarily come from composition and writing center theory about new media, these theories are shaped by their conversations with scholars from a range of disciplines. Thus, we include in our collection a selection of works that encourage readers to see the interdisciplinary nature of new media and the

movement of these ideas across time and fields. This historical focus emphasizes the identification of trends and developments of new media ideas that are seeded in computer science, education, and new media studies and cross-pollinate in the fields of composition and
writing center studies since the 90s. Our hope, moreover, is that the path of cross-pollination
will flow in only one direction—that this book will help writing center studies generate its
own knowledge through research and its unique opportunities for pedagogic application
and practice and that it will contribute significantly to written, oral, visual, and multimodal
studies as a whole.

Rhetorical Theories of New Media in Writing Centers: The second objective of this collection is to provide readings that will inspire writing center administrators and students new to
the field to deepen their perspective and understanding of rhetorical theories of new media.
Key issues and debates on new media in the field of writing center studies and composition
can point to productive tensions that encourage further discussions among tutors, administrators, and scholars. To achieve our objective, we include chapters that explore and test the
boundaries of new media composition. These chapters include essays by authors such as Lev
Manovich as well as works by composition scholars like Cynthia Selfe that prompt readers to
raise pressing questions related to current and future writing practices.

Pedagogical Value: Finally, we hope that the readings will provide theoretical grounding. The literature in this book can help writing centers become more comfortable with
new media composition and take risks by thinking of "remediating" tutoring practices. Not
only can tutors reflect on digital media writing as combining old practices with new, but
whether new media tutoring is "refashioning" traditional approaches or whether it imagines
an entirely new paradigm of aesthetic, rhetorical, or communication principles. We provide
an important pedagogical feature called "Reading Connections" to help tutors and scholars
reflect critically and rhetorically on the readings. Our "Reading Connections," found at the
end of this Introduction, clusters chapters as they relate and engage one another through
dialogue on specific topics, especially as they pertain to writing center theory or work. The
themes are:

- Digital and Visual Expression and Technology
- Fractal Structure of New Media
- Multimodal Learning and Multiliteracies
- Communities of Practice
- Infrastructure of New Media Writing and Writing Centers
- New Media Tutor Training

These texts are particularly generative when read together and may further conversations on
writing issues in writing center spaces. We hope, too, that these readings will provide practical guidance for thinking about approaches to new media writing.

Finally, this collection asks readers to take this moment to look both to our history and
our future, reconsidering not only what new media composition looks like in the writing
center now but also what the writing center may look like in the future through the lens of
new media. In a sense, we hope to provide writing center practitioners and students of writing with a new knowledge base, complementary to foundations in rhetoric and composition.
The Routledge Reader on Writing Centers and New Media encourages readers to consider
fundamental questions such as:

- What is new media "writing"?
- How do we communicate in multiple modes and how shall we tutor new media compositions?
- What do writing or communication center spaces look like now, and what should they look like in the future?

We expect that our readers will situate their writing center work within the context of these readings, including challenges, successes, interests, and failures. While moving the conversation forward, we hope that readers will also take this opportunity to situate their work within the rhetoric and composition literature, along with foundational concepts of writing center work—higher-order-concerns, lower-order-concerns, editing, and overall tutoring approaches.

What Is New Media?

While defined and discussed in different ways by different fields, new media for writing centers and writing programs refers to the cultural objects that, as Manovich (2001) explains further in Chapter 2 of this collection, use digital technologies for distribution of information, communication, and data. It also encompasses the digital data and communication—from video to applications (apps) on cell phones. We might see new media as a mix of "old" media (visual reality and human experience) and "new" media (interactive forms of communication technology). It encourages collaboration and creation. New media involves the design of digital data. It means that consumers are also producers who can create, collaborate, and share content. The readings in this book are meant to help readers explore the meaning of new media and its ramifications for the future of digital composition.

While most of us agree with the assumption that writing comes in many modes and media, writing centers have mostly followed the trends in the writing field led by composition studies. One reason writing center practitioners were slower to address multimodal composition might lie in the very practical nature of our institutions: our student "clients" bring in university or college assignments in traditional print-based writing forms. However, across disciplines and beyond the composition classroom, more university courses are asking students to use technology in the design of their communication products, signaling a radical shift—shaped by our digital culture—from writing in print-based environments to visual and multimodal environments. While scholars like Bolter and Lanham discussed early on how the composing process moves beyond the printed word, writing centers are only now addressing how to support the academic and personal student projects that involve modes and media including videos, audio files, slideshow design, and electronic portfolios. As more and more students are required to design digital ethnographies, electronic portfolios, and moving visual displays in addition to PowerPoint presentations, YouTube videos, and websites, writing centers will be asked to respond to these texts and provide a sounding board for student and staff skill development in multiliteracies.

Multiliteracies in Multiple Disciplines

A discussion of new media in the writing center inevitably involves an exploration of "multiliteracies," a term coined by the New London Group (1996) in the article presented in

Chapter 3. The New London Group suggests the teaching of all representations of meaning including linguistic, visual, audio, spatial, gestural, and multimodal. While the New London Group had the classroom in mind, we believe that writing and communication centers must also respond to the needs of students designing 21st-century communication, which involves attention to the production of writing, images, audio, and multimodal information.

In addition to exploring the range of representational possibilities, writing centers working with new media will also discover that their practice of multimodal tutoring, though similar to practices in composition studies, also have some important differences. While we find that rhetorical concepts such as audience and context can be applied across modes (Griffin, 2007), multimodal assignments in composition classrooms usually ask students to reflect on elements of rhetoric, the needs of audiences, and the appeals of argument. Multimodal assignments created for different fields are designed with learning goals that may prioritize clarity and lessons in the discipline. As writing in the sciences differs from humanities in genre, style, and form, we may discover that our support of multimodal communication across disciplines will be shaped by the nuanced needs of the field. If we neglect these disciplinary differences, we risk the danger of being perceived as only humanistic in our approach (with our uniform application of "rhetoric") and providing material that is too general and not relevant to the other disciplines. This is not to say that concerns of rhetoric cannot apply to multimodal assignments across disciplines; however, writing centers may find themselves not only expanding on existing theories but also generating a new field of practice in multimodal communication that reflects the unique practice of writing center professionals in attending to the broader communication needs of academics and students.

Tutoring Multimodal Texts

Digital media tutoring, like traditional tutoring of writing, is context specific and depends on the writing center's size, staffing, and resources. Although every writing center differs, we believe that writing centers can offer tutorials in digital media composition by building on prior knowledge and existing pedagogical approaches to writing tutorials. The following are some general tutorial concepts that writing centers might use or adapt for their own particular needs. Writing centers might use these as "starter concepts," which can be shaped and refined by what they take from the readings in this collection.

What are digital media tutors? Like writing tutors, digital media tutors work with students to help them develop and improve the persuasive quality of the argument shaped by mode, genre, and audience. Many writing centers that offer digital media consultation services provide trained digital media tutors who can address arguments that are represented in singular or multiple modes—but more importantly, modes other than the traditional alphabetic form of writing. Thus, tutors might help students who visit with projects that, alongside the written mode, heavily emphasize visual and aural arguments such as PowerPoint or Keynote slides, print or web advertisements, videos, podcasts, and websites.

Digital media tutors (peer, graduate students, professionals, or full time-teachers) work with students in a one-to-one or group consultation to discuss students' multimodal composition in any stage of the process. As modes change in student composition, so will the nature of the tutorial itself. Instead of "outlines" of essays, students may bring in storyboards of their PowerPoint presentation or video project for tutors to look at. Instead of "reading" the revised essay, the tutor may be "watching" the animation or "listening" to an audio narrative.

The issue of tutor knowledge and training is one of the most hotly debated areas for tutoring new media composition. Each institution will have to consider its own constraints of human and electronic resources, but the readings can provide direction and serve as a guide for how this issue is being explored. Most institutions range from requiring digital media tutors to having no knowledge of technology and software to working knowledge and finally to possessing expertise in technology and software.

Although debated by some, the pedagogical principles of digital media tutors at a writing or multiliteracy center are usually similar to those of print-based tutors: they are "coaches and collaborators, not teachers" (Harris, 2011). Although some individual consultants may have expertise in software programs, digital media consultations are usually described as offering feedback on the "rhetoric" or the persuasive quality and/or effectiveness of a digital or multimodal project. These consultants help students explore the "what" and "why" of the project, rather than the "how" of technical production. Like writing tutors, digital media tutors engage the writer in conversations about their ideas and the composition process using a range of non-directive and directive strategies appropriate for the tutorial situation.

Recommendations for Digital Media Consultation Programs: Many writing centers work under the premise that rhetoric is the foundational communication theory underlying the principles of digital media tutoring. Digital media tutors are trained to understand rhetorical principles regarding audience, context, and appeal strategies and how they are complicated by different or multiple modes. Institutions, however, might prioritize the principles differently. For instance, digital media tutors at University of Michigan emphasize the acronym MAPS (Mode, Audience, Purpose, and Situation) when discussing digital form. Stanford University's Hume Writing Center and Eastern Kentucky University's Noel Studio, by contrast, do not promote a unified rule for discussing digital or visual genres, but instead draw attention to design principles such as focalization, salience, and balance in light of rhetorical objectives. Challenges for digital media tutors are different from traditional tutors of writing on two levels: in learning new modes of communication and understanding the dynamic of multimodal argumentation. The following are some ideas for how digital media consultation programs might be developed.

New Modes for Tutor Training: First, digital media tutors will be expected to address argument or composition formulated in singular or monomodal forms that are non-alphabetic. As noted earlier, these might be visual modes such as a photograph or oral modes such as an audio narrative. Readings from this collection such as Lanham's "Digital Rhetoric and the Digital Arts" (Chapter 1) and Selfe's "The Movement of Air, the Breath of Meaning" (Chapter 16) can help students consider the concepts of visual and oral modes. In discussing the rhetorical application of one mode, tutors can turn to the diagram of the rhetorical triangle, which writing centers have adopted from composition theory and are commonly presented in composition textbooks. The rhetorical triangle remains a useful tool to help tutors discuss communication strategies that take into account the relationships between the rhetor, subject, and audience (see Figure 0.1). The triangle is set in a circle representing the "context," which includes socially, historically, and culturally shaped discourse as well as medium and moment in time.

Figure 0.1 represents the approach to argument in one mode. For traditional writing tutorials, the tutor may be reading the verbal mode of the written piece. For digital media tutorials, the tutor may be listening to a spoken argument or looking at the design of a visual project. Because literacy in different modes also requires what the New London Group calls

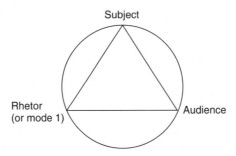

Figure 0.1 Monomodal Diagram of the Rhetorical Triangle.

"situated knowledge," writing centers may need to consider the assessment of how tutors themselves hone their practice of visual and/or vocal communication.

Multimodal Argumentation: The second challenge facing digital media tutors is in understanding how various media genres may work in two or more modes of argumentation. Through this collection, tutors and administrators are introduced to a range of scholars from educators in the New London Group (Chapter 3) to cognitive scientist Richard Mayer (Chapter 7), who explored how multimodal communication works differently for rhetors as well as for learners. In order to illustrate an aspect of this difference in terms of rhetorical strategies, we developed our own model (See Figure 0.2) that might help digital media tutors discuss the components of multimodal composition.

Figure 0.2 illustrates the rhetorical diamond for communication in multiple modes. Unlike the rhetorical triangle, the diamond visually displays how two or more "facets" or modes (M1, M2, and M3) interact with, connect to, and build on each other in a range of ways. While one mode may preside over other modes depending on media or genre, each mode works with the subject and audience in a distinct fashion. Secondly, the rhetorical diamond emphasizes how each mode may complement and play on the other—showing how

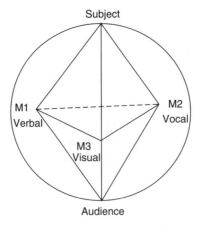

Figure 0.2 Multimodal Diagram of the Rhetorical Diamond.

modalities are choreographed to convey the rhetor's message. Moreover, we see the verbal, vocal, or visual modalities being replaced with other sensory dimensions such as kinesthetic, smell, and touch. More modalities might be added to expand on the three positions shown. Finally, the rhetorical diamond is situational like the rhetorical triangle; it is set in a sphere representing the "context," which includes socially, historically, and culturally shaped discourse, as well as medium and moment in time. This diagram of multimodal communication, which we introduce here, is one conceptual representation of how we communicate. The rhetorical diamond illustrates the way various modes might work together in order to help us understand and improve how we relay ideas and make meaning in multimodalities.

Chapters

In this introduction, we have attempted to set the tone for integrating new media into the writing center by offering perspectives on the rhetorical nature and context of this transition. It also frames the 19 chronological chapters in this book. We believe that these chapters will situate readers, from experienced writing center administrators to tutors in training, within the context of new media scholarship, with an eye toward application in writing centers. These seminal works provide a lens through which writing center scholars and students can read new media practices—from foundational theoretical writings that served as the catalyst for visual design thinking to more recent works that situate new media into the writing center space. Each chapter will encourage the reader to think about how new media theory is employed in the writing center.

Chapter 1 begins with one of the earliest reflections on digital rhetoric in English studies, Richard A. Lanham's "Digital Rhetoric and the Digital Arts" (1993). Lanham points to the rhetorical and expressive potential of the digital screen. As a foundational piece, Lanham helps readers explore the rhetorical potential as well as the classical rhetorical roots of "digital expression."

We transition from Lanham to Lev Manovich's "What Is New Media?" in Chapter 2, one of the most anthologized and read pieces on new media. Manovich provided two separate narratives of modern media and computers that help us understand the cultural form and history of new media. This history helps writing centers reflect on the relation between old and new cultural forms of technologies and the broader movements of these media forms.

In response to dramatic changes in writing and communication that were noted by scholars like Lanham and Manovich, Chapter 3 presents the New London Group's "A Pedagogy of Multiliteracies: Designing Social Futures," a must-read essay for scholars of multimodal composition. Publishing in the *Harvard Educational Review* in 1996, the New London Group argues for re-thinking of literacy pedagogy based on traditional language-based approaches to "multiliteracies" that include visual, cultural, and social literacies. Many composition and writing center scholars refer back to the New London Group when talking about multimodal discourse or new literacy in writing centers.

Chapter 4 presents a foundational theoretical reading in new media with Jay David Bolter and Richard Grusin's "Mediation and Remediation" (1999). In particular, Bolter and Grusin's essay establishes an excellent theoretical background for writing centers as the idea that remediation implies transformation or expansion of the previous medium. This essay may inspire writing centers to think of the work they do and the spaces they inhabit in terms of "remediation."

Chapter 5, John Trimbur's "Multiliteracies, Social Futures, and Writing Centers" (2000), introduces the article that first addresses multiliteracies to writing center studies and identifies writing center spaces by the functions they perform. It prompts a discussion of the appropriateness of the term "center" as in "writing center" and forsees a future that will include, as Trimbur explains, multimodal activity in which oral, written, and visual communication interact and integrate.

Chapter 6, Gunther Kress and Theo van Leeuwen's "Design" (2001), takes a look at visual arguments from the perspective of semiotics and communication theory. Central to Kress and van Leeuwen's argument is the idea of how modes contribute differently to meaning and that meanings may be better received in one mode than another. Their concepts of modal strategies and varying qualities of meaning in design can help tutors better understand and articulate choices in multimodal communication.

Chapter 7 adds the perspective of cognitive science and psychology to the discussion of visual argumentation with Richard E. Mayer's "A Cognitive Theory of Multimedia Learning" (2001). Unlike Kress and van Leeuwen, Mayer approaches visual language choices we make in multimedia platforms from the perspective of knowledge construction and viewer response. Mayer's research suggests that audiences not only learn better from words and pictures than words alone but also that visual and verbal arguments are "qualitatively different knowledge representation systems."

Chapter 8, N. Katherine Hayles's "Entering the Electronic Environment" (2002), explores, through a semi-biographical narrative, the frontier of electronic literature and the boundaries of the printed page as a writing environment. Ideas that her chapter provides will help writing center administrators and tutors approach new media composition from the perspective of its materiality and the challenges that may arise in new media studies.

Chapter 9, Michael A. Pemberton's "Planning for Hypertexts in the Writing Center … Or Not" (2003), can be seen as a seminal piece on new media tutoring from the perspective of writing center studies. Pemberton asks if writing centers should continue to dwell exclusively in the linear, non-linked page world of print or whether they should redefine themselves to take residence in the emerging world of multimodal hyperlinked digital texts.

In Chapter 10, LaGrandeur (2003) analyzes visual literacy from the perspective of composition studies and provides a practical approach towards designing visual arguments. LaGrandeur argues that we can read (and evaluate) new media images such as websites using principles of rhetoric. Interestingly, LaGrandeur proposes a model for assessing the persuasive impact of digital images using classical principles of rhetoric. This chapter provides an approach for applying classical rhetoric to digital images.

In Chapter 11, Stuart Selber's "Rhetorical Literacy" (2004) argues that computer-mediated communication design must be calculated in rhetorical terms, adding a creation-oriented context for the composition of multimodal texts. A scholar of computer literacies, information sciences, and technical communication, Selber puts into practice and makes accessible the multiliteracies pedagogy introduced by the New London Group.

Chapter 12, Dànielle Nicole DeVoss, Ellen Cushman, and Jeffrey T. Grabill's "Infrastructure and Composing: The *When* of New-Media Writing" (2005), alerts writing program administrators and composition teachers to the "structural aspects of new media composing" that place constraints on how they teach. The argument addresses an issue of *kairos* that limits pedagogy (i.e., software, student's understanding and experience with the software, campus server capacity, and university operating procedures). This essay on rhetorical choices shaped by infrastructure lays the groundwork for "material" writing center arguments such as David Sheridan's and the case for tutors to obtain technical knowledge alongside rhetorical expertise.

In Chapter 13, Lawrence Lessig's "RW, Revived" (2008) provides an important perspective of law and culture in new media studies. Lessig's chapter offers insight into our read/write culture; that is, reviving that culture for new media practices. In it, Lessig helps readers make the transition from reading and quoting from print texts (for writing) and visual texts (for new media compositions). Lessig's chapter will inspire critical conversation about ownership, authorship, and new media composition for further discussion among writing center scholars.

In Chapter 14, Russell Carpenter (2009) provides readers with a writing center perspective on how new media consultations transform consultant training. In "Writing Center Dynamics: Coordinating Multimodal Consultations," Carpenter highlights aspects of training consultants to work in and with new media in the writing center, including balancing new media practices with print-centric practices. Writing center practitioners will find this article interesting for developing a framework for consulting new media in the writing center.

In Chapter 15, "Among the Audience: On Audience in an Age of New Literacies" (2009), Andrea A. Lunsford and Lisa Ede revisit their earlier article on the role of audience in composition theory and pedagogy by taking into account multimodality and emerging technologies. Lunsford and Ede explore the changing role and place of audience in an age of social media (including Facebook and Twitter). Their revised theory of audience is critical for developing our own taxonomy for tutoring new media composition.

Chapter 16 approaches multimodal composition by addressing the important subject of aurality in Cynthia L. Selfe's "The Movement of Air, the Breath of Meaning: Aurality and Multimodal Composing" (2009). In this article, Selfe reminds us that voice, aurality, is central in multimodal composition. This chapter is valuable for writing center practitioners and students as it encourages them to see the critical rhetorical value and role of aurality.

Chapter 17 introduces readers to Jackie Grutsch McKinney's "New Media Matters: Tutoring in the Late Age of Print" (2009), which explicitly discusses the training of writing center tutors for new media or multimodal composition. McKinney argues that writing centers should train all tutors to consult new media, particularly in design knowledge; moreover, she makes the case that traditional methods will not provide tutors with the skills they need. Readers will appreciate McKinney's insight into tutor training and opens up a conversation on how writing centers should address new media writing.

In Chapter 18, Jennifer Sheppard in "Creating a Center for Communication Design: Negotiating Pedagogy, Disciplinarity, and Sustainability in Communities of Practice" (2010) examines the process of creating a new space dedicated to the development of the Center for New Media Communication Design (Design Center). Although not a writing center in a traditional sense, the Design Center offers valuable theoretical and practical frameworks that will prompt practitioners to think beyond print-based practices. Sheppard's chapter is practical, offering the perspective of a director and practitioner that complements other more theoretically grounded pieces offered in this collection.

Finally, in Chapter 19, David M. Sheridan's "All Things to All People: Multiliteracy Consulting and the Materiality of Rhetoric" (2010) approaches multiliteracies consulting by exploring experiences, practices, and theories that have informed the development of Michigan State University's Writing Center, specifically multiliteracies consulting and the materiality of rhetoric. This chapter will be valuable to writing center scholars and practitioners in its engagement of multiliteracies pedagogy and its recommendations for the training of writing center tutors.

Reading Connections

Digital and Visual Expression and Technology

The readings offered here contribute to preparing writing center practitioners for digital and visual compositions. These select readings will help readers prepare for working with digital and visual texts in writing center spaces. They are meant to be read through the lens of writing center work.

Chapter 1: Lanham, "Digital Rhetoric and the Digital Arts"

Chapter 4: Bolter and Grusin, "Mediation and Remediation"

Chapter 6: Kress and van Leeuwen, "Design"

Chapter 8: Hayles, "Entering the Electronic Environment"

Chapter 9: Pemberton, "Preparing for Hypertexts in the Writing Center … Or Not"

Chapter 11: Selber, "Rhetorical Literacy"

Fractal Structure of New Media

Manovich describes communication in new media as a "fractal structure" to highlight its modular nature. In new media, elements can be combined and recombined to form new meaning. This concept of new media variability is reviewed and explored by a range of authors in this collection.

Chapter 1: Lanham, "Digital Rhetoric and the Digital Arts"

Chapter 2: Manovich, "What Is New Media?"

Chapter 4: Bolter and Grusin, "Mediation and Remediation"

Chapter 13: Lessig, "RW, Revived"

Chapter 16: Selfe, "The Movement of Air, the Breath of Meaning"

Multimodal Learning and Multiliteracies

"Multiliteracies," a term coined by the New London Group, described an approach to literacy that explores visual, verbal, and vocal modalities and its multiple re-combinations. The scholars listed here explore the pedagogy involved in multiliteracies and communicating in multimodality.

Chapter 3: New London Group, "A Pedagogy of Multiliteracies"

Chapter 5: Trimbur, "Multiliteracies, Social Futures, and Writing Centers"

Chapter 6: Kress and van Leeuwen, "Design"

Chapter 7: Mayer, "A Cognitive Theory of Multimedia Learning"

Chapter 11: Selber, "Rhetorical Literacy"

Chapter 16: Selfe, "The Movement of Air, the Breath of Meaning"

Communities of Practice

Providing a new perspective on a familiar writing center topic, these readings offer insights into communities of practice for writing centers undertaking new media initiatives. This cluster of readings focuses on the social nature of new media work, to include the design of spaces and the multimodal communication within them.

Chapter 3: New London Group, "A Pedagogy of Multiliteracies"

Chapter 5: Trimbur, "Multiliteracies, Social Futures, and Writing Centers"

Chapter 14: Carpenter, "Writing Center Dynamics"

Chapter 15: Lunsford and Ede, "Among the Audience"

Chapter 17: McKinney, "New Media Matters"

Chapter 18: Sheppard, "Creating a Center for Communication Design"

Chapter 19: Sheridan, "All Things to All People"

Infrastructure of New Media Writing and Writing Centers

Readings in this cluster offer perspectives on the composing process of new media. With a focus on structure and infrastructure, these readings move from theoretical to practical applications. Infrastructures of new media can be dynamic, political, and cultural, as these chapters posit.

Chapter 2: Manovich, "What Is New Media?"

Chapter 8: Hayles, "Entering the Electronic Environment"

Chapter 9: Pemberton, "Planning for Hypertext in the Writing Center ... Or Not"

Chapter 12: DeVoss, Cushman, and Grabill, "Infrastructure and Composing"

Chapter 14: Carpenter, "Writing Center Dynamics"

New Media Tutor Training

The readings below support the training of writing center tutors in new media consultations. In particular, these readings may help undergraduate and graduate tutors rethink composition with technology in terms of what "writing" might mean, how to re-conceive "audience," and how to understand and approach new media text. Some readings may not directly discuss writing center practice but may be used to encourage tutors to think broadly by exploring textual composition across disciplines and outside of English studies.

Chapter 2: Manovich, "What Is New Media?"

Chapter 4: Bolter and Grusin, "Mediation and Remediation"

Chapter 6: Kress and van Leeuwen, "Design"

Chapter 7: Mayer, "A Cognitive Theory of Multimedia Learning"

Chapter 10: LaGrandeur, "Digital Images and Classical Persuasion"

Chapter 13: Lessig, "RW, Revived"

Chapter 15: Lunsford and Ede, "Among the Audience"

References

Cooper, M. M. (2007). Learning digital literacies. In C. Selfe (Ed.), *Multimodal composition: Resources for teachers* (pp. 181–191). Cresskill, NJ: Hampton.

Griffin, J. (2007). Making connections with writing centers. In C. Selfe (Ed.), *Multimodal composition: Resources for teachers* (pp. 153–165). Cresskill, NJ: Hampton.

Harris, M. (2011). SLATE (Support for the Learning and Teaching of English) statement: The concept of a writing center. *International Writing Center Association*. Retrieved from http://writingcenters.org/resources/writing-center-concept/. Web. 25 September 2012.

Lanham, R. A. (1993). *The electronic word: Democracy, technology, and the arts*. Chicago and London: The University of Chicago Press.

1
Digital Rhetoric and the Digital Arts

Richard A. Lanham

We have always, from Pascal to the present, thought of computers, especially digital computers, as logic machines. Whether they helped us with our weaving, our business tabulations, our artillery trajectories, or our atomic bombs, we have always located them where we locate logic: at the familiar Platonic, mathematical center of human reason. It was a Monster of Pure Reason that threatened to fold, spindle, and mutilate the riotous Berkeley students of the sixties. It was the same monster that prompted Hubert Dreyfus to write his equally riotous satire of artificial intelligence,[1] a modern *Dunciad* after which neither satirist nor satirized has ever been the same. I would like, as a supplement and complement to this view from philosophy and theory, to suggest that in practice, the computer often turns out to be a rhetorical device as well as a logical one, that it derives its aesthetic from philosophy's great historical opposite in Western thought and education, the world of rhetoric. I argue, at the same rime, that this fixation on logic has so bemused us that we have failed to notice the extraordinary way in which the computer has fulfilled the expressive agenda of twentieth-century art. It thus fulfills at the same time a very new visual agenda and a very old verbal one. I want to suggest some of these remarkable fulfillments here.

What happens when text moves from page to screen? First, the digital text becomes unfixed and interactive. The reader can change it, become writer. The center of western culture since the Renaissance—really since the great Alexandrian editors of Homer—the fixed, authoritative, canonical text, simply explodes into the ether. We can see that happening in a typographical explosion called *SCRABrrRrraaNNG*, from a 1919 manifesto by Filippo Tommaso Marinetti.

Italian Futurism, which began with Marinerri's famous *Futurist Manifesto* in 1909, was a complex, and as things turned out an extremely prophetic, movement that combined theatrical evenings very like the Happenings of fifty years later with political outpourings of an apocalyptically Fascist sort. It created a new, nonharmonic music which used both silence and noise in ways that foreshadowed John Cage, and argued for the primacy of vision over print in ways that point toward Marshall McLuhan. The final aim of all this was, or at least sometimes was, the conflation of the arts into a single theatrical whole, something Marinetti called "Il Teatro di Varietà," a theater that seemed, at least for him, to find its most natural future home not in live theater but in cinema—cinema being then the new technology. (He would now locate it, I think, in the digitally driven "theme park" events being designed by

Lucasfilm, Disney, and MCA. The perfect example of "Il Teatro di Varietà" would be the Disneyland space-travel attraction called "Star Tours.")

I want to single out from this prophetic mélange of violent theater and political rant only one of its dominant interests: the attack on the printed codex book and its typographical conventions, an attack symbolized by Marinetti's *esplosione*. In a tract called *La cinematografia futurista* Marinetti and some of his pals single out the books as the chief villain of the old order:

> The book, the most traditional means of preserving and communicating thought, has been for a long time destined to disappear, just like cathedrals, walled battlements, museums, and the ideal of pacificism. ... The Futurist Cinema will ... collaborate in a general renewal, substituting for the magazine—always pedantic—, for the drama—always stale—, and killing the book—always tedious and oppressive.[2]

The book is seen as static, inelastically linear, sluggish; the new cinematographic form as dynamic, interactive, simultaneous, swift. This war on the book chose as its immediate target typographical convention, with results like *SCRABrrRrraaNNG*. Here we see the book and all it represents in the act of deconstructing itself—all unawares the little children played, event as early as 1919—*esplosione* at its center literally shattering typographical convention into distended fragments.

Subsequent collage techniques from Dada to the present day have diffused the force and direction of this attack, but Marinetti was taking aim at the founding convention of a literate society. Eric Havelock's thesis is that a culture, to be truly literate, must possess an alphabet simple enough to be learned thoroughly in early youth and unobtrusive enough in its calligraphy that a reader forgets about its physical aspects and reads right through it to the meaning beneath. The written surface must be transparent. Transparent and unselfconscious. We must not notice the size and shape of the letters. We may in some subconscious way register the chirographic or typographic conventions but we must not *see* them. (Havelock, for example, points to early Greek vase-paintings where letters of the alphabet are used as decorative motifs, are noticed for their size and shape only, as registering the preliterate, still oral, use of the alphabet.)

It is to this stage that Marinetti—and electronic text—would return us. He seeks to make us aware of the enormous act of simplification that an ordinary printed text represents; he wants to make us self-conscious about a register of expressivity that as literate people we have abjured. It is common to call experiments of this sort "outrageous," but surely they aim at didacticism much rather. In a literate culture our conception of meaning itself—whether of logical argument or magical narrative—depends on this radical act of typographical simplification. No pictures; no color; strict order of left to right then down one line; no type changes; no interaction; no revision. In attacking this convention, Marinetti attacks the entire literate conception of humankind—the central self, a nondramatic society just out there waiting for us to observe it—and the purposive idea of language that rests upon it. He would urge us to notice that all this reality-apparatus is as conventional as the typography we are trained *not* to notice. There was a rime when it did not exist: in the oral culture, in fact, out of which Greek rhetoric developed.

Marinetti's techniques have been employed often since then. Ted Nelson's *Computer Lib/ Dream Machines* offers a handy example from the digital world.[3] Nelson's sometimes cutesy typographical games show more clearly than Marinetti the native didacticism of the genre. Here too, as often happens, the self-conscious typography advocates a theory of prose style— a campaign against "cybercrud" and for an unselfconscious prose style based on the "Clarity-Brevity-Sincerity" trinity—that the self-conscious typography contradicts at every point.

Concomitantly with the explosion of the authoritative text, electronic writing brings a complete renegotiation of the alphabet/icon ratio upon which print-based thought is built. We can detect this foregrounding of images over written words most clearly in the world of business and government communications, but it is happening everywhere. When the rich vocal and gestural language of oral rhetoric was constricted into writing and then print, the effort to preserve it was concentrated into something classical rhetoricians called *ecphrasis*, dynamic speaking-pictures in words. Through the infinite resources of digital image recall and manipulation, ecphrasis is once again coming into its own, and the pictures and sounds suppressed into verbal rhetorical figures are now reassuming their native places in the human sensorium. The complex icon/word interaction of oral rhetoric is returning, albeit *per ambages.*

The struggle between icon and alphabet is not, to be sure, anything new, as the history of illuminated manuscripts attests. This complex interaction of word and image never actually vanished; it only fell out of fashion. The tradition of mixing transparent alphabetic information with opaque pictures formed by the letters goes back at least to Simias, a Greek poet of the fourth century B.C.[4] It was revived first by Marinetti and then by the Dadaista, with a specifically aggressive purpose. And, to some degree, it lurks in any calligraphic tradition. Electronic display both invites manipulating the icon/alphabet mixture and makes it much easier to write.

As one instance of how such calligrams work, we might look at a prophetic pre-electronic example in Kenneth Burke's *Collected Poems, 1915–1967.*[5] Burke called these doodles "Flowerishes." The "text" of this particular typographical game is a series of comic apothegms: "In a world Full of problems he sat doing puzzles," "One must learn to be just morbid enough," "They liked to sit around and chew the phatic communion," and so on. The core of Burke's philosophy of rhetoric has been his discussion of "orientation," the self-conscious perception of paradigms for apprehending reality that we customarily push to the side, to our peripheral vision. In this doodle, he uses the conventions of typography to pun on orientation. To "orient" ourselves to this self-conscious form of proverbial wisdom, we must, like an illiterate pretending to read, turn the book round and round in an effort to make sense of it. We are made aware of the book as a physical presence in our hands. The printed surface is rendered opaque rather than transparent by changes in typeface, font size, and sequentiality. Text must be read top to bottom as well as left to right, back to front, in a circle, every which way. Type is "poured," as it is in a desktop publishing system such as *Quark XPress*, rather than set. Spec-ing type in such a frame becomes an aspect of meaning rather than merely a transparent window to it. Does "a grandfather clock, run by gravity," mean something different because the words are presented in Gothic type? Typography becomes allegorical, a writer-controlled expressive parameter, just as it does on an electronic screen. Here, though, as so often, the electronic screen fulfills an already existing expressive agenda rather than prophesying a new one.

The most revered and central function of the literary canon is to transmit the canonical wisdom found quintessentially in the proverb. Burke deliberately calls that tradition into question, breaking the "literacy compact" by introducing visual patterns and typographical allegories to suggest that proverbial wisdom never comes into the world purely transparent and disembodied, totally serious, unconditioned by game and play, by the gross physicality of its display. No formal cause without a material one. Again, the electronic parallels are manifest. The electronic universe's playful attitude toward typographical convention drives the print-based imagination mad.

All kinds of interesting conversions take place when we move from book to screen. Proverbial wisdom, for example, becomes visual. Digital expression has resurrected the world of proverbial wisdom, but through vast databanks of icons rather than words. We buy what are, in effect, catalogues representing commonplace situations and appropriate responses to them: faces, hand gestures, signage of all sorts. Our computer font menus regularly include printer's dingbats—❏▶❊▼◀◆❊✏✀—but the range of readily available proverbial icons now runs to thousands. The traditional dependence on commonplaces in rhetorical education has been transmuted from word to image.

The same wind that carried away the authoritative text has also ventilated the reverent solemnity with which we view it. Again we encounter the digital aesthetic charted much earlier in the visual arts. The canonical image of this anticanonicity is Marcel Duchamp's urinal. My favorite emblem of compromised canonicity, though, is John Baldessari's *Quality Material* from 1967, which consists of five lines of black alphabetic text on a white ground:[6]

QUALITY MATERIAL – – –
CAREFUL INSPECTION – –
GOOD WORKMANSHIP.

ALL COMBINED IN AN EFFORT TO
GIVE YOU A PERFECT PAINTING.

This textual painting does exactly what the computer screen does: it makes text into a painting, frames it in a new way, asks for a new act of attention—and smiles at the seriousness that text calls forth from us.

Baldessari, by a radical reversal of alphabetic and iconic information, denies an absolute beauty and fitness of things independent of humankind, a fitness we are first to discover and then breathlessly to adore. The painting would seem to suggest that such fitness is not out there in "reality," and it is not out there in sacred texts, either—timeless, unchangeable, self explanatory, and canonical—excerpts of which, duly presented as "touchstones," will impart the healing touch of sacred relics. Instead of a divine icon, we have a human text that substitutes the interpretation for the thing interpreted.

Doesn't electronic text often practice a similar comic reversal? The intrinsic motival structure of electronic text is as comic as print is serious. Let me illustrate this reversed polarity of seriousness by alluding to another familiar pre-electronic icon, Duchamp's most famous "Readymade," his mustachioed *Mona Lisa*. The title of this work, the letters L.H.O.O.Q., if pronounced in French, *yield* the words "Elle a chaud au cul," or in somewhat fractured French, "This chick has hot pants." What, in the process, has happened to "Mona Baby"? First of all, she seems to have undergone a devastatingly effective and economical sex-change operation. By desecrating Perfection, Duchamp has elicited a sexual ambiguity in the picture we had not seen before and could learn to see in no other way. Outrageous art as didactic criticism, once again. Second, Duchamp calls our attention to a powerful canonical constraint. The timeless perfection Mona Baby represents condemns us to passivity. No interaction allowed. Canonical vision moves in only one direction, does justice to an external reality that exists independent of us, bur never recreates that reality in the act of perceiving it. The traditional idea of an artistic canon brings with it, by the very "immortality" it strives for, both a passive beholder and a passive reality waiting out there to be perceived, the best that has been thought, said, or painted perhaps, but unchangeable in its perfection, a goddess we can adore but never ask out to play. And so Duchamp asks her out to play. Criticism again. And, again, not so much an attack on the artistic canon as a medication on the psychology of perception that canon implies. One perceptive critic has called this Readymade full of "quiet savagery." Not at all. Playful didacticism rather. Interactivity deflates solemnity—even as it does with electronic text. If we need a tutelary goddess for digital writing and reading, Mona Mustache is the perfect wo/man, or god/dess, for the job.

Electronic expression fulfills this deep urge in the modern visual arts; it asks the *Mona Lisa* out to play. It was not an accident that the hackers whom Steven Levy describes started out playing with model trains.[7] We can observe the interactive playful drive replacing Arnoldian solemnity in the work of the Swiss sculptor Jean Tinguely. Tinguely welded together junk contraptions that crash, bang, and thump, jiggle, make (for a small coin donation) an abstract drawing, and generally convert the museum into a combination toystore and playground. He took the world of civil engineering and converted it into game in much the same way that the personal compurer has begun to convert history into a game, letting us play our way into everything from the Battle of Britain to the fate of the human biosphere.

In photographs of Tinguely's exhibitions the people who come to see them often figure prominently. I saw why this was so in the autumn of 1982, when I spent an entranced afternoon in a huge Tinguely exhibit mounted at the Tate Gallery in London. Instead of a reverential art-gallery hush, the whole place was a symphony of sounds, the whangs, bangs, and whistles of the sculptures blending with the exclamations of the participants—for that is what we were—and the delighted outcries of the children. Most of them had speedily found the great *Rotozaza*, a huge sculpture that takes balls and, after moving them through a series of Rube Goldberg maneuvers, flings them out into the crowd. The viewers then retrieve them and feed them back into the machine.

Part of the show was that part of the Tate which was *not* part of the show, the galleries that still preserved the reverential quiet of a conventional exhibition. But now you heard this silence as one of Cage's "silences," something that you consciously attended to, that you began to "hear." Might I suggest that these conventional galleries allegorize the printed text, as read in a digital age? They are still the same, and yet we listen to them in a different way, and hear silences we have nor heard before. And in this new kind of gallery, this new kind of text, we hear voices and we move around.

With Tinguely's kind of junk sculpture comes, needless to say, a flood of Marxist moralizing. Behold the detritus of modern capitalism, the sordid remnants of a junk culture, and so on. The machines themselves, though, when they are working in their native environment—moving, clanking, and whistling, the spectators busy catching the balls, pushing the buttons, commissioning their abstract drawings for a sixpence—don't work this way at all. The machines exude high spirits and good humor. They do not damn a machine culture; like electronic text, they redeem it by returning it to play.

Let me, just for fun, report my own embodiment of this process, as I stood in the Tate exhibition before a machine called *Autoportrait Conjugal*, which dates from 1960. Two objects depend from the bottom of the machine. One is a weight, the other a stuffed bird. When the machine goes into action, a little ladder in the middle moves from side to side and the weight acts as a pendulum, imparting to the stuffed bird a pendulous twitch. I went to the exhibit with a very dear old friend, a remarkably tolerant and sophisticated woman with a wonderful sense of humor, who is also a keen bird-watcher. She had in fact arrived in London from a strenuous birding trip to the Pribilof Islands. She immediately noticed the dead bird and, after identifying it, began to excoriate Tinguely. She knows me extremely well, and when she saw me trying to flail my face into something resembling moral outrage, she remarked, "I'll bet you find this extremely funny, don't you?" Meaning by "this" both the stuffed bird swinging back and forth at the bottom of the bungee cord, and her outrage at it—which I anticipated—and my efforts to prevent her from seeing that I did indeed think that the dangling bird was, for reasons I could not explain, extremely funny. Finally I burst into laughter. And so did she. Tinguely had written a comedy and both of us had played our parts. *Autoportrait Conjugal* functioned as what the classical rhetoricians called a *chreia*, a little argumentative firecracker that got the argument of a speech going fast.

Electronic text contrives interactive events of precisely this sort, leavens with comedy the serious if not solemn business of clear, brief, and sincere human communication. Is it too fanciful to detect it supplying this comic leaven to the world of work? Aren't we finding that the world of computer-aided design and manufacture, for example, is deeply playful in the kinds of effort it calls forth? After all, screen space is free. You can make carefree mistakes and correct them, doodle with impudence.

Perhaps the most widely debated, though far from the most important, issue involving electronic text is whether writing on a computer creates verbal flatulence or not. Certainly it restores to centrality another element of classical rhetoric, the use of *topics*, of preformed arguments, phrases, discrete chunks of verbal boilerplate, which can be electronically cut, pasted, and repeated at will. Classical rhetoric argued that repetition, without intrinsically changing the object repeated, changes it absolutely, and modern philosophers like Andy Warhol have dwelt upon this theme, replicating everything from Brillo boxes and soup cans to rich and famous faces.

Think, since we have the *Mona Lisa* in mind, of Warhol's *Thirty Are Better Than One*, from 1963. In this painting, which gives us thirty Monas instead of one, her priceless canonical rarity vanishes even as we bring it to self-consciousness. The same aesthetic operates at the heart of electronic text, though we seldom notice it for what it is—an aesthetic of collage, the central technique of twentieth-century visual art. Collage is now a commonplace narrative technique too, as in David Hockney's recent work with photo collage and color photocopies; but my favorite example remains a golden oldie from the 1950s: Richard Hamilton's "Just What Is It That Makes Today's Homes So Different, So Appealing?" Couldn't this—collaged up as it is with clip art and advertising icons—just as well be called "Just What Is It That Makes Today's Desktop So Different, So Appealing?" Perhaps this technique of the *topos* ought not surprise us; the iconographic computer desktop, after all, was modeled after the memory system in classical Greek rhetoric, or so at least says Nicholas Negroponte of MIT. One can even obtain a startup icon (a *turn-on* icon perhaps we should call her) who looks like the lady in Hamilton's painting and who varies the size of her bosom to indicate the amount of data on the disk. *Gentilezza per gentilezza.*

To replicate and juxtapose at will, as collage does, is to alter scale, and scaling change is one of the truly enzymatic powers of electronic text. When you click in the zoom box, you make a big decision: you are deciding on the central decorum of a human event, on the boundary-conditions within which that event is to be staged, and hence on the nature of the event itself. Nobody has toyed with scale as much as Claes Oldenburg, whose gigantic pool balls, electric switches, umbrellas, and baseball bats reached a culmination of sorts in the Swiss Army knife made into a supersize Venetian gondola.[8] When I saw it, it was majestically rowing its way down the courtyard at the Museum of Contemporary Art in Los Angeles. As the oars moved, the viewer's scale switched back and forth from knife to gondola, and the plain courtyard became alternately trouser pocket and Venetian canal.

To change scale is, as with repetition, to transform reality utterly, without changing it at all. To make art of scaling changes means making us self-conscious about perceptual distance and the conventions, neural and social, that cluster around it. That distance itself can so change an object—give it, to use Duchamp's phrase, a "new idea"—locks us into a conception of art as essentially interactive. This interactivity is the very opposite of canonical passivity.

Oldenburg's *Batcolumn*, erected in Chicago in April 1977, shows how a scale-game works. To render a baseball bat epic in scale, as Oldenburg has done, perpetrates one of those play/ purpose reversals so common in Pop art and beyond, the same reversal we create when we zoom in on a letter until we dissolve its meaning into the abstract formal pleasure of the pixel patterns themselves—Havelock's decorative letters on Greek vases again. Oldenburg's bat ceases to be an instrument to hit a ball and becomes an object to be contemplated, to crane your neck up at, a skyscraper of a baseball bat. Yet the eye, less adaptive than the mind, still wants it to be a bat of normal size, and so yearns to make everything else increase in scale to fit it, conjuring up an enormous ball diamond with gigantic players scaled to fit the bat. If the skyscrapers surrounding it dwarf us, then the *Batcolumn* expands us again, restores a more equal relationship with our environment, a playful epic scale. The *Batcolumn* is a thing of beauty, a new shape, but also and more importane, it represents one of Duchamp's "new ideas," the idea of scale. Twentieth-century art has often aimed to recreate epic scale in a new form; the big bat does so by scaling up an everyday object. Epic scale, then, but radically democratized.

We do the same thing when we zoom on the screen—we draw far closer to the text than ever we could with the naked eye, and in the magic world we thus enter, the text becomes gigantic, enormously weighty, a physical space, a writing sheet large enough to wrap up the world. Language does indeed became a field of meaning over which we wander. A zooming session leaves the student of rhetoric with a renewed and expanded sense of how much the basic decisions about reading and writing and speaking have to do with scaling arguments, fitting them to time and place. Enlarging and diminishing them is what the basic figure/ground decision that empowers human vision is all about. The scaling powers of electronic text create an extraordinary allegory, almost a continual visual punning, of the stage sets implied by written discourse. The future of rhetorical figuration, which McLuhan in an inspired phrase called "the postures of the mind," looks, after a long hiatus, promising once again.

Scale-change stands at the heart of Roy Lichtenstein's comic-book paintings, too, and they tell us a good deal about how scale-change operartes on the images that electronic display can so easily mix with alphabetic text. Think for a moment of the well-known frame *Live Ammo* (1962). There, a form of commercial art usually presented in a format a couple of inches square suddenly finds a meticulous rendering almost six by eight feet. Again, an artifact of daily life is wrenched, through huge scale-change, into the domain of art. But another profound reversal operates. As these images appear in the funny papers, they function purely transparently, provide immediate access to the narrative they depict. They are the graphic equivalent of Havelock's "literate compact"; they trigger no self-consciousness, provide a pictographic "pure story," "romance" at its most mythically simplified, most unselfconscious. Lichtenstein reverses this convention. The surface is rendered maximally self-conscious. We look at the surface pattern, AT the design rather than THROUGH it. Lichtenstein points this out specifically in a small (sixteen by sixteen inches) black-and-white from 1962 called *Magnifying Glass*. In this small painting (shown most recently in the "High and Low" exhibition mounted by the Museum of Modern Art),[9] the *microdot* pattern, which in the comic-papers printing technique constitutes the transparent means for creating the narrative image, is deliberately framed in a magnifying glass, made into a self-conscious and opaque design motif, something we are forced to look AT and not THROUGH. So too with the characters in the narrative. "I use them for purely formal reasons," Lichtenstein has said, "and that's not what those heroes were invented for." This AT/THROUGH reversal appears in twentieth-century art in various guises, from the Italian Futurists onward. It is a favorite Lichtenstein motif. In his brushstroke paintings, for example, when he makes monumentality out of artistic means, the AT/THROUGH oscillation fairly jumps out at you.

Such an oscillation between looking AT the expressive surface and THROUGH it seems to me the most powerful aesthetic attribute of electronic text. Print wants the gaze to remain THROUGH and unselfconscious all the time. Lichtenstein's *Magnifying Glass*, like the electronic screen, insists on the continual oscillation between unselfconscious expression and self-conscious design that formed the marrow of the classical rhetorician's art and pedagogy. *Magnifying Glass* is a painting about a different kind of seriousness, a different kind of perception, one that *forgets intermittently*—but must never *forget forever*—the means of perception, the carefully tuned illusions from which Western social reality has always been constructed. It is a painting, too, about what happens to text when it is painted onto an electronic screen, when we can change fonts, zoom in on the pixels until their "meaning" metamorphoses into purely formal pleasure. Again, this oscillation happens continually in electronic text without our recognizing it for what it is, or seeing how deeply runs its cardinal allegory.

Some of Lichtenstein's paintings seem as if created by and for electronic means. I am thinking now of the "Haystack" paintings or the series of Rouen Cathedral, where the microdot technique resembles a pixeled screen seen very close up and the series of paintings seems a series of screen-prints of a dynamically changing electronic representation. One of Lichtenstein's commentators, Lawrence Alloway, remarks that he was "interested in the paradox of a systematically executed Impressionism."[10] That systematic creation has now found electronic expression in a computer program called Monet that paints impressionistic pictures by means of digital algorithms.[11] Perhaps not every aspect of contemporary art will find such heady digital fulfillment, but it is certainly tempting to think of all the series paintings—not only of Lichtenstein, but of Warhol and others—as prophetic. They seem to reach out for the dynamic image as much as Marinetti sought the dynamic word.

It is not accidental, I think, that *animation* has come to be so dominated by digital techniques. Traditional gel-animation takes much longer than its computer-graphic successor, but more important than that, it creates action out of a medium static to begin with. Computer graphics emerge from a medium in itself dynamic. This difference leaps out in the stylistic evolution of comic-book graphics. Even print-based comics exude a computer-graphics feeling. They look like printouts from a program-in-progress. A journal like *RAW*, a folio-sized compendium of "serious" comics, looks like a Marinetti typographical explosion, but in color and ten seconds later. It illustrates the profound remixture of the alphabet/icon ratio that awaits printed text. When Lichtenstein picked out comics, he was being prophetic as a great artist should; it was the narrative/iconic relationship that he zoomed in on.

Serious comics teach one important lesson so obvious that we don't notice it: the impact of adding color to the alphabet/image mix. Both newspapers and magazines are developing the habitual use of color in new ways. But we are only beginning to understand how the black-and-white convention of print will be changed by a color display. The history of typography is another story but clearly every aspect of it has been revolutionized by digital technology. Hot type was *set*. Digital typesetting programs *pour* or *flow* it. We encounter this change in liquidity everywhere in contemporary printed texts, especially in the relation between words and pictures.

Clearly every stage of this revolution has been predicated by the postmodern visual arts. What has collage done from the beginning but imitate this pouring of text around image? What are Jasper Johns's letter painting but invitations to look AT letters rather than THROUGH them, to think of letters as three-dimensional visual images in color? Oldenburg makes the page three-dimensional by taking letters and numbers and inflating them like overstuffed chairs, as in *Soft Calendar for the Month of August* (1962). Edward Ruscha painted a big red *Annie* over a yellow ground, as the top half of a square whose bottom half was plain blue, making a simple word vibrate against a color exercise à la Josef Albers. And in 1961 Lichtenstein painted a four-foot-square comic-book canvas showing a man looking into a completely dark, wholly black room through a round peephole. Through the peephole we glimpse a man, and a bright yellow background. The caption reads, "I can see the whole room *and there's nobody in it!*" Surely here is the electronic world of three-dimensional color looking back into the world of black-and-white print!

The sheer dynamic power of zooming in and zooming out on an image, this transformatory power of scale-change, seems frozen into a series of snapshots in the tremendous, and tremendously large, paintings of James Rosenquist. When I saw the Rosenquist exhibition in Denver, I felt as if I were a homunculus walking inside a gigantic, multifaceted computer display. The computer's power to transform the imagistic clutter of modern visual life by zooming in very close to it seemed to be what Rosenquist's paintings were about. Rosenquist started out as a billboard painter. His heroic efforts to bring commercial signage into the art gallery (I am not being ironic; *F-111* is a genuinely epic painting) find an exact counterpart on the electronic screen. Rosenquist flies us through the air up to one of his enormous billboards hanging over the city street and then rubs out noses in the billboard. We see it as line and shape and color and pattern, we look AT it rather than THROUGH it. The electronic screen allows us to practice this transformation on the images it displays. It flies us magically through the air, allows us to get closer to an image than normal human focus allows. It can and often does do what Rosenquist's paintings do—transform the public commercial landscape by scale-change, by flying us through and around it. Don't we witness the same process when a life scientist uses computer graphics and virtual-reality goggles to walk into a complex molecule the size of a room, wander around it and try, as it were, various possible junctures on for size?

We might reflect, too, on how easily another dominant theme of contemporary art—quotation—finds expression on an electronic screen. The storehouses of graphic images that all of us now have on our machines at home are, in effect, mass-produced and copyright-legal quotation devices. Our startup screens are often shifting art galleries of personal quotation—mine today started up with a Ferrari Testa Rossa—and iconic badges. When we have "quoted" the image we want, we can now process it in the same way we process words; we can, that is, "quote" it in the same way one painter quotes another. And the same democratization of "originality" takes place. Electronic display, in fact, spells out the pun in "original." It can easily call up the "original-as-root image" (the *least* original or most topical version) and make it, through now-commonplace manipulation routines, into an "original" in the Romantic "never-seen-before" sense of the word. The digital computer seems a machine created for Art-about-Art.

It also seems created to provide the perfect means for another contemporary artistic technique—the creativity of chance. The genuine ghost in this machine is the spirit not of Alan Turing but of John Cage. Even the simplest computer painting program builds in enormous resources for chance generation that seem taken right out of Cage's exhortation and practice. Take as an unpretentious example a program called Kid Pix.[12] It is as antilinear as Cage himself could have wished. When it is running in "Small Kids Mode," the user need not even know how to read. Scale-manipulation is a principal means of creation in the program—it has a built-in magnifying glass, à la Lichtenstein—but its many kinds of drawing implements depend on random variation. Patterns can be created, enhanced, juxtaposed, dynamically mixed, timed to fade in and out, poured in and out and away, all by random methods. Alphabetic information, in the Kid Pix environment, becomes iconic in the way it does on a Greek vase or in a medieval manuscript. And the program makes possible the three-dimensional layering that so many contemporary painters and collage-makers have striven for. It does so in reverse, going into the surface rather than out from it to build up layers. Kid Pix offers to kids a three-dimensional writing space—it comes with the territory.

We can study an architectural version of the basic electronic AT/THROUGH oscillation in one of the most controversial attempts at postmodern monumentality, the now-famous Centre Pompidou in Paris, the "Beaubourg" as it is called, designed by Richard Rogers and Renzo Piano. The façade reenacts a ritual in contemporary architecture, the reversal of use and ornament. The architects have turned the building inside out, put its plumbing on the outside instead of hiding it in utility shafts. They have made decoration out of ducts, play out of purpose, much as Duchamp did with *Fountain*. The building becomes an allegory of motive as well as a museum, a visual representation of the play/purpose reversal at the heart of postmodem architecture.

This oscillation between use and ornament, between purpose and play, pops out everywhere you look in the history of computers, and especially of private desktop ones. Play continually animates the operant purpose, indeed often becomes it. I have mentioned Steven Levy's history of the personal computer, *Hackers*, which recaptures this motivational mood perfectly. The play impulse symbolized purity of motive to the computer world (as so often to the academic world), and its loss has seemed the loss of innocence itself. I would urge the opposite case—play is as native to electronic text as it is to rhetoric. The purposive Suits and Bean-counters mistake the spirit of the place.

This motivational struggle is dramatized in the long-running struggle between the IBM world and the Apple world. The Apple world, born in personal computers not mainframes, has from the beginning been dominated by the play impulse. It colored motive, style, mood, personality type. Apple's graphics-based computers were built upon, assumed, a transformed alphabet/icon ratio. IBM—serious, indeed humorless—still cannot understand the revolution of electronic text or what it means to their business. Characteristic motivation, not technology, separates the two camps. The quarrel opposes an old way of looking at the world's business and a new way. About how the new way works, the postmodern arts have everything to tell us. The themes we are discussing—judgments about scale, a new icon/alphabet ratio in textual communication, nonlinear collage and juxtapositional reasoning, that is to say bottom-up rather than top-down planning, coaxing change so as to favor the prepared mind—all these constitute a new theory of management. The graphics-based digital computer—the computer as an instrument and work of art—implies this new theory at every point. Apple, because of the circumstances of its creation, knows this and IBM has yet to learn it. That's the real difference between them.

Classical rhetoric, and hence all of classical education, was built on a single dominant exercise: modeling. The key form was the oration, and it was rehearsed again and again in every possible form and context. *Declamatio*, as the modeling of speeches came to be called, stood at the hub of Western education, just as computer modeling is coming to do today. The world of electronic text has reinstated this centrality of modeled reality. The computer has adopted once again, as the fundamental educational principle the dramatizing of experience; most important, it has dramatized the world of work. Today we model everything digitally, and usually visually, before we build it, manufacture it, or embrace it as policy or sales program. This ubiquitous modeling has reintroduced into the world of work literary and artistic coordinates which had been, as much as possible, banished from industrial enterprise in the mechanical age. It is not in the museum but in the marketplace, as a managerial agenda, that the extraordinary convergence of artistic impulse with its electronic expression has found its most striking instantiation.

Nothing in the world of postmodern art better illustrates this convergence than the work of the environmental artist Christo Javacheff. His *Running Fence, Sonoma and Marin Counties, California, 1972–76* embodies this rehearsal-reality and everything it implies. It is an epic *declamatio* of the modern integrated visual arts, a didactic rehearsal-reality event of the greatest scale, grandeur, beauty, and meaning. It allegorizes perfectly the influence that electronic expression is now having on the world of work.

In October 1972 Christo made the first drawings of a gigantic "fence" projected to run through farmland and end in the sea. He began to look for a site in northern California or Oregon. The fence was to run for twenty-four-and-a-half miles and to be built in segments eighteen feet high and sixty to eighty feet wide. By July of the following summer he had settled on an area around Petaluma, California, formed the Running Fence Corporation, and placed an order for 165,000 yards of woven nylon fabric. The period from July 1973 to April 1976 was taken up by eighteen public hearings to get the permits to build the fence, by several court sessions, a huge Environmental Impact Statement, and applications to fifteen government agencies, these activities all made possible through the kind offices of nine lawyers. Finally, after a tense final hearing, the project was free to proceed. On 7 September 1976, the part-time army of fabric-installation workers, 360 strong, began to deploy the fence. *Running Fence* turned out to be even more beautiful than Christo had imagined, sailing through the early morning fog, celebrating cows in their fields and the rolling hills in their glory, sailing like a silver ribbon toward the sea, punctuating the day from the dusk, scaling, scaling, forever scaling the landscape with its band of silver white, making from the air a ribbon of light across the earth, until at dusk it plunged into the sea.

Running Fence sounded all the notes in our current aesthetic chord. It was calculated to be of an age and not for all time, mortal rather than immortal, to represent what we cannot do forever, and should not do for long, to the land, to allegorize not our vain glory but our solemn sense of our own limitations. It was completed at noon on 10 September. On 21 September the dismantling began and by 23 October, eight days ahead of schedule, the entire fence had been removed and the pole anchors each driven three feet into the ground.

This powerful allegory of the world of work was not lost on the beholders. As one businessman wrote in the local paper, "the Running Fence will depict the evolution of man from the sea, his enormous efforts to survive and build on the land, and the ultimate destruction of that for which he has strived with such intensity for so very long. It is, indeed, a true artist and businessman that can conceive and execute so huge a philosophical symbol of the determination of man and the futile and transitory nature of his efforts. ... In all this I know whereof I speak. I am retired after forty years as an industrialist and rancher and all the businesses and enterprises that I developed are now gone. Little remains to show they were ever here. I have no regrets, it was great fun, but that is the way it is."[13]

Christo earned praise as a businessman by financing this project, as he does all his gargantuan projects, entirely himself. A huge book was published about the making of the fence.[14] Christo signed 3,000 copies of the book, which includes, besides all the gorgeous photographs of the project, a full history of it, copies of the relevant-government documents, film stills, and—a relic of the project—a small square of its nylon cloth. I own copy number 133, and what a book it is! For it is no more a normal codex book than the Fence was a normal fence. Like the square of cloth it contains, it is not a book about a work of art which it describes, a work past or present which remains detached from it. The book is part of the work of art, formed part of its essence and design from the beginning. Christo has reached out in time as well as space, included in his work of art the object itself and all the processes, from the beginning, that brought it into, and out of, being. This insistence on art as process rather than product, interactive temporal event rather than untouchable timeless masterpiece, I take to stand at the center of contemporary thinking about art, and about more than art.

I take the *Running Fence* book as a model of how codex books will work in an electronic world. We will construe them not as absolute entities but as part of an expressive process both alphabetic and iconic, an entity whose physicality is manifest, whose rhetoric is perfectly self-conscious, that is to say whose place in a complex matrix of behavior forms a native part of its expression. Most students of the matter agree that books will not vanish. They will, however, like the *Running Fence* book, send out nerve-tendrils to the complex expressive world surrounding them. The book for *Running Fence* is one kind of "printout" among many, which, taken together, form a record of the artistic event.

I would also take the *Running Fence* itself as a model for how the digital computer might function in the everyday world of work. Christo testified before the Sonoma County Board of Supervisors that "the work is not only the physical object of the fence. The work of art is really right now, and here [that hearing itself]. Everybody is a part of the art, that is, through the project of the *Running Fence*, and it is a most exciting thing, and there is not one single element in this project that is make-believe."[15] Christo has chosen to work in behavior, in human motive, as well as in canvas and light; he has chosen to make art out of economic cooperation, out of the processes of collective work. In America nowadays, these are all bureaucratic processes, and Christo has transformed them into self-conscious art. By subtracting the practical purpose, the enduring object—fence, pipeline, building, whatever—from the process, he has allowed everyone involved (and that includes all of us) to focus on, to become self-conscious about, the process involved, the process of human cooperation. To look AT it rather than THROUGH it. I think we can use electronic text in the same way and for the same purpose.

The self-consciousness of the device at least beckons us along this path far more cordially than ever print did.

I suggest, then, that we can use the digital computer, and more specifically electronic text, as a work of art very like Christo's *Running Fence*. It is always inviting us to play with ordinary experience rather than exploit it, to tickle a text or an image a little while using it, to defamiliarize it into art. And, as with scaling-change, as with both the objects and the actors in *Running Fence*—the hearing, the plan, the rendering, the Environmental Impact Statement; the construction worker, the councilman, the artist—human purpose will be both the same and utterly transformed. Is this radical democratization of art, this interweaving of play and purpose, so different from the range of hopes that computers inspired in the first generation of hackers who developed them?

I have been using some examples from the visual arts to sketch out what is sometimes called the postmodern critique, an argument whose elements we have now before us: art defined as attentton, beholder as well as object; thus an art that includes its beholder, and the beholder's beholder, an outward frame-expanding, an infinite *progress* rather than *regress*; interactive text, that is, art and criticism mixed together, and so art and life as well; a continually shifting series of scale-changes, of what literary theory would call contextualisms; a resolute use of self-consciousness to turn transparent attention to opaque contemplation, especially, as we began by noting, in regard to the typographical conventions of fully literate reading; above all, a pervasive reversal of use and ornament, a turning of purpose to play and game, a continual effort not, as wich the Arnoldian canon, to purify our motives, but to keep them in a roiling, rich mixture of play, game, and purpose. All of this yields a body of work active not passive, a canon not frozen in perfection but volatile with contending human motive.

Is this not the aesthetic of the personal computer? And is such an aesthetic not part of a world view larger still—as I have tried to suggest by choosing my illustrative images from the pre-electronic world? This larger world view occurs not only in the visual arts from which I have taken my examples, but in perception psychology from the transactionalists onward (the work upon which the Pop artists drew so heavily), in American role theory from George Herbert Mead to Erving Goffman, in evolutionary biology from the New Darwinian Synthesis onward, in Havelock's and Ong's formulation of the literate-oral polarity in Western discourse from classical Greece to the present day, in the East-West polarity which, using Balinese culture as ur-type, first Margaret Mead and Gregory Bareson and then Clifford Geertz have established, and in literary theory, which encapsulates much of this thinking. It occurs, indeed, practically everywhere we care to look in the contemporary intellectual landscape.

I have been suggesting that technology isn't *leading* us in these new directions. The arts, and the theoretical debate that tags along after them, have done the leading, and digitization has emerged as their condign embodiment. We needn't worry about digital determinism. We must explain, instead, the extraordinary convergence of twentieth-century thinking with the digital means that now give it expression. It is the *computer as fulfillment of social thought* that requires explanation.

How find a frame wide enough to provide such explication? To explain reading and writing on computers, we need to go back to the original Western thinking about reading and writing—the rhetorical paideia that provided the backbone of Western education for 2,000 years. Digital expression indeed fulfills the postmodern aesthetic, but also a much larger movement that comprehends and explains that aesthetic—a return to the traditional pattern of Western education through words. We are still bemused by the three hundred years of Newtonian simplification that made "rhetoric" a dirty word, but we are beginning to outgrow it. Digital expression, in such a context, becomes not a revolutionary technology but a conservative one. It attempts to reclaim, and rethink, the basic Western wisdom about words. Its perils prove to be the great but familiar perils that have always lurked in the divided, unstable, protean Western self.

Notes

1. Hubert L. Dreyfus, *What Computers Can't Do: The Limits of Artificial Intelligence* (1972; rev. ed., New York: Harper and Row, 1979).
2. Luciano De Maria, ed., *Marinetti e il Futurismo* (Milan; Mondadori, 1973), 189–90; my translation.
3. Ted Nelson, *Computer Lib/Dream Machines* (Redmond, Wash.: Microsoft Press, 1974; rev. ed. 1987). 27.
4. See, in this regard, Albertine Gaur's discussion in *A History of Writing*, rev. ed. (New York: Abbeville, Cross River), 179–81.
5. Kenneth Burke, *Collected Poems, 1915–1967* (Berkeley and Los Angeles: University of California Press, 1968), 88–92; fig. 3 reproduces p. 88.
6. John Baldessari, *Quality Material*, reproduced in Jean Lipman and Richard Marshall, *Art about Art* (New York: Dutton, 1978), 51.
7. Steven Levy, *Hackers: Heroes of the Computer Revolution* (Garden City, N.Y.: Anchor Press/Doubleday, 1984), 6–11.
8. See Claes Oldenburg, Coosje van Bruggen, and Frank O. Gehry, *Il Corso del Coltello/The Course of the Knife* (New York: Rizzoli, 1987).
9. Roy Lichtenstein, *Magnifying Glass*, reproduced in Kirk Varnedoe and Adam Gopnik, *High & Low, Popular Culture & Modern Art* (New York: Museum of Modern Art, 1990), 229.
10. Lawrence Alloway, *Roy Lichtenstein* (New York: Abbeville, 1983), 53.
11. Monet (Delta Tao Software, 1992).
12. Kid Pix (Broderbund Software, 1991).
13. Werner Spies, *The Running Fence Project: Christo*, rev. ed. (New York: Abrams, 1980), unpaged.
14. *Christo: Running Fence, Sonoma and Marin Counties, California 1972–76* (New York: Abrams, 1978).
15. Spies (n. 13 above).

2
What Is New Media?

Lev Manovich

What is new media? We may begin answering this question by listing the categories commonly discussed under this topic in the popular press: the Internet, Web sites, computer multimedia, computer games, CD-ROMs and DVD, virtual reality. Is this all there is to new media? What about television programs shot on digital video and edited on computer workstations? Or feature films that use 3-D animation and digital compositing? Shall we also count these as new media? What about images and text-image compositions—photographs, illustrations, layouts, ads—created on computers and then printed on paper? Where shall we stop?

As can be seen from these examples, the popular understanding of new media identifies it with the use of a computer for distribution and exhibition rather than production. Accordingly, texts distributed on a computer (Web sites and electronic books) are considered to be new media, whereas texts distributed on paper are not. Similarly, photographs that are put on a CD-ROM and require a computer to be viewed are considered new media; the same photographs printed in a book are not.

Shall we accept this definition? If we want to understand the effects of computerization on culture as a whole, I think it is too limiting. There is no reason to privilege the computer as a machine for the exhibition and distribution of media over the computer as a tool for media production or as a media storage device. All have the same potential to change existing cultural languages. And all have the same potential to leave culture as it is.

The last scenario is unlikely, however. What is more likely is that just as the printing press in the fourteenth century and photography in the nineteenth century had a revolutionary impact on the development of modern society and culture, today we are in the middle of a new media revolution—the shift of all culture to computer-mediated forms of production, distribution, and communication. This new revolution is arguably more profound than the previous ones, and we are just beginning to register its initial effects. Indeed, the introduction of the printing press affected only one stage of cultural communication—the distribution of media. Similarly, the introduction of photography affected only one type of cultural communication—still images. In contrast, the computer media revolution affects all stages of communication, including acquisition, manipulation, storage, and distribution; it also affects all types of media—texts, still images, moving images, sound, and spatial constructions.

Principles of New Media

The identity of media has changed even more dramatically than that of the computer. Below I summarize some of the key differences between old and new media. In compiling this list of differences, I tried to arrange them in a logical order. That is, the last three principles are dependent on the first two. This is not dissimilar to axiomatic logic, in which certain axioms are taken as starting points and further theorems are proved on their basis.

Not every new media object obeys these principles. They should be considered not as absolute laws but rather as general tendencies of a culture undergoing computerization. As computerization affects deeper and deeper layers of culture, these tendencies will increasingly manifest themselves.

1. Numerical Representation

All new media objects, whether created from scratch on computers or converted from analog media sources, are composed of digital code; they are numerical representations. This fact has two key consequences:

1. A new media object can be described formally (mathematically). For instance, an image or a shape can be described using a mathematical function.
2. A new media object is subject to algorithmic manipulation. For instance, by applying appropriate algorithms, we can automatically remove "noise" from a photograph, improve its contrast, locate the edges of the shapes, or change its proportions. In short, *media becomes programmable.*

When new media objects are created on computers, they originate in numerical form. But many new media objects are converted from various forms of old media. Although most readers understand the difference between analog and digital media, a few notes should be added on the terminology and the conversion process itself. This process assumes that data is originally *continuous*, that is, "the axis or dimension that is measured has no apparent indivisible unit from which it is composed."[1] Converting continuous data into a numerical representation is called *digitization*. Digitization consists of two steps: sampling and quantization. First, data is *sampled*, most often at regular intervals, such as the grid of pixels used to represent a digital image. The frequency of sampling is referred to as *resolution*. Sampling turns continuous data into *discrete* data, that is, data occurring in distinct units: people, the pages of a book, pixels. Second, each sample is *quantified*, that is, it is assigned a numerical value drawn from a defined range (such as 0–255 in the case of an 8-bit greyscale image).[2]

While some old media such as photography and sculpture are truly continuous, most involve the combination of continuous and discrete coding. One example is motion picture film: each frame is a continuous photograph, but time is broken into a number of samples (frames). Video goes one step further by sampling the frame along the vertical dimension (scan lines). Similarly, a photograph printed using a halftone process combines discrete and continuous representations. Such a photograph consists of a number of orderly dots (i.e., samples), although the diameters and areas of dots vary continuously.

As the last example demonstrates, while modern media contain levels of discrete representation, the samples are never quantified. This quantification of samples is the crucial step accomplished by digitization. But why, we may ask, are modern media technologies often in part discrete? The key assumption of modern semiotics is that communication requires discrete units. Without discrete units, there is no language. As Roland Barthes put it, "Language is, as it were, that which divides reality (for instance, the continuous spectrum of the colors is verbally reduced to a series of discontinuous terms)."[3] In assuming that any form of communication requires a discrete representation, semioticians took human language as the prototypical example of a communication system. A human language is discrete on most scales: We speak in sentences; a sentence is made from words; a word consists of morphemes, and so on. If we follow this assumption, we may expect that media used in cultural communication will have discrete levels. At first this theory seems to work. Indeed, a film samples the continuous time of human existence into discrete frames; a drawing samples visible reality into discrete lines; and a printed photograph samples it into discrete dots. This assumption does not universally work, however: Photographs, for instance, do not have any apparent units. (Indeed, in the 1970s semiotics was criticized for its linguistic bias, and most semioticians came to recognize that a language-based model of distinct units of meaning cannot be applied to many kinds of cultural communication.) More important, the discrete units of modern media are usually not units of meanings in the way morphemes are. Neither film frames nor halftone dots have any relation to how a film or photograph affects the viewer (except in modern art and avant-garde film—think of paintings by Roy Lichtenstein and films of Paul Sharits—which often make the "material" units of media into units of meaning).

The most likely reason modern media has discrete levels is because it emerged during the Industrial Revolution. In the nineteenth century, a new organization of production known as the factory system gradually replaced artisan labor. It reached its classical form when Henry Ford installed the first assembly line in his factory in 1913. The assembly line relied on two principles. The first was standardization of parts, already employed in the production of military uniforms in the nineteenth century. The second, newer principle was the separation of the production process into a set of simple, repetitive, and sequential activities that could be executed by workers who did not have to master the entire process and could be easily replaced.

Not surprisingly, modern media follows the logic of the factory, not only in terms of division of labor as witnessed in Hollywood film studios, animation studios, and television production, but also on the level of material organization. The invention of typesetting machines in the 1880s industrialized publishing while leading to a standardization of both type design and fonts (number and types). In the 1890s cinema combined automatically produced images (via photography) with a mechanical projector. This required standardization of both image dimensions (size, frame ratio, contrast) and temporal sampling rate. Even earlier, in the 1880s, the first television systems already involved standardization of sampling both in time and space. These modern media systems also followed factory logic in that, once a new "model" (a film, a photograph, an audio recording) was introduced, numerous identical media copies would be produced from this master. As I will show, new media follows, or actually runs ahead of, a quite different logic of post-industrial society—that of individual customization, rather than mass standardization.

2. Modularity

This principle can be called the "fractal structure of new media." Just as a fractal has the same structure on different scales, a new media object has the same modular structure throughout. Media elements, be they images, sounds, shapes, or behaviors, are represented as collections of discrete samples (pixels, polygons, voxels, characters, scripts). These elements are assembled into larger-scale objects but continue to maintain their separate identities. The objects themselves can be combined into even larger objects—again, without losing their independence. For example, a multimedia "movie" authored in popular Macromedia Director software may consist of hundreds of still images, QuickTime movies, and sounds that are stored separately and loaded at run time. Because all elements are stored independently, they can be modified at any time without having to change the Director "movie" itself. These "movies" can be assembled into a larger "movie," and so on. Another example of modularity is the concept of "object" used in Microsoft Office applications. When an "object" is inserted into a document (for instance, a media clip inserted into a Word document), it continues to maintain its independence and can always be edited with the program originally used to create it. Yet another example of modularity is the structure of an HTML document: With the exemption of text, it consists of a number of separate objects—GIF and JPEG images, media clips, Virtual Reality Modeling Language (VRML) scenes, Shockwave and Flash movies—which are all stored independently, locally, and/or on a network. In short, a new media object consists of independent parts, each of which consists of smaller independent parts, and so on, down to the level of the smallest "atoms"—pixels, 3-D points, or text characters.

The World Wide Web as a whole is also completely modular. It consists of numerous Web pages, each in its turn consisting of separate media elements. Every element can always be accessed on its own. Normally we think of elements as belonging to their corresponding Web sites, but this is just a convention, reinforced by commercial Web browsers. The Netomat browser by artist Maciej Wisnewski, which extracts elements of a particular media type from different Web pages (for instance, images only) and displays them together without identifying the Web sites from which they are drawn, highlights for us this fundamentally discrete and nonhierarchical organization of the Web.

In addition to using the metaphor of a fractal, we can also make an analogy between the modularity of new media and structured computer programming. Structural computer programming, which became standard in the 1970s, involves writing small and self-sufficient modules (called in different computer languages *subroutines, functions, procedures, scripts*), which are then assembled into larger programs. Many new media objects are in fact computer programs that follow structural programming style. For example, most interactive multimedia applications are written in Macromedia Director's Lingo. A Lingo program defines scripts that control various repeated actions, such as clicking on a button; these scripts are assembled into larger scripts. In the case of new media objects that are not computer programs, an analogy with structural programming still can be made because their parts can be accessed, modified, or substituted without affecting the overall structure of an object. This analogy, however, has its limits. If a particular module of a computer program is deleted, the program will not run. In contrast, as with traditional media, deleting parts of a new media object does not render it meaningless. In fact, the modular structure of new media makes such deletion and substitution of parts particularly easy. For example, since an HTML document consists of a number of separate objects each represented by a line of HTML code, it is very easy to delete, substitute, or add new objects. Similarly, since in Photoshop the parts of a digital image usually kept placed on separate layers, these parts can be deleted and substituted with a click of a button.

3. Automation

The numerical coding of media (principle 1) and the modular structure of a media object (principle 2) allow for the automation of many operations involved in media creation, manipulation, and access. Thus human intentionality can be removed from the creative process, at least in part.[4]

Following are some examples of what can be called "low-level" automation of media creation, in which the computer user modifies or creates from scratch a media object using templates or simple algorithms. These techniques are robust enough so that they are included in most commercial software for image editing, 3-D graphics, word processing, graphics layout, and so forth. Image-editing programs such as Photoshop can automatically correct scanned images, improving contrast range and removing noise. They also come with filters that can automatically modify an image, from creating simple variations of color to changing the whole image as though it were painted by Van Gogh, Seurat, or another brand-name artist. Other computer programs can automatically generate 3-D objects such as trees, landscapes, and human figures as well as detailed ready-to-use animations of complex natural phenomena such as fire and waterfalls. In Hollywood films, flocks of birds, ant colonies, and crowds of people are automatically created by AL (artificial life) software. Word processing, page layout, presentation, and Web creation programs come with "agents" that can automatically create the layout of a document. Writing software helps the user to create literary narratives using highly formalized genre conventions. Finally, in what may be the most familiar experience of automated media generation, many Web sites automatically generate Web pages on the fly when the user reaches the site. They assemble the information from databases and format it using generic templates and scripts.

Researchers are also working on what can be called "high-level" automation of media creation, which requires a computer to understand, to a certain degree, the meanings embedded in the objects being generated, that is, their semantics. This research can be seen as part of a larger project of artificial intelligence (AI). As is well known, the AI project has achieved only limited success since its beginnings in the 1950s. Correspondingly, work on media generation that requires an understanding of semantics is also in the research stage and is rarely included in commercial software. Beginning in the 1970s, computers were often used to generate poetry and fiction. In the 1990s, frequenters of Internet chat rooms became familiar with "bots"—computer programs that simulate human conversation. Researchers at New York University designed a "virtual theater" composed of a few "virtual actors" who adjusted their behavior in real-time in response to a user's actions.[5] The MIT Media Lab developed a number of different projects devoted to "high-level" automation of media creation and use: a "smart camera" that, when given a script, automatically follows the action and frames the shots;[6] ALIVE, a virtual environment where the user interacts with animated characters;[7] and a new kind of human-computer interface where the computer presents itself to a user as an animated talking character. The character, generated by a computer in real-time, communicates with the through user natural language; it also tries to guess the user's emotional state and to adjust the style of interaction accordingly.[8]

The area of new media where the average computer user encountered AI in the 1990s was not, however, the human-computer interface, but computer games. Almost every commercial game included a component called an "AI engine," which stands for the part of the game's computer code that controls its characters—car drivers in a car race simulation, enemy forces in a strategy game such as *Command and Conquer*, single attackers in first-person shooters such as *Quake*. AI engines use a variety of approaches to simulate human intelligence, from rule-based systems to neural networks. Like AI expert systems, the characters in computer games have expertise in some well-defined but narrow area such as attacking the user. But because computer games are highly codified and rule-based, these characters function very effectively; that is, they effectively respond to the few things the user is allowed to ask them to do: run forward, shoot, pick up an object. They cannot do anything else, but then the game does not provide the opportunity for the user to test this. For instance, in a martial arts fighting game, I can't ask questions of my opponent, nor do I expect him or her to start a conversation with me. All I can do is "attack" my opponent by pressing a few buttons, and within this highly codified situation the computer can "fight" me back very effectively. In short, computer characters can display intelligence and skills only because programs place severe limits on our possible interactions with them. Put differently, computers can pretend to be intelligent only by tricking us into using a very small part of who we are when we communicate with them, At the 1997 SIGGRAPH (Special Interest Group on Computer Graphics of the Association for Computing Machinery) convention, for example, I played against both human and computer-controlled characters in a VR simulation of a nonexistent sports game. All my opponents appeared as simple blobs coveting a few pixels of my VR display; at this resolution, it made absolutely no difference who was human and who was not.

Along with "low-level" and "high-level" automation of media creation, another area of media use subjected to increasing automation is media access. The switch to computers as a means of storing and accessing enormous amounts of media material, exemplified by the "media assets" stored in the databases of stock agencies and global entertainment conglomerates, as well as public "media assets" distributed across numerous Web sites, created the need to find more efficient ways to classify and search media objects. Word processors and other text-management software has long provided the capacity to search for specific strings of text and automatically index documents. The UNIX operating system also included powerful commands to search and filter text files. In the 1990s software designers started to provide media users with similar abilities. Virage introduced Virage VIR Image Engine, which allows one to search for visually similar image content among millions of images as well as a set of video search tools to allow indexing and searching video files.[9] By the end of the 1990s, the key Web search engines already included the option to search the Internet by specific media such as images, video, and audio.

The Internet, which can be thought of as one huge distributed media database, also crystallized the basic condition of the new information society: overabundance of information of all kinds. One response was the popular idea of software "agents" designed to automate searching for relevant information. Some agents act as filters that deliver small amounts of information given the user's criteria. Others allow users to tap into the expertise of other users, following their selections and choices. For example, the MIT Software Agents Group developed such agents as BUZZ watch, which "distills and tracks trends, themes, and topics within collections of texts across time" such as Internet discussions and Web pages; Letizia, "a user interface agent that assists a user browsing the World Wide Web by ... scouting ahead from the user's current position to find Web pages of possible interest"; and Footprints, which "uses information left by other people to help you find your way around."[10]

By the end of the twentieth century, the problem was no longer how to create a new media object such as an image; the new problem was how to find an object that already exists somewhere. If you want a particular image, chances are it already exists—but it may be easier to create one from scratch than to find an existing one. Beginning in the nineteenth century, modern society developed technologies that automated media creation—the photo camera, film camera, tape recorder, video recorder, etc. These technologies allowed us, over the course of 150 years, to accumulate an unprecedented amount of media materials—photo archives, film libraries, audio archives. This led to the next stage in media evolution—the need for new technologies to store, organize, and efficiently access these materials. The new technologies are all computer-based—media databases; hypermedia and other ways of organizing media material such as the hierarchical file system itself; text management software; programs for content-based search and retrieval. Thus automation of media access became the next logical stage of the process that had been put into motion when the first photograph was taken. The emergence of new media coincides with this second stage of a media society, now concerned as much with accessing and reusing existing media objects as with creating new ones.[11]

4. Variability

A new media object is not something fixed once and for all, but something that can exist in different, potentially infinite versions. This is another consequence of the numerical coding of media (principle 1) and the modular structure of a media object (principle 2).

Old media involved a human creator who manually assembled textual, visual, and/or audio elements into a particular composition or sequence. This sequence was stored in some material, its order determined once and for all. Numerous copies could be run off from the master, and, in perfect correspondence with the logic of an industrial society, they were all identical. New media, in contrast, is characterized by variability. (Other terms that are often used in relation to new media and that might serve as appropriate synonyms of *variable* are *mutable* and *liquid*.) Instead of identical copies, a new media object typically gives rise to many different versions. And rather than being created completely by a human author, these versions are often in part automatically assembled by a computer. (The example of Web pages automatically generated from databases using templates created by Web designers can be invoked here as well.) Thus the principle of variability is closely connected to automation.

Variability would also not be possible without modularity. Stored digitally, rather than in a fixed medium, media elements maintain their separate identities and can be assembled into numerous sequences under program control. In addition, because the elements themselves are broken into discrete samples (for instance, an image is represented as an array of pixels), they can be created and customized on the fly.

The logic of new media thus corresponds to the postindustrial logic of "production on demand" and "just in time" delivery logics that were themselves made possible by the use of computers and computer networks at all stages of manufacturing and distribution. Here, the "culture industry" (a term coined by Theodor Adorno in the 1930s) is actually ahead of most other industries. The idea that a customer might determine the exact features of her desired car at the showroom, transmit the specs to the factory, and hours later receive the car, remains a dream, but in the case of computer media, such immediacy is reality. Because the same machine is used as both showroom and factory, that is, the same computer generates and displays media—and because the media exists not as a material object but as data that can be sent through wires at the speed of light, the customized version created in response to the user's input is delivered almost immediately. Thus, to continue with the same example, when you access a Web site, the server immediately assembles a customized Web page.

Here are some particular cases of the variability principle:

1. Media elements are stored in a *media database*; a variety of end-user objects, which vary in resolution and in form and content, can be generated, either beforehand or on demand, from this database. At first, we might think that this is simply a particular technological implementation of the variability principle, but, in a computer age the database comes to function as a cultural form in its own right. It offers a particular model of the world and of the human experience. It also affects how the user conceives the data it contains.

2. It becomes possible to separate the levels of "content" (data) and interface. *A number of different interfaces can be created from the same data.* A new media object can be defined as one or more interfaces to a multimedia database.[12]

3. *Information about the user can be used by a computer program to customize automatically the media composition as well as to create elements themselves.* Examples: Web sites use information about the type of hardware and browser or user's network address to customize automatically the site the user will see; interactive computer installations use information about the user's body movements to generate sounds, shapes, and images, or to control the behavior of artificial creatures.

4. A particular case of this customization is *branching-type interactivity* (sometimes also called *"menu-based* interactivity"). The term refers to programs in which all the possible objects the user can visit form a branching tree structure. When the user reaches a particular object, the program presents her with choices and allows her to choose among them. Depending on the value chosen, the user advances along a particular branch of the tree. In this case the information used by a program is the output of the user's cognitive process, rather than the network address or body position.

5. *Hypermedia* is another popular new media structure, which is conceptually close to branching-type interactivity (because quite often the elements are connected using a branch tree structure). In hypermedia, the multimedia elements making a document are connected through hyperlinks. Thus the elements and the structure are independent of each other—rather than hard-wired together, as in traditional media. The World Wide Web is a particular implementation of hypermedia in which the elements are distributed throughout the network. Hypertext is a particular case of hypermedia that uses only one media type—text. How does the principle of variability work in this case? We can think of all possible paths through a hypermedia document as being different versions of it. By following the links, the user retrieves a particular version of a document.

6. Another way in which different versions of the same media objects are commonly generated in computer culture is through *periodic updates*. For instance, modern software applications can periodically check for updates on the Internet and then download and install these updates, sometimes without any action on the part of the user. Most Web sites are also periodically updated either manually or automatically, when the data in the databases that drive the sites changes. A particularly interesting case of this "updateability" feature is those sites that continuously update information such as stock prices or weather.

7.   One of the most basic cases of the variability principle is *scalability*, in which different versions of the same media object can be generated at various sizes or levels of detail. The metaphor of a map is useful in thinking about the scalability principle. If we equate a new media object with a physical territory, different versions of this object are like maps of this territory generated at different scales. Depending on the scale chosen, a map provides more or less detail about the territory. Indeed, different versions of a new media object may vary strictly qualitatively, that is, in the amount of detail present: For instance, a full-size image and its icon, automatically generated by Photoshop; a full text and its shorter version, generated by the "Autosummarize" command in Microsoft Word; or the different versions that can be created using the "Outline" command in Word. Beginning with version 3 (1997), Apple's QuickTime format made it possible to embed a number of different versions that differ in size within a single QuickTime movie; when a Web user accesses the movie, a version is automatically selected depending on connection speed. A conceptually similar technique called "distancing" or "level of detail" is used in interactive virtual worlds such as VRML scenes. A designer creates a number of models of the same object, each with progressively less detail. When the virtual camera is close to the object, a highly detailed model is used; if the object is far away, a less detailed version is automatically substituted by a program to save unnecessary computation of detail that cannot be seen anyway.

New media also allow us to create versions of the same object that differ from each other in more substantial ways. Here the comparison with maps of different scales no longer works. Examples of commands in commonly used software packages that allow the creation of such qualitatively different versions are "Variations" and "Adjustment layers" in Photoshop 5 and the "writing style" option in Word's "Spelling and Grammar" command. More examples can be found on the Internet where, beginning in the mid-1990s, it become common to create a few different versions of a Web site. The user with a fast connection can choose a rich multimedia version, whereas the user with a slow connection can choose a more bare-bones version that loads faster.

Among new media artworks, David Blair's *WaxWeb*, a Web site that is an "adaptation" of an hour-long video narrative, offers a more radical implementation of the scalability principle. While interacting with the narrative, the user can change the scale of representation at any point, going from an image-based outline of the movie to a complete script or a particular shot, or a VRML scene based on this shot, and so on.[13] Another example of how use of the scalability principle can create a dramatically new experience of an old media object is Stephen Mamber's database-driven representation of Hitchcock's *The Birds*. Mamber's software generates a still for every shot of the film; it then automatically combines all the stills into a rectangular matrix one shot per cell. As a result, time is spetialized, similar to the process in Edison's early Kinetoscope cylinders. Spatializing the film allows us to study its different temporal structures, which would be hard to observe otherwise. As in *WaxWeb*, the user can at any point change the scale of representation, going from a complete film to a particular shot.

As can be seen, the principle of variability is useful in allowing us to connect many important characteristics of new media that on first sight may appear unrelated. In particular, such popular new media structures as branching (or menu) interactivity and hypermedia can be seen as particular instances of the variability principle. In the case of branching interactivity, the user plays an active role in determining the order in which already generated elements are accessed. This is the simplest kind of interactivity; more complex kinds are also possible in which both the elements and the structure of the whole object are either modified or generated on the fly in response to the user's interaction with a program. We can refer to such implementations as *open interactivity* to distinguish them from the *closed interactivity* that uses fixed elements arranged in a fixed branching structure. Open interactivity can be implemented using a variety of approaches, including procedural and object-oriented computer programming, AI, AL, and neural networks.

As long as there exists some kernel, some structure, some prototype that remains unchanged throughout the interaction, open interactivity can be thought of as a subset of the variability principle. Here a useful analogy can be made with Wittgenstein's theory of family resemblance, later developed into the theory of prototypes by cognitive psychologists. In a family, a number of relatives will share some features, although no single family member may possess all of the features. Similarly, according to the theory of prototypes, the meanings of many words in a natural language derive not through logical definition but through proximity to a certain prototype.

Hypermedia, the other popular structure of new media, can also be seen as a particular case of the more general principle of variability. According to the definition by Halasz and Schwartz, hypermedia systems "provide their users with the ability to create, manipulate and/or examine a network of information-containing nodes interconnected by relational links."[14] Because in new media individual media elements (images, pages of text, etc.) always retain their individual identity (the principle of modularity), they can be "wired" together into more than one object. Hyperlinking is a particular way of achieving this wiring. A hyperlink creates a connection between two elements, for example, between two words in two different pages or a sentence on one page and an image in another, or two different places within the same page. Elements connected through hyperlinks can exist on the same computer or on different computers connected on a network, as in the case of the World Wide Web.

If in old media elements are "hardwired" into a unique structure and no longer maintain their separate identity, in hypermedia elements and structure are separate from each other. The structure of hyperlinks—typically a branching tree—can be specified independently from the contents of a document. To make an analogy with the grammar of a natural language as described in Noam Chomsky's early linguistic theory,[15] we can compare a hypermedia structure that specifies connections between nodes with the deep structure of a sentence; a particular hypermedia text can then be compared with a particular sentence in a natural language. Another useful analogy is computer programming. In programming, there is clear separation between algorithms and data. An algorithm specifies the sequence of steps to be performed on any data, just as a hypermedia structure specifies a set of navigation paths (i.e., connections between nodes) that potentially can be applied to any set of media objects.

The principle of variability exemplifies how, historically, changes in media technologies are correlated with social change. If the logic of old media corresponded to the logic of industrial mass society, the logic of new media fits the logic of the postindustrial society, which values individuality over conformity. In industrial mass society everyone was supposed to enjoy the same goods—and to share the same beliefs. This was also the logic of media technology. A media object was assembled in a media factory (such as a Hollywood studio). Millions of identical copies were produced from a master and distributed to all the citizens. Broadcasting, cinema, and print media all followed this logic.

In a postindustrial society, every citizen can construct her own custom lifestyle and "select" her ideology from a large (but not infinite) number of choices. Rather than pushing the same objects/information to a mass audience, marketing now tries to target each individual separately. The logic of new media technology reflects this new social logic. Every visitor to a Web site automatically gets her own custom version of the site created on the fly from a database. The language of the text, the contents, the ads displayed—all these can be customized. According to a report in *USA Today* (9 November 1999), "Unlike ads in magazines or other real-world publications, 'banner' ads on Web pages change with every page view. And most of the companies that place the ads on the Web site track your movements across the Net, 'remembering' which ads you've seen, exactly when you saw them, whether you clicked on them, where you were at the time, and the site you have visited just before."[16]

Every hypertext reader gets her own version of the complete text by selecting a particular path through it. Similarly, every user of an interactive installation gets her own version of the work. And so on. In this way new media technology acts as the most perfect realization of the utopia of an ideal society composed of unique individuals. New media objects assure users that their choices—and therefore, their underlying thoughts and desires—are unique, rather than preprogrammed and shared with others. As though trying to compensate for their earlier role in making us all the same, descendants of the Jacquard loom, the Hollerith tabulator, and Zuse's cinema-computer are now working to convince us that we are all unique.

The principle of variability as presented here has some parallels to the concept of "variable media," developed by the artist and curator Jon Ippolito.[17] I believe that we differ in two key respects. First, Ippolito uses variability to describe a characteristic shared by recent conceptual and some digital art, whereas I see variability as a basic condition of all new media, not only art. Second, Ippolito follows the tradition of conceptual art in which an artist can vary any dimension of the artwork, even its content; my use of the term aims to reflect the logic of mainstream culture in that versions of the object share some well-defined "data." This "data," which can be a well-known narrative (*Psycho*), an icon (Coca-Cola sign), a character (Mickey Mouse), or a famous star (Madonna), is referred to in the media industry as "property." Thus all cultural projects produced by Madonna will be automatically united by her name. Using the theory of prototypes, we can say that the property acts as a prototype, and different versions are derived from this prototype. Moreover, when a number of versions are being commercially released based on some "property," usually one of these versions is treated as the source of the "data," with others positioned as being derived from this source. Typically, the version that is in the same media as the original "property" is treated as the source. For instance, when a movie studio releases a new film, along with a computer game based on it, product tie-ins, music written for the movie, etc., the film is usually presented as the "base" object from which other objects are derived. So when George Lucas releases a new *Star Wars* movie, the original property—the original *Star Wars* trilogy—is referenced. The new movie becomes the "base" object, and all other media objects released along with it refer to this object. Conversely, when computer games such as *Tomb Raider* are remade into movies, the original computer game is presented as the "base" object.

Although I deduce the principle of variability from more basic principles of new media— numerical representation and modularity of information—the principle can also be seen as a consequence of the computer's way of representing data—and modeling the world itself—as variables rather than constants. As new media theorist and architect Marcos Novak notes, a computer—and computer culture in its wake—substitutes every constant with a variable.[18]

In designing all functions and data structures, a computer programmer tries always to use variables rather than constants. On the level of the human-computer interface, this principle means that the user is given many options to modify the performance of a program or a media object, be it a computer game, Web site, Web browser, or the operating system itself. The user can change the profile of a game character, modify how folders appear on the desktop, how files are displayed, what icons are used, and so forth. If we apply this principle to culture at large, it would mean that every choice responsible for giving a cultural object a unique identity can potentially remain always open. Size, degree of detail, format, color, shape, interactive trajectory, trajectory through space, duration, rhythm, point of view, the presence or absence of particular characters, the development of plot—to name just a few dimensions of cultural objects in different media—can all be defined as variables, to be freely modified by a user.

Do we want, or need, such freedom? As the pioneer of interactive filmmaking Grahame Weinbren argues, in relation to interactive media, making a choice involves a moral responsibility.[19] By passing on these choices to the user, the author also passes on the responsibility to represent the world and the human condition in it. (A parallel is the use of phone or Web-based automated menu systems by big companies to handle their customers; while companies have turned to such systems in the name of "choice" and "freedom," one of the effects of this type of automation is that labor is passed from the company's employees to the customer. If before a customer would get the information or buy the product by interacting with a company employee, now she has to spend her own time and energy navigating through numerous menus to accomplish the same result.) The moral anxiety that accompanies the shift from constants to variables, from traditions to choices in all areas of life in a contemporary society, and the corresponding anxiety of a writer who has to portray it, is well rendered in the closing passage of a short story by the contemporary American writer Rick Moody (the story is about the death of his sister):[20]

> I should fictionalize it more, I should conceal myself. I should consider the responsibilities of characterization, I should conflate her two children into one, or reverse their genders, or otherwise alter them, I should make her boyfriend a husband, I should explicate all the tributaries of my extended family (its remarriages, its internecine politics), I should novelize the whole thing, I should make it multigenerational, I should work in my forefathers (stonemasons and newspapermen), I should let artifice create an elegant surface, I should make the events orderly, I should wait and write about it later, I should wait until I'm not angry, I shouldn't clutter a narrative with fragments, with mere recollections of good times, or with regrets, I should make Meredith's death shapely and persuasive, not blunt and disjunctive, I shouldn't have to think the unthinkable, I shouldn't have to suffer, I should address her here directly (these are the ways I miss you), I should write only of affection, I should make our travels in this earthly landscape safe and secure, I should have a better ending, I shouldn't say her life was short and often sad, I shouldn't say she had demons, as I do too.

5. Transcoding

Beginning with the basic, "material" principles of new media—numeric coding and modular organization—we moved to more "deep" and far-reaching ones—automation and variability. The fifth and last principle of cultural transcoding aims to describe what in my view is the most substantial consequence of the computerization of media. As I have suggested, computerization turns media into computer data. While from one point of view, computerized media still displays structural organization that makes sense to its human users—images feature recognizable objects; text files consist of grammatical sentences; virtual spaces are defined along the familiar Cartesian coordinate system; and so on—from another point of view, its structure now follows the established conventions of the computer's organization of data. Examples of these conventions are different data structures such as lists, records, and arrays; the already-mentioned substitution of all constants by variables; the separation between algorithms and data structures; and modularity.

The structure of a computer image is a case in point. On the level of representation, it belongs on the side of human culture, automatically entering in dialog with other images, other cultural "semes" and "mythemes." But on another level, it is a computer file that consists of a machine-readable header, followed by numbers representing color values of its pixels. On this level it enters into a dialog with other computer files. The dimensions of this dialog are not the image's content, meanings, or formal qualities, but rather file size, file type, type of compression used, file format, and so on. In short, these dimensions belong to the computer's own cosmogony rather than to human culture.

Similarly, new media in general can be thought of as consisting of two distinct layers—the "cultural layer" and the "computer layer." Examples of categories belonging to the cultural layer are the encyclopedia and the short story; story and plot; composition and point of view; mimesis and catharsis, comedy and tragedy. Examples of categories in the computer layer are process and packet (as in data packets transmitted through the network); sorting and matching; function and variable; computer language and data structure.

Because new media is created on computers, distributed via computers, and stored and archived on computers, the logic of a computer can be expected to significantly influence the traditional cultural logic of media; that is, we may expect that the computer layer will affect the cultural layer. The ways in which the computer models the world, represents data, and allows us to operate on it; the key operations behind all computer programs (such as search, match, sort, and filter); the conventions of HCI—in short, what can be called the computer's ontology, epistemology, and pragmatics—influence the cultural layer of new media, its organization, its emerging genres, its contents.

Of course, what I call "the computer layer" is not itself fixed but rather changes over time. As hardware and software keep evolving and as the computer is used for new tasks and in new ways, this layer undergoes continuous transformation. The new use of the computer as a media machine is a case in point. This use is having an effect on the computer's hardware and software, especially on the level of the human-computer interface, which increasingly resembles the interfaces of older media machines and cultural technologies—VCR, tape player, photo camera.

In summary, the computer layer and the culture layer influence each other. To use another concept from new media, we can say that they are being composited together. The result of this composite is a new computer culture—a blend of human and computer meanings, of traditional ways in which human culture modeled the world and the computer's own means of representing it.[…]

[…]In new media lingo, to "transcode" something is to translate it into another format. The computerization of culture gradually accomplishes similar transcoding in relation to all cultural categories and concepts. That is, cultural categories and concepts are substituted, on the level of meaning and/or language, by new ones that derive from the computer's ontology, epistemology, and pragmatics. New media thus acts as a forerunner of this more general process of cultural reconceptualization.

Given the process of "conceptual transfer" from the computer world to culture at large, and given the new status of media as computer data, what theoretical framework can we use to understand it? On one level new media is old media that has been digitized, so it seems appropriate to look at new media using the perspective of media studies. We may compare new media and old media such as print, photography, or television. We may also ask about the conditions of distribution and reception and patterns of use. We may also ask about similarities and differences in the material properties of each medium and how these affect their aesthetic possibilities.

This perspective is important and I am using it frequently, but it cannot address the most fundamental quality of new media that has no historical precedent—programmability. Comparing new media to print, photography, or television will never tell us the whole story. For although from one point of view new media is indeed another type of media, from another it is simply a particular type of computer data, something stored in files and databases, retrieved and sorted, run through algorithms and written to the output device. That the data represent pixels and that this device happens to be an output screen is beside the point. The computer may perform perfectly the role of the Jacquard loom, but underneath it is fundamentally Babbage's Analytical Engine—after all, this was its identity for 150 years. New media may look like media, but this is only the surface.

Notes

1. Isaac Victor Kerlov and Judson Rosebush, *Computer Graphics for Designers and Artists* (New York: Van Nostrand Reinhold, 1986), 14.
2. Ibid., 21.
3. Roland Barthes, *Elements of Semiology*, trans. Annette Lavers and Colin Smith (New York: Hill and Wang, 1968), 64.
4. I discuss particular cases of computer automation of visual communication in more detail in "Automation of Sight from Photography to Computer Vision," *Electronic Culture: Technology and Visual Representation*, ed. by Timothy Druckrey and Michael Sand (New York: Aperture, 1996), 229–239; and in "Mapping Space: Perspective, Radar, and Computer Graphics," *SIGGRAPH '93 Visual Proceedings*, ed. by Thomas Linehan (New York: ACM, 1993). 143–147.
5. http://www.mrl.nyu.edu/improv/.
6. http://www-white.media.mit.edu/vismod/demos/smartcam/.
7. http.//pattie.www.media.mit.edu/people/pattie/CACM-95/dife-cacm95.html.
8. This research was pursued at different groups at the MIT lab, Sec, for instance, the home page of the Gesture and Narrative Language Group, http://gn.www.media.mit.edu/groups/gn/.
9. See http://www.virage.com/products.
10. http://agents.www.media.mir.edu/groups/agents/projects/.
11. See my "Avant-Garde as Software," in *Ostranenie*, ed. Stephen Kovats (Frankfurt and New York: Campus Verlag, 1999) (htrp://visarts.ucsd.edu/-manovich).
12. For an experiment in creating different multimedia interfaces to the same text, see my *Freud-Lissitzky Navigator* (http://visarts.ucsd.edu/-manovich/FLN).
13. http://jefferson.village.virginia.edu/wax/.
14. Frank Halasz and Mayer Schwartz, "The Dexter Hypertext Reference Model," *Communication of the ACM* (New York: ACM, 1994), 30.
15. Noam Chomsky, *Syntactic Structures* (The Hague and Paris: Mouton, 1957).
16. "How Marketers 'Profile' Users," *USA Today* 9 November 1999, 2A.
17. See http://www.three.org. Our conversations helped me to clarify my ideas, and I am very grateful to Jon for the ongoing exchange.
18. Marcos Novak, lecture at the "Interactive Frictions" conference, University of Southern California, Los Angeles, 6 June 1999.
19. Grahame Weinbren, "In the Ocean of Streams of Story," *Millennium Film Journal* 28 (Spring 1995), http://www.sva .edu/MFJ/journalpages/MFJ28/GWOCEAN.HTML.
20. Rick Moody, *Demonology*, first published in *Conjunctions*, reprinted in *The KGB Bar Reader*, quoted in Vince Passaro, "Unlikely Stories," *Harper's Magazine* vol. 299, no. 1791 (August 1999), 88–89.

3
A Pedagogy of Multiliteracies
Designing Social Futures

New London Group[1]

In this article, the New London Group presents a theoretical overview of the connections between the changing social environment facing students and teachers and a new approach to literacy pedagogy that they call "multiliteracies." The authors argue that the multiplicity of communications channels and increasing cultural and linguistic diversity in the world today call for a much broader view of literacy than portrayed by traditional language-based approaches. Multiliteracies, according to the authors, overcomes the limitations of traditional approaches by emphasizing how negotiating the multiple linguistic and cultural differences in our society is central to the pragmatics of the working, civic, and private lives of students. The authors maintain that the use of multiliteracies approaches to pedagogy will enable students to achieve the authors' twin goals for literacy learning: creating access to the evolving language of work, power, and community, and fostering the critical engagement necessary for them to design their social futures and achieve success through fulfilling employment.

If it were possible to define generally the mission of education, one could say that its fundamental purpose is to ensure that all students benefit from learning in ways that allow them to participate fully in public, community, and economic life. Literacy pedagogy is expected to play a particularly important role in fulfilling this mission. Pedagogy is a teaching and learning relationship that creates the potential for building learning conditions leading to full and equitable social participation. Literacy pedagogy has traditionally meant teaching and learning to read and write in page-bound, official, standard forms of the national language. Literacy pedagogy, in other words, has been a carefully restricted project—restricted to formalized, monolingual, monocultural, and rule-governed forms of language.

In this article, we attempt to broaden this understanding of literacy and literacy teaching and learning to include negotiating a multiplicity of discourses. We seek to highlight two principal aspects of this multiplicity. First, we want to extend the idea and scope of literacy pedagogy to account for the context of our culturally and linguistically diverse and increasingly globalized societies, for the multifarious cultures that interrelate and the plurality of texts that circulate. Second, we argue that literacy pedagogy now must account for the burgeoning variety of text forms associated with information and multimedia technologies. This includes understanding and competent control of representational forms that are becoming increasingly significant in the overall communications environment, such as visual images and their relationship to the written word—for instance, visual design in desktop publishing or the interface of visual and linguistic meaning in multimedia. Indeed, this second point relates closely back to the first; the proliferation of communications channels and media supports and extends cultural and subcultural diversity. As soon as our sights are set on the objective of creating the learning conditions for full social participation, the issue of differences becomes critically important. How do we ensure that differences of culture, language, and gender are not barriers to educational success? And what are the implications of these differences for literacy pedagogy?

This question of differences has become a main one that we must now address as educators. And although numerous theories and practices have been developed as possible responses, at the moment there seems to be particular anxiety about how to proceed. What is appropriate education for women, for indigenous peoples, for immigrants who do not speak the national language, for speakers of non-standard dialects? What is appropriate for all in the context of the ever more critical factors of local diversity and global connectedness? As educators attempt to address the context of cultural and linguistic diversity through literacy pedagogy, we hear shrill claims and counterclaims about political correctness, the canon of great literature, grammar, and back-to-basics.

The prevailing sense of anxiety is fueled in part by the sense that, despite goodwill on the part of educators, despite professional expertise, and despite the large amounts of money expended to develop new approaches, there are still vast disparities in life chances—disparities that today seem to be widening still further. At the same time, radical changes are occurring in the nature of public, community, and economic life. A strong sense of citizenship seems to be giving way to local fragmentation, and communities are breaking into ever more diverse and subculturally defined groupings. The changing technological and organizational shape of working life provides some with access to lifestyles of unprecedented affluence, while excluding others in ways that are increasingly related to the outcomes of education and training. It may well be that we have to rethink what we are teaching, and, in particular, what new learning needs literacy pedagogy might now address.

The ten authors of this text are educators who met for a week in September 1994 in New London, New Hampshire, in the United States, to discuss the state of literacy pedagogy. Members of the group had either worked together or drawn from each other's work over a number of years. The main areas of common or complementary concern included the pedagogical tension between immersion and explicit models of teaching; the challenge of cultural and linguistic diversity; the newly prominent modes and technologies of communication; and changing text usage in restructured workplaces. When we met in 1994, our purpose was to consolidate and extend these relationships in order to address the broader issue of the purposes of education, and, in this context, the specific issue of literacy pedagogy. It was our intention to pull together ideas from a number of different domains and a number of different English-speaking countries. Our main concern was the question of life chances as it relates to the broader moral and cultural order of literacy pedagogy.

Being ten distinctly different people, we brought to this discussion a great variety of national, life, and professional experiences. Courtney Cazden from the United States has spent a long and highly influential career working on classroom discourse, on language learning in multilingual contexts, and, most recently, on literacy pedagogy. Bill Cope, from Australia, has written curricula addressing cultural diversity in schools, and has researched literacy pedagogy and the changing cultures and discourses of workplaces. From Great Britain, Norman Fairclough is a theorist of language and social meaning, and is particularly interested in linguistic and discursive change as part of social and cultural change. James Gee, from the United States, is a leading researcher and theorist on language and mind, and on the language and learning demands of the latest "fast capitalist" workplaces. Mary Kalantzis, an Australian, has been involved in experimental social education and literacy curriculum projects, and is particularly interested in citizenship education. Gunther Kress, from Great Britain, is best known for his work on language and learning, semiotics, visual literacy, and the multimodal literacies that are increasingly important to all communication, particularly the mass media. Allan Luke, from Australia, is a researcher and theorist of critical literacy who has brought sociological analysis to bear on the teaching of reading and writing. Carmen Luke, also from Australia, has written extensively on feminist pedagogy. Sarah Michaels, from the United States, has had extensive experience in developing and researching programs of classroom learning in urban settings. Martin Nakata, an Australian, has researched and written on the issue of literacy in indigenous communities.

Creating a context for the meeting were our differences of national experience and differences of theoretical and political emphasis. For instance, we needed to debate at length the relative importance of immersion and explicit teaching; our differing expert interests in the areas of multimedia, workplace literacies, and cultural and linguistic diversity; and the issue of the extent to which we should compromise with the learning expectations and ethos of new forms of workplace organization. We engaged in the discussions on the basis of a genuine commitment to collaborative problem-solving, bringing together a team with different knowledge, experiences, and positions in order to optimize the possibility of effectively addressing the complex reality of schools.

Being aware of our differences, we shared the concern that our discussion might not be productive, yet it was: *because* of our differences, combined with our common sense of unease, we were able to agree on the fundamental problem—that is, that the disparities in educational outcomes did not seem to be improving. We agreed that we should get back to the broad question of the social outcomes of language learning, and that we should, on this basis, rethink the fundamental premises of literacy pedagogy in order to influence practices that will give students the skills and knowledge they need to achieve their aspirations. We agreed that in each of the English-speaking countries we came from, what students needed to learn was changing, and that the main element of this change was that there was not a singular, canonical English that could or should be taught anymore. Cultural differences and rapidly shifting communications media meant that the very nature of the subject—literacy pedagogy—was changing radically. This article is a summary of our discussions.

The structure of this article evolved from the New London discussions. We began the discussions with an agenda that we had agreed upon in advance, which consisted of a schematic framework of key questions about the forms and content of literacy pedagogy. Over the course of our meeting, we worked through this agenda three times, teasing out difficult points, elaborating on the argument, and adapting the schematic structure that had been originally proposed. One team member typed key points, which were projected onto a screen so we could discuss the wording of a common argument. By the end of the meeting, we developed the final outline of an argument, subsequently to become this article. The various members of the group returned to their respective countries and institutions, and worked independently on the different sections; the draft was circulated and modified; and, finally, we opened up the article to public discussion in a series of plenary presentations and small discussion groups led by the team at the Fourth International Literacy and Education Research Network Conference held in Townsville, Australia, in June-July 1995.

This article is the result of a year's exhaustive discussions, yet it is by no means a finished piece. We present it here as a programmatic manifesto, as a starting point of sorts, open and tentative. The article is a theoretical overview of the current social context of learning and the consequences of social changes for the content (the "what") and the form (the "how") of literacy pedagogy. We hope that this article might form the basis for open-ended dialogue with fellow educators around the world; that it might spark ideas for possible new research areas; and that it might help frame curriculum experimentation that attempts to come to grips with our changing educational environment.

We decided that the outcomes of our discussions could be encapsulated in one word—multiliteracies—a word we chose to describe two important arguments we might have with the emerging cultural, institutional, and global order: the multiplicity of communications channels and media, and the increasing saliency of cultural and linguistic diversity. The notion of multiliteracies supplements traditional literacy pedagogy by addressing these two related aspects of textual multiplicity. What we might term "mere literacy" remains centered on language only, and usually on a singular national form of language at that, which is conceived as a stable system based on rules such as mastering sound-letter correspondence. This is based on the assumption that we can discern and describe correct usage. Such a view of language will characteristically translate into a more or less authoritarian kind of pedagogy. A pedagogy of muliliteracies, by contrast, focuses on modes of representation much broader than language alone. These differ according to culture and context, and have specific cognitive, cultural, and social effects. In some cultural contexts—in an Aboriginal community or in a multimedia environment, for instance—the visual mode of representation may be much more powerful and closely related to language than "mere literacy" would ever be able to allow. Multiliteracies also creates a different kind of pedagogy, one in which language and other modes of meaning are dynamic representational resources, constantly being remade by their users as they work to achieve their various cultural purposes.

Two main arguments, then, emerged in our discussions. The first relates to the increasing multiplicity and integration of significant modes of meaning-making, where the textual is also related to the visual, the audio, the spatial, the behavioral, and so on. This is particularly important in the mass media, multimedia, and in an electronic hypermedia. We may have cause to be skeptical about the sci-fi visions of information superhighways and an impending future where we are all virtual shoppers. Nevertheless, new communications media are reshaping the way we use language. When technologies of meaning are changing so rapidly, there cannot be one set of standards or skills that constitute the ends of literacy learning, however taught.

Second, we decided to use the term "multiliteracies" as a way to focus on the realities of increasing local diversity and global connectedness. Dealing with linguistic differences and cultural differences has now become central to the pragmatics of our working, civic, and private lives. Effective citizenship and productive work now require that we interact effectively using multiple languages, multiple Englishes, and communication patterns that more frequently cross cultural, community, and national boundaries. Subcultural diversity also extends to the ever broadening range of specialist registers and situational variations in language, be they technical, sporting, or related to groupings of interest and affiliation. When the proximity of cultural and linguistic diversity is one of the key facts of our time, the very nature of language learning has changed.

Indeed, these are fundamental issues about our future. In addressing these issues, literacy educators and students must see themselves as active participants in social change, as learners and students who can be active designers—makers—of social futures. We decided to begin the discussion with this question of social futures.

Accordingly, the starting point of this article is the shape of social change—changes in our working lives, our public lives as citizens, and our private lives as members of different community lifeworlds. The fundamental questions is this: What do these changes mean for literacy pedagogy? In the context of these changes we then go on to conceptualize the "what" of literacy pedagogy. The key concept we introduce is that of Design, in which we are both inheritors of patterns and conventions of meaning and at the same time active designers of meaning. And, as designers of meaning, we are designers of social futures—workplace futures, public futures, and community futures. The article goes on to discuss six design elements in the meaning-making process: those of Linguistic Meaning, Visual Meaning, Audio Meaning, Gestural Meaning, Spatial Meaning, and the Multimodal patterns of meaning that relate the first five modes of meaning to each other. In its last major section, the article translates the "what" into a "how." Four components of pedagogy are suggested: Situated Practice, which draws on the experience of meaning-making in lifeworlds, the public realm, and workplaces; Overt Instruction, through which students develop an explicit metalanguage of Design; Critical Framing, which interprets the social context and purpose of Designs of meaning; and Transformed Practice, in which students, as meaning-makers, become Designers of social futures. In the International Multiliteracies Project upon which we are now embarking, we hope to set up collaborative research relationships and programs of curriculum development that test, exemplify, extend, and rework the ideas tentatively suggested in this article.

The Changing Present and Near Futures: Visions for Work, Citizenship, and Lifeworlds

The languages needed to make meaning are radically changing in three realms of our existence: our working lives, our public lives (citizenship), and our private lives (lifeworld).

Changing Working Lives

We are living through a period of dramatic global economic change, as new business and management theories and practices emerge across the developed world. These theories and practices stress competition and markets centered around change, flexibility, quality, and distinctive niches—not the mass products of the "old" capitalism (Boyett & Conn, 1992; Cross, Feather, & Lynch, 1994; Davidow & Malone, 1992; Deal & Jenkins, 1994; Dobyns & Crawford-Mason, 1991; Drucker, 1993; Hammer & Champy, 1993; Ishikawa, 1985; Lipnack & Stamps, 1993; Peters, 1992; Sashkin & Kiser, 1993; Senge, 1991). A whole new terminology crosses and re-crosses the borders between these new business and management discourses, on the one hand, and discourses concerned with education, educational reform, and cognitive science, on the other (Bereiter & Scardamalia, 1993; Bruer, 1993; Gardner, 1991; Lave & Wenger, 1991; Light & Butterworth, 1993; Perkins, 1992; Rogoff, 1990). The new management theory uses words that are very familiar to educators, such as knowledge (as in "knowledge worker"), learning (as in "learning organization"), collaboration, alternative assessments, communities of practice, networks, and others (Gee, 1994a). In addition, key terms and interests of various postmodern and critical discourses focusing on liberation, the destruction of hierarchies, and the honoring of diversity (Faigley, 1992; Freire, 1968, 1973; Freire & Macedo, 1987; Gee, 1993; Giroux, 1988; Walkerdine, 1986) have found their way into these new business and management discourses (Gee, 1994b).

The changing nature of work has been variously called "postFordism" (Piore & Sable, 1984) and "fast capitalism" (Gee, 1994b). *PostFordism* replaces the old hierarchical command structures epitomized in Henry Ford's development of mass production techniques and represented in caricature by Charlie Chaplin in *Modern Times*—an image of mindless, repetitive unskilled work on the industrial production line. Instead, with the development of postFordism or fast capitalism, more and more workplaces are opting for a flattened hierarchy. Commitment, responsibility, and motivation are won by developing a workplace culture in which the members of an organization identify with its vision, mission, and corporate values. The old vertical chains of command are replaced by the horizontal relationships of teamwork. A division of labor into its minute, deskilled components is replaced by "multi-skilled," well-rounded workers who are flexible enough to be able to do complex and integrated work (Cope & Kalantzis, 1995). Indeed, in the most advanced of postFordist, fast capitalist workplaces, traditional structures of command and control are being replaced by relationships of pedagogy: mentoring, training, and the learning organization (Senge, 1991). Once divergent, expert, disciplinary knowledges such as pedagogy and management are now becoming closer and closer. This means that, as educators, we have a greater responsibility to consider the implications of what we do in relation to a productive working life.

With a new worklife comes a new language. A good deal of this change is the result of new technologies, such as the iconographic, text, and screen-based modes of interacting with automated machinery; "user-friendly" interfaces operate with more subtle levels of cultural embeddedness than interfaces based on abstract commands. But much of the change is also the result of the new social relationships of work. Whereas the old Fordist organization depended upon clear, precise, and formal systems of command, such as written memos and the supervisor's orders, effective teamwork depends to a much greater extent on informal, oral, and interpersonal discourse. This informality also translates into hybrid and interpersonally sensitive informal written forms, such as electronic mail (Sproull & Kiesler, 1991). These examples of revolutionary changes in technology and the nature of organizations have produced a new language of work. They are all reasons why literacy pedagogy has to change if it is to be relevant to the new demands of working life, if it is to provide all students with access to fulfilling employment.

But fast capitalism is also a nightmare. Corporate cultures and their discourses of familiarity are more subtly and more rigorously exclusive than the most nasty—honestly nasty—of hierarchies. Replication of corporate culture demands assimilation to mainstream norms that only really works if one already speaks the language of the mainstream. If one is not comfortably a part of the culture and discourses of the mainstream, it is even harder to get into networks that operate informally than it was to enter into the old discourses of formality. This is a crucial factor in producing the phenomenon of the glass ceiling, the point at which employment and promotion opportunities come to an abrupt stop. And fast capitalism, notwithstanding its discourse of collaboration, culture, and shared values, is also a vicious world driven by the barely restrained market. As we remake our literacy pedagogy to be more relevant to a new world of work, we need to be aware of the danger that our words become co-opted by economically and market-driven discourses, no matter how contemporary and "post-capitalist" these may appear. The new fast capitalist literature stresses adaptation to constant change through thinking and speaking for oneself, critique and empowerment, innovation and creativity, technical and systems thinking, and learning how to learn. All of these ways of thinking and acting are carried by new and emerging discourses. These new workplace discourses can be taken in two very different ways—as opening new educational and social possibilities, or as new systems of mind control or exploitation. In the positive sense, for instance, the emphases on innovation and creativity may fit well with a pedagogy that views language and other modes of representation as dynamic and constantly being remade by meaning-makers in changing and varied contexts. However, it may well be that market-directed theories and practices, even though they sound humane, will never authentically include a vision of meaningful success for all students. Rarely do the proponents of these ideas seriously consider them relevant to people destined for skilled and elite forms of employment. Indeed, in a system that still values vastly disparate social outcomes, there will never be enough room "at the top." An authentically democratic view of schools must include a vision of meaningful success for all, a vision of success that is not defined exclusively in economic terms and that has embedded within it a critique of hierarchy and economic injustice.

In responding to the radical changes in working life that are currently underway, we need to tread a careful path that provides students the opportunity to develop skills for access to new forms of work through learning the new language of work. But at the same time, as teachers, our role is not simply to be technocrats. Our job is not to produce docile, compliant workers. Students need to develop the capacity to speak up, to negotiate, and to be able to engage critically with the conditions of their working lives.

Indeed, the twin goals of access and critical engagement need not be incompatible. The question is, how might we depart from the latest views and analyses of high-tech, globalized, and culturally diverse workplaces and relate these to educational programs that are based on a broad vision of the good life and an equitable society? Paradoxically, the new efficiency requires new systems of getting people motivated that might be the basis for a democratic pluralism in the workplace and beyond. In the realm of work, we have called this utopian possibility productive diversity, the idea that what seems to be a problem—the multiplicity of cultures, experiences, ways of making meaning, and ways of thinking—can be harnessed as an asset (Cope & Kalantzis, 1995). Cross-cultural communication and the negotiated dialogue of different languages and discourses can be a basis for worker participation, access, and creativity, for the formation of locally sensitive and globally extensive networks that closely relate organizations to their clients or suppliers, and structures of motivation in which people feel that their different backgrounds and experiences are genuinely valued. Rather ironically, perhaps, democratic pluralism is possible in workplaces for the toughest of business reasons, and economic efficiency may be an ally of social justice, though not always a staunch or reliable one.

Changing Public Lives

Just as work is changing, so is the realm of citizenship. Over the past two decades, the century-long trend towards an expanding, interventionist welfare state has been reversed. The domain of citizenship, and the power and importance of public spaces, is diminishing.

Economic rationalism, privatization, deregulation, and the transformation of public institutions such as schools and universities so that they operate according to market logic are
changes that are part of a global shift that coincides with the end of the Cold War. Until the
eighties, the global geopolitical dynamic of the twentieth century had taken the form of an
argument between communism and capitalism. This turned out to be an argument about the
role of the state in society, in which the interventionist welfare state was capitalism's compromise position. The argument was won and lost when the Communist Bloc was unable
to match the escalating cost of the capitalist world's fortifications. The end of the Cold War
represents an epochal turning point. Indicative of a new world order is a liberalism that
eschews the state. In just a decade or two, this liberalism has prevailed globally almost without exception (Fukuyama, 1992). Those of us who work either in state-funded or privately
funded education know what this liberalism looks like. Market logic has become a much
bigger part of our lives.

In some parts of the world, once strong centralizing and homogenizing states have all but
collapsed, and states everywhere are diminished in their roles and responsibilities. This has
left space for a new politics of difference. In worst case scenarios—in Los Angeles, Sarajevo,
Kabul, Belfast, Beirut—the absence of a working, arbitrating state has left governance in the
hands of gangs, bands, paramilitary organizations, and ethnonationalist political factions.
In best case scenarios, the politics of culture and identity have taken on a new significance.
Negotiating these differences is now a life and death matter. The perennial struggle for access
to wealth, power, and symbols of recognition is increasingly articulated through the discourse of identity and recognition (Kalantzis, 1995).

Schooling in general and literacy teaching in particular were a central part of the old
order. The expanding, interventionary states of the nineteenth and twentieth centuries used
schooling as a way of standardizing national languages. In the Old World, this meant impos-
ing national standards over dialect differences. In the New World, it meant assimilating
immigrants and indigenous peoples to the standardized "proper" language of the colonizer
(Anderson, 1983; Dewey, 1916/1966; Gellner, 1983; Kalantzis & Cope, 1993a).

Just as global geopolitics have shifted, so has the role of schools fundamentally shifted.
Cultural and linguistic diversity are now central and critical issues. As a result, the meaning
of literacy pedagogy has changed. Local diversity and global connectedness mean not only
that there can be no standard; they also mean that the most important skill students need to
learn is to negotiate regional, ethnic, or class-based dialects; variations in register that occur
according to social context; hybrid cross-cultural discourses; the code switching often to
be found within a text among different languages, dialects, or registers; different visual and
iconic meanings; and variations in the gestural relationships among people, language, and
material objects. Indeed, this is the only hope for averting the catastrophic conflicts about
identities and spaces that now seem ever ready to flare up.

The decline of the old, monocultural, nationalistic sense of "civic" has a space vacated that
must be filled again. We propose that this space be claimed by a civic pluralism. Instead of
states that require one cultural and linguistic standard, we need states that arbitrate differences. Access to wealth, power, and symbols must be possible no matter what one's identity
markers—such as language, dialect, and register—happen to be. States must be strong again,
but not to impose standards: they must be strong as neutral arbiters of difference. So must
schools. And so must literacy pedagogy. This is the basis for a cohesive sociality, a new civil-
ity in which differences are used as a productive resource and in which differences are the

norm. It is the basis for the postnationalist sense of common purpose that is now essential to a peaceful and productive global order (Kalantzis & Cope, 1993b).

To this end, cultural and linguistic diversity is a classroom resource just as powerfully as it is a social resource in the formation of new civic spaces and new notions of citizenship. This is not just so that educators can provide a better "service" to "minorities." Rather, such a pedagogical orientation will produce benefits for all. For example, there will be a cognitive benefit to all children in a pedagogy of linguistic and cultural pluralism, including for "mainstream" children. When learners juxtapose different languages, discourses, styles, and approaches, they gain substantively in meta-cognitive and meta-linguistic abilities and in their ability to reflect critically on complex systems and their interactions. At the same time, the use of diversity in tokenistic ways—by creating ethnic or other culturally differentiated commodities in order to exploit specialized niche markets or by adding festive, ethnic color to classrooms—must not paper over real conflicts of power and interest. Only by dealing authentically with them can we create out of diversity and history a new, vigorous, and equitable public realm.

Civic pluralism changes the nature of civic spaces, and with the changed meaning of civic spaces, everything changes, from the broad content of public rights and responsibilities to institutional and curricular details of literacy pedagogy. Instead of core culture and national standards, the realm of the civic is a space for the negotiation of a different sort of social order: where differences are actively recognized, where these differences are negotiated in such a way that they complement each other, and where people have the chance to expand their cultural and linguistic repertoires so that they can access a broader range of cultural and institutional resources (Cope & Kalantzis, 1995).

Changing Private Lives

We live in an environment where subcultural differences—differences of identity and affiliation—are becoming more and more significant. Gender, ethnicity, generation, and sexual orientation are just a few of the markers of these differences. To those who yearn for "standards," such differences appear as evidence of distressing fragmentation of the social fabric. Indeed, in one sense it is just this historical shift in which singular national cultures have less hold than they once did. For example, one of the paradoxes of less regulated, multi-channel media systems is that they undermine the concept of collective audience and common culture, instead promoting the opposite: an increasing range of accessible subcultural options and the growing divergence of specialist and subcultural discourses. This spells the definitive end of "the public"—that homogeneous imagined community of modern democratic nation states.

Yet, as subcultural differences become more significant, we also witness another, somewhat contradictory development—the increasing invasion of private spaces by mass media culture, global commodity culture, and communications and information networks. Childhood cultures are made up of interwoven narratives and commodities that cross TV, toys, fast-food packaging, video games, T-shirts, shoes, bed linen, pencil cases, and lunch boxes (Luke, 1995). Parents find these commodity narratives inexorable, and teachers find their cultural and linguistic messages losing power and relevance as they compete with these global narratives. Just how do we negotiate these invasive global texts? In some senses, the invasion of the mass media and consumerism makes a mockery of the diversity of its media and channels. Despite all the subcultural differentiation of niche markets, not much space is offered in the marketplace of childhood that reflects genuine diversity among children and adolescents.

Meanwhile, private lives are being made more public as everything becomes a potential subject of media discussion, resulting in what we refer to as a "conversationalization" of public language. Discourses that were once the domain of the private—the intricacies of the sexual lives of public figures, discussion of repressed memories of child abuse—are now made unashamedly public. In some senses, this is a very positive and important development, insofar as these are often important issues that need a public airing. The widespread conversationalization of public language, however, involves institutionally motivated simulation of conversational language and the personae and relationships of ordinary life. Working lives are being transformed so they operate according to metaphors that were once distinctively private, such as management by "culture," teams dependent on interpersonal discourses, and paternalistic relationships of mentoring. Much of this can be regarded as cynical, manipulative, invasive, and exploitative, as discourses of private life and community are appropriated to serve commercial and institutional ends. This is a process, in other words, that in part destroys the autonomy of private and community lifeworlds.

The challenge is to make space available so that different *lifeworlds*—spaces for community life where local and specific meanings can be made—can flourish. The new multimedia and hypermedia channels can and sometimes do provide members of subcultures with the opportunity to find their own voices. These technologies have the potential to enable greater autonomy for different life-worlds, for example, multilingual television or the creation of virtual communities through access to the Internet.

Yet, the more diverse and vibrant these lifeworlds become and the greater the range of the differences, the less clearly bounded the different lifeworlds appear to be. The word "community" is often used to describe the differences that are now so critical—the Italian-American community, the gay community, the business community, and so on—as if each of these communities had neat boundaries. As lifeworlds become more divergent in the new public spaces of civic pluralism, their boundaries become more evidently complex and overlapping. The increasing divergence of lifeworlds and the growing importance of differences is the blurring of their boundaries. The more autonomous lifeworlds become, the more movement there can be: people entering and leaving, whole lifeworlds going through major transitions, more open and productive negotiation of internal differences, freer external linkage and alliances.

As people are simultaneously members of multiple lifeworlds, so their identities have multiple layers that are in complex relation to each other. No person is a member of a singular community. Rather, they are members of multiple and overlapping communities—communities of work, of interest and affiliation, of ethnicity, of sexual identity, and so on (Kalantzis, 1995).

Language, discourse, and register differences are markers of lifeworld differences. As lifeworlds become more divergent and their boundaries more blurred, the central fact of language becomes the multiplicity of meanings and their continual intersection. Just as there are multiple layers to everyone's identity, there are multiple discourses of identity and multiple discourses of recognition to be negotiated. We have to be proficient as we negotiate the many lifeworlds each of us inhabits, and the many lifeworlds we encounter in our everyday lives. This creates a new challenge for literacy pedagogy. In sum, this is the world that literacy pedagogy now needs to address:

	Changing Realities		*Designing Social Futures*
Working Lives:	Fast Capitalism/PostFordism	>	Productive Diversity
Public Lives:	Decline of Public Pluralism	>	Civic Pluralism
Private Lives:	Invasion of Private Space	>	Multilayered Lifeworlds

What Schools Can Do

What Schools Do and What We Can Do in Schools

Schools have always played a critical role in determining students' life opportunities. Schools regulate access to *orders of discourse*—the relationship of discourses in a particular social space—to *symbolic capital*—symbolic meanings that have currency in access to employment, political power, and cultural recognition. They provide access to a hierarchically ordered world of work; they shape citizenries; they provide a supplement to the discourses and activities of communities and private lifeworlds. As these three major realms of social activity have shifted, so the roles and responsibilities of schools must shift.

Institutionalized schooling traditionally performed the function of disciplining and skilling people for regimented industrial workplaces, assisting in the making of the melting pot of homogenous national citizenries, and smoothing over inherited differences between lifeworlds. This is what Dewey (1916/1966) called the assimilatory function of schooling, the function of making homogeneity out of differences. Now, the function of classrooms and learning is in some senses the reverse. Every classroom will inevitably reconfigure the relationships of local and global difference that are now so critical. To be relevant, learning processes need to recruit, rather than attempt to ignore and erase, the different *subjectivities*—interests, intentions, commitments, and purposes—students bring to learning. Curriculum now needs to mesh with different subjectivities, and with their attendant languages, discourses, and registers, and use these as a resource for learning.

This is the necessary basis for a pedagogy that opens possibilities for greater access. The danger of glib and tokenistic pluralism is that it sees differences to be immutable and leaves them fragmentary. Insofar as differences are now a core, mainstream issue, the core or the mainstream has changed. Insofar as there cannot be a standard, universal, national language and culture, there are new universale in the form of productive diversity, civic pluralism, and multilayered lifeworlds. This is the basis for a transformed pedagogy of access—access to symbolic capital with a real valence in the emergent realities of our time. Such a pedagogy does not involve writing over existing subjectivities with the language of the dominant culture. These old meanings of "access" and "mobility" are the basis for models of pedagogy that depart from the idea that cultures and languages other than those of the mainstream represent a deficit. Yet in the emergent reality, there are still real deficits, such as a lack of access to social power, wealth, and symbols of recognition. The role of pedagogy is to develop an epistemology of pluralism that provides access without people having to erase or leave behind different subjectivities. This has to be the basis of a new norm.

Transforming schools and schooled literacy is both a very broad and a narrowly specific issue, a critical part of a larger social project. Yet there is a limit to what schools alone can achieve. The broad question is, what will count for success in the world of the imminent future, a world that can be imagined and achieved? The narrower question is, how do we transform incrementally the achievable and apt outcomes of schooling? How do we supplement what schools already do? We cannot remake the world through schooling, but we can instantiate a vision through pedagogy that creates in microcosm a transformed set of relationships and possibilities for social futures, a vision that is lived in schools. This might involve activities such as simulating work relations of collaboration, commitment, and creative involvement; using the school as a site for mass media access and learning; reclaiming the public space of school citizenship for diverse communities and discourses; and creating communities of learners that are diverse and respectful of the autonomy of lifeworlds.

In the remainder of this article, we develop the notion of pedagogy as design. Our purpose is to discuss the proposition that *curriculum is a design for social futures* and to debate the overall shape of that design as we supplement literacy pedagogy in the ways indicated by the notion of multiliteracies. In this sense, this article is not immediately practical: it is more in the nature of a programmatic manifesto. The call for practicality is often misconceived insofar as it displaces the kind of foundational discussions we have here. There is another sense, however, in which discussion at this level is eminently practical, albeit in a very generai way. Different conceptions of education and society lead to very specific forms of curriculum and pedagogy, which in turn embody designs for social futures. To achieve this, we need to engage in a critical dialogue with the core concepts of fast capitalism, of emerging pluralistic forms of citizenship, and of different lifeworlds. This is the basis for a new social contract, a new commonwealth.

The "What" of a Pedagogy of Multiliteracies

In relation to the new environment of literacy pedagogy, we need to reopen two fundamental questions: the "what" of literacy pedagogy, or what it is that students need to learn; and the "how" of literacy pedagogy, or the range of appropriate learning relationships.

Designs of Meaning

In addressing the question of the "what" of literacy pedagogy, we propose a metalanguage of multiliteracies based on the concept of "design." Design has become central to workplace innovations, as well as to school reforms for the contemporary world. Teachers and managers are seen as designers of learning processes and environments, not as bosses dictating what those in their charge should think and do. Further, some have argued that educational research should become a design science, studying how different curricular, pedagogical, and classroom designs motivate and achieve different sorts of learning. Similarly, managers have their own design science, studying how management and business theories can be put into practice and continually adjusted and reflected on in practice. The notion of design connects powerfully to the sort of creative intelligence the best practitioners need in order to be able, continually, to redesign their activities in the very act of practice. It connects as well to the idea that learning and productivity are the results of the designs (the structures) of complex systems of people, environments, technology, beliefs, and texts.

We have also decided to use the term design to describe the forms of meaning because it is free of the negative associations for teachers of terms such as "grammar." It is a sufficiently rich concept upon which to found a language curriculum and pedagogy. The term also has a felicitous ambiguity: it can identify either the organizational structure (or morphology) of products, or the process of designing. Expressions like "the design of the car," or "the design of the text," can have either sense: the way it is—has been—designed, or the process of designing it. We propose to treat any semiotic activity, including using language to produce or consume texts, as a matter of Design involving three elements: Available Designs, Designing, and The Redesigned. Together these three elements emphasize the fact that meaning-making is an active and dynamic process, and not something governed by static rules.

This framework is based upon a particular theory of discourse. It sees semiotic activity as a creative application and combination of conventions (resources—Available Designs) that, in the process of Design, transforms at the same time it reproduces these conventions (Fairclough, 1992a, 1995). That which determines (Available Designs) and the active process of determining (Designing, which creates The Redesigned) are constantly in tension. This theory fits in well with the view of social life and social subjects in fast-changing and culturally diverse societies, which we described earlier.

Available Designs

Available Designs—the resources for Design—include the "grammars" of various semiotic systems: the grammars of languages, and the grammars of other semiotic systems such as film, photography, or gesture. Available Designs also include "orders of discourse" (Fairclough, 1995). An *order of discourse* is the structured set of conventions associated with semiotic activity (including use of language) in a given social space—a particular society, or a particular institution such as a school or a workplace, or more loosely structured spaces of ordinary life encapsulated in the notion of different lifeworlds. An order of discourse is a socially produced array of discourses, intermeshing and dynamically interacting. It is a particular configuration of Design elements. An order of discourse can be seen as a particular configuration of such elements. It may include a mixture of different semiotic systems—visual and aural semiotic systems in combination with language constitute the order of discourse of TV, for instance. It may involve the grammars of several languages—the orders of discourse of many schools, for example.

Order of discourse is intended to capture the way in which different discourses relate to (speak to) each other. Thus, the discourse of African American gangs in Los Angeles is related to the discourse of L.A. police in historical ways. They and other related discourses shape and are shaped by each other. For another example, consider the historical and institutional relations between the discourse of biology and the discourse of religious fundamentalism. Schools are particularly crucial sites in which a set or order of discourses relate to each other—disciplinary discourses, the discourses of being a teacher (teacher culture), the discourse of being a student of a certain sort, community discourses, ethnic discourses, class discourses, and public sphere discourses involving business and government, for instance. Each discourse involves producing and reproducing and transforming different kinds of people. There are different kinds of African Americans, teachers, children, students, police, and biologists. One and the same person can be different kinds of people at different times and places. Different kinds of people connect through the intermeshed discourses that constitute orders of discourse.

Within orders of discourse there are particular Design conventions—Available Designs— that take the form of discourses, styles, genres, dialects, and voices, to name a few key variables. A *discourse* is a configuration of knowledge and its habitual forms of expression, which represents a particular set of interests. Over time, for instance, institutions produce discourses—that is, their configurations of knowledge. *Style* is the configuration of all the semiotic features in a text in which, for example, language may relate to layout and visual images. *Genres* are forms of text or textual organization that arise out of particular social configurations or the particular relationships of the participants in an interaction. They reflect the purposes of the participants in a specific interaction. In an interview, for example, the interviewer wants something, the interviewee wants something else, and the genre of interview reflects this. *Dialects* may be region or age related. *Voice* is more individual and personal, including, of course, many discursive and generic factors.

The overarching concept of orders of discourse is needed to emphasize that, in designing texts and interactions, people always draw on systems of sociolinguistic practice as well as grammatical systems. These may not be as clearly or rigidly structured as the word "system" suggests, but there are nevertheless always some conventional points of orientation when we act semiotically. Available Designs also include another element: the linguistic and discoursal experience of those involved in Designing, in which one moment of Designing is continuous with and a continuation of particular histories. We can refer to this as the intertextual context (Fairclough, 1989), which links the text being designed to one or more series ("chains") of past texts.

Designing

The process of shaping emergent meaning involves re-presentation and recontextualization. This is never simply a repetition of Available Designs. Every moment of meaning involves the transformation of the available resources of meaning. Reading, seeing, and listening are all instances of Designing.

According to Halliday (1978), a deep organizing principle in the grammars of human languages is the distinction among macrofunctions of language, which are the different functions of Available Designs: ideational, interpersonal, and textual functions. These functions produce distinctive expressions of meaning. The ideational function handles the "knowledge," and the interpersonal function handles the "social relations." As for orders of discourse, the generative interrelation of discourses in a social context, their constituent genres can be partly characterized in terms of the particular social relations and subject positions they articulate, whereas discourses are particular knowledges (constructions of the world) articulated with particular subject positions.

Any semiotic activity—any Designing—simultaneously works on and with these facets of Available Designs. Designing will more or less normatively reproduce, or more or less radically transform, given knowledges, social relations, and identities, depending upon the social conditions under which Designing occurs. But it will never simply reproduce Available Designs. Designing transforms knowledge in producing new constructions and representations of reality. Through their co-engagement in Designing, people transform their relations with each other, and so transform themselves. These are not independent processes. Configurations of subjects, social relations, and knowledges are worked upon and transformed (becoming The Redesigned) in the process of Designing. Existing and new configurations are always provisional, though they may achieve a high degree of permanence. Transformation is always a new use of old materials, a re-articulation and recombination of the given resources of Available Designs.

The notion of Design recognizes the iterative nature of meaning-making, drawing on Available Designs to create patterns of meaning that are more or less predictable in their contexts. This is why The Redesigned has a ring of familiarity to it. Yet there is something ineluctably unique to every utterance. Most written paragraphs are unique, never constructed in exactly that way ever before and—bar copying or statistical improbability—never to be constructed that way again. Similarly, there is something irreducibly unique about every person's voice. Designing always involves the transformation of Available Designs; it always involves making new use of old materials.

It is also important to stress that listening as well as speaking, and reading as well as writing, are productive activities, forms of Designing. Listeners and readers encounter texts as Available Designs. They also draw upon their experience of other Available Designs as a resource for making new meanings from the texts they encounter. Their listening and reading is itself a production (a Designing) of texts (though texts-for-themselves, not texts-for-others) based on their own interests and life experiences. And their listening and reading in turn transforms the resources they have received in the form of Available Designs into The Redesigned.

The Redesigned

The outcome of Designing is a new meaning, something through which meaning-makers remake themselves. It is never a reinstantiation of one Available Design or even a simple recombination of Available Designs. The Redesigned may be variously creative or reproductive in relation to the resources for meaning-making available in Available Designs. But it is neither a simple reproduction (as the myth of standards and transmission pedagogy would have us believe), nor is it simply creative (as the myths of individual originality and personal voice would have us believe). As the play of cultural resources and uniquely positioned subjectivity, The Redesigned is founded on historically and culturally received patterns of meaning. At the same time it is the unique product of human agency: a transformed meaning. And, in its turn, The Redesigned becomes a new Available Design, a new meaning-making resource.

Through these processes of Design, moreover, meaning-makers remake themselves. They reconstruct and renegotiate their identities. Not only has The Redesigned been actively made, but it is also evidence of the ways in which the active intervention in the world that is Designing has transformed the designer.

Designs of Meaning

Available Designs: Resources for meaning; Available Designs of meaning
Designing: The work performed on/with Available Designs in the semiotic process
The Redesigned: The resources that are reproduced and transformed through Designing

Dimensions of Meaning

Teachers and students need a language to describe the forms of meaning that are represented in Available Designs and The Redesigned. In other words, they need a *metalanguage*—a language for talking about language, images, texts, and meaning-making interactions.

One objective of the International Multiliteracies Project, as initiated and planned during the New London meeting and as it is now entering a collaborative research and experimental curriculum phase, is to develop an educationally accessible functional grammar; that is, a metalanguage that describes meaning in various realms. These include the textual and the visual, as well as the multimodal relations between the different meaning-making processes that are now so critical in media texts and the texts of electronic multimedia.

Any metalanguage to be used in a school curriculum has to match up to some taxing criteria. It must be capable of supporting sophisticated critical analysis of language and other semiotic systems, yet at the same time not make unrealistic demands on teacher and learner knowledge, and not immediately conjure up teachers' accumulated and often justified antipathies towards formalism. The last point is crucial, because teachers must be motivated to work on and work with the metalanguage.

A metalanguage also needs to be quite flexible and open ended. It should be seen as a tool kit for working on semiotic activities, not a formalism to be applied to them. We should be comfortable with fuzzy-edged, overlapping concepts. Teachers and learners should be able to pick and choose from the tools offered. They should also feel free to fashion their own tools. Flexibility is critical because the relationship between descriptive and analytical categories and actual events is, by its nature, shifting, provisional, unsure, and relative to the contexts and purposes of analysis.

Furthermore, the primary purpose of the metalanguage should be to identify and explain differences between texts, and relate these to the contexts of culture and situation in which they seem to work. The metalanguage is not to impose rules, to set standards of correctness, or to privilege certain discourses in order to "empower" students.

The metalanguage we are suggesting for analyzing the Design of meaning with respect to orders of discourse includes the key terms "genres" and "discourses," and a number of related concepts such as voices, styles, and probably others (Fairclough, 1992a; Kress, 1990; van Leeuwen, 1993). More informally, we might ask of any Designing, What's the game? and What's the angle?

"The game" points us in the direction of purpose, and the notion of genre. Sometimes the game can be specified in terms of a clearly defined and socially labeled genre, like church liturgy; sometimes there is no clear generic category. Semiotic activity and the texts it generates regularly mixes genres (for example, doctor-patient consultations, which are partly like medical examinations and partly like counseling sessions, or even informal conversations).

In trying to characterize game and genre, we should start from the social context, the institutional location, the social relations of texts, and the social practices within which they are embedded. Genre is an intertextual aspect of a text. It shows how the text links to other texts in the intertextual context, and how it might be similar in some respects to other texts used in comparable social contexts, and its connections with text types in the order(s) of discourse. But genre is just one of a number of intertextual aspects of a text, and it needs to be used in conjunction with others, especially discourses.

A *discourse* is a construction of some aspect of reality from a particular point of view, a particular angle, in terms of particular interests. As an abstract noun, discourse draws attention to use of language as a facet of social practice that is shaped by—and shapes—the orders of discourse of the culture, as well as language systems (grammars). As a count noun (discourses in the plural rather than discourse in general), it draws attention to the diversity of constructions (representations) of various domains of life and experience associated with different voices, positions, and interests (subjectivities). Here again, some discourses are clearly demarcated and have conventional names in the culture (for example, feminist, party-political, or religious discourses), whereas others are much more difficult to pinpoint. Intertextual characterizations of texts in terms of genres and discourses are best regarded as provisional approximations, because they are cultural interpretations of texts that depend on the analyst's fuzzy but operationally adequate feel for the culture, as well as for specialist knowledges.

Design Elements

One of the key ideas informing the notion of multiliteracies is the increasing complexity and inter-relationship of different modes of meaning. We have identified six major areas in which functional grammars—the metalanguages that describe and explain patterns of meaning—are required: Linguistic Design, Visual Design, Audio Design, Gestural Design, Spatial Design, and Multimodal Design. Multimodal Design is of a different order to the other five modes of meaning; it represents the patterns of interconnection among the other modes. We are using the word "grammar" here in a positive sense, as a specialized language that describes patterns of representation. In each case, our objective is to come up with no more than approximately ten major Design elements.

Linguistic Design

The metalanguage we propose to use to describe Linguistic Design is intended to focus our attention on the representational resources. This metalanguage is not a category of mechanical skills, as is commonly the case in grammars designed for educational use. Nor is it the basis for detached critique or reflection. Rather, the Design notion emphasizes the productive and innovative potential of language as a meaning-making system. This is an action, a generative description of language as a means of representation. As we have argued earlier in this article, such an orientation to society and text will be an essential requirement of the economies and societies of the present and the future. It will also be essential for the production of particular kinds of democratic and participatory subjectivity. The elements of Linguistic Design that we foreground help describe the representational resources that are available, the various meanings these resources will have if drawn upon in a particular context, and the innovative potential for reshaping these resources in relation to social intentions or aims.

Consider this example: "Lung cancer death rates are clearly associated with increased smoking," and "Smoking causes cancer." The first sentence can mean what the second means, though it can mean many other things as well. The first sentence is more explicit in some ways than the second (e.g., reference to lung cancer), and less explicit in other ways (e.g., "associated with" versus "cause"). Grammar has been recruited to design two different instruments. Each sentence is usable in different discourses. For example, the first is a form typical of much writing in the social sciences and even the hard sciences. The second is a form typical of public health discussion. Grammar needs to be seen as a range of choices one makes in designing communication for specific ends, including greater recruitment of nonverbal features. These choices, however, need to be seen as not just a matter of individual style or intention, but as inherently connected to different discourses with their wider interests and relationships of power.

Our suggested metalanguage for analyzing the designs of language is built around a highly selective checklist of features of texts, which experience has shown to be particularly worth attending to (see also Fowler, Hodge, Kress, & Trent, 1979; Fairclough, 1992a). The following table lists some key terms that might be included as a metalanguage of Linguistic Design. Other potentially significant textual features are likely to be alluded to from time to time, but we think that a facility in using the features on the checklist itself constitutes a substantive, if limited, basis for critical language awareness.

We will examine two of these now in order to illustrate our notion of Linguistic Design: nominalization and transitivity. *Nominalizalion* involves using a phrase to compact a great deal of information, somewhat like the way a trash compactor compacts trash. After compacting, you cannot always tell what has been compacted. Consider the expression, "Lung cancer death rates." Is this "rates" at which people die of lung cancer, or rates at which lungs die from cancer? You can't know this unless you are privy to what the discussion has been.

Nominalizations are used to compact information—whole conversations—that we assume people (or at least "experts") are up on. They are signals for those "in the game" and thus are also ways to keep people out.

Transitivity indicates how much agency and effect one designs into a sentence. "John struck Mary" has more effect (on Mary) than "John struck out at Mary," and "John struck Mary" has more agency than "Mary was struck." Since we humans connect agency and effect with responsibility and blame in many domains (discourses), these are not just matters of grammar. They are ways of designing language to engage in actions like blaming, avoiding blame, or backgrounding certain things against others.

Some Elements of Linguistic Design

Delivery:	Features of intonation, stress, rhythm, accent, etc.
Vocabulary and Metaphor:	Includes colocation, lexicalization, and word meaning.
Modality:	The nature of the producer's commitment to the message in a clause.
Transitivity:	The types of process and participants in the clause. Vocabulary and metaphor, word choice, positioning, and meaning.
Nominalization of Processes:	Turning actions, qualities, assessments, or logical connecion into nouns or states of being (e.g., "assess" becomes "assessment"; "can" becomes ability).
Information Structures:	How information is presented in clauses and sentences.
Local Coherence Relations:	Cohesion between clauses, and logical relations between clauses (e.g., embedding, subordination).
Global Coherence Relations:	The overall organizational properties of texts (e.g., genres).

Designs for Other Modes of Meaning

Increasingly important are modes of meaning other than Linguistic, including Visual Meanings (images, page layouts, screen formats); Audio Meanings (music, sound effects); Gestural Meanings (body language, sensuality); Spatial Meanings (the meanings of environmental spaces, architectural spaces); and Multimodal Meanings. Of the modes of meaning, the Multimodal is the most significant, as it relates all the other modes in quite remarkably dynamic relationships. For instance, mass media images relate the linguistic to the visual and to the gestural in intricately designed ways. Reading the mass media for its linguistic meanings alone is not enough. Magazines employ vastly different visual grammars according to their social and cultural content. A script of a sitcom such as *Roseanne* would have none of the qualities of the program if you didn't have a "feel" for its unique gestural, audio, and visual meanings. A script without this knowledge would only allow a very limited reading. Similarly, a visit to a shopping mall involves a lot of written text. However, either a pleasurable or a critical engagement with the mall will involve a multimodal reading that not only includes the design of language, but a spatial reading of the architecture of the mall and the placement and meaning of the written signs, logos, and lighting. McDonalds has hard seats—to keep you moving. Casinos do not have windows or clocks—to remove tangible indicators of time passing. These are profoundly important spatial and architectonic meanings, crucial for reading Available Designs and for Designing social futures.

In a profound sense, all meaning-making is multimodal. All written text is also visually designed. Desktop publishing puts a new premium on visual design and spreads responsibility for the visual much more broadly than was the case when writing and page layout were separate trades. So, a school project can and should properly be evaluated on the basis of visual as well as linguistic design, and their multimodal relationships. To give another example, spoken language is a matter of audio design as much as it is a matter of linguistic design understood as grammatical relationships.

Texts are designed using the range of historically available choices among different modes of meaning. This entails a concern with absences from texts, as well as presences in texts: "Why not that?" as well as "Why this?" (Fairclough, 1992b). The concept of Design emphasizes the relationships between received modes of meaning (Available Designs), the transformation of these modes of meaning in their hybrid and intertextual use (Designing), and their subsequent to-be-received status (The Redesigned). The metalanguage of meaning-making applies to all aspects of this process: how people are positioned by the elements of available modes of meaning (Available Designs), yet how the authors of meanings in some important senses bear the responsibility of being consciously in control of their transformation of meanings (Designing), and how the effects of meaning, the sedimentation of meaning, become a part of the social process (The Redesigned).

Of course, the extent of transformation from Available Designs to The Redesigned as a result of Designing can greatly vary. Sometimes the designers of meaning will reproduce the Available Designs in the form of The Redesigned more closely than at other times—a form letter as opposed to a personal letter, or a classified as opposed to a display advertisement, for instance. Some Designing is more premeditated—planned, deliberate, systematized—than other instances, for example, a conversation as opposed to a poem. At times, Designing is based on clearly articulated, perhaps specialist, metalanguages describing Design elements (the language of the professional editor or the architect), while other Designing may be no more or less transformative, even though the designers may not have an articulated metalanguage to describe the elements of their meaning-making processes (the person who "fixes up" what they have just written or the home renovator). Notwithstanding these different relationships of structure and agency, all meaning-making always involves both.

Two key concepts help us describe multimodal meanings and the relationships of different designs of meaning: hybridity and intertextuality (Fairclough, 1992a, 1992b). The term *hybridity* highlights the mechanisms of creativity and of culture-as-process particularly salient in contemporary society. People create and innovate by hybridizing—that is, articulating in new ways—established practices and conventions within and between different modes of meaning. This includes the hybridization of established ways modes of meaning (of discourses and genres), and multifarious combinations of modes of meaning cutting across boundaries of convention and creating new conventions. Popular music is a perfect example of the process of hybridity. Different cultural forms and traditions are constantly being recombined and restructured—where the musical forms of Africa meet audio electronics and the commercial music industry. And new relations are constantly being created between linguistic meanings and audio meanings (pop versus rap) and between linguistic/audio and visual meanings (live performance versus video clips).

Intertextuality draws attention to the potentially complex ways in which meanings (such as linguistic meanings) are constituted through relationships to other texts (real or imaginary), text types (discourse or genres), narratives, and other modes of meaning (such as visual design, architectonic or geographical positioning). Any text can be viewed historically in terms of the intertextual chains (historical series of texts) it draws upon, and in terms of the transformations it works upon them. For instance, movies are full of cross references, either made explicitly by the movie maker or read into the movie by the viewer-as-Designer: a role, a scene, an ambiance. The viewer takes a good deal of their sense of the meaning of the movie through these kinds of intertextual chains.

The "How" of a Pedagogy of Multiliteracies

A Theory of Pedagogy

Any successful theory of pedagogy must be based on views about how the human mind works in society and classrooms, as well as about the nature of teaching and learning. While we certainly believe that no current theory in psychology, education, or the social sciences has "the answers," and that theories stemming from these domains must always be integrated with the "practical knowledge" of master practitioners, we also believe that those proposing curricular and pedagogical reforms must clearly state their views of mind, society, and learning in virtue of which they believe such reforms would be efficacious.

Our view of mind, society, and learning is based on the assumption that the human mind is embodied, situated, and social. That is, human knowledge is initially developed not as "general and abstract," but as embedded in social, cultural, and material contexts. Further, human knowledge is initially developed as part and parcel of collaborative interactions with others of diverse skills, backgrounds, and perspectives joined together in a particular epistemic community, that is, a community of learners engaged in common practices centered around a specific (historically and socially constituted) domain of knowledge. We believe that "abstractions," "generalities," and "overt theories" come out of this initial ground and must always be returned to it or to a recontextualized version of it.

This view of mind, society, and learning, which we hope to explicate and develop over the next few years as part of our joint international project, leads us to argue that pedagogy is a complex integration of four factors: Situated Practice based on the world of learners' Designed and Designing experiences; Overt Instruction through which students shape for themselves an explicit metalanguage of Design; Critical Framing, which relates meanings to their social contexts and purposes; and Transformed Practice in which students transfer and re-create Designs of meaning from one context to another. We will briefly develop these themes below.

Recent work in cognitive science, social cognition, and sociocultural approaches to language and literacy (Barsalou, 1992; Bereiter & Scardamalia, 1993; Cazden, 1988; Clark, 1993; Gardner, 1991; Gee, 1992; Heath, 1983; Holland, Holyoak, Nisbett, & Thagard, 1986; Lave & Wenger, 1991; Light & Butterworth, 1993; Perkins, 1992; Rogoff, 1990; Scollon & Scollon, 1981; Street, 1984; Wertsch, 1985) argues that if one of our pedagogical goals is a degree of mastery in practice, then immersion in a community of learners engaged in authentic versions of such practice is necessary. We call this Situated Practice. Recent research (Barsalou, 1992; Eiser, 1994; Gee, 1992; Harre & Gillett, 1994; Margolis, 1993; Nolan, 1994) argues that the human mind is not, like a digital computer, a processor of general rules and decontextualized abstractions. Rather, human knowledge, when it is applicable to practice, is primarily situated in sociocultural settings and heavily contextualized in specific knowledge domains and practices. Such knowledge is inextricably tied to the ability to recognize and act on patterns of data and experience, a process that is acquired only through experience, since the requisite patterns are often heavily tied and adjusted to context, and are, very often, subtle and complex enough that no one can fully and usefully describe or explicate them. Humans are, at this level,

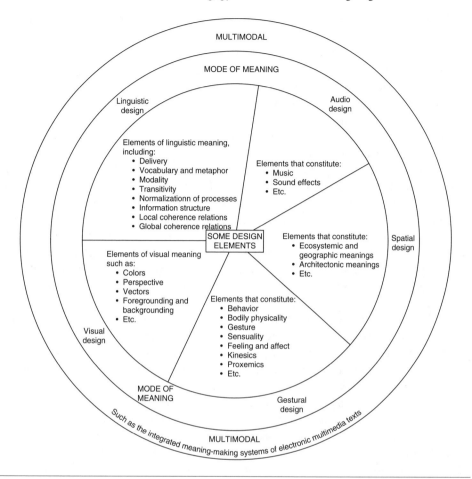

Figure 3.1 Multiliteracies: Metalanguages to Describe and Interpret the Design Elements of Different Modes of Meaning.

contextual and sociocultural "pattern recognizors" and actors. Such pattern recognition underlies the ability to act flexibly and adaptably in context—that is, mastery in practice.

However, there are limitations to Situated Practice as the sole basis for pedagogy. First, a concern for the situatedness of learning is both the strength and the weakness of progressivist pedagogies (Kalantzis & Cope, 1993a). While such situated learning can lead to mastery in practice, learners immersed in rich and complex practices can vary quite significantly from each other (and from curricular goals), and some can spend a good deal of time pursuing the "wrong" leads, so to speak. Second, much of the "immersion" that we experience as children, such as in acquiring our "native" language, is surely supported by our human biology and the normal course of human maturation and development. Such support is not available in later school immersion in areas such as literacy and academic domains, since these are far too late on the human scene to have garnered any substantive biological or evolutionary support. Thus, whatever help biology and maturation give children in their early primary socialization must be made up for—given more overtly—when we use "immersion" as a method in school. Third, Situated Practice does not necessarily lead to conscious control and awareness of what one knows and does, which is a core goal of much school-based learning. Fourth, such Situated Practice does not necessarily create learners or communities who can critique what they are learning in terms of historical, cultural, political, ideological, or value-centered relations. And, fifth, there is the question of putting knowledge into action. People may be able to articulate their knowledge in words. They could be consciously aware of relationships, and even able to engage in "critique." Yet they might still be incapable of reflexively enacting their knowledge in practice.

Thus, Situated Practice, where teachers guide a community of learners as "masters" of practice, must be supplemented by several other components (see Cazden, 1992). Beyond mastery in practice, an efficacious pedagogy must seek critical understanding or cultural understanding in two different senses. Critical in the phrase "critical understanding" means conscious awareness and control over the intra-systematic relations of a system. Immersion, notoriously, does not lead to this. For instance, children who have acquired a first language through immersion in the practices of their communities do not thereby, in virtue of that fact, become good linguists. Vygotsky (1978, 1987), who certainly supported collaboration in practice as a foundation of learning, argued also that certain forms of Overt Instruction were needed to supplement immersion (acquisition) if we wanted learners to gain conscious awareness and control of what they acquired.

There is another sense of "critical," as in the ability to critique a system and its relations to other systems on the basis of the workings of power, politics, ideology, and values (Fairclough, 1992b). In this sense, people become aware of, and are able to articulate, the cultural located-ness of practices. Unfortunately, neither immersion in Situated Practices within communities of learners, nor Overt Instruction of the sort Vygotsky (1987) discussed, necessarily gives rise to this sort of critical understanding or cultural understanding. In fact, both immersion and many sorts of Overt Instruction are notorious as socializing agents that can render learners quite uncritical and unconscious of the cultural locatedness of meanings and practices.

The four components of pedagogy we propose here do not constitute a linear hierarchy, nor do they represent stages. Rather, they are components that are related in complex ways. Elements of each may occur simultaneously, while at different times one or the other will predominate, and all of them are repeatedly revisited at different levels.

Situated Practice

This is the part of pedagogy that is constituted by immersion in meaningful practices within a community of learners who are capable of playing multiple and different roles based on their backgrounds and experiences. The community must include experts, people who have mastered certain practices. Minimally, it must include expert novices, people who are experts at learning new domains in some depth. Such experts can guide learners, serving as mentors and designers of their learning processes. This aspect of the curriculum needs to recruit learners' previous and current experiences, as well as their extra-school communities and discourses, as an integral part of the learning experience.

There is ample evidence that people do not learn anything well unless they are both motivated to learn and believe that they will be able to use and function with what they are learning in some way that is in their interest. Thus, the Situated Practice that constitutes the immersion aspect of pedagogy must crucially consider the affective and sociocultural needs and identities of all learners. It must also constitute an arena in which all learners are secure in taking risks and trusting the guidance of others—peers and teachers.

Within this aspect of pedagogy, evaluation, we believe, should never be used to judge, but should be used developmentally, to guide learners to the experiences and the assistance they need to develop further as members of the community capable of drawing on, and ultimately contributing to, the full range of its resources.

Overt Instruction

Overt Instruction does not imply direct transmission, drills, and rote memorization, though unfortunately it often has these connotations. Rather, it includes all those active interventions on the part of the teacher and other experts that scaffold learning activities, that focus the learner on the important features of their experiences and activities within the community of learners, and that allow the learner to gain explicit information at times when it can most usefully organize and guide practice, building on and recruiting what the learner already knows and has accomplished. It includes centrally the sorts of collaborative efforts between teacher and student wherein the student is both allowed to accomplish a task more complex than they can accomplish on their own, and where they come to conscious awareness of the teacher's representation and interpretation of that task and its relations to other aspects of what its being learned. The goal here is conscious awareness and control over what is being learned—over the intra-systematic relations of the domain being practiced.

One defining aspect of Overt Instruction is the use of metalanguages, languages of reflective generalization that describe the form, content, and function of the discourses of practice. In the case of the multiliteracies framework proposed here, this would mean that students develop a metalanguage that describes both the "what" of literacy pedagogy (Design processes and Design elements) and the scaffolds that constitute the "how" of learning (Situated Practice, Overt Instruction, Critical Framing, Transformed Practice).

Much assessment in traditional curriculum required replication of the generalities of Overt Instruction. As in the case of Situated Practice, evaluation in Overt Instruction should be developmental, a guide to further thought and action. It should also be related to the other aspects of the learning process—the connections, for example, between evolving metalanguages as they are negotiated and developed through Overt Instruction, on the one hand, and Situated Practice, Critical Framing, and Transformed Practice, on the other hand.

Critical Framing

The goal of Critical Framing is to help learners frame their growing mastery in practice (from Situated Practice) and conscious control and understanding (from Overt Instruction) in relation to the historical, social, cultural, political, ideological, and value-centered relations of particular systems of knowledge and social practice. Here, crucially, the teacher must help learners to denaturalize and make strange again what they have learned and mastered.

For example, the claim "DNA replicates itself" framed within biology is obvious and "true." Framed within another discourse in the following way, it becomes less natural and less "true": Put some DNA in some water in a glass on a table. It certainly will not replicate itself, it will just sit there. Organisms replicate themselves using DNA as a code, but that code is put into effect by an array of machinery involving proteins. In many of our academic and Western discourses, we have privileged information and mind over materials, practice, and work. The original claim foregrounds information and code and leaves out, or backgrounds, machinery and work. This foregrounding and backgrounding becomes apparent only when we reframe, when we take the sentence out of its "home" discourse and place it in a wider context. Here, the wider context is actual processes and material practices, not just general statements in a disciplinary theory (the DNA example is from Lewontin, 1991).

Through critical framing, learners can gain the necessary personal and theoretical distance from what they have learned, constructively critique it, account for its cultural location, creatively extend and apply it, and eventually innovate on their own, within old communities and in new ones. This is the basis for Transformed Practice. It also represents one sort of transfer of learning, and one area where evaluation can begin to assess learners and, primarily, the learning processes in which they have been operating.

Transformed Practice

It is not enough to be able to articulate one's understanding of intra-systematic relations or to critique extra-systematic relations. We need always to return to where we began, to Situated Practice, but now a re-practice, where theory becomes reflective practice. With their students, teachers need to develop ways in which the students can demonstrate how they can design and carry out, in a reflective manner, new practices embedded in their own goals and values. They should be able to show that they can implement understandings acquired through Overt Instruction and Critical Framing in practices that help them simultaneously to apply and revise what they have learned. In Transformed Practice we are offered a place for situated, contextualized assessment of learners and the learning processes devised for them. Such learning processes, such a pedagogy, needs to be continually reformulated on the basis of these assessments.

In Transformed Practice, in one activity we try to re-create a discourse by engaging in it for our own real purposes. Thus, imagine a student having to act and think like a biologist, and at the same time as a biologist with a vested interest in resisting the depiction of female things—from eggs to organisms—as "passive." The student now has to both juxtapose and integrate (not without tension) two different discourses, or social identities, or "interests" that have historically been at odds. Using another example, how can one be a "real" lawyer and, at the same time, have one's performance influenced by being an African American. In his arguments before the U.S. Supreme Court for desegregating schools, Thurgood Marshall did this in a classic way. And, in mixing the discourse of politics with the discourse of African American religion, Jesse Jackson has transformed the former. The key here is juxtaposition, integration, and living with tension.

Situated Practice:	Immersion in experience and the utilization of available discourses, including those from the students' lifeworlds and simulations of the relationships to be found in workplaces and public spaces.
Overt Instruction:	Systematic, analytic, and conscious understanding. In the case of multiliteracies, this requires the introduction of explicit metalanguages, which describe and interpret the Design elements of different modes of meaning.
Critical Framing:	Interpreting the social and cultural context of particular Designs of meaning. This involves the students' standing back from what they are studying and viewing it critically in relation to its context.
Transformed Practice:	Transfer in meaning-making practice, which puts the transformed meaning to work in other contexts or cultural sites.

The International Multiliteracies Project

Let us tie the "what" and the "how" of literacy pedagogy back to the large agenda with which we began this article: focusing on Situated Practices in the learning process involves the recognition that differences are critical in workplaces, civic spaces, and multilayered lifeworlds. Classroom teaching and curriculum have to engage with students' own experiences and discourses, which are increasingly defined by cultural and subcultural diversity and the different language backgrounds and practices that come with this diversity. Overt Instruction is not intended to tell—to empower students in relation to the "grammar" of one proper, standard, or powerful language form. It is meant to help students develop a metalanguage that accounts for Design differences. Critical Framing involves linking these Design differences to different cultural purposes. Transformed Practice involves moving from one cultural context to another; for example, redesigning meaning strategies so they can be transferred from one cultural situation to another.

The idea of Design is one that recognizes the different Available Designs of meaning, located as they are in different cultural contexts. The metalanguage of multiliteracies describes the elements of Design, not as rules, but as an heuristic that accounts for the infinite variability of different forms of meaning-making in relation to the cultures, the subcultures, or the layers of an individual's identity that these forms serve. At the same time, Designing restores human agency and cultural dynamism to the process of meaning-making. Every act of meaning both appropriates Available Designs and recreates in the Designing, thus producing new meaning as The Redesigned. In an economy of productive diversity, in civic spaces that value pluralism, and in the flourishing of interrelated, multilayered, complementary yet increasingly divergent lifeworlds, workers, citizens, and community members are ideally creative and responsible makers of meaning. We are, indeed, designers of our social futures.

Of course, the necessary negotiation of differences will be difficult and often painful. The dialogue will encounter chasms of difference in values, grossly unjust inequalities, and difficult but necessary border crossings. The differences are not as neutral, colorful, and benign as a simplistic multiculturalism might want us to believe. Yet as workers, citizens, and community members, we will all need the skills required to negotiate these differences.

This article represents a statement of general principle. It is highly provisional, and something we offer as a basis for public debate. The objective of the International Multiliteracies Project is to test and develop these ideas further, particularly the metalanguage of Design and the pedagogy of Situated Practice, Overt Instruction, Critical Framing, and Transformed Practice. We also want to establish relationships with teachers and researchers, developing and testing curriculum and revising the theoretical propositions of the project.

This article is a provisional statement of intent and a theoretical overview of the connections between the changing social environment and the "what" and the "how" of literacy pedagogy. As the project moves into its next phase, the group that met in New London is writing a book that explores the ideas of multiliteracies further, relating the idea to classrooms and our own educational experiences. We are also beginning to conduct classroom-based research, experimenting with multiliteracies as a notion that might supplement and support literacy curriculum. And we are actively engaged in ongoing public dialogue. In September 1996, the group will be opening the argument up to public discussion once again at the Domains of Literacy Conference at London University, and again in 1997 at the Literacy and Education Research Network Conference in Australia. We want to stress that this is an open-ended process—tentative, exploratory, and welcoming of multiple and divergent collaborations. And above all, our aim is to make some sort of difference for real children in real classrooms.

These activities will be informed by a number of key principles of action. First, the project will supplement, not critique, existing curricula and pedagogical approaches to the teaching of English language and literacy. This will include further developing the conceptual framework of the International Multiliteracies Project, and mapping this against existing curriculum practices in order to extend teachers' pedagogical and curriculum repertoires. Second, the project team will welcome collaborations with researchers, curriculum developers, teachers, and communities. The project framework represents a complex and difficult dialogue; these complexities and difficulties will be articulated along with an open invitation for all to contribute to the development of a pedagogy that does make some difference. And third, it will strive continually towards reformulations of theory that are of direct use in educational practice.

This article is a tentative starting point for that process.

Note

1. This discussion of the future of literacy pedagogy is coauthored by: Courtney Cazden, Harvard University, Graduate School of Education, USA; Bill Cope, National Languages and Literacy Institute of Australia, Centre for Workplace Communication and Culture, University of Technology, Sydney, and James Cook University of North Queensland, Australia; Norman Fairclough, Centre for Language in Social Life, Lancaster University, UK; Jim Gee, Hiatt Center for Urban Education, Clark University, USA; Mary Kalantzis, Institute of Interdisciplinary Studies, James Cook University of North Queensland, Australia; Gunther Kress, Institute of Education, University of London, UK; Allan Luke, Graduate School of Education, University of Queensland, Australia; Carmen Luke, Graduate School of Education, University of Queensland, Australia; Sarah Michaels, Hiatt Center for Urban Education, Clark University, USA; Martin Nakata, School of Education, James Cook University of North Queensland, Australia.

References

Anderson, B. (1983). *Imagined communities: Reflections on the origin and spread of nationalism.* London: Verso.

Barsalou, L. W. (1992). *Cognitive psychology: An overview for cognitive scientists.* Hillsdale, NJ: Lawrence Erlbaum.

Bereiter, C., & Scardamalia, M. (1993). *Surpassing ourselves: An inquiry into the nature and implications of expertise.* Chicago: Open Court.

Boyett, J. H., & Conn, H. P. (1992). *Workplace 2000: The revolution reshaping American business.* New York: Plume/Penguin.

Bruer, J. T. (1993). *Schools for thought: A science of learning in the classroom.* Cambridge, MA: MIT Press.

Cazden, C. (1988). *Classroom discourse: The language of teaching and learning.* Portsmouth, NH: Heinemann.

Cazden, C. (1992). *Whole language plus: Essays on literary in the United States and New Zealand.* New York: Teachers College Press.

Clark, A. (1993). *Associative engines: Connections, concepts, and representational change.* Cambridge, Eng.: Cambridge University Press.

Cope, B., & Kalantzis, M. (1995). *Productive diversity: Organizational life in the age of civic pluralism and total globalisation.* Sydney: Harper Collins.

Cross, K. F., Feather, J. J., & Lynch, R. L. (1994). *Corporate renaissance: The art of reengineering.* Oxford, Eng.: Basil Blackwell.

Davidow, W. H., & Malone, M. S. (1992). *The virtual corporation: Structuring and revitalizing the corporation for the 21st century.* New York: Harper Business.

Deal, T. E., & Jenkins, W. A. (1994). *Managing the hidden organization: Strategies for empowering your behind-the-scenes employees.* New York: Warner.

Dewey, J. (1966). *Democracy and education.* New York: Free Press. (Original work published 1916)

Dobyns, L., & Crawford-Mason, C. (1991). *Quality or else: The revolution in world business.* Boston: Houghton Mifflin.

Drucker, P. F. (1993). *Post-capitalist society.* New York: Harper.

Eiser, J. R. (1994). *Attitudes, chaos, and the connectionist mind.* Oxford, Eng.: Basil Blackwell.

Faigley, L. (1992). *Fragments of rationality: Postmodernity and the subject of composition.* Pittsburgh: University of Pittsburgh Press.

Fairclough, N. (1989). *Language and power.* London: Longmans.

Fairclough, N. (1992a). *Discourse and social power.* London: Polity Press.

Fairclough, N. (1992b). Discourse and text: Linguistic and intertextual analysis within discourse analysis. *Discourse and Society, 3,* 193–217.

Fairclough, N. (1995). *Critical discourse analysis.* London: Longmans.

Fowler, R., Hodge, R., Kress, G., & Trent, T. (1979). *Language and control.* London: Routledge.

Freire, P. (1968). *Pedagogy of the oppressed.* New York: Seabury Press.

Freire, P. (1973). *Education for critical consciousness.* New York: Seabury Press.

Freire, P., & Macedo, D. (1987). *Literacy: Reading the word and the world.* South Hadley, MA: Bergin & Garvey.

Fukuyama, F. (1992). *The end of history and the last man.* London: Penguin.

Gardner, H. (1991). *The unschooled mind: How children think and how schools should teach.* New York: Basic Books.

Gee, J. P. (1992). *The social mind: Language, ideology, and social practice.* New York: Bergin & Garvey.

Gee, J. P. (1993). Postmodernism, discourses, and linguistics. In C. Lankshear & P. McLaren (Eds.), *Critical literacy: Radical and postmodernist perspectives* (pp. 271–295). Albany: State University of New York Press.

Gee, J. P. (1994a). *Quality, science, and the lifeworld: The alignment of business and education* (Focus: Occasional Papers in Adult Basic Education, No. 4). Leichhardt, Australia: Adult Literacy and Basic Skills Action Coalition.

Gee, J. P. (1994b). New alignments and old literacies: From fast capitalism to the canon. In B. Shortland-Jones, B. Bosich, & J. Rivalland (Eds.), *Conference papers: 1994 Australian Reading Association Twentieth National Conference* (pp. 1–35). Carlton South: Australian Reading Association.

Gellner, E. (1983). *Nations and nationalism.* London: Basil Blackwell.

Giroux, H. (1988). *Schooling and the struggle for pedagogies: Critical and feminist discourses as regimes of truth.* New York: Routledge.

Halliday, M. A. K. (1978). *Language as social semiotic.* London: Edward Arnold.

Hammer, M., & Champy, J. (1993). *Reengineering the corporation: A manifesto for business revolution.* New York: Harper Business.

Harre, R., & Gillett, G. (1994). *The discursive mind.* Thousand Oaks, CA: Sage.

Heath, S. B. (1983). *Ways with words: Language, life, and work in communities and classrooms.* Cambridge, Eng.: Cambridge University Press.

Holland, J. H., Holyoak, K. J., Nisbett, R. E., Thagard, P. R. (1986). In J. H. Holland, K.J. Holyoak, R. E. Nisbett, & P. R. Thagard (Eds.), *Induction: Processes of inference, learning, and discovery.* Cambridge, MA: MIT Press.

Ishikawa, K. (1985). *What is total quality control? The Japanese way.* Englewood Cliffs, NJ: Prentice Hall.

Kalantzis, M. (1995). The new citizen and the new state. In W. Hudson (Ed.), *Rethinking Australian citizenship.* Sydney: University of New South Wales Press.

Kalantzis, M., & Cope, B. (1993a). Histories of pedagogy, cultures of schooling. In B. Cope & M. Kalantzis (Eds.), *The powers of literacy* (pp. 38–62). London: Falmer Press.

Kalantzis, M., & Cope, B. (1993b). Republicanism and cultural diversity. In W. Hudson & D. Carter (Eds.), *The Republicanism debate* (pp. 118–144). Sydney: University of New South Wales Press.

Kress, G. (1990). *Linguistic process and sociocultural change.* Oxford, Eng.: Oxford University Press.

Lave, J., & Wegner, E. (1991). *Situated learning: legitimate peripheral participation.* Cambridge, Eng.: Cambridge University Press.

Lewontin, R. C. (1991). *Biology as ideology: The doctrine of DNA.* New York: Harper.

Light, P., & Butterworth, G. (Eds.). (1993). *Context and cognition: Ways of learning and knowing.* Hillsdale, NJ: Lawrence Erlbaum.

Lipnack, J., & Stamps, J. (1993). *The team net factor: Bringing the power of boundary crossing into the heart of your business.* Essex Junction, VT: Oliver Wright.

Luke, C. (1995). Media and cultural studies. In P. Freebody, S. Muspratt, & A. Luke (Eds.), *Constructing critical literacies.* Crosskill, NJ: Hampton Press.

Margolis, H. (1993). *Paradigms and barriers: How habits of mind govern scientific beliefs.* Chicago: University of Chicago Press.

Nolan, R. (1994). *Cognitive practices: Human language and human knowledge.* Oxford, Eng.: Blackwell.

Piore, M., & Sable, C. (1984). *The second industrial divide.* New York: Basic Books.

Perkins, D. (1992). *Smart schools: From training memories to educating minds.* New York: Free Press.

Peters, T. (1992). *Liberation management: Necessary disorganization for the nanosecond nineties.* New York: Vintage Books.

Rogoff, B. (1990). *Apprenticeship in thinking.* New York: Oxford University Press.

Sashkin, M., & Kiser, K. J. (1993). *Putting total quality management to work.* San Francisco: Berrett-Koehler.

Scollon, R., & Scollon, S. B. K. (1981). *Narrative, literacy, and face in interethnic communication.* Norwood, NJ: Ablex.

Senge, P. M. (1991). *The fifth discipline: The art and practice of the learning organization.* New York: Doubleday.

Sproull, L., & Kiesler, S. (1991). *Connections: New ways of working in the networked organization.* Cambridge, MA: MIT Press.

Street, B. V. (1984). *Literacy in theory and practice*. Cambridge, Eng.: Cambridge University Press.

van Leeuwen, T. (1993). Genre and field in critical discourse analysis. *Discourse and Society. 4*, 193–223.

Vygotsky, L. S. (1978). *Mind in society: The development of higher psychological processes*. Cambridge, MA: Harvard University Press.

Vygotsky, L. S. (1987). *The collected works of L. S. Vygotsky: Vol. 1. Problems of general psychology, including the volume thinking and speech* (R. W. Ricber & A. S. Carton, Eds.; Trans. N. Minick). New York: Plenum.

Walkerdine, V. (1986). *Surveillance, subjectivity and struggle: Lessons from pedagogic and domestic practices*. Minneapolis: University of Minnesota Press.

Wertsch, J. V. (Ed.). (1985). *Culture, communication, and cognition: Vygotskian perspectives*. Cambridge, Eng.: Cambridge University Press.

This article and the collaborative work upon which it is based were made possible in a significant part by the support of the National Languages and Literacy Institute of Australia and the Spencer Foundation.

4
Mediation and Remediation

Jay David Bolter and Richard Grusin

It is easy to see that hypermedia applications are always explicit acts of remediation: they import earlier media into a digital space in order to critique and refashion them. However, digital media that strive for transparency and immediacy (such as immersive virtual reality and virtual games) also remediate. Hypermedia and transparent media are opposite manifestations of the same desire: the desire to get past the limits of representation and to achieve the real. They are not striving for the real in any metaphysical sense. Instead, the real is defined in terms of the viewer's experience; it is that which would evoke an immediate (and therefore authentic) emotional response. Transparent digital applications seek to get to the real by bravely denying the fact of mediation; digital hypermedia seek the real by multiplying mediation so as to create a feeling of fullness, a satiety of experience, which can be taken as reality. Both of these moves are strategies of remediation.[1]

There are two paradoxes at work here. One is that hypermedia could ever be thought of as achieving the unmediated. Consider again the music spectacle CD-ROMs like the *Emergency Broadcast Network* with its surfeit of images and sounds that bombard the viewer. The idea of excess has been part of the popular music culture for decades. At first the excess was achieved simply by turning up the volume, until the sound could be felt as well as heard. More recently, the stage productions of popular musicians have emphasized visual spectacle and the acknowledgment of multiple media. The excessive, highly self-conscious video style of MTV is one result, and the music spectacle CD-ROMs obviously remediate MTV. The excess of media becomes an authentic experience, not in the sense that it corresponds to an external reality, but rather precisely because it is does not feel compelled to refer to anything beyond itself. As with MTV, the viewer experiences such hypermedia not through an extended and unified gaze, but through directing her attention here and there in brief moments. The experience is one of the glance rather than the gaze, a distinction that Bryson (1983) has drawn in order to understand the semiotics of Western painting (cf. Bryson 1981). The aesthetic of the glance also makes the viewer aware of the process rather than just the product—both the process of creation and the process of viewing. For example, the Emergency Broadcast Network's CD-ROM conveys the feeling that we are witnessing, and in a way participating in, the process of its own construction. By emphasizing process, digital hypermedia become self-justifying. With their constant references to other media and their contents, hypermedia ultimately claim our attention as pure experience. In this claim, and perhaps only in this claim, hypermedia remind us of high modern art.

High modern visual art was also self-justifying, as it offered the viewer an experience that he was not expected to validate by referring to the external world. Modern art also promised authenticity of experience, and it emphasized the process of putting paint on canvas. As Greenberg (1986) described it, "[modern] painting and sculpture can become more completely nothing but what they do; like functional architecture and the machine, they *look* what they *do*" (34).[2] Digital hypermedia also look what they do. On the other hand, modern art often worked by reduction and simplification rather than excess. In that sense, digital hypermedia (and MTV) are closer in spirit to the excessive rhetoric of early modernism than to the visual practice of high modernism. The rhetoric of cyberspace is reminiscent of the manifestos of Filippo Tommaso Marinetti and the futurists. Moreover, the cyberspace enthusiasts have a similar relationship to technologies of representation that Marinetti and the futurists had to technologies of motive power (race cars, airplanes, etc.).

The second paradox is that just as hypermedia strive for immediacy, transparent digital technologies always end up being remediations, even as, indeed precisely because, they appear to deny mediation. Although transparent technologies try to improve on media by erasing them, they are still compelled to define themselves by the standards of the media they are trying to erase. The wire, Lenny claims, "is not like TV only better"; in saying this, of course, he affirms the comparison that he denies. The wire does improve on television, because it delivers "lived" experience, as television promises and yet fails to do. Similarly, interactive computer games such as *Myst* (and its sequel *Riven*) and *Doom* define their reality through the traditions of photography and film. *Doom* is regarded as authentic because it places the user in an action-adventure movie, *Myst* and *Riven* because of the near photorealism of their graphics and their cinematic use of sound and background music. In general, digital photorealism defines reality as perfected photography, and virtual reality defines it as first-person point-of-view cinema.

It would seem, then, that *all* mediation is remediation. We are not claiming this as an a priori truth, but rather arguing that at this extended historical moment, all current media function as remediators and that remediation offers us a means of interpreting the work of earlier media as well. Our culture conceives of each medium or constellation of media as it responds to, redeploys, competes with, and reforms other media. In the first instance, we may think of something like a historical progression, of newer media remediating older ones and in particular of digital media remediating their predecessors. But ours is a genealogy of affiliations, not a linear history, and in this genealogy, older media can also remediate newer ones.[3] Television can and does refashion itself to resemble the World Wide Web, and film can and does incorporate and attempt to contain computer graphics within its own linear form. No medium, it seems, can now function independently and establish its own separate and purified space of cultural meaning.

To suggest that at our present moment all mediation is remediation is not, however, to suggest that all of our culture's claims of remediation are equally compelling or that we could necessarily identify all of the strategies through which digital media remediate and are remediated by their predecessors. The double logic of remediation can function explicitly or implicitly, and it can be restated in different ways:

- *Remediation as the mediation of mediation.* Each act of mediation depends on other acts of mediation. Media are continually commenting on, reproducing, and replacing each other, and this process is integral to media. Media need each other in order to function as media at all.

- *Remediation as the inseparability of mediation and reality.* Although Baudrillard's notion of simulation and simulacra might suggest otherwise, all mediations are themselves real. They are real as artifacts (but not as autonomous agents) in our mediated culture. Despite the fact that all media depend on other media in cycles of remediation, our culture still needs to acknowledge that all media remediate the real. Just as there is no getting rid of mediation, there is no getting rid of the real.
- *Remediation as reform.* The goal of remediation is to refashion or rehabilitate other media. Furthermore, because all mediations are both real and mediations of the real, remediation can also be understood as a process of reforming reality as well.

Remediation as the Mediation of Mediation

Readers may already see an analogy between our analysis of media and poststructuralist literary theory of the past four decades, for Derrida and other poststructuralists have argued that all interpretation is reinterpretation. Just as for them there is nothing prior to writing, so for our visual culture there is nothing prior to mediation. Any act of mediation is dependent on another, indeed many other, acts of mediation and is therefore remediation. In his work on postmodernism. Fredric Jameson (1991) has traced out the connection between the "linguistic turn" and what he calls "mediatization." Jameson describes the spatialization of postmodern culture as "the process whereby the traditional fine arts are *mediatized*: that is, they now come to consciousness of themselves as various media within a mediatic system in which their own internal production also constitutes a symbolic message and the taking of a position on the status of the medium in question" (162). Jameson's mediatizarían of the traditional fine arts is a process of remediation, in which media (especially new media) become systematically dependent on each other and on prior media for their cultural significance. What Jameson describes as mediatization may be true not only of postmodern new media but also of prior visual media as well. What he identifies as new and truly postmodern in fact reflects an attitude toward mediation that, while dominant today, has expressed itself repeatedly in the genealogy of Western representation.

Jameson himself seems to recognize this genealogy.

> It is because we have had to learn that culture today is a matter of media that we have finally begun to get it through our heads that culture was always that, and that the older forms or genres, or indeed the older spiritual exercises and meditations, thoughts and expressions, were also in their very different ways media products. The intervention of the machine, the mechanization of culture, and the mediation of culture by the Consciousness Industry are now everywhere the case, and perhaps it might be interesting to explore the possibility that they were always the case throughout human history, and within even the radical difference of older, precapitalist modes of production.
>
> (68)

Jameson still insists that there is something special about the mediatization of our current culture: visual media are challenging the dominance of older linguistic media. The most powerful form of this "critical and disruptive challenge" is video, whose "total flow" threatens the physical and temporal differences that constitute linguistic meaning—even as the "available conceptualities for analyzing" media like video "have become almost exclusively linguistic in orientation."[4] Proclaimed by Jameson the dominant medium of our postmodern age, video simultaneously depends on and disrupts literary and linguistic theory. For Jameson, literary theory, and by extension the traditional humanist enterprise, is redefined by popular visual culture. In fact, television, film, and now computer graphics threaten to remediate verbal text both in print and on the computer screen—indeed, to remediate text so aggressively that it may lose much of its historical significance.[5]

In *We Have Never Been Modern* (1993), Bruno Latour takes us further in understanding the role of postmodern theory in our media-saturated, technological culture. For Latour, as for Jameson, contemporary theory gives a special status to language and interpretation: "Whether they are called 'semiotics,' 'semiology' or 'linguistic turns,' the object of all these philosophies is to make discourse not a transparent intermediary that would put the human subject in contact with the natural world, but a mediator independent of nature and society alike" (62). Contemporary theory thus makes it difficult to believe in language as a neutral, invisible conveyor of fully present meaning either between speaker/writer and listener/reader or between subjects and objects, people and the world. Instead, language is regarded as an active and visible mediator that fills up the space between signifying subjects and nature. But language is not the only mediator; it operates just as visual media operate in their tasks of remediation. Postmodern theory errs in trying to isolate language as a cultural force, for it fails to appreciate how language interacts with other media, other technologies, and other cultural artifacts. For Latour, the phenomena of contemporary technoscience consist of intersections or "hybrids" of the human subject, language, and the external world of things, and these hybrids are as real as their constituents—in fact, in some sense they are more real because no constituent (subject, language, object) ever appears in its pure form, segregated from the other constituents.[6] The events of our mediated culture are constituted by combinations of subject, media, and objects, which do not exist in their segregated forms. Thus, there is nothing prior to or outside the act of mediation.

Remediation as the Inseparability of Reality and Mediation

Media function as objects within the world—within systems of linguistic, cultural, social, and economic exchange.[7] Media are hybrids in Latour's sense and are therefore real for the cultures that create and use them. Photography is real—not just as pieces of paper that result from the photographic process, but as a network of artifacts, images, and cultural agreements about what these special images mean and do. Film is real; its reality is constituted by the combination of the celluloid, the social meaning of celebrity, the economics of the entertainment industry, as well as the techniques of editing and compositing. The reality of digital graphics and the World Wide Web is attested to by the web of economic and cultural relationships that have grown up in a few years around the products from Netscape and Microsoft.

Modern art played a key role in convincing our culture of the reality of mediation. In many cases, modern painting was no longer about the world but about itself. Paradoxically, by eliminating "the real" or "the world" as a referent, modernism emphasized the reality of both the act of painting and its product. Painters offered us their works as objects in the world, not as a representation of an external world. By diminishing or denying painting's representational function, they sought to achieve an immediacy of presentation not available to traditional painting, where immediacy had been achieved by concealing signs of mediation. Modern art was often regarded as real or authentic, precisely because it refused to be realistic, and the example of modern art reminds us of the need to distinguish mediation and remediation from representation. Although the real and the representational are separated in modern art, modern art is not therefore less immediate. Modern painting achieves immediacy not by denying its mediation but by acknowledging it. Indeed, as Cavell has noted, building on the work of Greenberg and Michael Fried, one of the defining characteristics of modernist painting is its insistence on acknowledging the conditions of its own mediation.[8]

The reality of modernist painting extends beyond the work itself to the physical space that surrounds it. As Philip Fisher (1991) has argued, "The colonizing of this space between the surface of the canvas and the viewer has been one of the most aggressive features of the 20th century" (37). As we can learn from a visit to any traditional museum, the space between viewer and canvas is controlled, institutionalized, and policed as a special, real kind of space, which people walk around or wait before entering. The colonization of museum space has extended to the space between a photographer or videographer and the object of her mediating technology. When a tourist is taking a photograph or making a video, for example, we treat the line of sight between the camera and the object as if it were a real obstruction; we walk around it, bend under it, or wait until it is gone. We make these gestures not only out of politeness, but also to acknowledge the reality of the act of mediation that we are witnessing. In this case, the act of mediation functions in a system of pedestrian traffic circulation like a tree, a wire, or a traffic light (which is also an act of mediation whose reality we acknowledge). Mediations are real not only because the objects produced (photos, videos, films, paintings, CD-ROMS, etc.) circulate in the real world, but also because the act of mediation itself functions as a hybrid and is treated much like a physical object.

Finally, just as there is nothing prior to the act of mediation, there is also a sense in which all mediation remediates the real. Mediation is the remediation of reality because media themselves are real and because the experience of media is the subject of remediation.

Remediation as Reform

The word *remediation* is used by educators as a euphemism for the task of bringing lagging students up to an expected level of performance and by environmental engineers for "restoring" a damaged ecosystem. The word derives ultimately from the Latin *remederi*—"to head, to restore to health." We have adopted the word to express the way in which one medium is seen by our culture as reforming or improving upon another. This belief in reform is particularly strong for those who are today repurposing earlier media into digital forms. They tell us, for example, that when broadcast television becomes interactive digital television, it will motivate and liberate viewers as never before; that electronic mail is more convenient and reliable than physical mail; that hypertext brings interactivity to the novel; and that virtual reality is a more "natural" environment for computing than a conventional video screen.[9] The assumption of reform is so strong that a new medium is now expected to justify itself by improving on a predecessor: hence the need for computer graphics to achieve full photorealism. The assumption of reform has not been limited to digital media. Photography was seen as the reform of illusionist painting and the cinema, as the reform of the theater (in the sense that early films were once called "photoplays").

It is possible to claim that a new medium makes a good thing even better, but this seldom seems to suit the rhetoric of remediation and is certainly not the case for digital media. Each new medium is justified because it fills a lack or repairs a fault in its predecessor, because it fulfills the unkept promise of an older medium. (Typically, of course, users did not realise that the older medium had failed in its promise until the new one appeared.) The supposed virtue of virtual reality of videoconferencing and interactive television, and of the World Wide Web is that each of these technologies repairs the inadequacy of the medium or media that it now supersedes. In each case that inadequacy is represented as a lack of immediacy, and this seems to be generally true in the history of remediation. Photography was supposedly more immediate than painting, film than photography, television than film, and now virtual reality fulfills the promise of immediacy and supposedly ends the progression. The rhetoric of remediation favors immediacy and transparency, even though as the medium matures it offers new opportunities for hypermediacy.

Remediation can also imply reform in a social or political sense, and again this sense has emerged with particular clarity in the case of digital media. A number of American political figures have even suggested that the World Wide Web and the Internet can reform democracy by lending immediacy to the process of making decisions. When citizens are able to participate in the debate of issues and possibly even vote electronically, we may substitute direct, "digital" democracy for our representational system. Here too, digital media promise to overcome representation. Even beyond claims for overt political reform, many cyberenthusiasts assert that the web and computer applications are creating a digital culture that will revolutionize commerce, education, and social relationships. Thus, broadcast television is associated with the old order of hierarchical control, while interactive media move the locus of control to the individual. That digital media can reform and even save society reminds us of the promise that has been made for technologies throughout much of the twentieth century: it is a peculiarly if not exclusively, American promise. American culture seems to believe in technology in a way that European culture, for example, may not Throughout the twentieth century, or really since the French Revolution, salvation in Europe has been defined in political terms: finding the appropriate (radical left or radical right) political formula. Even traditional Marxists, who believed in technological progress, subordinated that progress to political change. In America, however, collective (and perhaps even personal) salvation has been thought to come through technology rather than through political or even religious action.

Contemporary American culture claims to have lost much of its naive confidence in technology. Certainly postmodern theory is ambivalent about, if not hostile to, technology, but postmodern theory is European, and largely French, in its origins and allegiances. On the other hand, the whole fringe of rhetorical hangers-on that has grown up around computer technology is defined by its commitment to technological salvation. What remains strong in our culture today is the conviction that technology itself progresses through reform: that technology reforms itself. In our terms, new technologies of representation proceed by reforming or remediating earlier ones, while earlier technologies are struggling to maintain their legitimacy by remediating newer ones. The cyberenthusiasts argue that in remediating older media the new media are accomplishing social change. The gesture of reform is ingrained in American culture, and this is perhaps why American culture takes so easily to strategies of remediation.

Finally, remediation is reform in the sense that media reform reality itself. It is not that media merely reform the appearance of reality. Media hybrids (the affiliations of technical artifacts, rhetorical justifications, and social relationships) are as real as the objects of science. Media make reality over in the same way that all Western technologies have sought to reform reality. Thus, virtual reality reforms reality by giving us an alternative visual world and insisting on that world as the locus of presence and meaning for us. Recent proposals for "ubiquitous" or "distributed" computing would do just the opposite, but in the service of the same desire for reform. Instead of putting ourselves in the computer's graphic world, the strategy of ubiquitous computing is to scatter computers and computational devices throughout our world—to "augment reality" with digital artifacts and so create a "distributed cyberspace." Its advocates see such a strategy "as a way to improve on the 'flawed' design in ordinary reality," in which "objects are largely 'dead' to distinctions we care about. Television sets and stereo systems are socially insensitive; they do not turn themselves down when we talk on the phone" (Kellogg, Carroll, and Richards 1991, 418). Latour has argued, however, that for hundreds of years we have been constructing our technologies precisely to take our cultural distinctions seriously. Although he would probably agree with the enthusiasts for distributed computing that "the 'distinctions' people care about can be viewed as virtual worlds, or … information webs," these enthusiasts miss the point when they want to make a categorical distinction between distributed cyberspace and other current and past technologies (Kellogg, Carroll, and Richards 1991, 418). For Latour (1992) the idea of technologies that embody our cultural values or distinctions has been a feature not only of modern but of "amodern" or "premodern" societies as well.

The advocates of ubiquitous computing express grandiloquently the implied goal of all advocates and practitioners of digital media: to reimagine and therefore to reform the world as a mediated (and remediated) space. Again this is not new. For hundreds of years, the remediation of reality has been built into our technologies of representation. Photography, film, and television have been constructed by our culture to embody our cultural distinctions and make those distinctions part of our reality; digital media follow in this tradition. Nor will ubiquitous computing be the last expression of remediation as reform—as the burgeoning promises made on behalf of "push media" already remind us.

Notes

1. The logic of remediation we describe here is similar to Derrida's (1981) account of mimesis, where mimesis is defined not ontologically or objectively in terms of the resemblance of a representation to its object but rather intersubjectively in terms of the reproduction of the feeling of imitation or resemblance in the perceiving subject. "Mimesis here is not the representation of one thing by another, the relation of resemblance or identification between two beings, the reproduction of a product of nature by a product of art. It is not the relation of two products but of two productions. And of two freedoms. … 'True' *mimesis* is between two producing subjects and not between two produced things" (9).

2. Greenberg's account of modernism has been challenged by many critics, among them T. J. Clark (1983), who criticizes Greenberg for not recognizing what Clark sees as modernism's essential qualities of negation and ideological critique. Clark's argument is refuted by Michael Fried (1983), who sees Clark as subscribing to a kind of essentialism that Greenberg too endorses. For Fried, modernism is not about "the irreducible essence of *all* painting," but rather "those conventions which, at a given moment, alone are capable of establishing [a] work's identity as painting" (227). In arguing that all mediation is remediation, we do not mean that remediation is the irreducible essence of either digital media or mediation generally, but rather that at our historical moment, remediation is the predominant convention at work in establishing the identity of new digital media.

3. It is in this sense of older media remediating newer ones that our notion of remediation can be distinguished from the Hegelian concept of sublation (*Aufhebung*), in which prior historical formations (like pagan religions) are sublated or incorporated by newer formations (like Christianity). But as Slavoj Žižek (1993) points out, the interesting move in thinking about Hegelian sublation is to look at those moments when the newer formation is still "in its becoming," when it is perceived as something of a scandal.

4. Jameson's (1991) concept of "total flow" relates to the concept of the "televisual," which Tony Fry (1993) describes as "an ontological domain" of which "almost everyone, everywhere," lives within its reach. For Fry, and for the other authors collected in *RUA/TV*, the "televisual" signals "the end of the medium, in a context, and the arrival of television as the context" (11–13). Where Jameson still sees video as a medium, Fry aims to offer new "conceptualities" for analyzing the ontology of the televisual. (For a critique of this ontological argument, see Auslander, 1997a.)

5. In *Teletheory*, published in 1989 and therefore before the advent of the World Wide Web, Gregory Ulmer made an influential attempt ta refashion academic discourse for what he characterized as the "age of video." In this new, highly mediated environment, he argued, academic discourse must abandon its claim to critical distance and become more like television (10–11). He has subsequently revised his argument to take in new media as well.

6. Prior to *We Have Never Been Modern* (1993). Latour's fullest account of the heterogeneous network that links together humans, language, and the external world is in *Science in Action* (1987).

7. In *The Media Equation* (1996), Byron Reeves and Clifford Nass argue not only that media are real objects in the world, but that "media equal real life" (6). Drawing on their own extensive empirical research, the authors have conclusively demonstrated that people relate to media in the same way in which they relate to other people or places. For Reeves and Nass, the media equation has five variables: manners, personality, emotion, social roles, and form. Each of these variables, they argue, affects the way in which people relate to media and should inform the design choices made by media technologists and developers. This important book supports and complements our contention that media and reality are inseparable. Where Reeves and Nass focus largely on the psychological and sociological implications of how people relate to media, our concern is primarily with the cultural, historical, and formal relationships between people and media, and, more important, among media themselves.

8. For Cavell on modernist painting and acknowledgment, *see The World Viewed* (1979, 108–118). The relations among Cavell, Fried, and Greenberg are complex. See note 2 For Fried's Cavell-inspired criticism of Greenberg and T. J. Clark.

9. In *The Soft Edge* (1997), Paul Levinson uses the term *remediation* to describe how one medium reforms another (104–114). Levinson's intriguing theory is teleological: media develop "anthropotropically"—that is, to resemble the human. For Levinson, remediation is an agent of this teleological evolution, as we invent media that improve on the limits of prior media. Thus, writing makes speech mote permanent; the VCR makes TV more permanent; hypertext makes writing more interactive; and so on. The development Levinson describes, however, is always progressive. We are arguing that remediation can work in both directions: older media can also refashion newer ones. Newer media do not necessarily supersede older media because the process of reform and refashioning is mutual.

References

Baudrillard, Jean. *Simulations*. Trans. Paul Foss, Paul Patton, and Philip Beitchman. New York: Semiotext(e), 1983.

Bryson, Norman. *Vision and Painting: The Logic of the Gaze*. New Haven: Yale University Press, 1983.

——. *Word and Image French Painting of the Ancien Régime*. Cambridge: Cambridge University Press, 1981.

Cavell, Stanley. *The World Viewed: Reflections on the Ontology of the Cinema*. Cambridge, Mass.: Harvard University Press, 1979.

Clark, T. J. "Clement Greenberg's Theory of Art." In W. J. T. Mitchell, ed. *The Politics of Interpretation*, pp. 203–220. Chicago: University of Chicago Press, 1983.

Derrida, Jacques. "Economimesis." *Diacritics*. 11: 3–25. 1981.

Fisher, Philip. *Making and Effacing Art: Modern American Art in a Culture of Museums*. New York: Oxford University Press, 1991.

Fried, Michael. "How Modernism Works: A Response to T.J. Clark." In W. J. T. Mitchell, ed. *The Politics of Interpretation*, pp. 221–238. Chicago: University of Chicago Press, 1983.

Fry, Tony, ed. *RUA/TV? Heidegger and the Televisual*. Sydney: Power Institute of Fine Arts, 1993.

Greenberg, Clement. "Towards a Newer Laocoon." In John O'Brien, ed., *Clement Greenberg: The Collected Essays and Criticism*, vol 1, pp. 23–38. Chicago: University of Chicago Press, 1986.

Jameson, Fredric. *Postmodernism: Or the Cultural Logic of Late Capitalism*. Durham, NC: Duke University Press, 1991.

Kellogg, Wendy A., John M. Carroll, and John T. Richards. "Making Reality a Cyberspace." In Michael Benedikt, ed., *Cyberspace: First Steps*, pp. 411–433. Cambridge, Mass: MIT Press, 1993.

——. "Making Reality a Cyberspace." In Michael Benedikt, ed. *Cyberspace: First Steps*, pp. 411–433. Cambridge, Mass.: MIT Press, 1991.

Latour, Bruno. *We Have Never Been Modern*. Trans. Catherine Porter. Cambridge, Mass.: Harvard University Press, 1993.

——. "Where Are the Missing Masses? The Sociology of a Few Mundane Artifacts." In W. E. Bijker and J. Law, eds., *Shaping Technology/Building Society: Studies in Sociotechnical Change* pp. 225–258. Cambridge, Mass: MIT Press, 1992.

Levinson, Paul. *The Soft Edge: A Natural History and Future of the Information Revolution.* London: Routledge. 1997.

Reeves, Byron, and Clifford Nass. *The Media Equation: How People Treat Computers, Televisions, and New Media Like Real People and Places.* Stanford, Calif.: CSLI Publications; New York: Cambridge University Press, 1996.

Ulmer, Gregory. *Teletheory: Grammatology in the Age of Video.* New York: Routledge, 2004.

Zizek, Slavoj. *Tarrying with the Negative: Kant, Hegel, and the Critique of Ideology.* Durham, NC: Duke University Press, 1993.

5

Multiliteracies, Social Futures, and Writing Centers

John Trimbur

You can tell quite a bit from the names writing centers give themselves—"lab," "clinic," "center," "place," "studio," "workshop." Of course, there's the old debaie *WCJ* readers are likely to remember (and perhaps have taken part in) about whether the names "lab" and "clinic" carry pathologizing overtones. For as important as that debate was to the formation of writing center identities, I'm interested here in something else: namely, that the term "writing" seems to be taken for granted in all the names we've been using. At any rate, this came to mind recently when at Worcester Polytechnic Institute (WPI) we renamed the Writing Center (itself a renaming of the original Writing Resource Center—whatever a writing "resource" might be) the Center for Communication Across the Curriculum.[1] The new name we came up with, after considerable and sometimes heated discussion, is meant to signify the Center's commitment not just to writing but to multiliteracies, as an umbrella term under which appear three "workshops"—the Writing Workshop, the Oral Presentation Workshop, and (in planning) a Visual Design Workshop.

I mention our own experience at WPI because I think it's fairly indicative of recent trends in writing center theory and practice to see literacy as a multimodal activity in which oral, written, and visual communication intertwine and interact. This notion of multiliteracies[2] has to do in part with new text forms and new means of communication associated with the information age and knowledge economies of the globalized markets and societies of late capitalism. Now I'm not one who wanted to follow Bill Clinton across the bridge to the 21th century, but I am aware that these changes in how we read and write, do business, and participate in civic life have some pretty serious implications for our work in writing centers. Just as important, the notion of multilileracies also signals that writing itself has always amounted to the production of visible language and isn't just the invisible composing process we sometimes imagine it to be. For these reasons, at least for our purposes at WPI, where there's no required first-year course and we tutor lots of project work, the notion of multiliteracies offers a way to think about working on everything from essays and project reports to Powerpoint™ presentations to web page and poster design.

My guess is that writing centers will more and more define themselves as multiliteracy centers. Many are already doing so—tutoring oral presentations, adding online tutorials, offering workshops in evaluating web sources, being more conscious of document design. To my mind, the new digital literacies will increasingly be incorporated into writing centers not just as sources of information or delivery systems for tutoring but as productive arts in their own right, and writing center work will, if anything, become more rhetorical in paying attention to the practices and effects of design in written and visual communication—more product oriented and perhaps less like the composing conferences of the process movement.

Linked to the notion of multiliteracies is the challenge to develop more equitable social futures by redistributing the means of communication. In a sense, of course, social justice and the democratization of higher education have always been parts of the mission of writing centers, from the GI Bill of the postwar period to open admissions in the 1970s to the latest struggles to defend access in the CUNY schools and elsewhere. At present, there are important initiatives going on to keep education available and to extend the writing center's reach into the community. As work at Michigan State University shows, the notion of community service is an important legacy of the land-grant universities that imagines a continuity between the academy and civic life (Stock)—and implicitly raises questions for many writing centers whose primary constituency is students in a required first-year course. My feeling is that writing centers have a lot to gain by expanding their work beyond campus but, at the same time, need to expand it on campus as well, so that centers are not just support services to one required English course. In my view, one of the most glaring oversights in writing center practice—and more generally in writing program design—is the neglect of writing in languages other than English. There is important work to be done correcting this First Worldist deviation by making alliances with modem language teachers, promoting bilingualism in writing, and transforming writing centers from English Only to multilingual ones.

Finally, I want to mention, at least briefly, the issue of professional status and writing center administration. I worry that at too many colleges and universities. WPI included, the person who directs the writing center is still non-tenure track staff (and that writing center work is thereby regarded as akin to other types of "support services"), or a recent tenure track hire who directs the writing center for a few years (before, presumably, getting on with the "real" work). Two recent counterexamples, which I point to based on anecdotal evidence, suggest that things could be otherwise—that we could regard writing center work as more than an entry level position and early stage in a professional career. At the University of Maine, after two terms as English department chair, Harvey Kail returned to his former position as writing center director, and at the University of New Hampshire, Robert J. Connors, award-winning historian of composition and rhetoric (and former writing center director at LSU), became the first director of a new writing center. These moves indicate, I think, how writing center work can figure not as a peripheral, passing involvement but a professional activity central to the study and teaching of writing.

Work Cited

Stock, Patricia Lambert. "Reforming Education in the Land-Grant University: Contributions from a Writing Center." *The Writing Center Journal* 18.1 (1997): 7–29.

Notes

1. The "we" here refers largely to me and Lisa Lebduska, director of the Center for Communication Across the Curriculum.
2. I take the terms "multiliteracies" and "social futures" from the New London Group's report/manifesto "A Pedagogy of Multiliteracies: Designing Social Futures," *Harvard Educational Review* 66.1 (1996): 60–92; and Gunther Kress's *Writing the Future: English and the Making of a Culture of Innovation*, Urbana: NCTE, 1997.

6
Design

Gunther Kress and Theo van Leeuwen

Design in the Contemporary Period

The term 'design' is currently hugely fashionable. Whenever an idea becomes so ubiquitous that it has entered common parlance to such an extent it is time to ask why. Why is this idea everywhere? Why does it pop up in the most unlikely places? And in particular, why am *I* using this word, this idea? Am I simply caught up in a trend?

Fashions always speak of something real, which may not, however, be quite on the surface of the debate, there for all to see. One answer to the questions we have just posed seems ready to hand: it is the fact of multimodality itself which needs the notion of design. If the awareness of multimodality, and of its move into the centre of theoretical attention in communication and representation, is a recent phenomenon, as we suggest it is, then the emphasis on and interest in the concept of design is, we think, at least in part a consequence of that.

To explain. In an era when monomodality was an unquestioned assumption (or rather, when there simply was no such question, because it could not yet arise), all the issues clustering around the idea of design—a deliberateness about choosing the modes for representation, and the framing for that representation—were not only not in the foreground, they were not even about. Language was (seen as) the central and only full means for representation and communication, and the resources of language were available for such representation. Where now we might ask 'Do you mean language as speech or as writing?', there was then simply 'language'. Of course there was attention to 'style', to the manner in which the resources of 'language' were to be used on particular occasions. And of course there *were* other modes of representation, though they were usually seen as ancillary to the central mode of communication and also dealt with in a monomodal fashion. Music was the domain of the composer; photography was the domain of the photographer, etc. Even though a multiplicity of modes of representation were recognised, in each instance representation was treated as monomodal: discrete, bounded, autonomous, with its own practices, traditions, professions, habits.

By contrast, in an age where the multiplicity of semiotic resources is in focus, where multimodality is moving into the centre of practical communicative action and, though much more slowly, of theoretical attention, and in which it is becoming, palpably, a fact of the everyday communicational life of post-industrial societies, the question 'What mode for what purpose?' has become the central one. In the era of multimodality semiotic modes other than language are treated as fully capable of serving for representation *and* for communication. Indeed language, whether as speech or as writing, may now often be seen as ancillary to other semiotic modes: to the visual for instance. Language may now be 'extravisual'. The very facts of the new communicational landscape have made that inescapably the issue.

There are many other reasons. One has to do with what we might call 'the spirit of the age'. The era of late modernity is, by common consent, regarded as a period of fragmentation, of disparateness, of dispersion. We would not expect representational practices to be immune from this phenomenon. In an earlier period, that of seeming monomodality, representation was seen as coherent, as integrated, and as cohesive, as a reflex of social arrangements and practices which were similarly cohesive and stable. In the domain of work and of the professions, for instance, 'lines of demarcation' were clear and were kept clear (and conflicts were precisely about ensuring that the lines, the boundaries, were clear, hence the prevalence then of 'demarcation disputes'). Mass media production processes were an example of that. The reporter reports, the sub-editor sub-edits, the picture editor selects the pictures, the typesetter sets the pages of the paper, and so on. The practices of each profession, journalist, sub-editor, picture editor, typesetter, are clearly understood and follow well-established practices. In such contexts design is not (seen as) a necessary concept, because 'scripts' exist which are stable, and the stability of these scripts is supervised even when the scripts themselves are never made overt. Most trades prided themselves on the saying—adapted to the trade—that 'journalists (furriers, tailors, teachers) are born, not made', naturalising the scripts. Or else, design was seen to exist, but at a different, hierarchically *higher* institutional level: the editorial group might decide to change the house style; they had *the* right to (re)design (aspects of) the paper, and of the practices fundamental to its production. The age of desktop publishing and website design has blurred such lines of demarcation, and in many cases has already done away with them altogether.

The scripts underlying traditionally demarcated practices tended to be invisible. Their emergence as an issue of theoretical debate (sometime in the late 1960s and in the 1970s) coincided with the increasing insecurity of their existence. By the 1980s the notion of a script, just like the notion of genre (Van Dijk and Kintsch, 1983; Cope and Kalantzis, 2000), had become a central theoretical concern, reflecting, in the case of genres just as much as in the case of scripts, the phenomenon of the increased instability and fragmentation of these structures. Theoretical debates on genre and on the stability of genres became most insistent at the very moment when the phenomenon itself had begun to become highly problematic.

Today, by contrast, the notion of design is foregrounded: the organisation of what is to be articulated is overtly an issue. As we have said, the previously secure 'scripts' have become and are becoming unstable, and new practices for which no scripts as yet exist are coming into being. Previously distinct practices, the domains of distinct professions, the clear boundaries, all of these have begun to unravel. New domains of practice are in the process of being constituted, and new sets of practices are emerging or will undoubtedly emerge in time; and with these new practices will emerge new, not yet consolidated professions. The practitioner in this new domain now has to take a multiplicity of decisions, in relation to a multiplicity of modes and areas of representation which were previously the domain of discrete professions and their practices.

The former boundaries between certain sets of professions and trades have become weakened, permeable, or have, in many cases, disappeared under the pressure of quite new representational arrangements. Formerly, professions established themselves in relation to *one mode*, or around what was seen as one mode, and developed their practices around that. The issue of choice did not arise in this context. Instead of choice there was competence, and competent practice in relation to one mode—whether that was the mode of writing, as in the production of a film script for instance; of image production, as in cinematography; of acting, or of musical composition, to name but some of the distinct competencies that traditionally go into the production of films. In the case of industrial modes of semiotic production such as film production, one person then *integrated* the various practices of a group of professionals into one coherent performance—the conductor of the orchestra (from the mid-eighteenth century onwards), or the editor (and the editorial team) of the newspaper, or the director of the film. Digital technology, however, has now made it possible for one person to manage all these modes, and to implement the multimodal production single-handedly.

The previous monomodal world and its arrangement gave rise to the hierarchies needed for the implementation of 'orchestrated' performance: conductor, leader of the orchestra, first violin, etc. The new arrangements have, as contemporary management jargon has it, 'flattened' that hierarchy. The previously monomodally conceived arrangements (one profession deals with one mode and in that profession there are hierarchically differentiated practices and jobs) gave rise to highly articulated and stable design practices (scripts) in relation to the use of one mode, and, of necessity, to practices for the integration of these discrete practices, when they were joined with other discrete practices. The new multimodal arrangements have not yet given rise to new stable arrangements: the new 'scripts' are yet to be written. The fact that contemporary management everywhere, whether in semiotic or in industrial processes, is subject to the same forces, indicates that this phenomenon is deeply ramified in larger-scale economic and social changes.

When practices, habits and traditions persist and come to be closely supervised, two directions might be taken: they may remain inexplicit, implicit, passed on by osmosis, or by the 'mimicking' of observed practices (the professional common sense will then be as we said above: 'You can't teach creative writing', 'Journalists are born, not made', etc., both the subject of fierce debates in the 1970s and early 1980s) or they may be made explicit, articulated, formulated as overtly stated rules or as examples of 'best practice'. 'Cookery' as a social practice took the latter route sometime in the eighteenth and early nineteenth centuries, with the emergence of the first cookery books. In each case the practices exist as 'scripts', either held implicitly by those who are accomplished practitioners, or made overt and available in explicitly stated form, as instructions for production from design.

As with any semiotic practice, the semiotic means involved in design practice may become formulated in terms which are increasingly generalised, increasingly abstracted from the (repeated) instances of the practice, that is, they may become formulated as 'grammar-like' sets of rules. 'Grammars' of design, like the grammars of semiotic modes, may remain at the level of 'habit', or they may be brought into consciousness and deliberateness as overt, codified prescriptions. Whether this happens or not is a historical/cultural matter. What is or becomes 'elevated' into formally codified grammar (for instance the rules of writing, as *style* or as *genre;* the rules of musical composition, as *script*, or *score*, the rules of cooking, as *recipe*) or what is left as implicit and yet well understood (for instance patterns of jazz improvisation, or the 'rules' of home cooking) are matters of the social, and of the politics of social evaluation, of aesthetics, of 'taste', and relate to larger-level social trends and to the ideologies and politics of particular societies, and of particular periods—they are the stuff of the histories of semiotic practice.

At the moment Western, post-industrial societies are in a period of profound transition, in which formerly stable semiotic (and social, professional, institutional) arrangements and framings are coming undone, or are quite deliberately being disassembled, while new assemblings are, as we suggested, also emerging. We have already mentioned teaching as an example of the move from the assemblage of complex practices in one profession—where it seemed like a single practice—to its dis-articulation. Teaching, in England, has over the last eighty years or so been a profession in which the teacher had (relative) control over the shaping of curriculum, and over the pedagogic practices involved in teaching. At the moment this complex is being dis-assembled: more and more, the curricular content is being centrally prescribed, and the role of the teacher is becoming one of retailing that centrally produced content.

With the increasing availability of electronic technologies, and its promises of 'more effective' teaching, this process will accelerate in the near future. The new and the planned 'learning centres' will not have teachers in that older, now still recognisable form. 'Facilitator' is the vogue word which may more nearly describe the new role. At the same time, we need to be aware of the social and historical specificity of these arrangements. No teacher in France (or Germany, or Greece) would, during that same period, have assumed that they should have control over curricular content and structure. These matters are historical, social, contingent. Nevertheless, teaching, in England, is moving from being multi-skilled to becoming specialised. The elements of significant design still adhering to the role of teacher are diminishing. On the other side, as an example of the move in the opposite direction, stands (print) journalism. Here a relatively specialised profession, based on the mode of writing (and increasingly on that of image), is undergoing a change in the other direction. In many contexts, reporting, writing, (sub)editing, layout, publishing, are all merging into a single new practice, through the availabilities and affordances of electronic technologies.

In other words, the process does not move uniformly in the direction of disarticulation. In the case of industrial semiotic production processes such as newspaper production, movie production and the symphony orchestra, it moves towards re-articulation and integration. In the case of traditionally independent professions (in certain countries), such as teaching, the law, medicine, etc., it moves towards disarticulation. It is instructive to consider such cases in detail and to reflect on the causes for these dis-articulations and re-articulations. All are bound up, even if at first puzzlingly, with the move from the monomodal representational world (think of the figure of the mid to late 1950s pop singer) to the multimodal representational world of the present (think of Michael Jackson). New semiotic, social, political, institutional arrangements are beginning to take shape, and are quite knowingly being shaped. This process is extending and encompassing (engulfing, if you take an apocalyptic view) more and more of the formerly settled semiotic practices. One result is the foregrounding of design: we might say that we are living in a new age of design.

Coupling and Uncoupling of Semiotic Practices: Monomodality and Multi-Modality

[...]

Design, we suggested in the previous section, is the organisation of what is to be articulated into a blueprint for production. In that definition the task of the designer is seen as 'architectural': the shaping of available resources into a framework which can act as the 'blueprint' for the production of the object or entity or event. The cookery book is about design; the cooking from the book is not, though the person hosting a dinner party can expend their design energies in small modifications ('Yes, I always like to add some coriander, it just gives it a lift') or in other aspects of the event. The architect who designs the blueprint/plans for a house is a designer; the builder who comes along to 'produce' it should, ideally, not be a designer, but someone who fully reads and understands the printed plans and needs no further assistance in building from them—without change.

The example on which we wish to focus just now is that of an (actual) science teacher—one year qualified—who is teaching a series of lessons on blood circulation. This 'unit of work', comprising four lessons, is not designed by (let us call him) David. 'Blood circulation' is a topic within the science curriculum, as prescribed in the National Curriculum in England. It exists as a topic in various designs: as a sketched topic in the National Curriculum; as a topic in textbooks designed by commercial publishers for this curriculum; and as a topic for the grade he is teaching (a class of 13–14 year olds). It also exists in the practices and the traditions of this school's Science Department, both in the form of advice, of 'core' practices, and of materials: printed, 3D and others.

In other words, major aspects of the curriculum are delineated and even prescribed in quite significant detail. This might suggest that this teacher's role is simply that of executor, or of producer. However, he remains responsible in a significant way for 'the organisation of that which is to be articulated', and this is due, largely, we think, to two factors: first, to the facts of multimodality, and second, to a more general principle of semiosis.

We will take the second point first. One assumption of the monomodal communicational world is that the move from design to production is simply one of instantiation realisation. In other words, a design is held to be specific to such an extent and in such detail that no decision of any significant kind is left to the producer. Examples might be, in some versions of this, the performance of a piece of classical music (as contrasted with the freedom of the jazz improvisation); the architect's design and the builder's execution of the design; the design of a car and its manufacture; and so on. However, the general principle of semiosis which we adopt is that every act of realisation involves processes of transformation. For one thing, it involves a shift of a modal kind, from a general schema (realised in one mode) to its instantiation in another mode or modes. That process of *transduction* is itself transformative.

Putting it crudely, a blueprint is not the house, however detailed the former may be. This is where the current preoccupation with 'quality control' stems from: the car manufacturer of course has to accept transduction, but wants to keep transformative action to the absolute minimum. And yet we know that some cars are 'duds' from the moment they leave the production line. The extension of the notion of quality control from this domain to nearly all others (teaching, publication, the prison service, hospitals, religion, etc.) is, in this context, *the* interesting phenomenon. For another thing, every act of realisation, from design through to production, involves choices, even in a monomodal conception of the world.

In the case of the science teacher, David may be intending to articulate a particular auricular design (a discourse of the body and its textual structures) in speech; but that leaves open an unlimited number of choices. These include the rhetorical/epistemological position that he chooses to adopt: 'This is the case, and here is a demonstration to show you', versus 'Here is a textbook; it is an authoritative source of knowledge; it tells you what it is like', or 'You know from your own experience what this domain of science is like—you've seen mould growing on your sandwiches when you forgot to take them out of your lunchbox'. (These are referred to as 'rhetorical frames' in Kress *et al.*, 2000.) After this initial semiotic decision, in itself of great consequence for what a scientist is or will strive to be (or, an episternologically driven decision, with rhetorical/semiotic consequences), a whole range of choices have to be made by her/him, which are about the ultimate instantiation or articulation, the ultimate performance/production of this lesson.

As a question of *design* this involves issues such as what *modes* to use for what segments of the curricular content; how to arrange the content, for instance whether to devise a (largely) sequential structure for it; how to arrange the ensemble of modes in the structure; and, as we said, the initial decision as to the rhetorical *and* epistemological starting point. In this sequence of lessons, the teacher chose the approach of 'this is the case in nature and here are a series of different illustrations of this'. To give an indication of the overall shape of this design we describe its actualisation here, in part, over one lesson. The modes involved were the visual, as image; language, largely as speech, but, in some small part, also as writing, in the form of 'labels' both on the drawn diagram on the blackboard and in a textbook used in the lesson; gesture; the teacher's body (in the space of the classroom); and a physical, material model.

Not all of these were co-present at all times, but several of them were always involved. The manner in which the lesson unfolded was as follows: the teacher had drawn a circle on the whiteboard, with an outer and an inner edge, to indicate a tube-like entity (mode: visual image). This was on the board when the students came into the room. Once the class had settled, the teacher, who had stood perfectly still (mode: body in space), walked deliberately across the podium, in front of the board, turned (mode: body in space) and, halfway back, began to speak (mode: language as speech). His talk concerned the diagram: what it stood for, namely, a highly abstracted image of the path of the blood's circulation around the body, with an abstract image element indicating the heart as pump. He proceeded to make the image more complicated by adding a second, smaller circle to the top (mode: image), a second loop which, he explained, showed the blood's path more accurately: around the body, to the head, and back to heart and lungs.

In elaborating the newly complex model in speech, he used gestures (mode: gesture) to make signs indicating the pumping action of the heart (rhythmically pushing his semi-raised arms against his body), and in repeating the account of the blood's circulation, using the diagram, he both used his hands to indicate the motion of the blood (mode: gesture) and at the same time wrote names as labels on parts of the diagram; 'The blood moves around the body, from the heart to the *lungs*, to the small *intestine*, to the *cells*, to the …' (mode: language as writing). When the diagram had been fully articulated and labelled, he lifted a plastic model of the upper part of a human torso on to the bench in front of him, and, in taking apart the model (mode: model), he stood behind the model, establishing a parallel, so to speak, between his actual, real body and the plastic non-real, regularised body: the model-body as a projection of the real body.

He provided spoken labels (mode: speech) of the parts as he took them from the model (mode: model) and indicated with hands and fingers (mode: gesture) how the blood would move in and around various parts of the model. In this sequence/structure, as we have indicated it so far, it can be seen how different modes are brought together and orchestrated by the teacher, with different modes acting as the major 'carriers' of content at different times and with the modes always drawn in to the semiotic ensemble for quite specific representational/communicational support. At the conclusion of this lesson sequence, David picked up a textbook which had several pages devoted to blood circulation. He pointed to a diagram in the book and then read from the book.

The (Two) Boundaries of Design

What of this sequence/structure had been designed and what not? Our response is that it is not possible to say just from witnessing and describing the lesson. Had we had David's lesson plan, we would have been able to see what was designed—which modes had been deliberately selected, which were to be foregrounded, what the overall sequence was to be. As it is, we must infer from performance/production back to design. But we might suppose, nevertheless, that not all the features of this production had, in fact, been 'designed'. Do we assume, for instance, that gestures-as-mode would have featured in his lesson-plan/design? Do we assume that the precise moments of the arm-pumping action would have been indicated in the design, the 'score' of the lesson? We might assume that the stages and their sequence would have been pre-designed, and that the foregrounded modes might have been indicated, though perhaps not all of these—image, yes; body, perhaps not; gesture, probably not; model, yes; image and writing in the textbook, yes.

All this draws attention to several crucial points about the border between design and production: there need not be, in fact there is unlikely ever to be, a full specification of all of the elements of the eventual production; and there is unlikely to be a full specification of their orchestration. Even in a situation where the teacher's actions and practices are seemingly heavily circumscribed (in England, at least, relative to previous decades), this circumscription captures only parts of what is in fact finally produced/performed. Does this point to the absence of (fully) developed grammars in the area of social practice, to an absence of a grammar of design? Well, maybe yes, and maybe no. Clearly a lesson plan, if demanded, or if made, can encompass modes and structures, though foregrounded modes might actually remain quite invisible even to the maker of the lesson plan: they are 'naturally there'. She or he would not state that they were 'using speech', and the model torso, for instance, might be treated, not as means of communication, but as a 'teaching aid'.

Even so, what is or is not a formally, officially acknowledged mode in a given domain of practice can change over time. Gesture may not, at present, be recognised as a mode in the domain of teaching. But once the psychologist's expertise on 'body language' is drawn into the training of teachers, as it already is in the training of interviewers, interviewees, appraisers, etc., gesture, too, will become more codified. Yet, despite ever-tightening prescription, that which is collected up by 'grammars' of various kinds will always only ever be a fraction, sometimes quite small, of that which appears in performance/production. In our next example we will discuss this question in part in relation to the grammar of writing.

Of course, David had the possibility of other designs: there was no need necessarily for the image on the whiteboard. The fact that he started with that image was an effect of his epistemological/pedagogic decision to begin this 'unit of work' with a high degree of sparse abstraction and work from there both towards ever greater complexity and ever greater realism—until the very end, when he turns to use the textbook, to anchor the knowledge he has developed in its canonical expression.

But given the degree of curriular prescription within which he is working, and even given his epistemological/rhetorical starting point, there was no requirement for him to start with the sparse abstraction of the image of the circular tube. He could have started with the canonical form of knowledge of the textbook; or he could have started with the plastic model. However, within his epistemological/rhetorical framework he could not, we believe, plausibly have started with his own body as the site of demonstration and explanation. He could have made much greater use of the mode of writing, relegating image or 3D model very much to secondary, backgrounded status. And he could have varied the sequential structuring in a number of ways: moving, for instance, from linguistic description to exemplification with the model, and from there to the abstraction of the circle. All these choices of course imply a somewhat different rhetoric and with that some variation within the epistemological position that he has adopted. Each implies a differing pedagogical relation to his audience. But all of these could have been accommodated within his overall epistemological, rhetorical, pedagogical and curricular framework.

One real limitation to his possibilities of choice lies, or lay, within his awareness of what resources are, or were, actually available to him. Here we move to that other boundary of design—the boundary between resources and design. The boundary between design and production is, we said, blurry: usually designs underspecify elements and structures relative to what is to be produced/performed. This is so even in the case of an architect's design of a house, where, depending of course on the particular case, vast ranges of decisions may be left to the builder; though we also assume that there are cases where design is fully specific—in the case of the car assembly plant, or similar high tech instances—hence the concern with quality assurance. At the boundary of resources and design this issue emerges in a related yet distinct form: only those resources which are officially recognised, which are visible as communicational and representational resources, whether highly abstract, such as 'discourses', or entirely materially concrete, such as the materials for making a wall in a house, can become subject to (conscious) design. Semiotic modes which are not in the official, public inventory of modes of a culture or a domain of practice, cannot be drawn into the process of design. Only recognised modes are available as elements for the design process. Similarly, only recognised structures and sequences (syntagms), whether as 'script' or as 'genre', are available to the design process. In the case of David's lesson, this then raises the question of where the other elements and the other scripts come from. Clearly, they are 'there': the gestures are there, the sequencing of modes is clear, once we attend to it; and, moreover, we assume that these 'invisible' elements and structures are understood—even if not in full awareness—by those to whom they are communicated.

For us it suggests that out of the semiotic modes which exist in any one culture only some are officially recognised and therefore available to design processes. These modes are (likely to be) highly developed—with an awareness by members of that culture of their grammar-like organisation. Other modes are not recognised, or are recognised only in relation to certain specific domains, or are semi-recognised. These modes may be well developed, that is, quite fully articulated as semiotic resources, or they may be less so. Similarly with scripts and the rules of genre. Clearly, David can draw on available scripts which are not consciously present for design, in this domain of practice: those involving the semiotic mode of gesture, of the use of his body in space, perhaps in part that of image. What then can be 'designed' (rather than created in the process of the actual, physical production of the semiotic object or event) varies from instance to instance—not haphazardly, but in accord with cultural regularities involving the visibility and recognition of the resources available for design. A discussion such as ours here may have the effect of changing this visibility: for instance, it may be that teacher training courses might include focus on the mode of bodily action. That would bring teaching closer to a domain of practice such as acting, or performance in other fields, in which bodily action is visible, recognised and available for design.

It may be that we can treat the design process as that process which acts deliberately, with awareness, on visible, recognised, 'available' resources in a particular domain, in order to make the blueprint of that which is to be produced. This makes design always contingent: contingent on domain of practice, contingent on the specific stage in a long chain of design-production, where at any point the implementer of a design can become a designer in respect to a particular facet of the productive process.

Grammars for Design

We turn now to examine this question of the regularities of design from a slightly shifted perspective. We are aware that design has to be discussed in relation to a specific domain of practice; in relation to what the resources available for design are; and in relation to the regularities which surround this, both in terms of the modes involved, and in terms of design practice. Design practices, operating over extended periods, and in periods of stability, give rise, not only to the regularities of design itself, but also to the specific use of the modes involved in the design. That is, modes become shaped in response to *discourse*, where discourse itself is the effect of the socially shaped design practices. Here we want to discuss these issues in relation to two examples: one a small card, the size and shape of a credit card, which came (as one of three) inside a leather purse; and the other, revisiting an example from the previous chapter, the pages of two 'home' magazines, one French, one English. We will start with the latter, and investigate the matter of colour in relation to the question of mode and the question of the available resources, and of their shape.

As we pointed out, both magazines explicitly declare their interest in colour. The French magazine, *Maison Française*, in its summer issue has as its theme, stated on the front page, 'Rêve d'été' ('Summer Dream') and it is about 'choosing well': 'Bien choisir: des meubles mobiles, des tapis végétaux, des rotins malins, des tables de jardin' ('Choosing well: lightweight furniture, natural fibre floor coverings, garden tables') and 'living well': 'Bien vivre: les plaisirs de la douche, le charme des vérandas, les nouvelles maisons en bois' ('Living well: the pleasures of the shower, the charm of verandas, and new timber houses'). And it speaks 'du soleil, de l'ombre, de l'eau, de l'aire, du bleu, du blanc' ('of sun and shade, water and air, blue and white'). *Home Flair* has as its theme—its 'cover look'—'dreaming in colour, a country kitchen with a modern taste'. Here we focus, initially, on the French magazine's engagement with *bleu* and *blanc* (in the context of its other stated interests). In one feature in the magazine, 'Le Bleu du Ciel' blue is the dominant colour: 'Entre ciel et mer une couleur s'impose tout naturellement: le bleu. Serein mais dynamique, il encadre, relie, souligne l'architecture pure et dure de cette maison …' (131) ('Between sky and sea one colour imposes itself naturally, blue. Serene yet dynamic, it frames, connects and emphasises the pure and hard architecture of this house …').

Our question is: 'Is colour a mode?' That is, is it semiotically organised, is it a regularised means of representation (in the way sound-as-music, for instance, is)? Does it have a cultural history which has made it into a representational resource? What are its regularities, and how might they be described? Another of our questions can be answered straight away: we are in a specific, specialised domain of practice—that of advertising/publishing/marketing)—with its clear aesthetic requirements and values (of course, in our scheme, aesthetics can be seen to be explicable through a conjunction of the concepts of mode, design and discourse).

In linguistics, one of the formal tests for establishing whether there are regularities is to see if there are irregularities. That is, do members of the culture (or, in this case, of the specialised domain of practice) recognise a rule that has been broken? The test derives from Noam Chomsky's distinction, made in his *Syntactic Structures* (1957), between grammatical and non-grammatical 'strings', well-formed and not well-formed utterances. It is clear, on this criterion, that there can be, and are, ill-formed colour structures, that the colours which co-occur across a page (or a double page spread, or a whole feature article) obey 'rules' of collocation, of what can appropriately go with what.

In the French magazine the *bleu* goes with *blanc* (in various shades of the *bleu*) and with shadings of (off-) white and green. Colour here has a textual function. It forms a cohesive device across the eight pages of this feature article, providing cohesion (and *coherence*) every bit as clearly and as strongly as do the cohesive devices of lexis in language. The text of the magazine explicitly states this ('the blue *frames*, *connects* and *emphasises* the architecture ...'—our italics), which shows that 'grammatical' descriptions are not always written in the register of academic linguistics. This cohesive effect spills over into the adjoining feature advertisement on household goods; crockery, soft furnishings, glassware, napery, etc.: 'Du bleu, du blanc, des rayures, des motifs naifs: ils mettent en beauté, l'été, les objets de tous les jours' ('Blue and white, stripes, simple motifs: they beautify the summer and everyday objects').

Colour clearly functions as a formal semiotic device to provide cohesion and coherence; and this function is active across quite large spans, what in (functional) linguistics is called *colligation*. To test for either, all one needs to do is to take a page from the English magazine, by contrast, and to interleave it with the pages of the French magazine. The entirely differing rules are immediately apparent: the one does not fit with the other; interleaving produces an 'ungrammatical' structure. The precision and the clarity of the rule system of each becomes immediately apparent. There is also cohesion *across* modes. We won't focus on this here although both magazines do: the *textures* of fabrics and ceramics; the *shapes* of glasses, bowls, jugs; the patterns and designs on chair covers, towels, serviettes, plates; the materiality of rock, timber, cement, earthenware, etc. All these are cohesive and provide coherence. In the French magazine the *bleu* and the *blanc* cohere with natural rock, timber, grasses. In the English magazine the oranges and greens cohere with the checks of tablecloths and curtains, and with the turned legs of tables and chairs.

But for colour to be fully a mode, it has to be a resource for making signs: that is, it has to be the signifier-material (the 'stuff', the material, the form) which can be used to carry the signifieds (the 'meanings') of sign-makers. Are colours here used as signs? The choice of colours as signifiers occurs within already established, existent, and well-understood discourses. Colour as signifier is drawn into these discourses, in this case discourses around lifestyle: 'Ce bleu essential donne le tempo et, la maison ayant changé des mains, ses nouveaux propriétaires se sont laissé subjuger comme les précédents' ('This essential blue provides the tempo, and, after the house recently changed hands, the new owners have allowed themselves to be subjected to this like the previous ones'). The point however is that it is not discourse through language which provides the meaning, or shapes these signs, but that the discourse is directly realised in colour (as it is in writing or speech or in other modes).

To side-track for just a moment. For us this is a crucial point, because it promises the key to unlock the barriers to an understanding of colour. That key has so far eluded all those who sought to find it. To put it in our terms, we do not treat colour as sign. We do not say '*Bleu* means *serein*' or '*bleu* means *dure*', or 'green is the colour of hope'. Rather we see colour as a signifier (in the way in which we see all semiotic resources as signifiers at the point of sign-making), which is drawn into sign-making, and is given its signified by the maker of the sign in the context of specific discourses in which and through which the sign-making happens. This means that, as with all signifiers, the signifier material neither fully specifies what the signs which are made can be or will be (e.g. 'green means hope'), nor means that the potentials of the signifier material are completely open ('pink can mean anything you want it to mean, there are no rules'). Rather, a specific colour, as signifier, has, first of all, of itself, a potential for meaning as a signifier due to and in its materiality and interaction with the physiology of bodies. Second, it also has meaning potential because of its cultural history. How that potential will be realised in an actual sign is a matter, jointly, of the interests of the maker of the sign, of the potentials of the signifier material, of the cultural history of that colour (e.g. what specific colours have been given what meanings in what contexts in a given culture, e.g. 'pink is for girls'), and of the discourses within which the sign is articulated. So in the house with the 'minimalist heritage' of *Maison Française* there is a pink table: 'à l'acier … et [à] la table signée Bernard Venet répondent les rayures rouges et marines des toiles de Buren et le rose d'une table-sablier en plexiglas d'Yves Klein' ('to the steel … and the Bernard Venet table correspond the red and blue stripes of the Buren fabric and the pink sand of the Yves Klein plexiglas coffee table'). In this 'geometrically minimalist' house, pink is clearly not the pink of thousands of congratulations cards welcoming the birth of a baby girl in Anglophone societies. Its use in an architectural and lifestyle discourse, an aesthetic discourse of minimalism 'qui ordonne et rythme l'espace', makes this pink into a quite different sign.

This is, for us, the key: colours are not signs (the common-sense and mistaken assumption of art history and psychology alike); colours are signifiers. As such they become signs—enter into meaning—in the same way as other signifier material does. Where colour is drawn into design, as mode, it is brought in in the manner we have just described: the discourses which exist in the domain of the specific design practice shape the meaning of the colour sign.

In concluding our discussion of the question of colour as mode, we can say that colour is a semiotic mode, and certainly so in specific domains of practice. It is thus one of the 'available resources' for design, sufficiently articulated as a mode, and able to be integrated into the discourses of the domain of practice.

In our next example, the Annapelle card, colour-as-available-resource is again an issue. However, with this example we wish to discuss the matter of 'grammar and design' more directly: the 'grammars' of the resources—the modes—deployed in a design, as much as the 'grammars', the organisation, the shapes, the discourses, which emerge in and which have a shaping effect on design.

The Annapelle card is the size of a credit card; it is made of firm olive-eucalyptus green paper card with a smooth glossy surface; and it has printed language on one side. It came, as one of three identical cards, stuck in a small leather purse, sent as a present from Australia to London in 1996. The modes involved in its design are, clearly, language-as-writing and colour. A question arises whether the card as 'card' has modal aspects—it has a cultural history, and it is related to other cards, to business cards, calling cards, loyalty cards, credit cards, membership cards, etc. The question 'Is this a grammatical (conventional) use of the card?' or 'Is this a membership (or 'business', or 'loyalty') card?' certainly could arise. Is the card-qua-card to be treated as an element of a mode? Our own response would be, as with the term mode (or grammar, or genre, or script), that it depends on the domain of practice, that is, on the precise cultural, social, economic location, and on the occasions in which it is used. Here, in this instance, it may be; in other domains it need not be. Is photography (rather than visual image as such) a mode? If you are a photographer, no doubt our tests would be answered positively; if you are the man or woman in the street, there may, in your practice, not be a modal/grammatical distinction between images in printing, etching, drawing, photography, etc. That is not to say, of course, that the ordinary person in everyday situations is not entirely aware of differences; it is to say that for her or him they do not have modal import.

Similarly with layout: layout is a noticeable feature on this card, so is layout a mode? For the practitioner of magazine, newspaper or textbook production it undoubtedly is: forms of layout are distinctive, regular practices, with regular effects, 'looks' and structures. The question becomes somewhat more difficult when we move to the materiality of the kind of card paper: the thickness of the 'card' as material, its degree of gloss. No doubt for paper manufacturers, as for designers with paper, there are established regularities. Were these known, understood, *available* to the designer?

For us these are questions of absolute significance. 'Our', the 'Western', recent history has left 'us', in the West, with views in which a representational resource (not the term used in that history—the term is our attempt, borrowing from the work of Michael Halliday, precisely to get away from the terminologies of that past with their baggage) either is or is not grammatical, subject to the rigidities, certainties and conventions which are caught up in the term 'grammar'. We think that that is no longer a tenable approach: in some domains a resource is treated as though it were subject to grammar; in others it is not. These boundaries shift over time, and they vary between social-cultural groups. And that which is seen as subject to grammar is constantly subject to the socially contingent transformative action of those who avail themselves of the resource. For us this is not an abandonment of the view that there are regularities (a radical postmodern view) but an assertion that to see representational resources (all the resources available for meaning-making) as subject to and part of social forces is to accept precisely this position.

In the case of the card, the available resources as modes are likely to be writing, layout, colour, card (as cultural/social object), card paper (as material stuff), perhaps in this order of decreasing modal articulation, along a range; writing, certainly, in all domains; card (as material stuff) barely, and only in bounded domains. But these modes were all available to the designer, and were, we believe, made use of by her or him in this instance.

The card is designed for an economic purpose. Reading its texts reveals what that might be. What is this card meant to achieve? Clearly, somehow, it is to add value, 'appeal', to the purse. The text makes it obvious that, apart from the card itself as object, the appeal lies, or is meant to lie, in making it clear that this purse is, despite the histories of its production (made *in* Italian leather, *manufactured* in China), an 'Australian' product. And as an Australian product it is more valuable to Australian consumers than it would be without that quality. To produce this effect, the designers do semiotic work. They draw on a number of discourses: of *nationalism* (the emphasis on Australianness; on Australian ownership; on Australian value and practices); of (mildly expressed) *racism* and *ethnic difference* (the nervousness about standards of manufacture in China, and by contrast the positive evaluation of European manufacture and Australian quality control); of *aesthetics/taste* (the evaluative adjective 'fine'; the term 'handcrafted'); of *economics* and *business* (the use of the jargon of contemporary practices, such as 'quality inspection', and the format of the 'business card'); and *heritage* (the invocation of Europe in the form of Italianness).

Each of these discourses represents organisations of knowledge, values and taste, and each therefore provides a kind of template into which that which is to be designed can be fitted. The ensemble of all these discourses together has to be designed so that at the very least a semblance of coherence exists in the material (textual) object which is its realisation. Together the design of this discursive ensemble has a shaping effect on the modal elements which are used to realise it. To put this simply, the various discourses are expressed (each differently) in a number of modes. For instance, the discourse of nationalism is expressed in writing and colour. The discourse of aesthetics is realised in colour, layout, writing. The demand to produce a coherent discursive ensemble has a shaping effect on how the modal resources are used. This applies to language-as-writing, but it applies equally to colour, as it does to the other modes.

Designing is active, agentive, yet also hedged by rules, constraints, conventionalised practices on two sides. On the side of resources for design, the modes have cultural articulation through their histories of social use, and these articulations mean that the elements of the modes, and the combinations in which they appear, have a (relative) stability. Design has to work with and against that stability. On the side of that which provides available shapings for the design, the discourses (as well as the scripts and the genres), there are shapings which provide the frames; that which is to be designed has to negotiate with these—broadly these are the frames within which the to-be-designed has to be accommodated.

Here we briefly illustrate what we mean. Take the shaping effect of discourse on the one hand (let us say, the aesthetic discourse) and the constraints of the mode of writing, the *grammar of writing*, on the other hand. The aesthetic discourse emerges, as we said, in the selection of the adjectives 'fine' and 'handcrafted'; but it emerges also in the use of the grammar of this mode. Consider two instances: the use of the relative clause 'which is made in Italian leather' and the use of the preposition 'in' in that clause. This relative clause would normally be a non-restrictive clause; here it is treated as a restrictive relative clause (the distinction between 'a star, which, on a good night, is easily visible' and 'the star which outshines every other near sunset'). The latter makes the object named by the head noun unique, the former does not. 'Uniqueness' is here a sign produced with the resources of the grammar in order to play a part in realising the aesthetic discourse; but it happens somewhat against the grain of normal grammatical usage. That is, this is precisely an instance when in the process of design the constraints are worked against as a result of the demands of the discourse.

A very similar effect is produced, we feel, by the use of the preposition 'in'. This, we feel, would normally be—ought normally to be—the preposition 'of ('made of Italian leather'), or perhaps 'from' ('made from Italian leather'). 'In' gives a quite special feel, perhaps derived from its qualities as 'container metaphor', to use the Lakoff/Johnson parlance. We are, precisely, 'in' a world of craft, of quality, of tradition, of leather as aesthetic material. And 'in' is also connected to the world of art, in which a sculptor can be said to work 'in bronze' or 'in wood'. Both in the case of the relative clause and in the case of the preposition, grammar, as one aspect of mode, is drawn on as part of the realisational resources for this discourse.

Similarly with punctuation. A linguist's pedantic urge might be to punctuate this brief passage 'properly', with a comma after *company, produce, leather, China*, leaving the other two commas where they are. Again, we feel that the exceedingly sparse punctuation (including the omission of the possessive apostrophe in *People' s*) is there as an effect of a design decision: the 'proper' punctuation would make the text look fussy, fiddly. As it is the text looks clean, clear. Punctuation is used as a mode to play its part in the realisation of the aesthetic discourse.

To conclude this discussion, a word or two on the use of colour in this object. One of the discourses at work here is, as we said, that of nationalism. The eucalypt-green colour of the card may therefore be one of the expressions of that discourse in this small text. A different choice might have been made: Australianness could also have been signalled using the red, black and gold colours of the Australian Aboriginal flag. Of course, that choice would have foregrounded the highly political character of choosing colour (another sign of its function as mode): this is decidedly not the Australianness which these designers wished to evoke. Their Australianness is the green of the bush—the colour of 'natural' Australia, standing for an equally specific politics (the ostensive avoidance of the political, but also the politics of Australian environmentalism). But this green can also be read as olive green, and it then 'goes with' the Italianness of the leather, the style of the text, its layout. In other words, colours can have several distinct readings and functions, including, here too, the function of realising the discourse of aesthetics. Lexis, colour, grammar, punctuation, layout, logo, paper are all drawn into the realisation of this discourse. Or, to see it from the point of view of the designer, this discourse (once the design decision has been made to use it) provides a powerful constraining and shaping effect. On the one hand are the available resources, with their 'resistances', on the other hand stand the discourses, offering to shape design decisions in any number of modes. In the centre stands the designer: free yet not free; constrained and hemmed in; and yet creative and transformative. The elements and rules of the semiotic modes have shape and are resistant to a greater or lesser degree to the shaping of the designer; the discourses (and scripts and genres) strongly press in on possible design decisions and suggest how the modes are to be used in actual new designs. The designer works in this confined 'space'—creatively, agentively, transformatively.

Designing as Transformation: The Shaping of Modes and Discourse

The purposive process of design works with and on available resources and does so in the environment of the more or less strongly enforced and felt already existing shaping of discourses. In a sense this process might be simply reproductive: the modes are already shaped, and that shape imposes ite constraints as well as its affordances on specific discourses and designs. This is perhaps one restatement of what has, in the period of structuralism, been the accepted common sense of representation and communication. Design, however, takes place in the field of social action, and with the agentive force of individual (even if socially/ historically shaped) interests. The response to the demands of a new situation requires design decisions which are always significantly different from those taken before. The specific discourses with which a design will be realised will very likely be different from one time to another. New ensembles of discourses ensure that the resultant material semiotic object, whether 'textual' or other, is always new in some significant respect. The appearance of the discursive ensemble and its materialisation as text or other object has its effect on each of the co-present discourses. In the compromise of accommodation to each of the co-present discourses, each discourse is transformed.

There is, equally, transformation of discourse in relation to the modes used: the design process in the multimodal world involves selection of discourses and selection of modes through which content-in-discourse will be realised. To use the mode of image to represent certain information means that the mode of writing is not used for that purpose. That will have an effect on the (elements of the) mode writing. Writing will come to be used for specific purposes, and that shift in use will have its inevitable effects on the shape of signs made in that mode, and therefore on the signifier material. In work we have done elsewhere (Kress and van Leeuwen, 1996) it is clear that the uses of writing in textbooks have undergone a remarkable shift. Where thirty, forty or fifty years ago writing 'carried' all the informational load, with consequent effects on forms of syntax (sentence complexity, forms and frequencies of nominalisation, etc.), in contemporary textbooks there is *functional specialisation*. Language-as-writing is now used to describe (pedagogically salient) actions, events, in quasi-narrative form; image is used to describe the 'shape' of phenomena (circuits, magnetic fields, digestive mechanisms, the carbon cycle) which are the stuff of curricular content.

The design process reshapes, transforms, both writing and image, both as realisational material and as discourses (as well as scripts and genre), and as existent potential shapings.

We will conclude this section with a brief discussion of another example. It may be that the issue of the constant transformation of modal resources in design is uncontentious when it is applied to modes such as writing, speech, image, gesture, etc. We wish to assert that it applies to all cultural objects, and so return once more to that seemingly implausible subject, the house.

The ordinary, common, late nineteenth-century terrace house was built, let us say in 1888, in Sydney or London, to a broadly common design. Despite this common design it had vast variations of overall size, sizes of rooms, and smaller details in the dispositions of rooms, etc.; not to mention the addition of verandas in Australia, the effect there both of climate and a mixture of Indian colonial and Italianate discourses. But such a house, once built, is surely beyond transformation? Yet, as we mentioned in the previous chapter, houses of this kind have been subject to constant transformation. In the 1950s and 1960s bathrooms and indoor toilets were added, and in the 1970s and through the 1980s the dividing walls between the front room and the back room were knocked out, and scullery, kitchen, and outhouse were unified into a single space, while the insertion of glass doors at the back of the house permitted vision and movement into the garden, 'let light into the house', and so on.

These changes were not accidental, they were not arbitrary, nor were they 'individual', even though each individual imagined that she or he was doing this redesign as the expression of individual taste. The changes reflected changed notions of the family, of divisions of public and private—in Australia as in England. They involved a migration from the front of the house to the back, away from the public street to the private garden. They both reflected and produced changing lifestyles, in which, perhaps, a changing climate played its part. They were founded not so much on more leisure as on changed discourses of leisure. And they reflected, precisely, the importation of new discourses of aesthetics, for instance inspired by holidays taken around the Mediterranean.

But, it might be said, these changes happen so infrequently, they are hardly constant transformations. Consider then the minor, the lesser transformations, the decision as to which room will be the parents' bedroom, upstairs at the front of the house or at the back, and which will be the children's rooms, of whether there will be a dining room or just an eating corner in the kitchen, etc. Choices of colours for different rooms are also transformations, related, engendered by discourses of lifestyle, which, in their turn, relate to discourses of the family, of the economy, of work and of leisure. The decision to have the evening meal in the eating comer, with or without the tablecloth, is another transformation, as is the decision to have Sunday lunch in the dining room. Each use of space of the house is transformative—of course made in the light of discourses, as we said in the previous chapter, of family, of work, of leisure, of aesthetics. And the home magazines and television programmes are there to supply, incessantly, designs for this process. These designs are not prescriptive in any strict sense, but they are nevertheless presented as taken up or endorsed by television personalities and other celebrities, and by various kinds of 'model' families, and they come with all the authority of the designers who are constantly presented to the public as the ultimate arbiters of good taste.

References

Chomsky, N. (1957) *Syntactic Structures*, The Hague, Mouton.

Cope, B. and Kalantzis, M. (2000) *Multiliteracies*, London, Routledge.

Kress, Gunther, and Theo van Leeuwen. (1996). *Reading Images: The Grammar of Visual Design*, New York, Routledge.

Kress, G.R., Jewit, C., Ogborn, J. and Tsatsarelis, C. (2000) *Multimodal Teaching and Learning*, London, Continuum.

Lakoff, G. and Johnson, M. (1980) *Metaphors We Live By*, Chiago, University of Chicago Press.

Van Dijk, T.A. and Kintsch, W. (1983) *Strategies of Discourse Comprehension*, New York, Academic Press.

7

A Cognitive Theory of Multimedia Learning

Richard E. Mayer

Multimedia messages that are designed in light of how the human mind works are more likely to lead to meaningful learning than those that are not. A cognitive theory of multimedia learning assumes that the human information processing system includes dual channels for visual/pictorial and auditory/verbal processing, that each channel has limited capacity for processing, and that active learning entails carrying out a coordinated set of cognitive processes during learning. The five steps in multimedia learning are selecting relevant words from the presented text or narration, selecting relevant images from the presented illustrations, organizing the selected words into a coherent verbal representation, organizing selected images into a coherent visual representation, and integrating the visual and verbal representations and prior knowledge. Processing of pictures occurs mainly in the visual/pictorial channel and processing of spoken words occurs mainly in the auditory/verbal channel, but processing of printed words takes place initially in the visual/pictorial channel and then moves to the auditory/verbal channel.

[...]

In this chapter, I spell out a cognitive theory of multimedia learning—that is, a cognitive theory of how people construct knowledge from words and pictures. First, I explore three fundamental assumptions underlying the theory, and second, I examine each of five steps in meaningful multimedia learning based on the theory.

Three Assumptions of a Cognitive Theory of Multimedia Learning

[...]

What is the role of a theory of learning in multimedia design? Decisions about how to design a multimedia message always reflect an underlying conception of how people learn, even when the underlying theory of learning is not stated. Designing multimedia messages is always informed by the designer's conception of how the human mind works. For example, when a multimedia presentation consists of a screen overflowing with multicolored words and images flashing and moving about, this reflects the designer's conception of human learning. The designer's underlying conception is that human learners possess a single-channel, unlimited-capacity and passive-processing system. First, by not taking advantage of auditory modes of presentation, this design is based on a single-channel assumption—that all information enters the cognitive system in the same way regardless of its modality. It follows that it does not matter which modality—such as presenting words as sounds or text—is used to present information, just as long as the information is presented. Second, by presenting so much information, this design is based on an unlimited-capacity assumption—that humans can handle an unlimited amount of material. It follows that the designer's job is to present information to the learner. Third, by presenting many isolated pieces of information, this design is based on a passive-processing assumption—that humans act as tape recorders who add as much information to their memories as possible. It follows that learners do not need any guidance in organizing and making sense of the presented information.

What's wrong with this vision of learners as possessing a single-channel, unlimited-capacity, passive processing system? Current research in cognitive psychology paints a quite different view of how the human mind works (Bransford, Brown, & Cocking, 1999; Lambert & McCombs, 1998). Thus, the difficulty with this commonsense conception of learning is that it conflicts with what is known about how people learn. In this chapter, I explore three assumptions underlying a cognitive theory of multimedia learning—*dual channels, limited capacity*, and *active processing*. These assumptions are summarized in Figure 7.1.

Figure 7.2 presents a cognitive model of multimedia learning intended to represent the human information processing system. The boxes represent memory stores, including sensory memory, working memory, and long-term memory. Pictures and words come in from the outside world as a multimedia presentation (indicated in the left side of the figure) and enter sensory memory through the eyes and ears (indicated in the **Sensory Memory** box). Sensory memory allows for pictures and printed text to be held as exact visual images for a very brief time period in a visual sensory memory (at the top) and for spoken words and other sounds to be held as exact auditory images for a very brief time period in an auditory sensory memory (at the bottom). The arrow from Pictures to Eyes corresponds to a picture

Assumption	Description	Related Citations
Dual Channels	Humans possess separate channels for processing visual and auditory information	Paivio, 1986; Baddeley, 1992
Limited Capacity	Humans are limited in the amount of information that they can process in each channel at one time	Baddeley, 1992; Chandler and Sweller, 1991
Active Processing	Humans engage in active learning by attending to relevant incoming information, organizing selected information into coherent mental representation with other knowledge	Mayer, 1999c; Wittrock, 1989

Figure 7.1 Three Assumptions of a Cognitive Theory of Multimedia Learning.

being registered in the eyes; the arrow from Words to Ears corresponds to spoken text being registered in the ears; and the arrow from Words to Eyes corresponds to printed text being registered in the eyes.

The central work of multimedia learning takes place in working memory, so let's focus there. Working memory is used for temporarily holding and manipulating knowledge in active consciousness. For example, in reading this sentence, you may be able to actively concentrate on only some of the words at one time, or in looking at Figure 7.2, you may be able to hold the images of only some of the boxes and arrows in your mind at one time. This kind of processing—of which you are consciously aware—takes place in your working memory. The left side of the box labeled *Working Memory* in Figure 7.2 represents the raw material that comes into working memory—visual images of pictures and sound images of words—so it is based on the two sensory modalities that I called visual and auditory in chapter 1; in contrast, the right side of the *Working Memory* box represents the knowledge constructed in working memory—visual and verbal mental models and links between them—so it is based on the two representation modes that I called pictorial and verbal. The arrow from Sounds to Images represents the mental conversion of a sound (such as the spoken word *cat*) into a visual image (such as an image of a cat)—that is, when you hear the word *cat*, you might also form a mental image of a cat The arrow from Images to Sounds represents the mental conversion of a visual image (such as a mental picture of a cat) into a sound image (such as the sound of the word *cat*)—that is, you may mentally hear the word *cat* when you see a picture of one. These processes may occur by mental association in which the spoken word *cat* primes the image of a cat and vice versa. The major cognitive processing required for multimedia learning is represented by the arrows labeled Selecting images, Selecting sounds, Organizing images, Organizing words, and Integrating, which are described in the next section.

Finally, the box on the right is labeled *Long-Term Memory* and corresponds to the learner's storehouse of knowledge. Unlike working memory, long-term memory can hold large amounts of knowledge over long periods of time, but for a person to actively think about material in long-term memory, it must be brought into working memory (as indicated by the arrow from *Long-Term Memory* to *Working Memory*).

In accord with the dual-channel assumption, I have divided *Sensory Memory* and *Working Memory* into two channels: The one across the top deals with auditory sounds and eventually with verbal representations, whereas the one across the bottom deals with visual images and eventually with pictorial representations. In this way, I try to compromise between the

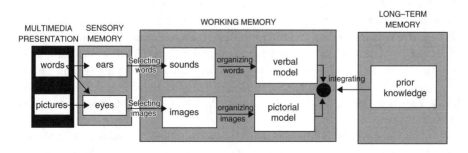

Figure 7.2 Cognitive Theory of Multimedia Learning.

sensory modality view, which I use to create two channels in the left side of *Working Memory*, and the presentation mode view, which I use to create two channels on the right side of *Working Memory*. In accord with the limited-capacity assumption, working memory is limited in the amount of knowledge it can process at one time, so that only a few images can be held in the visual channel of working memory and only a few sounds can be held in the auditory channel of working memory. In accord with the active-processing assumption, I have added arrows to represent cognitive processes for selecting knowledge to be processed in working memory (i.e. arrows labeled Selecting that move from the presented material to *Working Memory*), organizing the material in working memory into coherent structures (i.e., arrows labeled Organizing that move from one kind of representation in *Working Memory* to another), and integrating the created knowledge with other knowledge, including knowledge brought in from long-term memory (i.e., arrow labeled Integrating that moves from *Long-Term Memory* to *Working Memory* and between the visual and auditory representations in Working Memory).

Dual-Channel Assumption

The dual-channel assumption is that humans possess separate information processing channels for visually represented material and auditorily represented material. The dual-channel assumption is summarized in Figure 7.3: Figure 7.3A shows the auditory/verbal channel highlighted and Figure 7.3B shows the visual/pictorial frame highlighted. When information is presented to the eyes (such as illustrations, animation, video, or on-screen text), humans begin by processing that information in the visual channel; when information is presented to the ears (such as narration or nonverbal sounds), humans begin by processing that information in the auditory channel. The concept of separate information processing channels has a long history in cognitive psychology and currently is most closely associated with Paivio's dual-coding theory (Clark & Paivio, 1991; Paivio, 1986) and Baddeley's model of working memory (Baddeley, 1986, 1992, 1999).

What Is Processed in Each Channel?

There are two ways of conceptualizing the differences between the two channels—one based on *sensory modalities* and one based on *presentation modes*. The sensory-modality approach focuses on whether learners initially process the presented materials through their eyes (such as for pictures, video, animation, or printed words) or ears (such as for spoken words or background sounds). According to the sensory-modality approach, one channel processes visually represented material and the other channel processes auditorily represented material. This conceptualization is most consistent with Baddeley's (1986, 1992, 1999) distinction between the visuospatial sketchpad and the articulatory (or phonological) loop.

In contrast, the presentation-mode approach focuses on whether the presented stimulus is verbal (such as spoken or printed words) or nonverbal (such as pictures, video, animation, or background sounds). According to the presentation-mode approach, one channel processes verbal material and the other channel processes pictorial material and nonverbal sounds. This conceptualization is most consistent with Paivio's (1986) distinction between verbal and nonverbal systems.

Whereas the sensory-modalities approach focuses on the distinction between auditory and visual representations, the presentation-mode approach focuses on the distinction between verbal and nonverbal representations. The major difference concerning multimedia learning

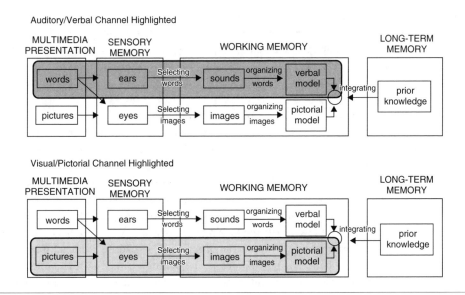

Figure 7.3 (A) The Auditory/Verbal Channel (Top Frame) and (B) Visual/Pictorial Channel (Bottom Frame) in a Cognitive Theory of Multimedia Learning.

rests in the processing of printed words (i.e., on-screen text) and background sounds. On-screen text is initially processed in the verbal channel in the presentation-mode approach but in the visual channel in the sensory-modality approach; background sounds, including nonverbal music, are initially processed in the nonverbal channel in the presentation-mode approach but in the auditory channel in the sensory-mode approach.

For purposes of the cognitive theory of multimedia learning, I have opted for a compromise in which I use the sensory-modalities approach to distinguish between visually presented material (such as pictures, animation, video, and on-screen text) and auditorily presented material (such as narration and background sounds) as well as a presentation-mode approach to distinguish between the construction of pictorially based and verbally based models in working memory. Thus, I distinguish between an auditory/verbal channel and a visual/pictorial channel. However, additional research is needed to clarify the nature of the differences between the two channels.

What Is the Relation between the Channels?

Although information enters the human information system via one channel, learners may also be able to convert the representation for processing in the other channel. When learners are able to devote adequate cognitive resources to the task, it is possible for information originally presented to one channel to also be represented in the other channel. For example, on-screen text may initially be processed in the visual channel because it is presented to the eyes, but an experienced reader may be able to mentally convert images into sounds that are processed through the auditory channel. Similarly, an illustration of an object or event such as a cloud's rising above the freezing level may initially be processed in the visual channel, but the learner may also be able to mentally construct the corresponding verbal description in the auditory channel. Conversely, a narration describing some event such as "the cloud rises above the freezing level" may initially be processed in the auditory channel because it is presented to the ears, but the learner may also form a corresponding mental image that is processed in the visual channel. Such cross-channel representations of the same stimulus play an important role in Paivio's (1986) dual-coding theory.

Limited-Capacity Assumption

The second assumption is that humans are limited in the amount of information that can be processed in each channel at one time. When an illustration or animation is presented, the learner is able to hold only a few images in working memory at any one time. These images reflect portions of the presented material rather than an exact copy of the presented material. For example, if an illustration or animation of a tire pump is presented, the learner may be able to focus on building mental images of the handle going down, the inlet valve opening, and air moving into the cylinder. When a narration is presented, the learner is able to hold only a few words in working memory at any one time. These words reflect portions of the presented text rather than a verbatim recording. For example, if the spoken text is "When the handle is pushed down, the piston moves down, the inlet valve opens, the outlet valve closes, and air enters the bottom of cylinder," the learner may be able to hold the following verbal representations in auditory working memory: "handle goes up," "inlet valve opens," and "air enters cylinder." The conception of limited capacity in consciousness has a long history in psychology, and some modern examples are Baddeley's (1986, 1992, 1999) theory of working memory and Chandler and Sweller's (1991; Sweller, 1999) cognitive load theory.

What Are the Limits on Cognitive Capacity?

If we assume that each channel has limited processing capacity, it is important to know just how much information can be processed in each channel. The classic way to measure someone's cognitive capacity is to give him or her a memory span test (Miller, 1956; Simon, 1974). For example, in a digit span test, I can read a list of digits at the rate of one digit per second (such as 8-7-5-3-9-6-4) and ask you to repeat them back in order. The longest list that you can recite without making an error is your memory span for digits (or digit span). Alternatively, I can show you a series of line drawings of simple objects at the rate of one per second (such as moon-pencil-comb-apple-chair-book-pig) and ask you to repeat them back in order. Again, the longest list you can recite without making an error is your memory span for pictures. Although there are individual differences, average memory span is fairly small-approximately five to seven chunks.

With practice, of course, people can learn techniques for chunking the elements in the list, such as grouping the seven digits 8-7-5-3-9-6-4 into three chunks, 875-39-64 (e.g., "eight seven five"—pause—"three nine"—pause "six four"). In this way, the cognitive capacity remains the same (e.g., five to seven chunks), but more elements can be remembered within each chunk. Researchers have developed more refined measures of verbal and visual working memory capacity but continue to show that human processing capacity is severely limited.

What Are the Sources of Cognitive Load?

Sweller and Chandler (1994) and Sweller (1999) have distinguished between intrinsic and extraneous sources of cognitive load during learning. *Intrinsic cognitive had* depends on the inherent difficulty of the material—how many elements there are and how they interact with each other. When there are many elements in the material and they are related to one another in complex ways, intrinsic cognitive load is high. In contrast, intrinsic cognitive load is low when the material is not complicated, such as when each element in the material can be learned separately. *Extraneous cognitive load* depends on the way the instructional message is designed—that is, on the way material is organized and presented. When the message is poorly designed, learners must engage in irrelevant or inefficient cognitive processing; when it is well designed, extraneous cognitive load is minimized.

How Are Limited Cognitive Resources Allocated?

The constraints on our processing capacity force us to make decisions about which pieces of incoming information to pay attention to, the degree to which we should build connections among the selected pieces of information, and the degree to which we should build connections between selected pieces of information and our existing knowledge. *Metacognitive strategies* are techniques for allocating, monitoring, coordinating, and adjusting these limited cognitive resources. These strategies are at the heart of what Baddeley (1992, 1999) has called the *central executive*—the system that controls the allocation of cognitive resources—and play a central role in modern theories of intelligence (Sternberg, 1990).

Active-Processing Assumption

The third assumption is that humans actively engage in cognitive processing to construct a coherent mental representation of their experiences. These active cognitive processes include paying attention, organizing incoming information, and integrating incoming information with other knowledge. In short, humans are active processors who seek to make sense of multimedia presentations. This view of humans as active processors conflicts with a common view of humans as passive processors who seek to add as much information as possible to memory—that is, as tape recorders who file copies of their experiences in memory to be retrieved later.

What Are the Major Ways that Knowledge Can Be Structured?

Active learning occurs when a learner applies cognitive processes to incoming material—processes that are intended to help the learner make sense of the material. The outcome of active cognitive processing is the construction of a coherent mental representation, so active learning can be viewed as a process of model building. A *mental model* (or *knowledge structure*) represents the key parts of the presented material and their relations. For example, in a multimedia presentation of how lightning storms develop, the learner may attempt to build a cause-and-effect system in which a change in one part of the system causes a change in another part. In a lesson comparing and contrasting two theories, construction of a mental model involves building a sort of matrix structure that compares the two theories along several dimensions.

If the outcome of active learning is the construction of a coherent mental representation, it is useful to explore some of the typical ways that knowledge can be structured. Some basic knowledge structures include *process, comparison, generalization, enumeration,* and *classification* (Chambliss & Calfee, 1998; Cook & Mayer, 1988). Process structures can be represented as cause-and-effect chains and consist of explanations of how some systems work. An example is an explanation of how the human ear works. Comparison structures can be represented as matrices and consist of comparisons among two or more elements along several dimensions. An example is a comparison between how two competing theories of learning view the role of the learner, the role of the teacher, and useful types of instructional methods. Generalization structures can be represented as a branching tree and consist of a main idea with subordinate supporting details. An example is a chapter outline for a chapter explaining the major causes for the American Civil War. Enumeration structures can be represented as lists and consist of a collection of items. An example is the names of principles of multimedia learning listed in this book. Classification structures can be represented as hierarchies and consist of a set and subsets. An example is a biological classification system for sea animals. These structures are summarized in Figure 7.4.

Understanding a multimedia message often involves constructing one of these kinds of knowledge structures. This assumption suggests two important implications for multimedia design: (1) the presented material should have a coherent structure and (2) the message should provide guidance to the learner for how to build the structure. If the material lacks a coherent structure, such as being a collection of isolated facts, the learner's model building efforts will be fruitless. If the message lacks guidance for how to structure the presented material, the learner's model-building efforts may be overwhelmed. Multimedia design can be conceptualized as an attempt to assist learners in their model-building efforts.

Type of structure	Description	Representation	Example
Process	Explain a cause-aand effect chain	**Flow chart**	Explaination of how the human ear works
Comparison	Compare and contrast two or more elements along several dimension	**Matrix**	Comparison of two theories of learning with respect to nature of the learner, teacher, and instructonal methods
Generalization	Describe main idea and supporting details	**Branching tree**	Presentation of thesis for the major causes of the American Civil War along with evidence
Enumeration	Present a list of items	**List**	List of the names of seven principals of multimedia design
Classification	Analyze a domain into sets and subsets	**Hierarchy**	Description of a biological classification system for sea animals

Figure 7.4 Five Kinds of Knowledge Structures.

What Are the Cognitive Processes Involved in Active Learning?
Three process that are essential for active learning are selecting relevant material, organizing selected material, and integrating selected material with existing knowledge (Mayer, 1996, 1999a, 1999b, 1999c; Wittrock, 1989). Selection of relevant material occurs when a learner pays attention to appropriate words and images in the presented material. This process involves bringing material from the outside into the working-memory component of the cognitive system. Organizing selected material involves building structural relations among the elements—such as one of the five kinds of structures described above. This process takes place within the working-memory component of the cognitive system. Integrating selected material with existing knowledge involves building connections between incoming material and relevant portions of prior knowledge. This process involves activating knowledge in long-term memory and bringing it into working memory. For example, in a multimedia message, learners must pay attention to certain words and images, arrange them into a cause-and-effect chain, and relate the steps to prior knowledge such as the principle that hot air rises. These processes are summarized in Figure 7.5.

In sum, the implicit theory of learning underlying some multimedia messages is that learning is a single-channel, unlimited-capacity, passive-processing activity. Thus, multimedia design is sometimes based on the empty-vessel view of learning—the idea that the learner lacks knowledge, so learning involves pouring information into the learner's empty mind. In contrast, I offer a cognitive theory of multimedia learning that is based on three assumptions about how the human mind works—namely, that the human mind is a dual-channel, limited-capacity, active-processing system.

Name	Description	Example
Selecting	Learners pays attention to relevent words and pictures in a multimedia message to create a word base and an image base	In viewing a narrated animation on lightning formation, learner pays attention to words and pictures describing each of the main steps
Organizing	Learner bulids internal connections among selected words to create a coherent verbal model and among pictures to create a coherent pictorial model	Learner organizes the steps into a cause-and-effect chain for the words and for the pictures
Integrating	Learner builds external connections between the verbal and pictorial models and with prior knowledge	Learner makes connections between corresponding steps in the verbal chain in the pictorial chain and justifies the steps on the basis of knowledge of electricity

Figure 7.5 Three Processes for Active Learning.

Five Steps in a Cognitive Theory of Multimedia Learning

Building on the three assumptions described in the previous section, Figure 7.2 presents a cognitive theory of multimedia learning. For purposes of this book, I define a multimedia environment as one in which material is presented in more than one format, such as in words and pictures. For meaningful learning to occur in a multimedia environment, the learner must engage in five cognitive processes: (1) selecting relevant words for processing in verbal working memory, (2) selecting relevant images for processing in visual working memory, (3) organizing selected words into a verbal mental model, (4) organizing selected images into a visual mental model, and (5) integrating verbal and visual representations as well as prior knowledge. Although I present these processes as a list, they do not necessarily occur in linear order, so a learner might move from process to process in many different ways. Successful multimedia learning requires that the learner coordinate and monitor these five processes.

Selecting Relevant Words

The first labeled step listed in Figure 7.2 involves a change in knowledge representation from a sensory representation of spoken sounds entering the ears to an internal representation of word sounds in working memory. The input for this step is a spoken verbal message that is received in the learner's ears. The output for this step is a word sound base—a mental representation in the learner's verbal working memory of selected words or phrases.

The cognitive process mediating this change is called *selecting relevant words* and involves paying attention to some of the words that are presented in the multimedia message as they pass through auditory sensory memory. If the words are presented as speech, this process begins in the auditory channel (as indicated by the arrow from Words to Ears to Sounds). However, if the words are presented as on-screen text or printed text, this process begins in the visual channel (as indicated by the arrows from Words to Eyes) and later may move to the auditory channel if the learner mentally articulates the printed words (as indicated by the arrow from Images to Sounds in the left side of *Working Memory*). The need for selecting only part of the presented message occurs because of capacity limitations in each channel of the cognitive system. If the capacity were unlimited, there would be no need to focus attention on only part of the verbal message. Finally, the selection of words is not arbitrary; the learner must determine which words are most relevant—an activity that is consistent with the view of the learner as an active sense maker.

For example, in the lightning lesson, one segment of the multimedia presentation contains the words "Cool moist air moves over a warmer surface and becomes heated," the next segment contains the words "Warmed moist air near the earth's surface rises rapidly," and the next segment has the words "As the air in this updraft cools, water vapor condenses into water droplets and forms a cloud." When a learner engages in the selection process, the result may be that some of the words are represented in verbal working memory—such as "Cool air becomes heated, rises, forms a cloud."

Selecting Relevant Images

The second step involves a change in knowledge representation from a sensory representation of unanalyzed visual stimulation entering the eyes to an internal representation of visual images in working memory, The input for this step is a pictorial portion of a multimedia message that is held briefly in visual sensory memory. The output for this step is a visual image base—a mental representation in the learner's working memory of selected images.

The cognitive process underlying this change is called *selecting relevant images* and involves paying attention to part of the animation or illustrations presented in the multimedia message. It is represented by the arrow from Eyes to Images. This process begins in the visual channel, but it is possible to convert part of it to the auditory channel (such as by mentally narrating an ongoing animation). The need to select only part of the presented pictorial material arises from the limited processing capacity of the cognitive system. It is not possible to process all parts of a complex illustration or animation segment, so learners must focus on only part of the incoming pictorial material. Finally, the selection process for images—like the selection process for words—is not arbitrary because the learner must judge which images are most relevant for making sense of the multimedia presentation.

In the lightning lesson, for example, one segment of the animation shows blue arrows (but no arrows are colored in this book)—representing cool air—moving over a heated land surface that contains a house and trees; another segment shows the arrows turning red and traveling upward above a tree; and a third segment shows the arrows changing into a cloud with lots of dots inside. In selecting relevant images, the learner may compress all this into images of a blue arrow pointing rightward, a red arrow pointing upward, and a cloud; details such as the house and tree on the surface, the wavy form of the arrows, and the dots in the cloud are lost.

Organizing Selected Words

Once the learner has formed a word sound base from the incoming words of a segment of the multimedia message, the next step is to organize the words into a coherent representation—a knowledge structure that I call a *verbal model*. The input for this step is the word sound base—the words and phrases selected from the incoming verbal message—and the output for this step is a verbal model—a coherent (or structured) representation in the learner's working memory of the selected words or phrases.

The cognitive process involved in this change is *organizing selected words*, in which the learner builds connections among pieces of verbal knowledge. It is represented by the arrow from Sounds to Verbal Model. This process is most likely to occur in the auditory channel and is subject to the same capacity limitations that affect the selection process. Learners do not have unlimited capacity to build all possible connections, so they must focus on building a simple structure. The organizing process is not arbitrary but rather reflects an effort at sense making—such as the construction of a cause-and-effect chain.

For example, in the lightning lesson, the learner may build causal connections between the selected verbal components: "First, cool air is heated; second, it rises; third, it forms a cloud." In mentally building a causal chain, the learner is organizing the selected words.

Organizing Selected Images

The process for organizing images parallels that for selecting words. Once the learner has formed an image base from the incoming pictures of a segment of the multimedia message, the next step is to organize the images into a coherent representation—a knowledge structure that I call a *pictorial model*. The input for this step is the image base—the pictures selected from the incoming pictorial message—and the output for this step is a pictorial model—a coherent (or structured) representation in the learner's working memory of the selected images.

This change from images to a pictorial model requires the application of a cognitive process that I call *organizing selected images*. It is represented by the arrow from Images to Pictorial Model. In this process, the learner builds connections among pieces of pictorial knowledge. This process occurs in the visual channel, which is subject to the same capacity limitations that affect the selection process. Learners lack the capacity to build all possible connections among images in their image base and rather must focus on building a simple set of connections. As in the process of organizing words, the process of organizing images is not arbitrary. Rather, it reflects an effort at building a simple structure-that makes sense to the learner, such as the cause-and-effect chain.

For example, in the lightning lesson, the learner may build causal connections between the selected images: The rightward-moving blue arrow horns into a rising red arrow, which turns into a cloud. In short, the learner builds causal links in which the first event leads to the second, and so on.

Integrating Word-Based and Image-Based Representations

Perhaps the most crucial step in multimedia learning involves making connections between word-based and image-based representations. This step involves a change from having two separate representations—a visual model and a verbal model—to having an integrated representation in which corresponding elements and relations from one model are mapped onto the other. The input for this step is the visual model and the verbal model that the learner has constructed so far, and the output is an integrated model, which is based on connecting the two representations. In addition, the integrated model includes connections with prior knowledge.

I refer to this cognitive process as *integrating* because it involves building connections between corresponding portions of the pictorial and verbal models as well as relevant existing knowledge from long-term memory. This process occurs in visual and verbal working memory and involves the coordination between them. It is represented by the arrows from the Verbal Model and the Pictorial Model as well as the arrow from *Long-Term Memory*. This is an extremely demanding process that requires the efficient use of cognitive capacity. The process reflects the epitome of sense making because the learner must focus on the underlying structure of the visual and verbal representations. The learner can use prior knowledge to help coordinate the integration process, as indicated by the arrow from Long-Term Memory to Working Memory.

For example, in the lightning lesson, the learner must see the connection between the verbal chain—"First, cool air is heated; second, it rises; third, it forms a cloud"—and the visual chain—the blue arrow followed by the red arrow followed by the cloud shape. In addition, prior knowledge can be applied to the transition from the first to the second event by remembering that hot air rises.

Each of the five steps in multimedia learning is likely to occur many times throughout a multimedia presentation. The steps are applied segment by segment, not to the entire message as a whole. For example, in processing the lightning lesson, learners do not first select all relevant words and images from the entire passage, then organize them into verbal and visual models of the entire passage, and then connect the completed models with one another at the very end. Rather, learners carry out this procedure on small segments: They select relevant words and images from the first sentence of the narration and the first few seconds of the animation; they organize and integrate them; and then this set of processes is repeated for the next segment, and so on.

In short, multimedia learning takes place within the learner's information processing system—a system that contains separate channels for visual and verbal processing, a system with serious limitations on the capacity of each channel, and a system that requires coordinated cognitive processing in each channel for active learning to occur. In particular, multimedia learning is a demanding process that requires selecting relevant words and images, organizing them into coherent verbal and pictorial representations, and integrating the verbal and pictorial representations.

Conclusion

[...]

The theme of this chapter is that the design of multimedia messages should be based on a satisfactory theory of how people learn and, in particular, on a cognitive theory of multimedia learning. In this chapter, I present a cognitive theory of multimedia learning based on three well-established ideas in cognitive science—what I call the dual-channel, limited-capacity, and active processing assumptions. I show how multimedia learning occurs when the learner engages in five kinds of processing—selecting words, selecting images, organizing words, organizing images, and integrating.

Works Cited

Baddeley, A. D. (1986). *Working memory*. Oxford, England: Oxford University Press.

Baddeley, A. D. (1992/1999). *Human memory*. Boston: Allyn & Bacon.

Baddeley, A. D. (1992). Working memory. *Science*, 255, 556–559.

Bransford, J. D., Brown, A. L., & Cocking, R. R. (1999). *How people learn*. Washington, DC: National Academy Press.

Chambliss, M. J. & Calfee R. C. (1998). *Textbooks for learning*. Oxford, England: Blackwell.

Chandler, P., & Sweller, J. (1991). Cognitive load theory and the format of instruction. *Cognition and Instruction*, 8, 293–332.

Clark, J. M., & Paivio, A. (1991). Dual coding theory and education. *Educational Psychology Review, 3*, 149–210.

Cook, L. K., & Mayer, R. E. (1998). Teaching readers about the structure of scientific text. *Journal of Educational Psychology*, 80, 448–456.

Lambert, N. M., & McCombs, B. L. (1998). *How students learn*. Washington, DC: American Psychological Association.

*Mayer, R. E. (1996). Learning strategies for making sense out of expository text: The SOI model for guiding three cognitive processes in knowledge construction. *Educational Psychology Review, 8*, 357–371.

*Mayer, R. E. (1999a). Multimedia aids to problem-solving transfer. *International Journal of Educational Research, 31*, 611–623.

*Mayer, R. E. (1999b). Research-based principles for the design of instructional messages. *Document Design, 3*, 7–20.

Mayer, R. E. (1999c). *The promise of educational psychology*. Upper Saddle River, NJ: Prentice Hall/Merrill.

Miller, G. A. (1956). The magic number seven, plus or minus two: Some limits on our capacity for processing information. *Psychological Review*, 63, 81–97.

Paivio, A. (1986). *Mental representations: A dual coding approach*. Oxford, England: Oxford University Press.

Simon, H. A. (1974). How big is a chunk? *Science*, 183, 482–488.

Sternberg, R. J. (1990). *Metaphors of mind: Conceptions of the nature of human intelligence*. Cambridge, England: Cambridge University Press.

Sweller, J. (1999). *Instructional design in technical areas*. Camberwell, Australia: ACER Press.

Sweller, J. & Chandler, P. (1994). Why some material is difficult to learn. *Cognition and Instruction*, 12, 185–233.

Wittrock, M. C. (1989). Generative processes of comprehension. *Educational Psychologist*, 24, 345–376.

Note

* Asterisk indicates that a portion of this chapter is based on this publication.

8

Entering the Electronic Environment

N. Katherine Hayles

Steeped in print literature, Kaye was like those of her generation who came to the computer as an adult. Even so, her somewhat idiosyncratic experience made her an early adopter. Her first encounter with computers predated the desktop variety by nearly two decades, for she used a computer interface to program electrodes in her scientific work. It is mind-numbingly difficult to program in ASSEMBLY CODE, and for Kaye it would always be associated with darkness. She arrived at the lab before the sun came up and left after the sun went down. Since the lab was in a sub-sub-basement, she saw precious little of that golden orb during the week. Only on weekends was she able to glory in the Southern California landscape drenched in sunlight, which soon became a second home to her.

At the Ivy League college where she served her academic apprenticeship, she encountered the equipment that before long would be called "dumb terminals," but at the time she found it thrilling to move from typewriters to this more flexible and powerful medium. At this early point terminals were not capable of full-screen response; she edited line-by-line using computer commands in a process users today would find unbearably primitive. Still idealistic enough to think she could change the world, she tried to recruit her English-Department colleagues to the medium. She has a vivid memory of demonstrating the technology to a senior professor to show how easy and fun it was compared to typing and retyping drafts. He was not persuaded, begging out after fifteen minutes, saying he had other things to do (he was too polite to say, *better* things). To find colleagues who shared her enthusiasm, she went to the mathematics/computer science department, where she suggested co-teaching a master's level summer course on "Computer Literacy." At this time in the early 1980s, MODULAR PROGRAMMING was a new idea, and she thought it had much in common with the composition techniques she used in her writing classes. Paragraphs were like modules; transitions were like comments and annotations; structure and organization were like flowcharts. Why not teach advanced writing in a context that drew parallels with the modular computer programming that participants could learn at the same time? And throw into the mix some texts that would stimulate discussion about the effects of the computer revolution on print culture? Without really understanding the implications, she already knew that the computer would dramatically change the dynamics of what she would later learn to call medial ecology.

The connection with literature came when she received in the mail an advertisement from Eastgate Systems for "serious hypertext." By this time she was back in the Midwest, teaching at the University of Iowa and debating postmodernism with the bright eager graduate students who turned up there. She had graduated from dumb terminals to a desktop computer and couldn't wait to order Joyce's *Afternoon, a story.* She devoured it in a single setting, the way she was accustomed to do with print novels. But then it occurred to her that she had missed the point, for her reading strategy had been to use the default, which soon took her to the end—or rather, an end. Further exploration showed that the default left untouched large portions of the text. So she went back, and this time read more systematically, using the NAVIGATION tool to read all the screens, or lexias as they were called. She soon arrived at the same conclusion Jane Yellowlees Douglas was to argue later in print—that the privileged lexia, "White Afternoon," allowed the reader to see that Peter, the protagonist, was responsible for causing the very accident he spends most of the narrative investigating. A clever strategy, she thought—but how would one teach a work such as this?

She tried it out with a group of college teachers from across the country when she was asked to conduct a weekend seminar for Phi Beta Kappa. Many of them made the same mistake she had, missing a lot of the text. Others argued vehemently that this electronic hypertext failed to deliver the immersion in a fictional world that for them was the main reason to read narrative literature. When she pointed out that many print texts, especially postmodern works, also failed to deliver this experience, they fell back on what Mark Bernstein would later call the "bathtub theory of literature," arguing that if you couldn't take the text into the bathtub with you, it wasn't worth reading. She was not entirely unsympathetic, for as noted earlier the tub was one of her favorite reading spots, along with being sprawled across the bed. But Kaye was not ready to concede the point. "Oh come on," she responded, "surely you cannot judge a piece of literature by such superficial standards. So what if you read it on the computer? Isn't it far more important what the language is like, the linking structure, the plot, the characters?" Later she would think back on this conversation as a classic case of the blind leading the blind, for without realizing it, she was continuing to judge this electronic text by the same criteria she used for print. It would take years and many more experiences with electronic texts before she began to understand that electronic literature operated m fundamentally different ways than print and required new critical frameworks to assess its reading and writing practices.

The mistake may have been unavoidable, not only because she had been raised on print but also because these first-generation hypertexts were largely comprised of text, making little or no use of graphics, animation, and sound. Moreover, they had relatively simple navigation systems that consisted largely of clicking on links to go from one lexia to another. Although early commentators claimed that the NONLINEAR structures and links made electronic literature qualitatively different than print books, in retrospect Kaye realized that these first-generation works were more like books than they were like second-generation electronic literature, because they operated by replacing one screen of text with another, much as a book goes from one page to another. Despite the hoopla, first-generation works left mostly untouched the unconscious assumptions that readers of books had absorbed through centuries of print. They were a brave beginning, but only a beginning. Not unlike the dumb terminals Kaye now thought of as quaint antiques, these works opened up pathways of change that would, when more fully exploited, make them seem obsolete.

Meanwhile, computer hardware and software were changing at exponential rates, and with them, ELECTRONIC LITERATURE. The text that heralded the transition to second-generation electronic literature for Kaye was Shelley Jackson's *Patchwork Girl*. It presented itself as a rewriting of Mary Shelley's *Frankenstein* in which the female monster, dismembered by a nauseated Victor in Mary's classic tale, is reassembled and made into the text's main narrator. Written in a later version of the Storyspace software that Joyce used for *Afternoon*, *Patchwork Girl* engaged the tool in significantly different ways. In an important innovation, it drew connections between the electronic text and the female monster's fragmented body. One of the screens showed a large head in profile, presumably the monster's, divided into sections after the style of a phrenology chart. Clicking on them took Kaye to the stories of the women whose body parts were used to make the monster. Navigation was envisioned as taking place not only between lexias but between images and words, and more profoundly between the text and the computer producing it. This was something very different than moving from lexia to lexia; it was an effect print could not duplicate. Jackson reinforced the point by writing passages that explicitly drew connections between the machinery and the text, asking what happened to consciousness when it existed discontinuously as screens with gaps in between. Where was the narrator's consciousness during the gaps, the microseconds that separated one screen from another? Did it dissolve into the noise of the machine, decomposed back into ones and zeros?

The speculation sent chills down Kaye's spine. It was her first glimpse into how significantly literature might change if the literary body was not a book but a computer. She could name dozens of print texts that played with connections between the book and a narrator's body, from Laurence Sterne's eighteenth-century masterpiece *Tristram Shandy*, to Italo Calvino's contemporary print hypertext novel *If on a Winter's Night a Traveler*. As a print lover, she had taken for granted that the book as a physical artifact would ground metaphoric networks connecting the print form with the bodies of characters and narrators, authors and readers. Authors regularly thought of their books as offspring; characters in metafiction often tried to peer out of the covers that contained them to see the book as an object; the human form converged with book technology even in such inert metaphors as footnotes, spine, and appendix. All this was obvious and known. But the trembler now rippling through her consciousness hinted at a shift in tectonic plates massive enough to send an earthquake roaring through the terrain of literary studies, for it implied that a shift in the material SUBSTRATE of the artifact would affect not just the mode of delivery but everything about the literary work. Like all really momentous changes, this realization came in fits and starts for Kaye, now clearly foreseen, now slipping into inarticulate intuition. She knew and yet she didn't know. It would take several shocks to her system before she grasped the fuller significances of moving from print to the computer.

The first shock was mild, even pleasant. She was invited by the University of Bergen to serve as the "First Opponent" on the dissertation defense of a young Norwegian scholar, Espen Aarseth. The procedure was a grueling full-day ordeal that bespoke the university's medieval origins. The candidate delivered a 45-minute lecture on his dissertation, which the committee judged satisfactory or not. If satisfactory, the defense proceeded to the second stage, which consisted of the First and Second Opponents questioning the candidate for a full hour each, probing for weaknesses, inconsistencies, and so on. She thought the dissertation was excellent, but she tried gamely to enter into the spirit of the exercise. When the candidate passed with flying colors, tradition called for him to host a dinner that evening, to which were invited friends, relatives, mentors, and of course the dissertation committee. Numerous toasts were made, all in Norwegian so she couldn't understand a word, but she gathered that the gist was to ridicule the academic proceedings, a sport she enjoyed even without knowing the language.

The dissertation was already accepted for publication by the Johns Hopkins University Press and would become an influential work in electronic literature. As noted earlier, Aarseth coined the term cybertext, clearing the field of previous work that had identified the link as the defining characteristic of hypertext. He argued for a computational perspective, a move that placed literary works on the same playing field as computer games and other combinatorial works. He made the important point that textual functions must not only be based an the marks appearing on screen but also had to take into account what was happening inside the machinery. To distinguish between screen display and underlying code, he coined the terms SCRIPTON and TEXTON. Here was a perspective and vocabulary that reinterpreted the print book in terms of the computer, rather than shoehorning electronic texts into categories derived from print.

The second shock came at a Digital Arts conference in Atlanta at which she had been invited to deliver a keynote address. Usually she prepared carefully for such occasions, but the week of the conference she came down with a violent flu and spent days shaking in bed with chills and fever. A sensible person would have cancelled, but she came from good German stock where phrases like "Your word is your bond" were not only intoned but actually practiced. So she gulped down the antibiotics that her doctor had predicted would do no good and boarded the plane. Her lecture passed in a daze; she could scarcely remember what she said, and no doubt it deserved to be forgotten. The discussion that followed, however, was memorable, for it marked a turning point for Kaye. In the audience were such luminaries as Michael Joyce of *Afternoon* fame and critic Janet Murray, author of *Hamlet on the Holodeck*. They took her to task for using vocabulary and concepts that were too *literary*—the opposite of Aarseth's computational approach. She was startled to hear this objection from someone like Joyce, who was, if possible, even more steeped in the literary tradition than she and constantly used allusions to literary works in his writing, including several lexias in *Afternoon* based on James Joyce's *Ulysses*. Surely, she objected, we cannot throw out everything four centuries of literary criticism has taught us about character, plot, narration, voice? He conceded the point but remained unconvinced. He wanted something more, though he could not say exactly what.

The next shock struck closer to home. Her close friend, M. D. Coverley, had given Kaye her electronic hypertext novel *Califfa*. To Kaye, M. was Margie, a wonderful person who was invariably warm and gracious, smart and perceptive. Kaye read the work and was not swept away by the narrative, finding it presentable but not overwhelming. When she conveyed this, Margie patiently pointed out features that Kaye had noticed but had not really integrated into her reading—the navigational structure, for example, which offered at least twenty different pathways on every screen and which, with two or three clicks, could be used to access any of the work's 800 screens. Only later, when Kaye returned to *Califia* after more than a year had passed, did she understand that her mistake had been precisely to *read* the work, concentrating mainly on the words and seeing the navigation as a way to access the words, the images as illustrations of the words. She thought more deeply about the nature of the *Califia* project, which drew connections between present-day narrators and a rich treasure trove of California history, including economics, water politics, and geology, using an astonishing variety of inscription surfaces including road maps, documents, letters, journals, and even star maps. Finally it hit her: the work embedded the verbal narrative in a topographic environment in which word was interwoven with world. The world contained the words but much else besides, including layered images, complex navigation functionalities, and simulated documents. By focusing on the words alone, she had missed the point. Now she was able to evaluate *Califia* in a different way, from an integrated perspective in which all components became SIGNIFYING PRACTICES. From this viewpoint, she could see not only that it was a ground-breaking work but also that the materiality of the text was integral to its project of connecting word with world.

This was a significantly different practice from a conventional print novel in which a world is evoked exclusively through words, and different also from an illustrated work in which words and images work together. She could not grasp the work as a whole without taking the computer into account, with its material specificity of hardware capabilities and software functionalities. Medium and work were entwined in a complex relation that functioned as a multilayered metaphor for the relation of the world's materiality to the space of simulation. "This is deep," she thought to herself in a dawning realization that was half perplexity, half illumination. "Material metaphor," a phrase casually dropped by her anthropologist husband, swam into consciousness as an appropriate expression to describe these complexities.

The point was driven home by her encounter with Diana Slattery's *Glide*, a beautifully designed piece that speculated about what it would be like to live in a culture that had developed a VISUAL LANGUAGE that could be written and enacted but not spoken. The *Glide* site was a fully multimedia work, displaying animated GLYPHS—the components of the Glide language—transforming into one another while deep resonant chords played on the soundtrack. The narrative, extracted from Slattery's full-length print novel, *The Maze Game* (soon to be published), depicted a culture whose central ritual is the titular Game, a contest between a Dancer who runs a maze that is also a Glide message and a Player who tries to solve the maze represented as a video game. Breaking the deep connection between written mark and spoken sound, *Glide* envisioned different connections emerging between language and vision, body movement and code. Kaye saw in it a parable about the profound changes afoot as the human sensorium was reconfigured by information technologies, including electronic literature.

Now she thought she had something worthwhile to say, and when the North American Association for the Study of Romanticism invited her to give a keynote lecture, she accepted despite knowing little about English Romantic literature. The conference topic was the materiality of Romanticism, and she figured to use the occasion to convey some of her hard-won insights about the importance of materiality in literary works, the necessity for MSA, and the ways in which thinking about electronic texts could illuminate print. Brimming with good health this time, she prepared her talk with care, using visuals from the magnificent William Blake Archive on the Web to show that the electronic Blake functioned in significantly different ways than Blake in print. She further made a point of the site's rhetoric, which emphasized rendering the print Blake as exactly as possible, providing users with a color calibration device so they could adjust their browsers. But these very functionalities were themselves part of what made the electronic Blake different than the print Blake. In her conclusion she drew the obvious moral that the literary community could no longer afford to treat text on screen as if it were print read in a vertical position. Electronic text had its own specificities, and a deep understanding of them would bring into view by contrast the specificities of print, which could again be seen for what it was, a medium and not a transparent interface.

By this time the argument was so obvious to her that she was afraid it might seem too simple. Her audience's reaction told her otherwise. As they moved into the discussion period, the room seemed to break out in a sweat. As the tension became palpable, one woman articulated it explicitly: "I want you to know how anxious you have made me," she said. Kaye was even more taken aback when W. J. T. Mitchell, the other keynote speaker whom she revered as a god, rose to express the opinion mentioned earlier: that the only two important signifying components of a literary text are words and images; nothing else really counts. Mitchell had authored the influential book *Picture Theory* arguing that literary criticism had to move away from the parochialism of considering literature to be only verbal structures; images too must be taken into account. Kaye was stunned to think he could not see that the arguments of *Picture Theory* made it important to think about a medium in all its specificity. She was sure his assertion that only words and images mattered did not hold true for electronic literature; *Califia* and *Glide* had taught her that. But she believed it did not hold true for print texts either, including virtually all artists' books.

She left the conference thinking she would have to learn more about why her audience had been so resistant to media specificity. She recalled a computer-phobic colleague who complained to Kaye about various outrages to which the computer subjected her. Kaye could sympathize to an extent; she had spent too many hours dealing with software glitches and hardware problems not to understand the woman's frustration. But she had no more power to stop the transformation of literary studies by information technology than her colleague— even if she wanted to, which she didn't. For literary people like her colleague, the computer was threatening because it demanded new skills and made traditional ones obsolete at an alarming rate. "I'm glad I am retiring soon," another colleague had remarked to her, "because now I won't have to deal with these changes."

She acknowledged the problems. It was not only the computer-phobic who suffered from their impact. She watched incredulously when Michael Joyce, a figure so esteemed in electronic literature that he was regularly referred to as "His Joyceness," announced he was leaving electronic literature and going back to print. When she wrote an urgent email asking why, he responded with an "open letter," sent to many of his colleagues and admirers, saying that he felt his continuing growth as a writer and thinker required it. Another blow was delivered by Robert Coover, a man she admired not only for his experimental print fiction but also for the stance he had taken in an influential *New York Times* article a decade ago in which he had put his considerable prestige at risk to come out in favor of hypertext literature. At the same Digital Arts conference where she had spoken, Coover stunned the audience of mostly younger writers and artists interested in pushing the envelope of the electronic medium by announcing that the Golden Age of hypertext was over and we were rapidly declining into the Silver Age, if not the Bronze and Iron.

She could not imagine why Coover would make this pronouncement, and it was several months before she had the chance to talk with him about it. He explained that for him literature was about the voice of the writer, and he feared that *voice* was being overwhelmed by the very developments that seemed so exciting to Kaye. She could see that if voice was what mattered most to you, second-generation electronic works generally had less of it than first-generation texts and so from this perspective could be seen as a decline. It came down, she realized, to a question of what constituted literature. She was less interested in reinforcing boundaries—a consistent theme in her life—than in seeing what happened if you romped over them, which second-generation works were exuberantly doing as they moved toward multimedia creating works that contained components drawn from literature, visual arts, computer games, and programming practices. To her, this was part of their appeal.

Coover also expressed concern about the relentless cycles of software innovation and obsolescence. He felt he could not continue to master all the new software programs coming out at an accelerating pace and still devote his energy to what he cared about most, crafting words. She could understand his reasoning and respect his position, for she knew as well as he that the marketplace was demanding and unforgiving. The personal decisions of Joyce and Coover foregrounded more general concerns that worried her about electronic literature—problems of access, obsolescence, and software compatibility, not to mention the fact it was a pricey enterprise for writers, and very few if any were making money from it.

Still, even considering these difficulties, she saw electronic literature as one of the most important literary developments since the mid-twentieth century, and she felt confident it would be a major component of the twenty-first century canon. Moreover, electronic textuality was here to stay as more print books were reconstructed for the Web, from medieval manuscripts, to illustrated works like William Blake's books, to multimedia sites devoted to such master texts as Joyce's *Ulysses*. Even if electronic literature crashed and burned, which she considered highly unlikely, literary studies could no longer pretend that electronic textuality was print on a screen. The desktop computer changed things forever. Print would never be the same as it was when she was programming assembly code in the sub-sub-basement—and neither would she.

9
Planning for Hypertexts in the Writing Center ... Or Not

Michael A. Pemberton

It will come as no surprise, perhaps, to say that writing centers have long been grounded in—some would say "bounded by"—the conventions of printed text. True, writing centers, like most of the rest of the world, have been influenced by advances in computer technology, most recently through the explosive growth of Online Writing Labs (OWLs) and computer-mediated conferencing with students, but fundamentally, most of the interactions between students and tutors still center on the handwritten or printed texts that are placed on a table between them or, perhaps, shared in a word-processed file. These texts are structured linearly and hierarchically, moving along a single path from beginning to end, following well-known and universally taught discourse forms that have emerged from a print-based rhetorical tradition.

But times may be changing. As we enter an era when, electronic publishing and computer-mediated discourse are the norm, an era when new literary genres and new forms of communication emerge on, seemingly, a weekly basis, we must ask ourselves whether writing centers should continue to dwell exclusively in the linear, non-linked world of the printed page or whether they should plan to redefine themselves—and retrain themselves—to take residence in the emerging world of multimedia, hyper-linked, digital documents. To put it plainly, should we be preparing tutors to conference with students about hypertexts? This is not a simple question to answer, but it is a question that may soon demand explicit answers as our students explore and experiment with hypermedia in greater numbers in the years to come.

There are certainly compelling reasons to believe that writing centers should learn more about digital texts and prepare themselves to help students both navigate and create them, and more than a few writing center scholars have urged the professional community to start their planning now. In an article on preparing for future technologies in the writing center, Muriel Harris warns her readers that writing center tutors will soon be conferencing with

> ... a clientele of students who are composing texts [...] in multimedia presentations, on Websites, in distance-learning projects, and so on. Computers as a technology interwoven in communication is a given, as is electronic communication across the curriculum.

Writing centers without the technology or staff to work with these students will find themselves no longer in sync with how writers write and with what writers need to know about writing processes as they are affected by technology.

(194)

For John Trimbur, this move toward technological expertise in the writing center is inevitable and will eventually force writing centers to accommodate new rhetorical theories and practices to deal with new types of documents. "To my mind," he says, "the new digital literacies will increasingly be incorporated into writing centers not just as sources of information or delivery systems for tutoring but as productive arts in their own right, and writing center work will, if anything, become more rhetorical in paying attention to the practices and effects of design in written and visual communication" (30). As a result, writing centers may soon find themselves conferencing with students about hypertexts in progress, confronting not only unfamiliar textual landscapes but also challenging problems in document design.

Trimbur's imagined future may be approaching us more swiftly than we realize, now that the Internet and the World Wide Web have become such pervasive features of our culture and our students' academic lives. Students are not only browsing Web documents with more frequency, they are using Web sites as primary research sources in their papers and often creating such documents themselves. James Inman, in fact, asserts that "[i]n many writing classes, whether first-year composition or other courses like technical writing and business writing … teachers assign websites, and students look to writing centers for help, as that's where they've most often turned for peer help with writing" (II.8.3).[1]

But even if writing centers "are well suited to guide the journey into the bumpy land of learning with technology" (Cummins 206), we should ask ourselves at least three important questions as we consider what our specific role should be in this moment of transition, both at a global level (in relation to writing center theory and practice overall) and at a local level (in relation to our home institutions):

- Are writing centers generally *willing* to accommodate hypertexts?
- Do writing centers need to *accommodate* hypertexts?
- If a need exists, how should writing centers *prepare* to accommodate hypertexts?

How Have Writing Centers Viewed New Technologies?

A brief look at the ways writing centers have responded to new technologies in the past may help us answer the first of these questions and provide a useful context for answering the other two as well. Computers have been a part of writing center work for the better part of forty years now, sometimes as writing tools, sometimes as teaching devices, sometimes as resource centers, and sometimes as communications media; yet the relationship between writing centers and computer technology has been, overall, only a cordial one, with occasional fluctuations ranging from wild enthusiasm to brooding antagonism. While computers and computer software have often been praised by writing center scholars for the educational benefits they provide, they have also been seen as incipient threats—not merely to the personal, interactive pedagogies that writing centers embrace, but also to the writing center's very existence, particularly in tough budget times when administrators may view CAI programs and other technological artifacts as cheap, efficient alternatives to the labor-intensive, individualized teaching model at the heart of writing center practice.

Neal Lerner's work on the history of technology in writing centers from the 1930s to the 1970s documents the roots of this ambivalence, illustrating how new technologies, despite their potential benefits, have often been used to reshape writing center pedagogy, sometimes insidiously and frequently in ways that centers would later want to repudiate. In "Drill Pads, Teaching Machines, and Programmed Texts: Origins of Instructional Technology in Writing Centers." Lerner traces the earliest origins of a "technological model" for writing center work to social and cultural pressures that manifested in the 1930s, including the tripling of college enrollments as the children of immigrant families turned to higher education as a means of social advancement, and the concomitant cry for massive remediation as administrators had to cope with a sudden influx of students from diverse economic and cultural backgrounds with widely varying degrees of preparation (121–22). Lerner, citing Rose (1985), argues that the "efficiency movement" in education, tremendously influential at this time, responded to this crisis by producing and promoting an assortment of programmed, quasi-individualized "drill and practice technologies" that could be applied to under-prepared nontraditional students *en masse* (123). Writing labs soon became the sites where such programmed instruction and remediation took place, and the focus of this remediation work was largely restricted to grammar, mechanics, and other easily-quantifiable matters of surface structure. Through the 1950s and 1960s, this model for writing center work found an easy confluence with Skinnerian behaviorism, current-traditionalism, and an instrumental view of computer technology to produce the "Comp-Lab" model for programmed learning, a pedagogy that was prevalent in writing centers by the 1970s. As in the drill and practice writing lab of the 1930s, the "Comp-Lab" model focused on lower-order deficiencies in student writing (marked primarily by observable errors in surface structure) and "remedied" them by carefully chosen computer programs that would—with drills, exercises, practice sets, and "rewards" for right answers—gradually modify the students' deviant linguistic behaviors. This approach to writing instruction soon became a source of irritation to writing center directors as its current-traditional focus on grammar and final products conflicted strongly with the writing process model embraced by scholars and practitioners in the burgeoning field of composition studies. Writing center directors found themselves increasingly at odds with the pedagogy they were expected to support, and computers—to some extent—became avatars of a stagnant tradition rather than icons of progress and change.

Peter Carino's "Computers in the Writing Center: A Cautionary History" takes up the story where Lerner leaves off, tracing the conflicts that arose between the uses of computer technology for writing instruction and an increasingly sophisticated writing center theory that developed from the 1970s through the 1990s.[2] During this time period, says Carino, discussions of technology in writing centers primarily addressed the utility of behaviorist CAI programs like those Lerner described in the Comp-Lab model, the effect of word processors on student writing processes, and the impact computer technologies would have on the day-to-day functions of writing centers. While a fair number of these pieces offered "success stories" that stressed the benefits of computers for writing instruction, equally often writers expressed concerns about how technology would affect the mission of the center and whether or not technology might eventually dominate the center and eliminate the need for tutors altogether. "This tension between technological endorsement and technological resistance," he says, "marks writing center discourse on computers since the early 1980s" (172), and though such conflict does nor, in itself, embody a master narrative for understanding the complex ways in which technology and writing center theory/practice interpenetrate one another, it is nevertheless a salient perspective from which to view and interpret what has been, historically, an uneasy relationship.

Carino's article, like Lerner's, makes several important points about technology's effects on writing center pedagogy and the corresponding positions that writing center professionals have taken in relation to those effects. Foremost among these points, perhaps, is the fact that writing centers have always maintained a healthy critical skepticism about the impact technology has had or should have on what they do. Writing centers have always wanted to be responsive to technology and the changes technology brings to the student populations they serve, but they also question whether the seductions of technology will end up diluting their core values or giving them responsibilities that they're not prepared to accept. As recently as 1995. Muriel Harris and I warned that "the lack of personal contact [in online tutorials] may seem to dehumanize a setting that writing centers have traditionally viewed as personal and warm" (156), and Nancy Grimm in that same year wrote that concerns about such dehumanization were still an "unresolved issue" (324).

The implication this history has for hypertexts, then, is that writing centers will—in principle—be willing to adjust to the demands that these new types of documents bring, but they will not do so uncritically, and they will likely remain wary. Though hypertexts, in and of themselves, may not represent the kind of depersonalizing influence (at least symbolically) that computers do, their metaphorical affiliation with a steadily encroaching technology—sometimes threatening, often unfamiliar—will probably exacerbate any hopes of easy accommodation.

What's Missing in Writing Center Discourse

Some evidence for the wariness writing center professionals feel about technology can be seen in the field's recent professional discourse about the impact of hypertexts—or rather, the near total lack of such discourse. Carino ends his historical review by noting that OWLs, LANs, MOOs and Webs have dominated the conversation in writing center discourse in recent years, but it's also worth noting that except for a smattering of writing center articles that have reflected on somewhat marginal technological issues[3], the substance of that conversation has fallen into one of two distinct threads: discussions of online tutoring—conferencing between tutor and tutee at remote sites, mediated by computers—or the design, purpose, and function of OWLs. Rarely has there been a discussion (even in the archives of WCENTER) of the impact that the Web is having on the very nature of what constitutes a "text" or the impact that the reconstituted shape of these texts might have on writing center training, conferences, or discourse.

Though writing centers hitched their wagons to the Internet train early on, their primary research interest in this area since the early 1990s has been the collaborative possibilities enabled by email, chatrooms, listservs, and the World Wide Web. In a 1995 special issue of *Computers and Composition,* edited by Joyce Kinkead and Christine Hult, fully a dozen articles appeared about computers and writing centers, most of them reflecting on the opportunities for computer-mediated tutoring made available via the Internet. The majority of these pieces concerned themselves with one of two possible topics: (1) the mechanics of creating systems for online tutoring (Harris and Pemberton, Nelson and Wambean, Healy) or (2) the textual features of the discourse produced by tutors and students in online environments (Coogan,

Wood, Chappell, Johanek and Rickly). At a time when the Internet was first making its power as an instructional delivery system felt, such research was absolutely necessary. People in the field needed to know the possibilities, and they had to be aware of the risks. Did writing centers want to develop an online presence? How should they go about doing it? What happens in online tutoring? What are the gains? What are the losses? These were the clear, important questions that writing center professionals needed answers to, and researchers regularly reported the results of their online experiences in journal publications and conference presentations.

From 1995 to the present, the substance and focus of writing center research as it relates to technology has remained largely unchanged. "How-to-build-an OWL" articles have begun to disappear in recent years as online writing labs have become the norm rather than the exception, and the sheer comprehensiveness of James Inman and Clint Gardner's recent CD-ROM, The *OWL Construction and Maintenance Guide,* may close the door on such articles for quite some time. Still, a good deal of technology-related writing center scholarship continues to focus on the textual features of dialogue produced in online collaborative exchanges between tutors and students. Sara Kimball's "Cybertext/Cyberspeech: Writing Centers and Online Magic," for example, investigates the nature of cybertext in online tutorials and discusses ways in which online identities are either constructed or obscured (see also Bell and Hübler). Recent descriptive studies of synchronous OWL conferences, the dynamics of email tutoring, and CMC interactions with distance-learning students have also employed this methodological focus in their studies of tutorial discourse (see also Monroe; Coogan; Gardner; Anderson). By no means do I wish to devalue this research or the knowledge it produces. These studies are often insightful and theoretically sophisticated, helping us to better understand the complex sociolinguistic structures inherent in the hybrid oral/textual environment of online conversation. My point here, however, is that they tend to investigate only one kind of technological "text" that writing centers are likely to generate or come in contact with.

When matters of tutor training are addressed with respect to technology, they tend to highlight how tutors can be trained to use technology effectively when working as OWL consultants, rather than how to critique HTML documents and guide students toward successful revisions. Breuch, Kastman, and Racine, for example, only encourage tutors to be sensitive to the distinctive nature of text-only environments, and offer several useful suggestions for structuring online responses and adopting appropriate tutoring roles. Similarly, three current tutoring manuals, *Tutoring Writing* (McAndrew & Reigstad), *A Tutor's Guide: Helping Writers One to One* (Rafoth), and the *Allyn and Bacon Guide to Peer Tutoring* (Gillespie and Lerner) include sections that address technology issues in writing centers, but they too focus on online tutoring alone—using email. OWLs, or synchronous chat systems to conference with students about their papers. Other sections in these texts contain advice for handling "difficult" discourse issues or conferencing sessions, but these chapters tend to focus on matters such as "what to do when a student has no draft" or "how to conference on unfamiliar subjects," rather than providing insights about how to help students whose drafts are constructed as hypermedia texts.

Do Writing Centers Need to Adjust Their Pedagogies?

If we believe that more and more writing classes will be taking Sean Williams' advice to "think out of the pro-verbal box" and allow students to write and create documents that incorporate more visual, multiliterate forms of communication, and if the Internet is spawning entirely new textual genres with their own sets of critical features, not all of which are common to print texts (Bauman), then the consequences for writing centers are clear: more students with different texts in unfamiliar genres will be making new demands on tutor expertise.

But what is the nature of these demands? What sorts of expertise will be necessary? What specific challenges do hypertexts entail, and must writing centers make significant changes in what they already do quite well—work with students, one-to-one, on papers that already span a wide range of discourse types across multiple disciplines?

Hypertexts can certainly present significant problems for writing centers, particularly with regard to the logistics of reading text itself. Hypertext documents complicate traditional rhetorical forms and can therefore subvert normal "print-based" reading strategies. Familiar notions of organization, argument, and thesis-support structures do not often translate well into Web space; comfortable understandings of format and conventions may no longer apply, and new schemas may take their place (Costanzo 13). "People write arguments in hypertext differently than they do in a more traditional format," notes Locke Carter. "When faced with the task of constructing single-author, self-contained arguments in a hypertext environment [he says], … authors must overcome the expectation of order" (3).[4] If what Carter says is true, then tutors would have to learn entirely new schemas for what hypertextual order entails, and at least in the short term, their ability to assess tests quickly and offer advice might be compromised. Imagine Michael Joyce coming into the writing center with a draft of his literary hypertext. *Afternoon,* a text whose opening page contains twenty possible links to other nodes or paths through the story. While many have lauded this work for breaking the shackles of conventional, linear narrative structure, a great many writing center tutors would probably find themselves disoriented and at a loss for how to give advice for revision. As Johndan Johnson-Eilola notes, a hypertext such as this "can give readers a rush of euphoria—or, for the same reasons, a rush of vertigo" (195). And though student writers may not bring hypertexts as complex or as challenging as Joyce's into the writing center, the ones they do bring in may well give tutors the same sense of vertigo, particularly if they are not trained to deal with them.

Preparing for Hypertext #7: Treat Hypertexts Like Any Other Texts

So how, then, should writing centers address hypertexts? How should they restructure their training schedules or reconfigure their theories to account for texts that elide linear patterns of organization in a digital environment? Interestingly enough, it's possible to build at least two lines of argument that maintain they shouldn't—that despite the likelihood that students will be writing hypertexts in growing numbers, there is no need for writing centers to change their pedagogies as a consequence.

The first line of argument would maintain that the problems hypertexts pose for tutors are essentially no different from the problems posed by any other texts, regardless of genre or discipline. Since there is no possibility that a tutor will be able to address all possible content or rhetorical features in a single writing center conference (or multiple conferences) anyway, then tutors should feel comfortable working with the aspects of writing they are already familiar with and not worry overmuch about those they aren't. Similar arguments have been made in writing center literature about questions of disciplinary expertise (Pemberton) and the relative benefits of having generalist or specialist tutors (Kiedaisch and Dinitz). James Inman summarizes this perspective with regard to technology when he says,

Just as writing centers do not claim to be founts of all knowledge that is great and good about essays and other more traditional writing challenges, so we should not feel pressure to know everything about technology. Consultants' general knowledge about textuality and investment in asking questions, listening carefully, and other non-directive pedagogical approaches is all they need to help clients, I believe, no matter the nature of their visits to the writing center.

(II.8.3)

It seems reasonable to claim, by extension, that despite the inflections hypertext introduces into print-based conceptions of argument and order, there will be other aspects of textual production and reception that apply across forms. Alan Rea and Doug White point out, for example, that issues of audience and purpose remain as important in web texts as in print texts (429–30), and all tutors in the writing center, regardless of their background or level of technological expertise, are capable of directing conferences to focus on these issues. Further, tutors, like most anyone else who browses the Web, comprise a legitimate audience for hypertext documents that will appear on the Internet, and their input and responses can therefore be informative, whatever their level of technical or hypertextual knowledge.

Larry Beason's experiences teaching "future English teachers" how to critique Web pages provide some support for this position. When describing an assignment sequence that he gives to his writing students. Beason suggests that they get feedback on their hypertexts from a variety of readers, presumably including writing center tutors, because "the most common concern [he found in the drafts he reviewed] was that the page authors were indeed not taking into account the varied ways in which readers might approach a page" (33). From this perspective, then, a writing center tutor's unfamiliarity with hypertext structure and design should be no more of a concern than their lack of familiarity with economic theory or the principles of civil engineering. No one can be an expert in everything; what's important in a conference is that writers receive a thoughtful response from an authentic audience.

Preparing for Hypertext #2: Hypertexts Will Rarely Appear in Writing Centers

A second rationale for opting to ignore the complications of hypertext in tutorials is that writing centers may not, in fact, see much of it. Despite the glowing successes experienced by a relatively small number of enthusiastic computer-literate instructors and the predictions of digital visionaries, it is possible that the majority of academics will continue to assign their students linear, print-centered papers and expect students to demonstrate mastery of those forms alone. The reasons for such persistent consistency can be many and varied, ranging from simple unfamiliarity with the medium to sophisticated theoretical stances on the nature of thinking processes and academic discourse.

To a great many academics, the linear, hierarchical nature of print texts is a virtue, not a weakness. David W. Chapman makes a case for this position in his *Computers and Composition* article, "A Luddite in Cyberland, Or How to Avoid Being Snared by the Web." Though his perspective seems astonishingly provincial at times, the point he makes here is cogent and is likely shared by a great many academics in both the humanities and the sciences:

... the nonlinearity of the reading experience, the widely acclaimed hypertext, undermines logicai patterns of reading and thinking. The linearity of a written text is not a limitation, it is its glory. ... No one needs to teach students to jump in random order from one "tickler" to the next. What students do need to learn is how to spend an hour or two in concentrated thought as they engage a work of complexity and depth. ... [K]nowing how to produce a Web page is a useful skill, but there is no indication that it will improve a student's ability to write.

(249–51)

Though some might well argue with this conclusion, there is no arguing the fact that the dominant discourse paradigm in academia is linear and print-based and that instructors will continue to teach that form to students, often to the exclusion of all other forms. This is not entirely a matter of clinging to tradition or resisting the need to learn something new. The controlled, linear flow of ideas through focal attention is, according to Davida Charney, one of the great strengths of print texts (243), and Clifford Lynch, the Director of the Coalition for Networked Information, believes that "some kinds of discourse—scholarly and otherwise—[may] he more effective using existing genres rooted in printed works (perhaps presented digitally as well as on paper) rather than in the new genres." For these reasons alone, most instructors in most courses could choose to rely on print text assignments for the foreseeable future.

On a more subtle yet influential level, it is also possible that some academics perceive hypertext as a threat to the educational and disciplinary goals they value and will resist it for that reason. As Stuart Moulthrop and Nancy Kaplan, two of the strongest proponents of hypertext, have observed, this threat may not be wholly imaginary. "[T]he more we experiment with hypertext in literature courses," they say, "the deeper our conviction grows that this new medium is fundamentally at odds with the aims and purposes of conventional literary education" (236). If this is true, and if it holds true for disciplines other than literary studies, then a natural response among those who are most deeply invested in a more conventional educational program would simply be to resist the incursions of hypertext whenever possible, meaning fewer hypertexts assigned or allowed, and therefore fewer students with hypertexts visiting the writing center.

But even if most instructors will not encourage hypertext papers or teach Web design in their courses, others certainly will. Technical writing classes now incorporate Web documents and design as a matter of course, and a great many information technology, journalism, and graphic design classes view Web design and hypertext as integral parts of their curricula. This being the case, writing centers may feel it is their responsibility to prepare tutors to meet these students' rhetorical needs as well as the needs of students with more traditional assignments.

Preparing for Hypertext #3: Use Specialist Tutors

If writing centers want to be proactive, to prepare for the hypertexts that students bring in—be they in small numbers (if the above writers are right) or large numbers (if the above writers are wrong)—and if they want tutors to be knowledgeable about the conventions and organizational schemas that hypertexts employ, then one way to accomplish this is to hire tutors who already have demonstrable expertise with these sorts of texts. Writing centers with a strong WAC focus often employ an analogous approach by seeking out and hiring tutors from multiple disciplines, thereby ensuring that one or more tutors will be able to respond knowledgeably to students' questions about discourse-specific rhetorical forms as well as content.

The tricky part of this solution is purely practical, however, and may be especially troublesome for writing centers in smaller schools or those with limited resources for training. Finding students who know how to create a basic Web page is easy: finding students who know—and can articulate—what makes a particular set of hypertext documents effective or ineffective as *hypertexts* may be far more difficult. Finding students who have a practical understanding of hypertextual design as well as the writing and rhetorical skills necessary to be effective tutors for conventional print texts may be nigh-on impossible. David Chapman, the self-proclaimed Luddite mentioned earlier, claims that "[r]eal expertise in document design is possessed [only] by a small vanguard of technical writing instructors, and even they are just coming to grips with the implication of Web documents" (251). If what he says is true, then any dreams of employing tutors with real expertise in hypertext may remain, as Hamlet intoned, merely "a consummation devoutly to be wished."

Nevertheless, a rich, detailed, sophisticated knowledge of hypertext structure and Web design is probably not a necessity for productive conferencing. A reasonable working knowledge of the principles of hypertext should be more than sufficient for all but the most complex and sophisticated documents, and that degree of knowledge can usually be achieved through a series of manageable, but well-focused workshops.

Preparing for Hypertext #4: Provide Specialized Training for Tutors

Workshops and training sessions on hypertext nevertheless presentsome problems for writing centers, partly because they represent just one more item on a continuously-expanding agenda of specialized knowledges that writing center tutors should know or learn. Already confronted with the diverse needs of ESL students, learning-disabled students, second-dialect students, nontraditional students, students from a variety of disciplines, students in first-year composition courses, graduate students, and students in professional writing classes, writing center directors may decide it's in their best interest to defer workshops on the intricacies of hypertext until the need becomes critical—or at least more critical than many of the other critical needs the writing center has to respond to. Randall Beebe and Mary Boneville recognize the pressing need for tutors to develop advanced computer literacies, to become "quite skilled in manipulating network technologies, designing Web pages, and answering computer-application questions," but they also admit that "because most tutors are overworked with face-to-face tutorials, adding another dimension to their job description hardly seems fair; many writing centers are already understaffed without the resources to provide extensive training" (47). In the face of such pressures and a relative paucity of students visiting the writing center with hypertexts, workshops on nonlinear electronic documents may quickly give way to other topics in tutor training sessions.

But if—in keeping with our general willingness to accommodate new rhetorical and digital forms—we do decide to devote at least part of our tutorial attentions to hypermedia, multimedia, and other "unconventional" electronic documents, where should we begin? What resources must we have on hand, and what training must we give our tutors—and ourselves—to meet our students' needs?

Fortunately, most tutors—as I mentioned earlier—will already have the expertise necessary to discuss hypertexts as informed, aware readers. They will know (or soon be trained in) the conventions of print texts, audience, organization, and argument, and they will also likely be skilled users of the World Wide Web, familiar with the basic conventions of linking, clicking, and scrolling. While this might not enable them to teach students about the subtleties of page design or Web site navigation strategies, their responses as users and readers of a Web page can nevertheless provide valuable guidance to hypertext authors.

Writing center directors who wish to train their tutors further in the basics of Web page design have a wealth of accessible (read: not jargony) resources available online that can be shared as training material in workshops. Among the most useful of these are the *Web Style Guide, 2nd Edition* by Patrick Lynch and Sarah Horton (http://www.webstyleguide.com), and Tammy Worcester's *Web Page Design—From Planning to Posting* (http://www.essdack. org/webdesign/). A great set of negative examples, guaranteed to make a dry training workshop hilarious and also raise important issues in Web site design, can be found at *Web Pages that Suck* (http://www.web-pagesthatsuck.com/). The information provided on these sites and others, as well as a host of trade books aimed at computer novices (such as *The Complete Idiot's Guide to Web Page Design* by Paul McFedries), can teach tutors how to identify and address some simple design issues—and common mistakes—that arise in student Web pages with some frequency.

Tutoring, Training, and Tough Questions

Although it would be easy to pursue this trail of possible resources further, identifying an assortment of sites and texts that could be used to teach tutors HTML and JavaScript, or how to use Microsoft FrontPage or Netscape Composer, we should stop and think carefully about how far we are really willing to go down this path in our quest to create "better" writing tutors. Ultimately, we have to ask ourselves whether it is really the writing center's responsibility to be all things to all people. There will always be more to learn. There will always be new groups making demands on our time and our resources in ways we haven't yet planned for. And there will never be enough time or enough money or enough tutors to meet all those demands all of the time. If we diversify too widely and spread ourselves too thinly in an attempt to encompass too many different literacies, we may not be able to address any set of literate practices particularly well.

The decision about whether to train tutors in the rhetoric of hypertext, then, must necessarily be inflected by local needs and resources. As James Inman notes, some writing centers offer "specialized training for consultants and the acquisition of software options like Macromedia Dreamweaver, Netscape Composer, and Microsoft FrontPage for website design" while others simply "choose not to support such website and desktop publishing assignments" (11.8.3). Each of these paths may be equally appropriate, depending on the institution, the student body, the writing center's mission, and contingencies involving time, money, and resources. The important thing for writing center directors and administrators to remember is that they should remain attuned to changes in their students' and institutions' needs and not let apprehensions about technology interfere with their efforts to learn and work with the new rhetorical forms that technology brings about.

Notes

1. Though I don't completely agree with Inman—I suspect that a great many students still see Web design and organization ss a technical rather than a rhetorical issue and do not automatically think of the writing center as

a primary resource—it would only take a relatively minor change in institutional culture or student culture to alter those circumstances dramatically.

2. Carino also argues that the conflicts over the uses of technology which arose in writing centers paralleled conflicts that took place in the larger field of composition studies, as described by Gail Hawisher, Paul Le Blanc, Charles Moran, and Cindy Selfe in *Computers and the Teaching of Writing in American Higher Education, 1979–1994: A History*.

3. Including such topics as the need to work closely with software designers (Selfe); to ensure adequate access for students, tutors, and necessary services (Harris): and to understand the intellectual property and plagiarism issues raised by inappropriate borrowing and linking to other texts (Haynes-Burton).

4. These articles include is not to say that disorder is the rule, of course. Carter goes on to describe a series of organizational and arrangement strategies that writers can use to guide readers through their hypertexts. Some of these articles draw on traditional rhetorical schemes: using an existing argumentative structure such as a Toulmin model, or "writing prose with an eye to fundamentals of textual coherence" (8).

Works Cited

Anderson, Dana. "Interfacing Email Tutoring: Shaping an Emergent Literate Practice." *Computers and Composition* 19 (2002): 71–87.

Bauman, Marcy Lassota. "The Evolution of Internet Genres." *Computers and Composition 16* (1999): 269–282.

Beason, Larry. "Preparing Future Teachers of English to Use the Web: Balancing the Technical with the Pedagogical." *Weaving a Virtual Web: Practical Approaches to New Information Technologies.* Ed. Sibylle Gruber. Urbana, IL: NCTE, 2000: 25–42.

Beebe, Randall L. and Mary J. Bonevelle. "The Culture of Technology in the Writing Center: Reinvigorating the Theory-Practice Debate." Inman and Sewall, 41–51.

Bell, Diana C. and Mike T. Hübter. "The Virtual Writing Center: Developing Ethos through Mailing List Discourse." *Writing Center Journal 21.2* (2001): 57–78.

Breuch, Lee-Ann M. Kastman and Sam Racine. "Developing Sound Tutor Training for Online Writing Centers: Creating Productive Peer Reviews." *Computers and Composition 17* (2000): 245–263.

Carino, Peter. "Computers in the Writing Center: A Cautionary History." Hobson. 171–193.

Carter, Locke, "Argument in Hypertext: Writing Strategies and the Problem of Order in a Nonsequential World." *Computers and Composition* 20 (2003): 3–22.

Chapman, David W. "A Luddite in Cyberland, Or How to Avoid Being Snared by the Web." *Computers and Composition 16* (1999): 247–252.

Chappell, Virginia A. "Theorizing in Practice: Tutor Training 'Live from the VAX' Lab." *Computers and Composition 12.2* (1995): 227–235.

Charney, David. "The Effect of Hypertext on Processes of Reading and Writing." Selfe and Hilligoss. 238–263.

Coogan, David. "E-Mail Tutoring, a New Way to Do New Work." *Computers and Composition 12.2* (1995): 171–181.

——. "Email 'Tutoring' as Collaborative Writing." *Wiring the Writing Center.* Hobson. 25–43.

Costanzo, William. "Reading, Writing, and Thinking in an Age of Electronic Literacy." Selfe and Hilligoss. 11–21.

Cummins, Gail. "Centering in the Distance: Writing Centers, Inquiry, and Technology." Inman and Sewell, 203–210.

Flanders, Vincent. *Web Pages That Suck.* 2003. 4 November 2003. <http://www.web-pagesthatsuck.com>.

Gardner, Clinton. "Have You Visited Your Online Writing Center Today?: Learning, Writing, and Teaching Online at a Community College." Hobson. 75–84.

Gillespie, Paula and Neal Lerner. *The Allyn and Bacon Guide to Peer Tutoring,* 2nd ed. Boston: Allyn & Bacon. 2003.

Grimm, Nancy Maloney. "Computer Centers and Writing Centers: An Argument for Ballast." *Computers and Composition 12* (1995): 323–29.

Harris, Muriel. "Making Up Tomorrow's Agenda and Shopping Lists Today: Preparing for Future Technologies in the Writing Center." Inman and Sewell, 193–202.

Harris, Muriel and Michael Pemberton. "Online Writing Labs (OWLS): A Taxonomy of Options and Issues." *Computers and Composition 12.2* (1995): 145–159.

Haynes-Burton, Cynthia. "Intellectual (Proper)ty in Writing Centers: Retro Texts and Positive Plagiarism." *Writing Center Perspectives* Eds. Byron Stay, Christina Murphy, and Eric H. Hobson. Emmitsburg, MD: NWCA Press, 1995. 84–93.

Healy, Dave. "From Place to Space: Perceptual and Administrative Issues in the Online Writing Center." *Computers and Composition 12.2* (1995): 183–193

Hobson, Eric, ed. *Wiring the Writing Center.* Logan, UT: Utah State University Press, 1998.

Inman, James A., and Clinton Gardner, eds. *The OWL Construction and Maintenance Guide.* CD-ROM. IWCA Press, 2002.

Inman James A. and Donna N. Sewell, eds. *Taking Flight With OWLs: Examining Electronic Writing Center Work.* Mahwah, NJ: Erlbaum, 2000.

Johanek, Cindy and Rebecca Rickly. "Online Tutor Training: Synchronous Conferencing in a Professional Community." *Computers and Composition 12.2* (1995): 237–246.

Johnson-Eilola, Johndan. "Reading and Writing in Hypertext: Vertigo and Euphoria." Selfe and Hilligoss. 195–219.

Kiedaisch, Jean and Sue Dinitz. "Look Back and Say 'So What': The Limitations of the Generalist Tutor." *Writing Center Journal 14.1* (1993): 63-74.

Kimball, Sara. "Cybertext/Cyberspeech: Writing Centers and Online Magic." *Writing Center Journal 18.*1 (1997): 30–49.

Lerner, Neal. "Drill Pads, Teaching Machines, and Programmed Texts: Origins of Instructional Technology in Writing Centers." Hobson. 119–136.

Lynch, Clifford. "The Battle to Define the Future of the Book in the Digital World." *First Monday 6.6* (June 2001). 9 May 2003. <http://www.firstmonday.dk/issues/issue6_6/lynch/>.

Lynch, Patrick J and Saran Horton. *Web Style Guide,* 2nd Edition. 2002. 4 November 2003. <http://www.websiyle-guide.com>.

McAndrew, Donald A. and Thomas J. Reigstad. *Tutoring Writing: A Practical Guide for Conferences.* Portsmouth, NH: Boynton/Cook-Heinemann, 2001.

McFedries, Paul. The *Complete Idiot' s Guide to Cresting a Web Page, 5th Edition.* Indianapolis, IN: Alpha Books, 2003.

Monroe, Barbara. "The Look and Feel of the OWL Conference." Hobson. 3–24.

Moulthrop, Stuart and Nancy Kaplan. "They Became What They Beheld: The Futility of Resistance in the Space of Electronic Writing." Selfe and Hilligoss. 220–237.

Nelson, Jane, and Cynthia A. Wambeam. "Moving Computers into the Writing Center: The Path to Least Resistance." *Computers and Composition 12.2* (1995): 135–143.

Pemberton, Michael. "Rethinking the WAC/Writing Center Connection." *Writing Center Journal 15.2* (1995): 116–133.

Rafoth, Ben, ed. *A Tutor' s Guide: Helping Writers One to One.* Portsmouth, NH: Boynton/Cook-Heinemann, 2000.

Rea, Alan and Doug White. "The Changing Nature of Writing: Prose or Code in the Classroom." *Computers and Composition 16* (1999): 421–436.

Rose, Mike. "The Language of Exclusion: Writing Instruction at the University." *College English 47* (1985): 341–59.

Selfe, Cynthia L., and Susan Hilligoss, eds. *Literacy and Computers: The Complications of Teaching and Learning with Technology.* New York: MLA, 1994.

Selfe, Dickie. "Surfing the Tsunami: Electronic Environments in the Writing Center." *Computers and Composition 12* (1995): 311–22.

Trimbur, John. "Multiliteracies, Social Futures and Writing Centers." *Writing Center Journal 20.2* (2000): 29–31.

Williams, Sean D. "Part I: Thinking Out of the Pro-Verbal Box." *Computers and Composition* (2001): 21–32.

Wood, Gail F. "Making the Transition from ASL to English: Deaf Students, Computers, and the Writing Center." *Computers and Composition 12.2* (1995): 219–226.

Worcester, Tammy. *Web Page Design—From Planning To Pasting.* 1999. 4 November 2003. <http://www. essdackorg/webdesign/>.

10
Digital Images and Classical Persuasion

Kevin LaGrandeur

> The digitization of images inevitably strips away their context and allows the machine, or rather its programmer, to define new contexts.
>
> —Jay David Bolter, *Writing Space*

Introduction

The abilities to digitize and contextualize images on the computer required, through the late 1980s, some degree of mathematical expertise. Digital graphics are really pictures made by equations and were originally constructed piece by piece. Now, however, the ease of digitizing photographs and drawings has made the Web's graphic landscape much more accessible to the average person. Thus, the statement by Bolter that begins the chapter now has added implications. Where once only words were malleable enough to be widely wielded as a rhetorical tool, in the latter half of the 1990s the digital image became prevalent, easy to manipulate, and consequently, easy to recontextualize, meaning that now just about any image is available to any computer user for any occasion. To use Bolter's terminology, the "interpenetration" of textual and pictorial space in digital environments, especially the World Wide Web, has increased markedly, so that the predominance of the digital image now rivals that of the digital word. Indeed, a number of thinkers have noted the digital imaged ascendancy in communicating information via the computer.[1] But how are we to think about, to analyze the rhetorical dimensions of these images? Both static and moving images can be intensely affective, of course, as print, film, and television have taught us; but what model can we use to assess the persuasive impact of the image in the realm of information technology—specifically, in environments like the Web, a realm where there is an interdependence between text and graphics, as well as an interactivity between reader and writer/programmer/rhetor?

Many have turned to postmodernism to theorize the digital medium in general. The gist of such theorization is that the characteristics of new media like the Web—collage, hypertextuality, multimodality, and nonlinearity, for instance—enact the postmodern *texte*. The focus of this thinking tends to be on aspects of chaos and fragmentation represented by such digital media. But one can also approach these media from another viewpoint, focusing on them as integrative, intertextual, and complex. Notable among those who have approached digital media from this angle are Gunther Kress, Jay David Bolter, Richard Lanham, and Kathleen Welch. The latter two authors, though they sometimes make use of postmodern theory, have successfully used classical rhetoric as their foundation for analyzing computer media. Lanham (1993) discussed digital textuality, including some focus on the digital image, in these terms back in *The Electronic Word.* More recently, Welch (1999) has explored how Isocratic rhetoric may provide a way to think about modern video-based communication, a category in which she includes computers. This chapter owes a debt to these others, and proceeds in their spirit, but focuses particularly on using classical rhetoric as a way of thinking about the persuasive power of computer-based images.

Why Refer to Classical Rhetoric?

There are good reasons for looking at the digital image in classical terms. In a general sense, as Lanham (1993) contends, few models provide a "frame wide enough" to explain the "extraordinary convergence of twentieth-century thinking with the digital means that now give it expression"; therefore, he continues, "to explain reading and writing on computers, we need to go back to the original Western thinking about reading and writing—the rhetorical paideia that provided the backbone of Western education for 2,000 years" (51). Because, with increasing bandwidth, images have become ever more integral to the computer-based reading and writing process since Lanham wrote this passage, I would argue that what he says applies to images, as well. Moreover, as Welch (1999) puts it, classical rhetoric is pertinent to the new communication technologies because "classical Greek rhetoric" is "intersubjective, performative, and a merger of oralism and literacy" (12), and these qualities are common to the technologies in question. I would add to her assertion that these qualities are especially common to the realm of Web-based presentation. For instance, as I shall discuss later, images on Web sites act as part of an argument by parataxis, which, as Eric Havelock has maintained, is characteristic of oral rhetoric, the heart of the classical system (see Lanham 1991, 108). Finally, there is good reason to redeploy classical rhetoric to examine the persuasive value of digital images because, as I intend to show by presenting the thoughts of some of its most notable thinkers, classical notions provide us with excellent, codified ways to think about the persuasive efficacy of images and words as interdependent and interactive things.

The Image and Classical Rhetoric

It might be extremely difficult to have a true argument, with the give and take that "argument" implies, using *only* visual images. Yet the potential of the image to move its viewers was recognized by ancient rhetoricians, and thus a correlation between it and verbal imagery has been an important component of persuasion since classical times. The theoretical basis for seeing images as modes of persuasion lies in Aristotelian rhetoric, which stipulates that the speaker's ability to arouse emotion in his audience and his ability to cultivate an impression of credibility with them are, in addition to evidence and logic, extremely important persuasive elements.

In practical terms, the precedents for the use of images and imagery to instill emotion or credibility can be found in two slightly different classical traditions. One tradition, stemming from Aristotle and continuing with the early Greek orator Gorgias, concerns the affective similarity of images and words: In his *Encomium of Helen,* Gorgias equates the emotive power of the image with that of persuasive speech. The other tradition, most famously associated with the Roman writer Horace, emphasizes how the poetic image can be persuasive: In discussing poetry's instructional potential, Horace mentions the similarity of poetry to pictures. This Horatian idea became very popular among literary critics and rhetoricians, especially those of the Neoclassical era. In fact, as is exemplified in the theories of the eighteenth-century rhetorician George Campbell, these slightly different traditions of Gorgias and Horace appear to have mingled together over time, so that poetry, visual images, and persuasive speech and composition became interdependent. In the age of the pixelated image, which has given rise to everything from television advertisements to hypermedia, the rhetorical principles codified by Aristotle are still important: Fluency with images and their use has become crucial to controlling credibility and creating emotional appeal, and even, to some extent, logical appeal.

The Aristotelian Basis for Linking Images and Persuasion

One reason Aristotelian rhetoric provides a good basis for discussing the image as a persuasive tool is that Aristotle's definition of rhetoric is broad enough to encourage it: He defines rhetoric as the art of finding "in any given case the available means of persuasion" (*Rhetoric* [1984b], bk. I, chap. 2.). In the years since he wrote those words, our "available means" have expanded considerably, especially with the advent of electronic gadgetry like the computer, which has evolved from a solely mathematical tool into, as Richard Lanham (1993) has proclaimed, a rhetorical medium.[2] In this respect, Aristotle's definition of the different means of proof available to the orator provides the most important means of discussing the persuasive image. Besides nonartistic proofs, or what we would call "hard evidence," Aristotle specifies that three artistic forms of proof are also important to argument: *logos* (an appeal to reason), *pathos* (an appeal to the emotions), and *ethos* (the appeal implicit in the speaker's character and credibility). Although he felt that only "the bare facts" *should* be weighed in any kind of decision and that a plain rhetorical style should suffice, Aristotle grudgingly conceded that because of the "defects of the hearers" such things as artistic appeals are necessary (bk. III, chap. 1). Accordingly, he devotes much of his discussion in the *Rhetoric* to examining artistic forms of appeal, their delivery, and how they may affect the psychology of a given audience. In this contest, he discusses the effects of images rendered in words. "Prose writers must," he says, "pay especially careful attention to metaphor" for it gives writing a "clearness, charm, and distinction as nothing else can" (bk. III, chap. 2).

The source of the image's power is clearly in its emotional appeal. As Aristotle points out in his *Poetics,* "Though the objects themselves may be painful to see, we delight to view the most realistic representations of them in art, the forms for example of the lowest animals and of dead bodies" (1984a, chap. 4). The source of the image's emotional appeal clearly depends on its mimetic quality; but it also depends significantly on the artist's manipulation of the image, on its rendering, not *just* on its "realistic" imitation of nature. This is why one may have no familiarity at all with the original object rendered in an image and still experience emotion when viewing the image. The emotion "will be due" says Aristotle, not to the realistic imitation of the object, but "to the execution, the coloring, or some similar cause" (chap. 4). Aristotle's own analysis of images and imagery is evidence not only of their similar emotional effects and potential persuasive value, but also of the necessity for a critical awareness of affective elements common to both, such as their execution, context and structure.

Gorgias: Linking the Persuasive Power of Words and Images

Although Aristotle's advocacy of the rhetorical use of artistic appeal, and therefore of images and imagery, is grudging, for other orators of Aristotle's era, such as the Sophists, artistic proof, images, and the corresponding use of imagery were very important. Gorgias, a Sophist who lived just before Aristotle began writing, put heavy emphasis on artistic elements such as delivery, style, and artistic modes of proof. His *Encomium of Helen* illustrates how he sees the image as a potential means of persuasion. In this work, Gorgias tries to exonerate Helen of Troy of starting the Trojan War by showing how her flight to Troy with Paris could be seen as a matter of compulsion. He begins by considering the possibility that Paris raped her and argues that she could not hove put up an effective resistance in such a case. He uses this argument as a premise to set up his succeeding contentions that, just as physical strength can ravish the body, so words and images can ravish one's reason. Gorgias argues that speech "has the form of necessity," and that, because it can "ravish" the mind, it is like magic or drugs in its effect on people (1972, 52). He proves this through some examples, the most central being that what Aristotle would call artistic appeal is sufficient to persuade a crowd to accept an argument for something that is logically false. Basing his reasoning on the affective power of poetry, Gorgias observes, "A single speech, written with art but not spoken with truth, bends a great crowd and persuades" (53). At this point one can recognize what Gorgias is getting at in his own speech. If a false speech relying on art—that is, on *ethos* and *pathos* can "constrain" the soul and blind one to *logos*, if a whole crowd can be swayed against reason by "artistic" means, then, implicitly, Helen should surely be considered blameless for what her culture would consider perfidious and unreasonable behavior.

Having illustrated the persuasive power of words, Gorgias then compares this power to that of images. He points out that "frightening sights" are capable of "extinguishing and excluding thought" and thus causing madness (1972, 53–54). Hence, he reasons, we must conclude that images and words are effectively equal; they are both able to "ravish" the soul, to cause blindness to reason and law. As he says, the emotion that is created by images is "engraved upon the mind" and "is exactly analogous to what is spoken" (54). Thus, Gorgias ultimately equates the persuasive power of the image to that of words. Moreover, as one can see by his arguments and examples, the thing that makes the two equal is their effect upon the emotions. (It is notable that he does not limit susceptibility to emotions, words, and images to women such as Helen but gives examples that include all people.)

Although he spends much time discussing the specific emotion of fear, Gorgias does not limit the appeal of images to this emotion: Images, like words, can create great desire, too. He demonstrates this in the last section of his *Encomium,* in which, in reference to the physical beauty of Paris, he argues that visual images—especially beautiful works of art—can cause irresistible desire for whatever they depict: "whenever pictures perfectly create a single figure and form from many colors and figures, they delight the sight, while the creation of statues and the production of works of art furnish a pleasant sight to the eyes. Thus it is natural for the sight to grieve for some things and to long for others" (54). Gorgias uses this example concerning artworks to show how Helen of Troy's longing for the delightful sight of Paris might have forced her into fleeing with him every bit as effectively as the drug like words or physical ravishment he referred to earlier.

Besides the overt purpose of exonerating Helen, Gorgias's discussion of the power of the image is meant to make his Greek audience—who are proud of their powers of reason, who indeed consider those powers the mark of their superiority to barbarians—aware of the sway that other modes of persuasion may have over that of reason. In essence, he is doing what a modern teacher might do in helping her students dissect the emotional appeal of a visual advertisement: showing the audience the power of something they might have considered inconsequential and, in the process, making them cognizant of their own susceptibility to it. Through such a process of exposition, both Gorgias and the modern rhetorician attempt to enable their listeners to defend themselves against *and* to use this kind of power. Understanding the image, in other words, means comprehending its dichotomous possibilities: Its persuasive power might add to an argument, but its force and nonrational nature can distract one from a message's logical appeal, or its lack thereof. I will return to this idea in the later sections of this chapter.

Horace: Linking Poetry, Pictures, and Persuasion

As we have seen, Gorgias points to the emotional force of poetry when discussing the power of persuasive speech. This is not coincidental. Indeed, Richard Lanham (1991) reminds us that "rhetorical theory has ... often in its history overlapped poetics," most clearly because of "the area where the two bodies of theory overlap—the connotative, suggestive, metaphoric use of language," but also because their purposes have so often coincided (131–132). As Lanham notes, Cicero maintained that the main functions of rhetoric were to teach, to please, and to move. Similarly, Cicero's contemporary, the Roman writer Horace, maintained the same mixture of persuasive, didactic and pleasing functions to be essential to poetry. As he argues in his *Ars Poetica,* that poet "has gained every vote who has mingled profit with pleasure by delighting the reader at once and instructing him" (1929/1978, 479).

More importantly, he is also the most famous classical source of the idea that poetry imitates visual images, though that idea may extend as far back as the fifth-century Greek poet Simonides (Adams 1971, 67). Horace's notion, expressed in his *Ars Poetica,* equates poetry and pictures (*ut pictura poesis*) (1929/1978, 481). Although this notion was not really meant to promote the power of visual imagery as much as to show how poems may be appreciated for different attributes, succeeding generations of poets and rhetoricians came to consider *ut pictura poesis* a dictum, encouraging the functional elision of words and images. The endurance of Horace's implicit idea of marrying the didactic, the poetic, and the visual provides a good example, along with Gorgias's linking of statues, desire, and persuasion, of the strength of the crossover between rhetoric, poetry and the visual arts.

The Adaptation and Blending of Horatian, Gorgian, and Aristotelian Concepts

Horace's concepts linking poetry, the visual image, and didactic purpose became especially popular among neoclassical thinkers (Adams 1971, 73). One such thinker, George Campbell (1719–1796), talks at length of the use of imagery in rhetoric, and in doing so expands both on Gorgias's implicit linking of images, rhetoric, and poetry and on Horaces linking of poetry, painting, and instructive persuasion. In Book I of his *Philosophy of Rhetoric,* Campbell asserts that "an harangue framed for affecting the hearts or influencing the resolve of an assembly, needs greatly the assistance both of intellect and of imagination," and that it is best to seize the attention of one's audience by appealing first to the imagination (1963, 2), The best way to do this, he contends, is through poetic imagery. Because Campbell considers poetry "one mode of oratory" (3), the methodology he encourages is one that connects this poetry-as-oratory directly to painting:

> The imagination is addressed by exhibiting to it a lively and beautiful representation of a suitable abject. As in this exhibition, *the task of the orator* may, in some sort, be said, *like that of the painter,* to consist in imitation, the merit of the work results entirely from these two sources; dignity, as well in the subject or thing imitated, as in the manner of imitation; and resemblance, in the portrait or performance.
>
> (3, emphasis added)

As one may see from this passage, imitation of the thing depicted is paramount. There are three reasons for this.

First, Campbell believes the use of images can provide a means of comparison for an audience and thus work upon their sense of reason. Thus, there is a precedent for considering images as a form of *logical* proof: "The connexion ... that generally subsisteth between vivacity and belief will appear less marvelous, if we reflect that there is not so great a difference between argument and illustration as is usually imagined" (1963, 74). This is because "reasoning," as he sees it, "is but a kind of comparison" (74). A second reason that a "painter-like" exactness of imitation is important—as is a poetic ability to create these word-images—is that imagery can produce a deep and persuasive affective response, which "assumes the denomination of *pathetic*" (4). Ultimately, Campbell says, "The ideas of the poet," expressed in this painterly way, "give greater pleasure, command closer attention, operate more strongly on the passions, and are longer remembered" than ideas expressed by more mundane writers (74).

So powerful are poetic images that they may serve to provide great sway to oratory; for, "when in suitable coloring [these images are] presented to the mind, [they] do, as it were, distend the imagination with some vast conception, and quite ravish the soul" (1963, 3). Here, we see a clear debt to Gorgias, as Campbell presents imagery as irresistible to the emotions, even going so far as to use Gorgias's terminology of "ravishment." Also, Campbell's classification of imagery under two different categories of argument, logical and emotional, follows Aristotle's system of rhetoric.

Analyzing the Web-Based Image

How are Horace's and Gorgias's precedents for blending the poetic, imagistic, and oratorical and Aristotle's ideas of rhetoric applicable to modern electronic images? I would like to propose the following analytical system. Using Aristotle's notions of rhetoric as a starting point for discussing modern digitally based presentations, one can argue that images on an electronic screen can serve as a form of *logos,* or rational proof, especially when they consist of such things as charts and graphs. For as Campbell might say, such images serve as a means of comparison (of data and so forth, in modem contexts) and thus, of rational judgment Also, in this mode, images can augment textual information via parataxis, that is, by being placed next to such information as a coordinate, supportive structure. Accordingly, and because the Web is intertextual by nature, some consideration of how well the text and graphics interrelate is important.[3] In terms of *logos,* this consideration is especially important, because digital graphics are sometimes used to replace written text.

There are also the appeals to *pathos* and *ethos* to consider. Just as Campbell, Gorgias, and Horace saw more value in the *pathetic* aspects of the image, so the persuasive "value of the digital image is perhaps more evident when one considers it in terms of *pathos* and *ethos*. This is especially true because the latter of these terms has expanded, with the evolution of rhetoric, to signify the rhetor's general credibility, rather than just serving to denote moral character. As Campbell's essay exemplifies, *ethos* and *pathos* have usually been seen, in a classical sense, as dependent upon the nature of the images the speaker "draws" with words, as well as on such things as hand gestures, facial expressions, voice modulation, clothing, and other subtleties. On the Web, however, as with printed compositions, these nonverbal cues are usually absent Thus, part of the judgment of the speaker's character and credibility becomes contingent, instead, upon the visual images she composes, chooses, and presents on the screen. Her choice of graphics and their nature, arrangement, and movement (if they are animated) not only are important to instilling the proper emotion in the audience (and thus elemental to *pathos*) but are also part of what the audience uses, consciously or unconsciously, to decide if she, and hence her presentation, are authoritative and believable (and thus integral to *ethos*).

In sum, I propose the following model, based on classical principles of rhetoric, to assess the persuasive impact of digital images:

1. Consider *logos*: How effectively do digital graphics work together with, or even replace, digital text to create an appeal to reason?
2. Consider *pathos*: As classical rhetoricians note, images are most powerful as a means of emotional appeal (which is why their cousins, metaphorical images, are so persuasive); thus, we should take into account how digital images work in concert with written text, or by themselves, to enhance the emotional appeal of digital messages. In particular, how effectively do the enhanced verisimilitude and vividness made possible by such digital innovations as 3-D, animated, computer-aided design (CAD), and interactive graphics and easily mastered, professional-looking layouts and fonts affect the emotional appeal of digital textuality? How do these enhanced graphic effects affect the readers perception of other modes of appeal, such as *logos* and *ethos?*
3. Consider *ethos*: How effectively do digital images work in concert with written text, or by themselves, to enhance the *ethical* appeal (credibility) of the makers of digital messages? In particular, how do the enhanced verisimilitude and vividness made possible by such digital innovations as 3-D, animated, CAD, and interactive graphics and easily mastered, professional-looking layouts and fonts affect the credibility of those who author digital texts?

Test Case 1: An "Informational" Web Page

We can look at part of a Web page to see how these analytical criteria might be applied. For instance, a Web page designed to persuade people to consider getting Lasik surgery—a type of corrective surgery for the eye—includes a series of images at the top of the figure explaining the surgical procedure and is an example of an attempt to use images as *logos*. Each image is paired with a caption, but it is the image, more than the caption, that carries the clearest explanation of the procedure. Phrases like "corneal flap," "excimer laser" and "steeper cornea" are explained visually rather than verbally. The captions merely help explain what is happening in the corresponding picture. Further indication of the predominance of the image in the explanatory process is the presence of a redundant, animated version of the surgical process, using the same four images, that one can access by clicking the animation button. Nevertheless, this page presents a good sample of intertextuality and parataxis at work. Is the page persuasive? Using our criteria, I would say it is. The pictures, aided by the words, act in concert to form the *logos* of the argument: that the surgical procedure is simple, straightforward, and clean. The pictures with their captions are eye catching (which goes to *pathos*), *easy* to understand, and located at the top of the Web page, so that they are seen immediately upon its loading, all of which is an attempt to make the pictorially presented rationale easier for the reader to follow and is therefore important to *logos*. Additionally, the maker of this page has used both images and words to enhance the credibility (*ethos*) of the presentation. Though it is an advertisement by a doctors' office meant to generate business, it avoids any overt sales tactics: no flashy color scheme, no exhortations or radical-sounding claims. Rather, the colors are muted, with a relaxing blue as the dominant hue; the text is spare and clinical, and the illustrations have a professional, scientific appearance. This all seems calculated to instill emotions of relaxation and an *ethos* of trust in the doctors' professionalism.

Test Case 2: Of Drugs and Magic—The Problem with Ravishing Images

As we have seen, rhetorical tradition recognizes the power of images and so promotes capturing the imagination of the audience quickly by using imagistic words. The digital age allows the same purpose to be served by a return to the source of power, by a creation of "lyrical" images that delight enrage, frighten, or excite. It seems that Web sites increasingly use this approach, and therein lies a problem, as Gorgias and his descendant Campbell warn us. The image can be seductive to the point of distraction, and this can be detrimental for both the authors and the audiences of Web sites.

About two years ago, when I began teaching basic Web design in my technical writing classes, the surprising seductiveness of some of my students' home pages got me thinking about the whole issue of using digital images as rhetorical tools. So I would like to turn to an example from one of my beginning classes to begin examining the darker side of the digital image.

Early in the semester, I always ask my students to form groups of four or five people and to devise and post a simple home page on the Internet to which they will link their succeeding assignments. This home page must be about new scientific developments related to the mind and body. Rhetorically, the aim of the homepage is to convince its visitors to stay and visit the other pages that students (eventually) post regarding these new developments. I expected, when I first tried this assignment, that these sites would be relatively unsophisticated in their rhetorical appeal and, because this was an intermediate composition class, in the development of their written content—and many of them were. But some of them astonished me with their reliance on, their preoccupation with, and the attractiveness of their graphics.

The photograph of the running cheetah a student's home page effectively "advertises" the rest of the site in ways that reflect the classical criteria I have been discussing. Specifically, it reflects the three classical criteria that Campbell uses: The image draws attention, invites comparison, and generates emotional response. First, the image catches the cheetah in a dramatic full sprint, which creates attentiveness. The same is true of the color scheme: Hot oranges blaze on a light background. In addition to focusing attention, the image of the cheetah could also persuade by paratactical association: The vitality of the cheetah not only invites analytical comparisons to the viewer's own vitality (or lack of it), it is also pertinent to the exercise-and-health theme of the page (if one reads and understands the text, a problem that I will return to in a moment). In terms of modern Web design, the web page includes some other elements of what might be called a good "rhetorico-graphic interface": The links are laid out well; they are placed where the eye of an English reader will focus first—in the upper left of the page. Indeed, the clean layout and flashy picture might forge an emotional impression that could linger long after the reader has left the page. The problem, however, is that the image is everything to this Web page. Though the writing shows some flair for emotional appeal in the first two sentences, the grammar, structure and clarity suffer afterward. Thus the images on this page offer no real paratactic for the words they accompany.

I had watched the students as they created this page. Fairly inexperienced at using computers, much less Web design tools, they were entranced by the image they had found and the relative ease with which they could fashion a page around it. Perhaps influenced by our immersion in a highly televisual culture, they clustered around the computer that had the image and worked on it eagerly. When I ventured over to remind them that they had to include some text, too, I watched them assign it to one reluctant person in their group, who promptly decided to put it off until later and went back to the image of the cheetah. This problem was not unique to this particular group. I have found that images—including format, layout, and even fonts for written text—take up so much of my students' attention that the idea of useful content, whether I based in image or word, suffers. One mark of this is that, though ours is a technical writing class, students are often shocked when I lower their grade for bad grammar on their Web sites (this could have to do with other factors, as well, I realize, but that is another chapter in a different book). Suffice it to say that I had a difficult time getting my students to see that though a good, vivid graphical image may be enough to make a person pause on a page, it takes more than that to keep her from leaving that page; it takes a good interweaving of text and image, along with usable content.

Test Case 3: Defending Ourselves against the Dark Side of Persuasive Digital Images

This kind of experience with my students, which left me feeling somewhat like a character in *The Sorcerer's Apprentice,* has made me dunk that it would be a good idea to use a classically based, analytical system like the one I proposed earlier in this chapter to teach the principles of a visual rhetoric along with the elements of Web design. Teaching an awareness of the power and effects of images would provide students of Web design with a better sense not only of how to use them, but also of how to defend themselves against their power.

Indeed, there are already numerous examples of dangerous, image-centered arguments proliferating on the Web. Perhaps Aristotle said it best when he noted, as I mentioned earlier, that "the defects of the hearers" are what make images so powerful and useful to rhetoricians. The reason that my students are easily awed by fancy-looking images lies partly in the wizardry that those images convey. They look so professional, so polished, so authoritative—yet they are so easy to manipulate, and it is so easy to learn how to do so. Not surprisingly, there is a negative side to the relative ease with which one can learn how to create impressive images in digital formats. Graphics sometimes lend undue credibility to otherwise weak arguments. Even sophisticated typography and layout, graphic elements that were, before the digital age, available mainly to professional publishers, can have this result. *NBC Nightly News* ran a segment on July 19, 2000, about the fact that rumors spread on the Internet are often granted more credibility than they are due. This effect was attributed not only to the speed of rumor propagation allowed by electronic media, but also to the persuasive effect of simply seeing something in print let alone with polished graphics) in a public venue. If an electronic document *looks* like one that has been published on paper, then, for many people, it carries the same authority. Thus, even the form and "look" of the print, on a Web page can have a credibility-increasing effect. One could argue that this "print effect" occurs not only because people are conditioned to put great trust in documents that are publicly disseminated, but also because people have been socially conditioned for over 500 years to place great credibility in the typographical forms that publishers have used. Now, with electronic fonts, those forms are available to anybody.

Thus, the *ethical* effect of electronic print is at least partially a function of the fact that, like calligraphy, electronic fonts are as much art as they are signifiers of sound and words.[4] Alphabets are, in essence, abbreviations of figural metaphors (think of the evolution of Chinese ideograms, for example) and, in the digital realm, there are multitudes of fonts, designed specifically for the screen, each with its own expressive style. Web designers have already begun using these fonts and other tricks of typography for their power to affect. The Web page of a well-known hate provide group provide an example of how images, including typography, when interlaced cunningly with textual content, can lend undue credibility and dangerous emotional force to a site.

The methodology of this Web site is to pitch its "product" without an appeal to logic, but instead to create a sort of sublime experience, a persuasive, horrifying, visual poem. If Gorgias is right, we have a particular emotional susceptibility to fearful images. Hate mongers know this and make use of it. The rumor and the frightening image are two of their favorite devices, and this is another reason to encourage an understanding of the workings of visual rhetoric. The main rhetorical appeal here is to *pathos,* to the emotion of fear; but, ironically, it is clear from the way the images and text are constructed that the primary aim in making the Web page fearsome is to provide an aura of power, and therefore lend credibility, to the group itself. So, ultimately, the central aim of the composite image of this Web page is to affect *ethos.* The topics in the menu bar are dominated by links that provide contact and ideological information for prospective members. Most importantly, the huge image of a wolf's eyes, in conjunction with the text under it that reads, "We're everywhere you are," is meant to give a false (I hope) sense of ubiquity and power to any secret racists who visit the site. This paratactic tie between the text and image is reinforced by the interactivity between them. When one uses the mouse to roll the cursor over the image of the wolf, textual elaboration pops up regarding "Lone Wolves"—evidently a metaphor for members of the group. This pop-up text reads, "Lone Wolves are everywhere. We're m your neighborhoods, financial institutions, police departments, military, and social clubs." Not only is the message contained in the image-word combination meant to convey power and, therefore, *ethical* e*f*fect, but so is the very sophistication of the page; the Java-based rollover function appears us a surprising, subtle—and chilling—piece of technological legerdemain.

This brings us to the secondary purpose of the page: to instill fear and intimidation in any enemies of the group who may view it; thus, its images also have a *pathetic* dimension. The typography conveys this; the font is boldface, italicized, and red to provide an image of aggressiveness, and the word "war" is written in capital letters. The Web designer's choice of a sans serif font could he seen as an attempt to accentuate the aggressive effect, as serif fonts tend to slow the eye down. The picture of a wolfs eyes and the hot, red-based colors convey aggressiveness. The kind of "published" look drat this site has would have been more expensive to attain in printed pamphlets and much more difficult to disseminate before the advent of the Web. Now that it is so easy to disseminate images and messages such as the one in this Web site, it is doubly important that we pay attention to how graphics and text interact in the networked environment.

Overuse: A Limit to the Digital Image's Persuasiveness?

The persuasiveness of digital images may be limited, paradoxically, by their own power and ubiquity. Complex, graphics-heavy Web sites take a long time to load and are not very "degradable"; that is, they do not look good on older browsers and computers. This limits accessibility to these sites. But perhaps the biggest limit to the rhetorical power of graphics, even on pages where their density is not a problem, is that they can distract the reader from the logical appeal of the Web site. A recent study done at Ohio State University found that, regardless of whether a Web site's fonts and other graphic images have authoritative *form*, people had trouble understanding and focusing on the site's content. The strong *pathetic* effect of digital images can distract one from any kind of *logos* that the site might convey. One of the students in the study complained about this: "There are all these great graphics, and it takes concentration to home in and focus on the actual information" (Greenman 2000, 11). Part of this student's problem also had to do with hyperlinks, which are, technically, a type of graphical image: He found himself "struggling to digest the information on a Web page before being lured away by links to other pages."

Casual Web users are not the only ones troubled by how its hypertextual nature reinforces a focus on the *pathetic* appeal of images over any form of logical content. At least one Web designer anticipated the complaints of the students in the Ohio State study. Writing in 1998, Jeffrey Veen lamented that "designers add links by inserting harsh blue underlined scars into the patterns of the paragraphs. The result? An overbearing distraction to the readers subconscious. Suddenly, that reader must decide: Do I stop here and click on to this link? Do I finish the sentence and come back? Do I finish the story and scroll back to the navigation element? Its a headachy mess" (1998a, lesson 3, 1). Note that, like the classical authors we have discussed, Veen sees the attraction of the image as a factor of the "subconscious, and so of *pathos.*"

The limits to digital graphics that this study exposes appear to inhere not only in the very *pathetic* power of such images, which distracted students from logical appeals contained in digital pages, but also in two other problems: the well-known difficulty of reading material on a computer screen, and an issue of image saturation. The second of these problems is particularly important: Because images in a Web environment are so emotionally appealing, they tend to be used too abundantly. As a result, as this study showed, they marginalize meaning carried in written text (which is what students in the study were asked to focus on). As Kress (1998) has pointed out, the marginalization of text by images is increasingly common in all types of printed media, and this practice has carried over to the Internet. The result appears to be an increasing reliance on digital imagery that is ever easier to manipulate and a consequent obstruction of logical appeal by emotional appeal in the digital realm. The more that this happens, the shallower the overall rhetorical appeal of digital messages becomes.[5]

Conclusion

Bizzell and Herzberg (1990) mention that Plato thought rhetoric "made a virtue of linguistic facility" by drawing attention to "the material effects of [language's] style and structure" (1165). Similarly, one could say that the integration of electronic media into the persuasive endeavor has made a virtue of digital facility by drawing attention to the material effects of graphical style and structure. When a Web site's images are especially polished, pleasing, and well arranged, its readers often cannot help but be attentive—and even impressed or moved.

The dominant effect of graphical elements may be leading to the adaptation of an advertiser-centered model of Web design, with its profusion of flashy images and persuasive appeals that work on a subconscious, emotional level, rather than on a rational one. The media critic David Shenk (1999) is skeptical about the image-rich environment of new media. He thinks that the moving image, as presented on television, and transferred thence to the Web, insidiously distracts from the substance of any message. He does not see images (he points to television as the model for the cybernetic image) as enhancing the message in any way. Shenk says, "Images captivate us effortlessly, and are difficult to filter our" (6). As an example, he uses Wim Wenders' 1991 film *Until the End of the World,* which depicts a world addicted to neurologically stimulating images. He notes that "Wenders calls this 'the disease of images,' the problem where 'you have too many images around so that finally you don't see anything anymore'" (5). The question that arises from Shenk's discussion, with regard to teaching, is: If we encourage students to include images (especially moving ones) in their Web work, are we discouraging appeals to rational thought (*logos*)? Perhaps, if, as Bolter (1991) says, "The digitization of images inevitably … allows the … programmer, to define new contexts" for them, the real answer to this question is that we must learn to build better contexts, ones in which images work in conjunction with rational thought (72). We can begin doing this by learning to understand the rhetorical context of digital images better, and a redeployment of classical notions such as those I suggest here could prove a great help.

Notes

1. Kress (1998) notes that there is, in "information technology circles," the acute awareness of a "trend towards the visual representation of information which was formerly coded solely in language" (77); see also Brown et al 1995, as well as Tufte 1990; Lanham 1994; and Stevens 1998, especially chap.11.
2. This is a formulation that Lanham (1993) mentions in various, slightly different ways; see xii and 31, especially.
3. There are numerous sources of information on the interrelation of graphics and text on the Web itself, one that is particularly helpful because of the breadth of its articles is a Web site For designers called Webmonkey <hotwired.lycos.corn/webmonkey>; see especially Frew 1997; Veen 1998a, 1998b; and Nichols 2000. My thanks, also, to Karin Kawamoto, Webmaster and technical writer, for her input on these matters.
4. See Lanham 1993, chap. 2, for a very interesting and detailed discussion of the connections between digital typography and art, as well as of art and rhetoric in the general digital realm.
5. Also, in reference to me merginalization of text by graphics, it seems that Web designers need to come up with some kind of adjustment to reduce the level of distraction hypertext links present to readers. Veen (1998a) mentions various solutions, including two interesting, low-tech ones: remarginalize some of the images by moving the hyperlinks to the margin of the text, so that they become like annotations, or move them all to the end of the document. He notes that these solutions have been tried by various companies, like the *New York Times,* but does not say how good the results have been.

References

Adams, Hazard. 1971. *Critical Theory since Plato.* New York: Harcourt Brace Jovanovich.

Aristotle. 1984a. *Poetics.* In *The Complete Works,* ed. Jonathan Barnes. 2 vols., 2316–2340. Princeton: Princeton University Press.

Aristotle. 1984b. *Rhetoric.* In *The Complete Works,* ed. Jonathan Barnes. 2 vols., 2152–2269. Princeton: Princeton University Press.

Bizzell, Patricia, and Bruce Herzberg, eds. 1990. *The Rhetorical Tradition: Readings from Classical Times to the Present.* Boston: St. Martin's.

Bolter, Jay David. 1991. *Writing Space: The Computer, Hypertext, and the History of Writing.* Hillsdale, NJ: Lawrence Erlbaum.

Brown, J. R., R. Earnshaw, M. Jern, and J. Vince. 1995. *Visualization: Using Computer Graphics to Explore Data and Present Information.* New York: John Wiley.

Campbell, George. 1963. *The Philosophy of Rhetoric,* ed. Lloyd F. Bitzer. Carbondale: Southern Illinois University Press.

Frew, Jim. 1997. "Design Basics" In *Webmonkey: The Web Developers Resource.* Terra Lycos Network. Available: <http://hotwired.rycos.cam/webmonkey/html/97/05/index2a.html?tw=design> (accessed February 1, 2002).

Gorgias. 1972. "Encomium of Helen," trans. George A. Kennedy. In *The Older Sophists,* ed. Rosamond Kent Sprague, 50–54. Columbia: University of South Carolina Press.

Greenman, Catherine. 2000. "Printed Page Beats PC Screen for Reading, Study Finds" *New York Times,* 10 August, p. Gl1.

Horace. [1929] 1978. *Ars Poetica.* In *Horace: Satires, Epistles and Ars Poetica.* trans. H. Rushton Fairclough, 442–89. Cambridge: Harvard University Press.

Kress, Guntfaer. 1998, "English at the Crossroads: Rethinking Curricula of Communication in the Context of the Turn to the Visual." In *Passions, Pedagogies, and 21st Century Technologies,* ed. Gail E. Hawisher and Cynthia L. Selfe, 66–88. Logan: Utah State University Press,

Lanham, Richard. 1991. *A Handlist of Rhetorical Terms,* 2nd ed. Berkeley and Los Angeles: University of California Press.

Lanham, Richard. 1993. *The Electronic Word: Democracy, Technology, and the Arts.* Chicago: University of Chicago Press.

Lanham, Richard. 1994. "The Implications of Electronic Information for the Sociology of Knowledge." *Leonardo* 27:155–163.

Nichols, Belinda. 2000. "Writing Web Documentation." In *Webmonkey: The Web Developers Resource's,* terra Lycos Network, Available: <hotwired.lycos.com/webmonkey/00/10/indes3a.html?twoebusiness> (accessed February 1, 2002).

Shenk, David. 1999. *The End of Patience: Cautionary Notes on the Information Revolution.* Bloomington: Indiana University Press.

Stevens, Mitchell. 1998. *The Rise of the Image, the Fall of the Word.* Oxford: Oxford University Press.

Tufte, E. R. 1990. *Envisioning Information.* Cheshire, CT: Graphics Press.

Veen, Jeffrey. 1998a. "The Foundations of Web Design." In *Webmonkey: The Web Developer' s Resource.* Terra Lycos Network, Available: <http://hoonred.Ivcos.corn/webmankey/design/site_bnilding/tutorials/tuD3riaI3.html> (accessed February 1, 2002).

Veen, Jeffrey. 1998b. "Big Minds on Web Design." In *Webmonkey: The Web Developers Resource.* Terra Lycos Network. Available: <http://hotwired.lyca5.com/webmonkey/98/13/index0a.html> (accessed February 1, 2002).

Welch, Kathleen E. 1999. *Electric Rhetoric: Classical Rhetoric, Oralism, and a New Literacy.* Cambridge: MIT Press.

11
Rhetorical Literacy

Stuart Selber

Computers as Hypertextual Media, Students as Reflective Producers of Technology

> If English is to remain relevant as the subject which provides access to participation in public forms of communication, as well as remaining capable of providing understandings of and the abilities to produce culturally valued texts, then an emphasis on language alone simply will no longer do. English will need to change.
>
> —Gunther Kress,
> "'English' at the Crossroads: Rethinking Curricula of
> Communication in the Context of the Turn to the Visual"

In "Negative Spaces: From Production to Connection in Composition," Johndan Johnson-Eilola encourages teachers to reconsider what in composition studies counts as a text. Although social construction and postmodernism in composition theory provide important ways to understand texts as inherently social artifacts, he argues, teachers still tend to privilege a vision of composition practice that "remains rooted in relatively concrete, individualist notions of authorship" (17). To support his assertion, Johnson-Eilola distinguishes between writing as production versus writing as connection. In the production paradigm, which usually prevails in composition studies, teachers embrace process models and even the social turn that the discipline has taken, yet they ultimately expect students to produce a thoroughly original text, one in which their own (if intertextualized) ideas and words become the discernable anchor of the discourse. The connection paradigm, in contrast, values the negotiation of contexts, the ability to "write with fragments" (24). In this approach, writers focus on reorganizing and rerepresenting existing (and equally intertextualized) texts—their own included—in ways that are meaningful to specific audiences. An example would be a hypertext that interprets and arranges relevant discussions of copyright for teachers of writing and communication. Johnson-Eilola does not dismiss the production paradigm, but he does find adequate justification for the connection paradigm in a postindustrial culture where linked information packets, not discrete concrete goods, increasingly assume key social and economic value (see also Negroponte; Reich).

Anyone who has been overwhelmed by the sheer volume of information on the Internet knows that the metatext—a heavily linked text that connects other texts and their contexts in imaginative and meaningful ways—has become an invaluable online genre, one that requires in its construction a sophisticated knowledge of audience, purpose, context, and the various organizational schemes that hypertext can support. But the node-link mechanism in hypertext is not the only feature that challenges teachers to expand their idea of what a text (or author) is, for computer-based texts not only accommodate automatic intertextual mechanisms but also encourage writers to function as designers of spatialized literacy environments.

Indeed, the World Wide Web has quickly become a popular instructional site in which rhetoric as it has been traditionally mapped out both illuminates and fails to illuminate the process of creating online texts. Hypermedia design often confounds print-reared teachers trained solely in verbal rhetoric (S. Williams), a fact borne out by two diametrically opposed approaches to what is already becoming a conventional assignment: the Website design project. The first approach asks students to create a Website that conforms to specific technical requirements. Reminiscent of the impoverished version of functional literacy, a standard assignment directs students to design a project that includes particular site elements: for example, five paragraphs of text, one ordered list, two unordered lists, three graphics, one image map or animated image, three internal links with anchors, three external links, and two manipulations of text attributes. It is the electronic equivalent of the five-paragraph essay assignment. If students are provided a context for their project, it is surely secondary to the correct execution of interface requirements in HTML. On the other end of the spectrum, the second approach emphasizes context but largely abandons all considerations of the medium, as if the technological environment of the Internet provides a neutral space for writers. It is the equivalent of an assignment inviting students to "write about anything." In this situation, students are typically asked to create Websites that demonstrate an awareness of stock concepts in composition: the canons of rhetoric, the elements of argument (logos, pathos, ethos), the rhetorical situation (audience, purpose, occasion). Criteria for evaluation are borrowed from the expository essay, which is to say that teachers focus on such areas as expression (Is the work expressed clearly and efficiently?), organization (Is the work organized logically?), content (Is the work presented thoroughly and accurately?), and context (Is the work addressed appropriately and persuasively to a specific audience for a specific purpose?). The not altogether bad outcome of this second approach is projects that privilege academic print literacies, those that pay homage to a history of rhetoric.

That instructional approaches to the design of online texts might be imagined in antithetical ways should not come as a complete surprise in departments of English, where multiple curricular visions coexist and sometimes conflict. In 1982, James Berlin admonished teachers to understand their roles and responsibilities in epistemic terms: "In teaching writing, we are not simply offering training in a useful technical skill that is meant as a simple complement to the more important studies of other areas" ("Contemporary" 776). Rather, Berlin continued, "We are teaching a way of experiencing the world, a way of ordering and making sense of it" (776). Yet a service-oriented culture in which teachers routinely fixate on vocational preparation thrives. In such a culture, technical considerations provide a natural focal point, especially in light of the facts that employers often organize job descriptions around software skills and programs and that students often expect teachers to offer vocationally serviceable instruction. On the other hand, some teachers are so insulated into the discipline that their investments in rhetoric properly understood limit the manner in which online texts are conceptualized and constructed. As Don Byrd and Derek Owens explain, "We bring a limited number of formal vocabularies to the new technologies, and instead of exploring how these technologies might create hybrid forms, often we use them to preserve old paradigms of rhetorical construction" (49). Although rhetoric should serve as a linchpin in the education of computer-literate students, redefinitions of rhetoric can take place at the nexus of literacy and technology.

Consider speed as a feature of computer-mediated communication. Readers in electronic environments expect them to be reasonably responsive, so writers must orchestrate the temporal dimensions of online texts. That is, they must become designers of information environments that span time as well as space. But this task involves competencies that transcend the familiar confines of the English curriculum. For example, on the Web, students need a certain level of domain knowledge from computer science in order to produce texts that are optimized for performance. Such technical awareness includes a basic comprehension of the client/server architecture that underlies the Internet, because the configurations of end-user computers (clients) help determine the speed with which texts are delivered over the internet (via servers). However, a fast text is not necessarily an effective text, so whenever possible speed must be calculated in rhetorical terms, even though a rhetoric of optimization has yet to be worked out. Numerous how-to guides advise students to design Web pages that download quickly, but what does that mean? Ten seconds? Twenty seconds? Thirty seconds? I agree with Jakob Nielsen that online environments can encourage impatience, yet is it so inconceivable that in certain contexts readers might be more or less patient given the nature of their task? In addition, is it so inconceivable that speed might be manipulated to achieve certain rhetorical effects, perhaps in a multimedia transition? The plot thickens as students consider issues of speed in a highly visual medium where images consume the bulk of the bandwidth. If the aforementioned tensions were not complicated enough, students must invent and produce visual representations that negotiate the design constraints of the Internet. This activity interlaces—and redefines—technical, rhetorical, and visual literacies in ways before not imaginable.

Speed, of course, is not the only feature online that expands textual parameters, nor are technical, rhetorical, and visual literacies the only literacies that inform the creation of online texts. Lee Brasseur has characterized electronic spaces as postmodern because in those spaces writers, readers, and software designers all collaborate on some level in the formation and interpretation of online texts. Nowhere is this more evident than in open hypertexts in which technical features support the physical collapse of writer-reader distinctions, although it should be noted that traces of collaboration can be found in almost any computer-mediated environment, as Johnson-Eilola argues in his proposal for a connection paradigm in composition studies. Yet for student writers, electronic spaces are also postmodern in a curricular sense. That is, the traditional categories that organize knowledge in academia are too rigid to explain texts that cast aside rigid genre distinctions. E-mail, for instance, is a genre that mixes oral and literate practices, and so because e-mail exchanges are primarily written, the discipline provides a foundation for the study and use of e-mail. However, where any one discipline thins is in the creation and evaluation of online texts that incorporate an array of data types and structures, particularly for networked environments.

This chapter assumes that one facet of a computer multiliteracies program should prepare students to be authors of twenty-first-century texts that in some measure defy the established purview of English departments. I start with an overview of interface design, tracing broad shifts in audience, genre, and context that have helped to move this activity into the territory of writing and communication teachers. Next I sketch out the terrain of rhetorical literacy by relating four parameters from rhetoric to interface design that constitute a rhetorically literate student: persuasion, deliberation, reflection, and social action. In the final section of the chapter, I consider computers as hypertextual media, the metaphor of identity that has become inextricably bounded up with the landscape of rhetorical literacy. Overall, this chapter insists that students who are rhetorically literate will recognize the persuasive dimensions of human-computer interfaces and the deliberative and reflective aspects of interface design, all of which is not a purely technical endeavor but a form of social action.

A Preliminary Note about Interface Design

Critical work on computer literacy often concludes with a call for action, a call that lays out concrete steps students and teachers might take to respond productively to the politics of technologies. One step frequently recommended is that students should become *producers* and not just users of computer-based environments, people who can contribute in unique ways to the design of literacy technologies. In "The Politics of the Interface: Power and Its Exercise in Electronic Contact Zones," Cynthia Selfe and Richard Selfe warn that if teachers fail to prepare students of writing and communication as architects of virtual spaces, "interface design will continue to be dominated primarily by computer scientists and will lack perspectives that could be contributed by humanist scholars" (498). Their warning here is clear: Interface design should be an enterprise the discipline influences because there is so much at stake in the representations of literacy online.

Interface design, however, may be a phrase that some teachers in departments of English are only vaguely familiar with, so let me clarify my use of the phrase. In a traditional sense, interface design concerns the front-end layer of computers that users manipulate in order to accomplish tasks (e.g., the keyboard, mouse, desktop, or the features of end-user applications). But interface design involves much more than that. As Michael Heim explains,

> Interface denotes a contact point where software links the human user to computer processors. This is the mysterious, nonmaterial point where electronic signals become information. It is our interaction with software that creates an interface. Interface means the human being is wired up. Conversely, technology incorporates humans.
>
> (78)

In other words, the interface is the place where different agents and contexts are connected to each other: it is where the communicative process is centered, spreading out from that contact point between texts and users. This definition is a sensible one for humanists because it transcends the design of functional screen elements into psychological and emotional considerations and because, unlike numerous other definitions, it includes social and political dimensions in that it defines human action as an essential element or condition of interfaces.

The academic roots of interface design can be traced to human-computer interaction (HCI), an area in computer science that since the 1950s has devoted itself to improvements in the ways people relate to computer technologies. In the evolution of computer interfaces—from command-line to menu-driven to graphical—it is not difficult to spot advances that have made computers easier to operate. In his history of human-computer interaction technologies, Brad Myers organizes such advances into three categories: basic interactions, computer applications, and software tools and architectures. Advances in basic interactions have included windows, icons, and other elements that allow for the direct manipulation of software programs. Ben Shneiderman argues that direct manipulation was a major breakthrough because it allowed cryptic command language syntax to be replaced by relatively straightforward visible screen objects. As a result, computer applications are now available for a wide range of users and uses. What is more, multimedia and gesture-recognition applications accommodate users who are differently abled (Slatin, "Art of ALT"). So for software tools and architectures, the programs used to create interfaces have been dramatically improved, to the point where utilities have even been created that allow users to adjust the look and feel of interfaces, a feature which, is crucial to a more effective approach to functional literacy. Anyone who has hand-coded Web pages and then switched over to a visual HTML editor appreciates the point Myers makes about the level of control that powerful development tools can provide. This is all to say that interface design has evolved out of computer science in at least one significant sense: The audience for computer interfaces is no longer solely, or even primarily, other computer scientists.

Although his history is valuable and useful, Myers stresses the computer side of the human-computer interaction dyad and thus elides other important ways interface design surpasses computer science contexts. Beth Kolko pinpoints one omission when she argues that in networked environments like the Internet, the concept of human-computer interaction should be reimagined as human-computer-human interaction, or HCHI (versus HCI). Kolko also traces technical developments in computer systems, particularly from stand-alone to globally wired machines, but the dynamic she highlights "speaks to more than the representation of objects and environments; it is the representation of people in interactional circumstances" (220). In other words, Kolko is interested in approaches that not only acknowledge the existence of others online but see the human-human relationship as the primary relationship around which interface design practices should revolve. Computers have been networked for decades (B. Myers), yet time and again the limelight remains on individual transactions with machines, a reality that underrates the value of social perspectives in HCI.

For the purposes of this chapter, which do not really deal directly with electronic exchanges, there are other ways for humanists to identify with interface design as an expansive activity. One straightforward avenue would be to enlarge the time-honored definition of software so that it covers electronic texts that are user centered. Most discussions in computer science divide software into two categories: system software, which controls hardware devices, and application software, which allows users to solve problems or accomplish targeted tasks. System software coordinates the relationship between hardware devices and software applications. This intermediary function is rather stable and hence not easily open to reinterpretation. But application software is a different story, at least in the realm of special-purpose programs. When most people think of software, the first things that probably come to mind are word-processing, spreadsheet, database, and e-mail programs, what Marilyn Meyer and Roberta Baber would call general-purpose programs (3–4). These programs do not really fit in here because it is unrealistic to think that students will be able to create them in writing and communication courses. Although students should interrogate the biases of general-purpose programs whenever possible and remap their interfaces to make them as meaningful as possible, it is more likely that our students will produce electronic texts that function as special-purpose programs—programs that solve specific communication problems for specific users. Realistic examples include informational Websites, hypertextual bibliographies, and online documents that serve instrumental purposes. In addition to content, such texts have interfaces, often intricate ones, that must be designed by their authors, our students.

If shifts in genre and audience have turned computer science outward and toward the business of humanists, so too has the realization that human-computer interfaces incorporate not only multiple users, as Kolko notes, but their social settings as well. This can perhaps best be illustrated by an attention to usability, a subfield in HCI concerned with the assessment of interfaces at both formative and summative stages of development. Usability is a complex area, but it can be addressed here by simply contrasting stereotypical descriptions of three basic approaches: heuristic evaluations, tests, and contextual inquiries. Although each of these approaches is profitable in its own right, and especially in combination, they make different assumptions about the scope of interfaces.

As the name implies, heuristic evaluations are conducted by usability experts who analyze an interface against the best practices reported in the HCI literature. In this case, experts speak to one another about the interface, which is limited to the software program. Usability tests attempt to open up this controlled feedback loop. There are too many types of tests to mention, but typically they ask real users (or user surrogates) to perform a set of authentic tasks that can be observed and measured. Here the actions and reactions of the user-tester, which are psychological and emotional and physical, constitute human layers of the interface. Contextual inquiries flesh out the human context because they jettison the controlled conditions of tests for the contingencies of user environments. Contextual inquiries attempt to understand a software program as it gets used in actual settings of work. This requires interface designers to obtain access to user sites, see users as collaborators in the design process, understand qualitative approaches to research, and recognize the fact that social, political, and institutional factors shape user actions and interpretations in central ways. This last point is paramount, for in the richly textured sites that users inhabit, human-computer interactions are composed of various cultural and technical forces.

Interface design has historically been the bailiwick of computer scientists, principally those in the area of human-computer interaction. Yet numerous changes have pushed out the boundaries of HCI and expanded the competencies needed to create intelligible interfaces. These changes have altered the ways interface designers must think about audiences (computer users have become heterogeneous), genres (electronic texts have become software programs), and contexts (user sites have become crucial to the signification of interface objects and actions). As should be evident, the competencies such new realities call for are largely rhetorical in nature.

The Parameters of a Rhetorical Approach

Rhetorical literacy as I envision it here has not been well articulated in the discourse of English studies. Teachers of writing and communication have concentrated on the assumptions and consequences of functional literacy, if mainly to reject shortsighted educational programs that cater to private interests. But there is an identifiable disciplinary narrative, one teachers continue to write and revise in a digital age in which students must learn to take advantage of computer technologies. In fact, it is unremarkable to claim that the values and directions of critical literacy have shaped the discipline in central ways. In the context of computers, critical approaches have provided a much-needed corrective to the emphases often placed on functional skills, as well as a socially comfortable framework. However, if discussions of functional and critical literacy construct a well-established dualism, teachers have just begun to define the parameters for rhetorical literacy, which at least partially mediates this dualism because rhetorical literacy insists upon praxis—the thoughtful integration of functional and critical abilities in the design and evaluation of computer interfaces.

In some measure, Daniel Boyarski and Richard Buchanan rough out aspects of a key parameter that should speak to teachers in departments of English. These two professors of design at Carnegie Mellon University have employed rhetorical studies to better understand effective human-computer interaction. Rhetoric has become indispensable because computer design problems must always be contextualized in social terms. In their words,

> Science is concerned with laws, rules, and other forms of universal regularity. In contrast, human-computer communication is a concrete problem, always situated in a particular environment of human experience. The concreteness of communication reminds us of a truth that is sometimes forgotten when scientists and engineers attempt to project their knowledge in practical application: there is no science of the particular.
>
> (32)

Boyarski and Buchanan rightly doubt that a "deductive and predictive science of HCI" can account for the "habits, desires, preferences, and values of the different types of human beings who use computers" (32). So they turn to rhetoric for insight into what orients computer users and encourages them to act—or not act—in specific situations. Toward this end, Boyarski and Buchanan model an approach that formulates interface design as persuasive communication. "HCI is like a persuasive speech" (34). Boyarski and Buchanan argue; "The user is led into the computer system and provided with every support deemed valuable for its use. A balance of reasoning, implied voice, and feeling (haptic as well as emotional) is critical to effective human-computer communication" (34). Such an argument, It should be emphasized, is atypical in a field that has overwhelmingly relied on either system-centered or text-centered models of human-computer interaction (Johnson).

Persuasion is indeed one fundamental parameter in the terrain of rhetorical literacy, and for this reason I want to unpack the persuasive dimensions of HCI in more detail. But once interfaces have been contextualized, understood as discursive technologies, and implicated in value systems, other parameters can be conceptualized. In addition to persuasion, deliberation, reflection, and social action are parameters that illuminate the role of rhetoric. Briefly, deliberation refers to the very real likelihood that in any situation there are no perfect solutions to interface design problems. Interface design problems are ill-defined problems, and therefore require designers to continuously engage in deliberative activities. Reflection could be discussed under deliberation, but because usability is such an important area, I isolate it to extend the analysis. Social action concerns the responsibilities of interface designers, who are in a position to help enact productive societal change. These four parameters—persuasion, deliberation, reflection, social action—delimit the terrain of rhetorical literacy and suggest the qualities of a rhetorically literate student (see Figure 11.1).

Parameters of a rhetorical approach to computer literacy

Parameters	Qualities of a Rhetorically Literate Student
Persuasion	A rhetorically literate student understands that persuasion permeates interface design contexts in both implicit and explicit ways and that it always involves larger structures and forces (e.g., use contexts, ideology).
Deliberation	A rhetorically literate student understands that interface design problems are ill defined problems whose solutions are representational arguments that have been arrived at through various deliberative activities.
Reflection	A rhetorically literate student articulates his or her interface design knowledge at a conscious level and subjects their actions and practices to critical assessment.
Social action	A rhetorically literate student sees interface design as a form of social versus technical action.

Figure11.1 Parameters of a Rhetorical Approach to Computer Literacy.

Persuasion

There are a number of levels on which interfaces are persuasive, yet only the most obvious ones have been generally recognized. Evidence to substantiate this claim abounds, but I reference captology, the study of computers as persuasive technologies, because this area of inquiry has been formalized in highly visible places (see <http://captology.stanford.edu>). Captologists are interested in the planned effects of computers, so they focus exclusively on those systems that attempt to modify attitudes or behaviors in explicit ways (Fogg). Technologies on the internet that would engage captologists include Websites that promote safe sex, educate voters, and calculate the benefits of individual retirement accounts. Phillip King and Jason Tester analyze the landscape of captology and offer these conclusions about its state of affairs: persuasive technologies flourish in certain domains, namely marketing, health, safety, and environmental conservation (32); persuasive technologies primarily target teen and pre-teen children (33); the physical manifestations of persuasive technologies vary, although the Internet has encouraged the development of systems that can be accessed through personal computers (36); and the persuasive strategies interface designers use are not necessarily novel (37). These observations, notably the first two, help delineate the boundaries of captology, for as researchers in this area fondly assert in no uncertain terms, "not all technologies are persuasive; in fact, only a small subset of today's computing technologies fit this category" (Fogg 27).

But is that really true? I take issue with this assertion and the assumptions it makes about persuasion, and I suspect others will too because persuasion involves symbolic gestures that can operate implicitly and subtly. I applaud captologists for their scholarly efforts, which have advanced persuasion as a quasi-legitimate topic in HCl. Perhaps their greatest contribution has been to challenge interface designers to think about ethics (Berdichevsky and Neun-schwander), a matter that cannot be dismissed in even the most impoverished conversations about persuasion. However, the standpoint that captologists have so far adopted is not plausible enough to account for the manifold ways that computer users are influenced in technological environments. William Nothstine and Martha Cooper oppose three perspectives toward persuasion—classical, symbolist, and institutional—that elucidate the concerns I have here. My aim is not to rehearse the nuances of theoretical discussions of persuasion, but to sketch in broad strokes the limitations I see in captology.

The first perspective, the classical, is the one captologists have adopted, but I will urge teachers of writing and communication to consider the explanatory power of the other two perspectives. Nothstine and Cooper write that the "paradigm and rationale of persuasion within the classical perspective," and by classical, they mean Aristotelian, "is the intentional and explicit attempt by an individual to influence matters of civic concern by directly addressing an audience" (506). The salient point to note is that this perspective "lays primary emphasis on strategic—hence, intentional—choices among persuasive strategies" (506). If persuasion is a premeditated and rational enterprise, as captologists maintain, then the job of interface designers is to construct software elements that appeal directly to their audiences. Fair enough.

But what about the unintentional effects of interfaces, as well as the more implicit forms of persuasion? What about, for example, the wildly different worldviews of computer users that have a direct bearing on how interfaces get interpreted? This is where the symbolist perspective enters in, a perspective that "centers on the notion that all persuasion is really to a significant extent self-persuasion, involving the active participation of an audience" (509). Nothstine and Cooper elaborate: "Because all symbols represent interests and motives, from the symbolic perspective all symbols, and all acts of interpretation, are considered inherently persuasive" (509). This perspective shifts the epistemological spotlight toward computer users, whose concerns, values, and skills ultimately determine what interfaces mean, a point Boyarski and Buchanan indirectly arrive at in their formulation of interface design as persuasive speech. The symbolist stance has numerous implications, but a major one is to erode unstudied distinctions between the two basic communication functions of online texts: to inform and to persuade.

The third perspective implicates institutions and thus extends the province of persuasion further still. Nothstine and Cooper stress that the context for the institutional perspective "is the modern society, moderated by mass media, which have become both extraordinarily pervasive and interpenetrated with other institutions, all of them large, enduring social collectives empowered by custom or law to perform important social functions" (511). Although the institutional perspective lacks a fully developed and coherent theory of persuasion, it deals with four interconnected spheres: campaigns, social movements, propaganda, and ideology. The relevant sphere for interface designers is the last one, and what is at issue are the formal and informal ways everyday institutions shape the manner in which computer technologies are developed and used. The keys to the institutional perspective are cultural values, shared myths, and power structures, all of which Nothstine and Cooper underscore because ideological persuasion ordinarily goes unnoticed.

Captologists are headed in the right direction insofar as they foreground persuasion, a move that is still uncommon in HCI. But, in point of fact, computers increasingly support overt persuasive activities, especially on the Internet where the "home-page-as-an-ad prop-osition" (Singh and Dalal 98) has captured the imagination of countless interface design-ers. So, on the one hand, it is common-sensical to consider the arguments and evidence that appeal to users and how these might be incorporated into computer interfaces. Some of the most profitable work in this vein has examined credibility issues online (Tseng and Fogg), the ways in which Aristotelian notions of drama can inform interface design practices (Laurel), and the "seductive" qualities of software—those things that connect with the goals and emotions of users (Khaslavsky and Shedroff). However, the symbolist and institutional perspectives suggest the limitations of a strictly classical approach. Persuasion operates on numerous levels, and not just those in the realm of interface designers. Research tells us, for instance, that the beliefs, attitudes, and perceptions of users, which can be deeply subjective and idiosyncratic, help determine the ways, and the extent to which, technological innova-tions are utilized (Xia and Lee). Research also tells us that Hollywood (Crane), the mass media (Poster), software companies (Spender), government agencies (Birkmaier), profes-sional societies (R. Rosenberg), worksites (De Young), educational institutions (Taylor), and the like exert substantial influence on both technology designers and users.

Two boiled-down examples should make this point concrete. Kathryn Henderson studied the situated practices of engineers and discovered that their visual culture, constructed in part from historically rooted organizational and disciplinary conventions, is not always con-gruent with the assumptions embodied in computer-graphics design. Similarly, Paul Sees-ing and Mark Haselkorn emphasized that public perceptions of the year 2000 problem, the so-called millennium bug, were driven at least as much by sensational stories as by more accurate understandings of what interface designers and users needed to do to protect them-selves. In short, persuasion permeates technological contexts in both obvious and not so obvious ways, yet those who are rhetorically literate, who understand that persuasion always involves larger structures and forces, will be in a unique position to design agreeable and worthwhile interfaces.

This is not an especially difficult point to make in the classroom. Indeed, in my courses I often use a warm-up assignment that asks students to quickly analyze a Website from clas-sical, symbolist, and institutional perspectives on persuasion. Students read an excerpt from Nothstine and Cooper that outlines the basic assumptions of these three perspectives and then identify concrete instances of the different levels on which persuasion operates in HCI. I usually select a Website for analysis that would appeal to captologists, one in which the attempts at persuasion are easily discernable: My objective is not to dismiss the classical perspective, but to gradually paint a more complicated picture of persuasion for budding interface designers. So we start with overt gestures and proceed toward more subtle forms of persuasion.

For example, I often ask students to analyze a United States government Website that encourages people to become organ and tissue donors (<http://organdonor.gov>). From the classical perspective, the analysis is rather straightforward because there is clearly a deliberale attempt on the part of the government to influence the attitudes and behaviors of its citizens. As students point out, explicit attempts at persuasion can be readily found in the introduc-tory paragraphs, in the highly personal testimonials, in the downloadable resources for fam-ily members, and in other site areas. Overall, I am sure captologists would agree that this site is persuasive. But is it as effective as possible? This is the question I pose to students in order to turn the analysis in the direction of the symbolist and institutional perspectives. These perspectives invite students to think about the ways the Web site might—or might not—tap into the concerns, perspectives, and values of potential donors as well as the larger cultural narratives that influence them. Because my students are rarely (if ever) actual registered donors, they are well positioned to discuss some of the implicit modes of persuasion that might be exploited. Although my students have tended to conclude that the site is fairly well designed, they have also noted some missed opportunities, such as more direct appeals to the best of American ideals (e.g., dignity, equality of opportunity, the willingness to engage in shared sacrifice) and ties to religious traditions, which overwhelmingly endorse organ and tissue donation as a selfless act of charity. On the whole, I agree with my students that an attention to ideology could help improve the effectiveness of the Website.

Deliberation

Deliberation is a parameter that teachers of writing and communication often associate with invention, with Aristotle, and with his special topics—deliberative oratory was a branch of classical oratory that dealt with legislative matters and the future of the Athenian state—but what I want to focus on here is the complexion of interface design problems and the concomitant deliberative activities. Nevertheless, this direction should resonate with teachers because there are similarities in the situations writers and interface designers come up against. Specifically, interface designers, like writers, tackle problems that have multiple, contradictory solutions, some of which are better than others, but none of which is absolutely best. That is, in particular cases, certain solutions could be considered more efficient or effective, persuasive or logical, but such judgments are always truth claims that cannot be proven definitively in the same way a math problem can. So, in essence, solutions to interface design problems are representational arguments that have been arrived at through various deliberative activities, through choices that honor one or another value above others.

I need to expound on this point because a tremendous amount of work in HCI has a rationalistic orientation (Winograd and Flores). Horst Rittel and Melvin Webber have explicated considerable variations in the nature of disciplinary problems. According to them, there are two broad classes of problems—tame and wicked—that are fundamentally different in kind. Tame problems are well-defined problems that can be separated from their contexts and from other problems, and thus easily solved. Scientists and engineers have been frequently enlisted to iron out tame problems, examples of which are provided by Rittel and Webber:

> Consider a problem of mathematics, such as solving an equation; or the task of an organic chemist in analyzing the structure of some unknown compound; or that of the chessplayer attempting to accomplish checkmate in five moves. For each the mission is clear. It is clear, in turn, whether or not the problems have been solved.
>
> (160)

Although tame problems can be enormously complex, their complexities are largely technical in character, as are their solutions. In contrast, wicked problems are more intractable in that they inherently involve social judgments. Rittel and Webber dwell on the Fact that wicked problems do not have single solutions, only interim and imperfect resolutions. Adjustments in tax rates, changes in school curricula, procedures to reduce crime—these problems can all be understood, addressed, and resolved in countless ways because there are elusive social dimensions that muddy the causal waters. Hence the label "wicked," a term that was adopted not because wicked problems are "ethically deplorable" in the slightest, but rather because such problems are "'malignant' (in contrast to 'benign') or 'vicious' (like a circle) or 'tricky' (like a leprechaun) or 'aggressive' (like a lion, in contrast to the docility of a lamb)" (160).

Rittel and Webber discuss properties that can help teachers realize that interface design problems are more like wicked than tame problems and that although all projects have intricate technical aspects, mathematical and scientific formalisms are inadequate in socially ambiguous situations. There are too many properties to recount here, so let me limit myself to the first three, which happen to be particularly instructive. First, "There is no definitive formulation of a wicked problem" (161). That is to say, the way one understands a problem suggests, and is suggested by the possible resolutions. Different interpretations of a problem and its context naturally lead to different decisions and actions, which in turn shed light on, and shape, the problem and its definition. So one does not "first understand, then solve" (162) interface design problems; rather, one constructs interface design problems and their resolutions, which are mutually constitutive, out of discursive processes that require "incessant judgment, subjected to critical argument" (162). The challenge, of course, is to figure out who profits from the various social constructions. Second, "Wicked problems have no stopping rule" (162). This property is well-known in departments of English, for writing and communication projects have no slopping rule either. In tame problems, there are criteria or conditions that signal when acceptable solutions have been reached. Not so with wicked problems. Interface designers finalize projects because "time, or money, or patience" have run out, "not for reasons inherent in the 'logic' of the problem" (162). In the same way that papers are never done, just due, interface designs can always be revisited and reconsidered. Third, "Solutions to wicked problems are not true-or-false, but good-or-bad" (162). Although interfaces are never perfected in objective terms, their effectiveness must still be judged. Yet there are no absolutely correct or false answers to interface design problems. This means that the perspectives of judges "are likely to differ widely to accord with their group or personal interests, their special value-sets, and their ideological predilections" (163); and it means that "assessments of proposed solutions are [therefore] expressed as 'good' or 'bad' or, more likely, as 'better or worse' or 'satisfying' or 'good enough'" (163). Such an assessment context is familiar to even first-time writing instructors, who quickly learn that it is difficult, if not impossible, to assess the work of one student apart from that of another or apart from the intended context of the paper or apart from the biases of the teacher. Thus, as the first three properties of wicked problems suggest, when it comes to interface design problems a more rhetorical and less rational view of things is needed. This kind of deliberation is a hallmark of interface design.

Armed with these theoretic insights, teachers might begin to question whether or not wicked problems can be taken up with any degree of precision. Phrased another way, can interface designers work systematically? The answer to this question is definitely yes, although I should spell out my conception of systematic work, which derives from research on the deliberative practices of experienced writers. In a nutshell, researchers have learned that experienced writers have recourse to rich literacy repertoires that can steer their discursive efforts in productive directions (Flower; Rose; Sommers). These writers recognize that on some level all communication situations are unique but that ad hoc approaches disregard what has been learned from ambitious research on advanced composition, while rules-based approaches are too inelastic to illuminate the contingencies of situated contexts. So one characteristic of experienced writers is that they deliberate over patterns, structures, and frameworks in strategic ways, treating schematized practices as heuristics, not formulas, which are open to analysis and change. In the same manner, interface designers can approach their tasks with analytic flexibility and aplomb. However, this assumes they have been exposed to rhetorical approaches, which are still relatively rare in HCI. An example of one such approach is the model of persuasively effective communication articulated by Boyarski and Buchanan or their more speculative model of mediation in which human-computer interaction is characterised "as a kind of dialogue focused on the phenomenology of the system" (35). This phenomenological approach presupposes that interfaces can always be multiply interpreted; therefore, interface designers should strive to help users understand all of the possibilities in a system, not one, ostensibly true interpretation of it. Nascent approaches like these are philosophically and methodologically different from traditional approaches in HCI, and their deliberative aspects are wholly consonant with academic programs that champion humanistic perspectives.

I suggest that one way to relate the parameter of deliberation is to have students design entirely different versions of the same Website. But as a preliminary activity, students can read and respond to case studies that illustrate the ill-defined nature of interface design problems. Two cases I use repeatedly have been posted at a government Website dedicated to the improvement of communication about cancer research (<http://usability.gov>). The first case study discusses the development of CancerNet, a Website that organizes a wide array of cancer information from the National Cancer Institute (NCI) for different types of users: patients and their families, health care providers, and researchers. The second case study discusses the development of LiveHelp, an instant largely tied to its ability to support personal ways of writing, reading, and structuring texts. Vannevar Bush, writing in the 1940s in response to the limitations that he saw in print-based indexing systems designed to handle increasingly vast and varied amounts of information, considered linking to be the central quality of the memex, the precursor to computer-based hypertext systems:

> It affords an immediate step, however, to associative indexing, the basic idea of which is a provision whereby any item may be caused at will to select immediately and automatically another. This is the essential feature of the memex. The process of tying two items together is the important thing.

(103)

Assuming that the human brain works by association, Bush argued that such an ability would allow scientists and scientific communities to work more naturally, to pursue and replicate thought processes common to their day-to-day work.

Building upon Bush's description of, and assumptions informing, the memex, Ted Nelson also urged an ambitious vision of hypertext, a *docuverse* containing all the world's literature online that could be connected and reconnected in an infinite number of ways. Central to this project, and to others in the hypertext community that employ World Wide Web resources, is the notion that print-based texts often fail to encourage nonlinear writing and reading, and therefore associative thinking. Nelson provides two general arguments to support his claim: The technology of print "spoils the unity and structure of interconnection" and "forces a single sequence for all readers which may be appropriate for none" (1/14). The former observation has also been made in social thought associated with rhetorical and writing studies.

Notions of intertextuality, multivocality, and decenteredness that privilege a kind of textual openness—where every text at least always refers to other related texts and contexts—underscore Nelson's concerns about the textual closeness encouraged by the technology of print. The latter claim about print's inability to accommodate diverse, complex, and multiple audiences has been discussed, at least in spirit, in the literature on audience analysis. For example, in their overview of common approaches to structuring printed functional documents for varied audiences, Melissa Holland, Veda Charrow, and William Wright advise that writers may need to develop separate documents that correspond to the different reading goals that audiences bring to reading tasks. And textbooks in technical writing have long noted how certain segments of reports are often designed to meet the needs of different readers.

However, even if writers can seemingly find ways of successfully structuring printed texts for different audiences or creating entirely separate texts for all audiences, these tasks still assume that writers can clearly identify some unified meaning for texts and that readers of an intended audience learn, problem-solve, and make meaning in the same ways. But, as Janice Redish notes,

> Meaning does not reside in the text of a document; it exists only in the minds of communicators who produce documents and readers who use documents. Because each reader is an individual with his or her own knowledge, interests, and skills, a text can have as many meanings as it has readers.
>
> (22)

Of course, this is also true of a fixed text; much hypertext theory assumes incorrectly that fixed texts always address a monadic, static, unified reader. Still, one promise of hypertext is that it can provide users with greater and perhaps even different opportunities in which to explore information and make meaning from texts by way of personal associations: Their writing, reading, and thinking patterns are made explicit and ultimately support individual learning styles and problem-solving strategies. Applications that provide such potentially customized learning spaces exist not only in corporate sites but in educational settings as well.

Despite the pedagogical promise of mapping user associations in hypertext, applications commonly privilege links or connections generated by teachers at the (unconscious or conscious) expense of those generated by students. An example of such an instance is outlined by David Jonassen, who describes hypertext-based tools for evoking semantic networks from subject-matter experts that can be used to shape a novice learner's understanding and experience of some new information. According to Jonassen and cognitive theory, as individuals go through life they develop schemata or mental models that organize their experiences and that help them understand and interpret new knowledge domains. The more associations that individuals can form between old and new knowledge, the better their understanding of that new knowledge is likely to be. One pedagogical assumption of such a position is that learning requires individuals to instantly restructure their schemata in response to new experiences. Another is that, in the process of learning, a novice's knowledge structure (or semantic network) increasingly resembles, to varying degrees, that of an expert's ("Semantic" 144). Ultimately, according to Jonassen, "the instructional process may be thought of as the mapping of subject matter knowledge (usually that possessed by the teacher or expert) onto the learner's knowledge structure" (144).

As opposed to supporting associative ways of learning, hypertext can paradoxically become a technology that unwittingly positions students in relatively passive rather than active roles. At the extreme, one could argue that the automation of expert knowledge in virtual space, combined with the authority often attributed to hypertext (and other "technologies of progress") in Western culture, encourage computer-based instructional approaches that actually limit rather than enrich student learning. In terms of Paulo Freire's banking concept of education, "in which the students are the depositories and the teacher is the depositor" (58), novices may be simply asked to reproduce the knowledge of an expert, which can at least be partially mapped and captured in hypertext systems. In this way, interface designers and other experts contributing to these systems centrally shape a subject area and the manner in which learners approach that area pedagogically and epistemologically:

> It follows logically from the banking notion of consciousness that the educator's role is to regulate the way the world "enters into" the students. His [or her] task is to organize a process which already occurs spontaneously, to "fill" the students by making deposits of information which he [or she] considers to constitute true knowledge.
>
> (Freire 63)

Although hypertext can encourage associative work, it can also support literacy practices that discourage students from pursuing this type of personal inquiry. In fact, as Alister Cumming and Gerri Sinclair argue,

> If teachers are prompted to determine the content and uses of hypermedia, following conventional practices, it is probable that the potential uses of hypermedia will be reduced to task routines which are not, fundamentally, unlike those now occurring in classrooms using less sophisticated media.
>
> (322)

Interface designers frequently rely on the metaphor of association as evidence of user control, but such a reliance may unintentionally mask the potential of hypertext to support control by experts rather than students.

The metaphors that define and describe texts, nodes, and links, then, encourage developments and uses of hypertext along particular axes of interest, and so the realms from which these metaphors are appropriated should therefore be considered in any rhetorical approach to computer literacy. To provide students with the theoretical lenses needed for such considerations, a crucial pedagogical activity is to conceptualize metaphor as a social force, that is, as a trope that filters and delimits experience, functions as a heuristic device, and helps constitute what a culture considers knowledge. From this epistemic viewpoint, metaphors are not simply stylistic devices or reducible to literal expressions without cognitive loss. Rather, as with other forms of language, they play a central role in how meaning is made discursively. And, because terrains mapped metaphorically are marked by preferred sets of beliefs and perspectives, they represent a useful area in which to examine social influences in HCI.

There are many theories that articulate how metaphors operate semantically, but Max Black's interactive view provides an account that highlights their filtering quality. According to Black, metaphors contain two constituent halves: a principal and subsidiary subject (or what I. A. Richards has termed a *tenor* and *vehicle*). A subsidiary subject filters our experience of a principal subject by providing contexts that impose an extension or change of meaning; this occurs when individuals attempt to connect or reconcile the realms of thought summoned by what a metaphor juxtaposes (73). As I demonstrated in the previous discussion, it is not difficult to identify subsidiary subjects that commonly influence the design and use of hypertext. And they each invoke a different "system of associated commonplaces" (74) or set of cultural connections. According to Black, these connections might include "half-truths or down-right mistakes (as when a whale is classified as a fish); but the important thing for the metaphor's effectiveness is not that the commonplaces be true, but that they should be readily and freely evoked" (74). Thus, this filtering process relies on cultural myths as well as on more accurate understandings of the relationships between things juxtaposed in metaphorical constructions. This is an important point that should be stressed to students.

Although metaphors for hypertextual media may be both productive and unproductive, as well as rich in contradiction, they are always significantly influential. Through these tropes and other social, political, and ideological forces, teachers help articulate forms to hypertext, mapping a wide range of potential uses within the territory of rhetorical literacy. However, as cartographer Dennis Wood notes, the making of these maps is never innocent—certain interests are always served through representational gestures. Because the effectiveness of metaphors is a direct result of their selectivity, they work to naturalise certain cultural perspectives on how hypertext might be best designed and employed. Teachers should therefore help students become critical readers of the metaphors that are commonly used to represent human-computer interfaces, a task that requires paying attention to their "absences" as well as "presences" (Wood).

Conclusion

Rhetorical literacy concerns the design and evaluation of online environments; thus students who are rhetorically literate can effect change in technological systems. Students should not be just effective users of computers, nor should they be just informed questioners. Although these two roles are essential, neither one encourages a sufficient level of participation. In order to function most effectively as agents of change, students must also become reflective producers of technology, a role that involves a combination of functional and critical abilities. Teachers who are responsible for helping students become rhetorically literate might feel nervous about this prospect, and indeed interface design is a brave new world for many humanists. However, interface design can be understood as largely a rhetorical activity, one that includes persuasion, deliberation, reflection, social action, and an ability to analyze metaphors. The key for teachers is to be flexible in their perspectives on literacy. As Kathleen Welch argues, "electric rhetoric is not a destroyer of literacy, as is commonly thought. It is, instead, an extension of literacy, a thrilling extension," one that "will bring about many important changes and may bring about good changes" (157). These changes include not only new definitions of literacy but also different decisions about who should have a say in the design of literacy technologies. The time is ripe for students and teachers in departments of English to have their say.

References

Adelson, Belth and Troy Jordan. "The Need for Negotiation in Cooperative Work." *Sociomedia: Multimedia, Multimedia, Hypermedia, and the Social Construction of Knowledge.* Ed. Edward Barrett. Cambridge: MIT P, 1992. 469–92.

Anderson, John R. *Language, Memory, and Thought*. Hillsdale: Erlbaum, 1976.

Beck, Kent. *Extreme Programming Explained: Embrace Change*. Boston: Addison, 2000.

Berdichevsky, Daniel, and Erik Neunschwander. "Toward an Ethics of Persuasive Technology." *Communications of the ACM* 42 (1999): 51–58.

Berk, Emily. "Hypertext Glossery." *Hypertext/Hypermedia Handbook*. Ed. Emily Berk and Joseph Devlin. New York: McGraw, 1991. 535–54.

Berk, Emily and Joseph Devlin. "What is Hypertext?" *Hypertext/Hypermedia Handbook*. Ed. Emily Berk and Joseph Devlin. New York: McGraw, 1991. 535–54.

Berlin, James A. "Contemporary Composition: The Major Pedagogical Theories." *College English* 44 (1982): 765–77.

Birkmaier, Craig. "Limited Vision: The Techno-Political War to Control the Future of Digital Mass Media." *Net-Worker: The Craft of Network Computing* 1 (1997): 36–52.

Black, Max. "Metaphor." *Philosophical Perspectives on Metaphor*. Ed. Mark Johnson. Minneapolis: U of Minnesota P, 1981. 63–82.

Bolter, J. David. "Literature in the Electronic Writing Space." *Literacy Online: The Promise (and Peril) of Reading and Writing with Computers*. Ed. Myron C. Tuman. Pittsburgh: U of Pittsburgh P, 1992.

Boyarski, Daniel and Richard Buchanan. "Exploring the Rhetoric of HCI." *Interactions* Apr. 1994: 24–35.

Boyle, Craig and Kelly Ratliff. "A Survey and Classification of Hypertext Document Systems." *IEEE Transactions on Professional Communication* 35 (1992): 98–111.

Bush, Vannevar. "As We May Think." *Atlantic Monthly* 176. 1 (1945): 641–649.

Byrd, Don and Derek Owens. "Writing in the Hivemind." *Literacy Theory in the Age of the Internet*. Ed. Todd Taylor and Irene Ward. New York: Columbia UP, 1998. 47–58.

Capron, H. L. *Computers: Tools for an Information Age*. Redwood: Benjamin, 1990.

Conklin, Jeff. "Hypertext: An Introduction and Survey." *IEEEComputer* Sept 1987: 17–41.

Crane, David. "In Medas Race: Filmic Representations, Networked Communication, and Racial Intermediation." *Race in Cyberspace*. Ed. Lisa Nakamura, Beth E. Kolko, and Gilbert B. Rodman. New York: Routledge, 2000. 87–115.

Cummin, Alister, and Gerri Sinclair. "Conceptualizing Hypermedia Curricula for Literary Studies in Schools." *Hypermedia and Literary Studies*. Ed. Paul Delany and George P. Landow. Cambridge: MIT P. 1990. 315–28.

Cushman, Ellen. "The Rhetorician as an Agent of Social Change." *College Composition and Communication* 47 (1996): 7–28.

De Young, Laura. "Organizational Support for Software Design." *Bringing Design to Software*. Ed. Terry Winograd. New York: ACM, 1996. 253–67.

Flower, Linda. *The Construction of Negotiated Meaning: A Social Cognitive Theory of Writing*. Carbondale: Southern Illinois UP, 1994.

Fogg, B. J. "Persuasive Technologies." *Communications of the ACM* 42 (1999): 27–29.

Fox, Edward, Qian Chen, and Robert France. "Integrating Search and Retrieval with Hypertext." *Hypertext/Hypermedia Handbook*. Ed. Emily Berk and Joseph Devlin. New York: McGraw, 1991. 329–55.

Friere, Paolo. *Pedagogy of the Oppressed*. New York: Herder, 1970.

Glushko, Robert J. "Seven Ways to Make a Hypertext Project Fail." *Technical Communication* 39 (1992): 226–30.

Heim, Michael. *The Metaphysics of Virtual Reality*. New York: Oxford UP, 1993.

Henderson, Kathryn. "The Visual Culture of Engineers." *The Cultures of Computing*. Ed. Susan Leigh Star. Cambridge: Blackwell, 1995. 196–218.

Hillocks, George. *Teaching Writing as Reflective Practice*. New York: Teachers College P, 1995.

Holland, Melissa, Veda R. Charrow, and William W. Wright. "How Can Technical Writers Write Effectively for Several Audiences at Once?" *Solving Problems in Technical Writing*. Ed. Lynn Beene and Peter White: New York: Oxford UP 1988, 27–55.

Horn, Robert E. *Mapping Hypertext: Analysis, Linkage, and Display of Knowledge for the Next Generation of On-Line Text and Graphics*. Lexington: Lexington Inst, 1989.

Horton, William. "Let's Do Away with Manuals … Before They Do Away With Us." *Technical Communication* 40 (1993): 26–34.

Irish, Peggy M., and Randall H. Trigg. "Supporting Collaboration in Hypermedia: Issues and Experiences." *The Society of Text: Hypertext, Hypermedia, and the Social Construction of Knowledge*. Ed. Edward Barrett. Cambridge: MIT P, 1989. 93–106.

Johnson, Jeff and Evelyn Pine. "Toward a Guide to Social Action for Computer Professionals." *SIGCHI Bulletin* 25 (1993): 23–27.

Johnson, Robert R. *User-Centered Technology: A Rhetorical Theory for Computers and Other Mundane Artifacts*. Albany: State U of New York P, 1998.

Johnson-Eilola, Johndan. "Hypertext and Print Culture: Some Possible Geometries for Cyberspace." Conference on College Composition and Communication Convention. Sheraton Harbor Island Hotel, San Diego. 1–3 Apr. 1993.

——. "Negative Spaces: From Production to Connection in Composition." *Literacy Theory in the Age of the Internet*. Ed. Todd Taylor and Irene Ward. New York: Columbia UP, 1998. 17–33.

Jonassen, David H. "Semantic Network Elicitation: Tools for Structuring Hypertext." *Hypertext: State of the Art*. Ed. Ray McAleese and Catherine Green. Oxford Intellect, 1990. 142–52.

Khaslavsky, Julie and Nathan Shedroff. "Understanding the Seductive Experience." *Communications of the ACM* 42 (1999): 45–49.

King, Philip and Jason Tester. "The Landscape of Persuasive Technologies." *Communications of the ACM* 42 (1999): 31–38.

Kolko, Beth. "Erasing @race: Going White in the (Inter)face." *Race in Cyberspace.* Ed. Lisa Nakamura, Beth Kolko, and Gilbert B. Rodman. New York: Routledge, 2000. 213–232.

Kolosseus, Beverly, Dan Bauer, and Stephen A. Bernhardt. "From Writer to Designer: Modeling Composing Processes in a Hypertext Environment." *Technical Communication Quarterly* 4 (1995): 79–93.

Kottkamp, Robert B. "Means for Facilitating Reflection." *Education and Urban Society* 22 (1990): 182–203.

Kress, Gunther. "'English' at the Crossroads: Rethinking Curricula of Communication in the Context of the Turn to the Visual." *Passions, Pedagogies, and Twenty-First Century Technologies.* Ed. Gail E. Hawisher and Cynthia L. Selfe. Logan: Utah State UP and NCTE, 1999. 66–88.

Landow, George and Paul Delany. "Hypertext, Hypermedia, and Literary Studies: The State of the Art." *Hypermedia and Literary Studies.* Ed. George P. Landow and Paul Delany. Cambridge: MIT P, 1991. 3–50.

Liu, Yameng. "Rhetoric and Reflexivity." *Philosophy and Rhetoric* 28 (1995): 333–49.

Markus, M. Lynne and Niels Bjorn-Anderson. "Power over Users: Its Exercise by System Professionals." *Communication of the ACM* 30 (1987): 498–504.

McLuhan, Marshall. *Understanding Media: The Extensions of Man.* New York: Penguin, 1964.

Meyer, Marilyn and Roberta Baber. *Computers in Your Future.* Indianpolis: Que, 1997.

Moulthrop, Stuart. "The Politics of Hypertext." *Evolving Perspectives on Computers and Composition Studies: Questions of the 1990s.* Ed. Gail E. Hawisher and Cynthia L. Selfe. Urbana: NCTE and Computers and Composition, 1991. 253–71.

Myers, Brad A. "A Brief History of Human-Computer Interaction Technology" *Communication* 2 (1998): 44–54.

Negroponte, Nicholas. *Being Digital.* New York: Knopf, 1995.

Nelson, Theodor Holm. *Literary Machines* 90.1. Sausalito: Mindful, 1990.

Nielsen, Jacob. "Be Succinct!" *Alertbox.* 15 Mar. 1997. 22 Feb 2002 <http://www.userit.com/alertbox/9703b.html>

Nothstine, William L. and Martha Cooper. "Persuasion." *Encyclopedia of Rhetoric and Composition: Communication from Ancient Times to the Information Age.* Ed. Theresa Enos. New York: Garland, 1996. 505–12.

Parunak, H. Van Dyke. "Ordering the Information Graph." *Hypertext/Hypermedia Handbook.* Ed. Emily Berk and Joseph Devlin. New York: McGraw, 1991. 299–325.

Poster, Mark. *The Second Media Age.* Cambridge: Polity, 1995.

Press, Larry. "Before the Altair: The History of Personal Computing." *Communications of the ACM* 36 (1993): 27–33.

Redish, Janice C. "Understanding Readers." *Techniques for Technical Communicators.* Ed. Carol M. Barnum and Saul Carliner. New York: MacMillan, 1993. 14–41.

Reich, Robert B. *The Work of Nations: Preparing Ourselves for Twenty-First Century Capitalism.* New York: Vintage, 1992.

Richards, I. A. *The Philosophy of Rhetoric.* New York: Oxford UP, 1936.

Rittel, Horst W. and Melvin M. Webber. "Dilemmas in a General Theory of Planning." *Policy Sciences* 4 (1973): 155–69.

Rose, Mike. *Writer's Block: The Cognitive Dimension.* Carbondale: Southern Illinois UP, 1984.

Rosenberg, Martin. "Contingency, Liberation, and the Seduction of Geometry: Hypertext as an Avant-Garde Medium." *Performations* 2.3 (1992): 1–12.

Rosenberg, Richard S. "Beyond the Code of Ethics: The Responsibility of Professional Societies." *ACM Proceedings of the Ethics and Social Impact Component on Shaping Policy in the Information Age.* Washington, DC, 10–12 May 1998. New York: ACM, 1998. 18–25.

Schoen, Donald. *The Reflective Practitioner: How Professionals Think in Action.* New York: Basic, 1983.

Seesing, Paul R. and Mark P. Haselkorn. "Communicating Technology Risk to the Public: The Year 2000 Example." *Proceedings of the 1998 IEEE Professional Communication Conference,* Quebec City, 23–25 September 1998. Piscataway: IEEE, 1998. 349–59.

Saussure, Ferdinand de. *Course in General Linguistics.* New York: McGraw, 1959.

Selber, Stuart A., Dan McGavin, William Klein, and Johndan Johnson-Eilola. "Key Issues in Hypertext-Supported Collaborative Writing." *Nonacademic Writing: Social Theory and Technology.* Ed. Ann Hill Duin and Craig J. Hansen. Hillsdale: Erlbaum, 1996. 257–80.

Selfe, Cynthia L. and Richard J. Selfe. "The Politics of the Interface: Power and Its Exercise in Electronic Contact Zones." *College Composition and Communication* 45 (1994): 480–504.

Shirk, Henrietta Nickels. "Technical Writing's Roots in Computer Science: The Evolution from Technician to Technical Writers." *Journal of Technical Writing and Communication* 18 (1988): 305–23.

Shneiderman, Ben. *Designing the User Interface: Strategies for Effective Human-Computer Interaction.* Reading: Addison, 1987.

Singh, Surendra N. and Nikunj P. Dalal. "Web Home Pages as Advertisements." *Communications of the ACM* 42 (1999): 91–98.

Slatin, John M. "The Art of ALT: Toward a More Accessible Web." *Computers and Composition* 18 (2001): 73–81.

Smyth, John. "Developing and Sustaining Critical Reflection in Teacher Education." *Journal of Teacher Education* 40 (1989): 2–9.

Sommers, Nancy. "Revision Strategies of Student Writers and Experienced Adult Writers." *College Composition and Communication* 31 (1980): 378–88.

Spender, Dale. *Nattering on the Net: Women, Power, and Cyberspace.* North Melbourne: Spinifex, 1995.

Taylor, Todd. "The Persistence of Authority: Coercing the Student Body." *Literacy Theory in the Age of the Internet.* Ed. Todd Taylor and Irene Ward. New York: Columbia UP, 1998. 109–21.

Tseng, Shawn and B. J. Fogg. "Credibility and Computing Technology." *Communications of the ACM* 42 (1999): 39–44.

Tuman, Myron C. *Word Perfect: Literacy in the Computer Age.* Pittsburgh: U of Pittsburgh P. 1992.

Weiser, Mark. "The Computer for the Twenty-First Century." *Scientific American* July 1991: 94–104.

Welch, Kathleen E. *Electric Rhetoric: Classical Rhetoric, Oralism, and a New Literacy.* Cambridge: MIT P, 1999.

Williams, Sean D. "Part 1: Thinking out of the Pro-Verbal Box." *Computers and Composition* 18 (2001): 21–32.

Winograd, Terry and Fernando Flores. *Understanding Computers and Cognition: A New Foundations for Design.* Reading: Addison, 1986.

Wood, Dennis. *The Power of Maps.* New York: Guilford, 1992.

Xia, Weidong and Gwanhoo Lee. "The Influence of Persuasion, Training, and Experience on User Perceptions and Acceptance of IT Innovations." *Proceedings of the Twenty-First ACM International Conference on Information Systems, Brisbane,* 10–13 December 2000. New York: ACM, 2000. 371–84.

Yancey, Kathleen Blake. *Reflection in the Writing Classroom.* Logan: Utah State UP, 1998.

12
Infrastructure and Composing
The When *of New-Media Writing*

Dànielle Nicole DeVoss, Ellen Cushman, and Jeffrey T. Grabill

New-media writing exerts pressure in ways that writing instruction typically has not. In this article, we map the infrastructural dynamics that support—or disrupt—new-media writing instruction, drawing from a multimedia writing course taught at our institution. An infrastructural framework provides a robust tool for writing teachers to navigate and negotiate the institutional complexities that shape new-media writing and offers composers a path through which to navigate the systems within and across which they work. Further, an infrastructural framework focused on the *when* of new-media composing creates space for reflection and change within institutional structures and networks.

Rebecca Leibing's digital composition "Sunoco" (Figure 12.1)—available as a QuickTime movie at the URL below—was created in the beginning weeks of a multimedia writing course; her composition is a digital movie composed from a rather traditional personal narrative essay about her first job at a gas station. Rebecca drew and colored a collection of

Figure 12.1 From "Sunoco," by Rebecca Leibing, a Digital Composition Available at http://www.wide.msu.edu/ccc.

still images, set them to a digital recording of her reading her paper, and contextualized the combination of images and voice with digital music clips. These media were then tracked together, with the addition of transitions and image pans, using digital video software. To create this piece, she used equipment (software and hardware), technical support, instruction, and different media choices—framed by decisions about color, texture, appeal, and other variables—to fuse what have traditionally been discrete media. Rebecca's composition could be remarked upon as a product in itself—it is funny, smart, and well-written. Certainly, many in the field of composition and rhetoric would choose to focus the analytical lens on this product of new media and for good reasons. However, what is remarkable to us about Rebecca's piece is the story behind its composition, which is revealing of a moment in time, space, institutional relations, and seemingly insurmountable obstacles.

Many researchers pay attention to the what and why of new media without paying attention to the *when* of new-media composing. For example, scholars have done important work that examines the blend of visual and verbal elements in the surfaces and structures of new-media compositions (e.g., Allen; Anson; Bernhardt, "Designing" and "Shape"; DeWitt; George; Handa; Hocks, "Feminist" and "Understanding"; Hocks and Kendrick; Kress "English" and "Visual"; Markel; Ruszkiewicz; Sirc; Ulmer; Wysocki and Johnson-Eilola).[1] All of these scholars have in common their focus on new-media writing products, an important topic to be sure. However, few offer frameworks for understanding the spaces for and practices of composing in contemporary, technology-mediated ways. To this growing conversation about new-media composing, we would like to add a focus on the institutional and political arrangements that—typically invisibly—allow these new-media products to emerge in the first place.

In this essay we focus on the institutional infrastructures and cultural contexts necessary to support teaching students to compose with new media.[2] These often invisible structures make possible and limit, shape and constrain, influence and penetrate all acts of composing new media in writing classes. Although these structural aspects of teaching new media might easily be dismissed as mere inconvenience when they break down or rupture entirely, they are, in fact, deeply embedded in the acts of digital-media composing. We argue that infrastructures are absolutely necessary for writing teachers and their students to understand if we hope to enact the possibilities offered by new-media composing.

Writing within digital spaces occurs within a matrix of local and more global policies, standards, and practices. These variables often emerge as visible and at times invisible statements about what types of work are possible and valuable (encoded, often, in curricula, assessment guidelines, standards, and policies). Some of these issues need the attention of teachers and of program administrators, but we would be miseducating student writers if we didn't teach them that these issues—that which we can too easily dismiss as "constraints"—are indeed deeply embedded in the decision-making processes of writing. If students are to be effective and critical new-media composers, they should be equipped with ways in which they can consider and push at practices and standards in strategic ways.

While the analytical lens that focuses on the *when* of new media keeps in focus the materiality of such media (e.g., the software, wires, and machines), it also brings to light the often invisible issues of policy, definition, and ideology. Indeed, the concept of infrastructure itself demands an integrative analysis of these visible and invisible issues; separations of these issues cannot persist if writing teachers are truly interested in making an impact in both how new media develop and how pedagogies and theories of multimedia composing come into being. We know many people, including ourselves, who have been prevented from working in certain ways as teachers and writers because it was infrastructurally impossible in a given context. Not intellectually impossible. Not even strictly technologically impossible. Something deeper.

Here we adapt Susan Leigh Star and Karen Ruhleder's definition of infrastructure to help us make visible the story behind Rebecca's digital composition. This infrastructural framework allows us to account for any number of "breakdowns" (cognitive, rhetorical, procedural, technical, and so on), to establish the importance of communities of practice, and perhaps most important of all, to focus our attention on the presence and operations of standards and classifications, which lean heavily on all writing practices—and on new-media practices in particular. An infrastructural analysis of the spaces and practices of composing new media gets at some basic and powerful issues with respect to new-media composing: the ways in which new-media writing becomes defined, shaped, accepted, rejected, or some combination of all of these (and more); who gets to do new media; who gets to learn it, where, and how; and what values get attached to this work (and to its writers and audiences). In these ways, we will show that analyzing the when of new-media composing is as important as analyzing the what and why of new-media composing.

Writing in Digital Environments, Writing with Multiple Sign Systems

We are interested in ways of understanding the contexts of new-media writing because our own experiences suggest that writing with multiple sign systems within technology-mediated environments pushes on systems and established ways of working with a pressure that other ways of writing don't exert.[3] Many of the writing teachers we work with indicate an interest in developing teaching practices that better attend to visual rhetorics and multimedia writing, but these teachers also voice the concern that such teaching is impossible because of the institutional resources currently available to them. This recognition of institutional and technological limitations suggests the need for analytical tools that might help us account for the contexts of new-media writing in ways that enable students and teachers to achieve what they can imagine in and for the composition classroom. But how best to account for the contexts of new-media composing?

Although previous scholars have not adopted the specific language we have here (i.e., "infrastructure"), computers and writing researchers have long paid attention to issues of digital writing environments. Teachers of writing in computer-mediated spaces have been attentive to the spaces in which they teach, and to the physical and digital spaces in which students work; for twenty years, composition scholars have published on possibilities and complications related to teaching in computer-mediated settings (for example, in technology classrooms: Bernhardt, "Designing" and "Shape"; Britton and Glynn; Dinan, Gagnon, and Taylor; Gruber; Haas; Kent-Drury; Moran, "Access" and "From"; Palmquist; Palmquist, Kiefer, Hartvigsen, and Godlew; Selfe, *Creating*, "Creating," and "Technology"; with/in electronic spaces like e-mail, bulletin board systems, and MOOs/MUDs: Cooper; Cooper and Selfe; Grigar; Holdstein; Kinkead; LeCourt; Moran and Hawisher; Rouzie; Sanchez; Spooner and Yancey; Thompson; and via distance- and online-education spaces: Buckley; Harris and Wambeam; Webb Peterson and Savenye).

Compositionists have also attended to issues of agency and subjectivity in regard to digital media and online spaces. For instance, Stephen Knadler, Heidi McKee, Teresa Redd, Elaine Richardson, Todd Taylor, and others have addressed issues of race and difference in digital spaces, both from an instructor standpoint and from a student perspective. A strong thread of composition scholarship has explored issues of gender in digital space, attending to the male-centered context of computing and to possible feminist interventions in electronic spaces (e.g., Brady Aschauer; Hocks, "Feminist"; Pagnucci and Mauriello; Rickly; L. Sullivan; Takayoshi, "Building" and "Complicated"; Takayoshi, Huot, and Huot; Webb; Wolfe). Access—an issue that often manifests itself at intersections of gender, class, and race—has also been addressed as an issue crucial to computers and composition scholarship. Jeffrey Grabill and Alison Regan and John Zuern have targeted issues of access by exploring the movement of computer-mediated composition outside of the classroom and into communities. Lester Faigley, Joseph Janangelo, Charles Moran, and Cynthia Selfe have studied issues of access and traced access across cultural, social, and historical trends.

New technologies have raised questions not only about manifestations of race and gender in the "bodiless" realm of cyberspace and about the real issues of access to machines and networks, but new technologies have also raised speculation about emergent and electronic literacy practices (see, for example, Bolter; Burbules; Heba; Holdstein and Selfe; Joyce; Selfe, "Technology and Literacy"; Tuman). Closely related is scholarship analyzing how specific interfaces potentially shape writing practices and processes (e.g., Condon; Curtis; "Forum"; LeBlanc; McGee and Ericsson; Selfe and Selfe; P. Sullivan; Vernon; Wysocki, "Impossibly" and "Monitoring"; Wysocki and Jasken); certainly, text messaging, blogs, and wikis are shaping research paths related to interfaces of/for writing. Framing all this work are examinations of institutional and political dynamics as they affect writing classrooms via, for example, policies, guidelines, and intellectual property laws (Gurak and Johnson-Eilola; Howard; Johnson-Eilola, "Living"; Kalmbach; Lang, Walker, and Dorwick; Porter, "Liberal" and *Rhetorical Ethics;* Porter, Sullivan, Blythe, Grabill, and Miles; CCCC Committee). These contributions are significant, and help situate composition scholars within emerging—and existing—issues of visual and digital rhetorics and possibilities for new-media production, or at least analysis. Specifically, these contributions help us to better understand the ways that composition researchers have made sense of past and current integrations of technology and writing.

Although the composition scholars mentioned above have noted the increasing prominence given to visual communication, online writing, and digital spaces, and although researchers are paying more attention to the blend of visual and verbal elements, few offer frameworks for understanding the spaces for and practices of composing new media. Issues such as the standards and policies of network use and the institutional locations of new-media curricula still remain invisible—and these issues are integral to understanding and enabling new-media composing. Here we attempt to make visible these and some of the other dynamics of new-media writing. An infrastructural framework helps not only to reveal these dynamics and their consequences, but also to identify access points for discursive agency and change-making within institutions. As an analytical framework, then, an understanding of infrastructure makes strange the taken-for-granted, often invisible, institutional structures implicit in the teaching of new-media composing. In the remainder of the essay, we'll outline this framework and apply it to the new-media writing class in which Rebecca's piece was produced. We demonstrate the utility of an infrastructural framework for writing teachers who hope to uncover the deeply embedded institutional, cultural, and political issues involved in teaching new media.

Infrastructure as Analytical Tool

When teachers express frustration with their ability to teach new-media writing, they often point toward specific and often physical infrastructural impediments—computers, software, and networks. An infrastructure of a computer lab certainly would include its server and network system, the machines and their monitors, and the wiring within the room. However, there is something more complex going on in any composing context—both in terms of what frustrates teachers and in terms of how we understand infrastructure itself. If we expand our notion of infrastructure, we would include the policies and standards that regulate the uses of the room. We would also include systems of support for the work that takes place in the room, and the budget and funding (and related decisions) for the material objects in the room. We would include structures for surveillance within the room and within the spaces to which the machines allow access (e.g., the security cameras found in many of the computer labs on our campus; the student tracking function in course-management software that allows teachers to see how often students have accessed a course site and what areas of the course site they have visited). We would consider the tasks and practices that occur within the room—how the material objects are used, to what end, and for what audiences. Our use of the term "infrastructure" reflects the work of Star and Ruhleder, who characterize infrastructure in the following way:

- *Embeddedness.* Infrastructure is "sunk" into, inside of, other structures, social arrangements and technologies;
- *Transparency.* Infrastructure is transparent to use, in the sense that it does not have to be reinvented each time or assembled for each task, but it invisibly supports those tasks;
- *Reach or scope.* This may be either spatial or temporal—infrastructure has reach beyond a single event or one-site practice;
- *Learned as part of membership.* The taken-for-grantedness of artifacts and organizational arrangements is a *sine qua non* of membership in a community of practice [...]. Strangers and outsiders encounter infrastructure as a target object to be learned about. New participants acquire a naturalized familiarity with its objects as they become members;
- *Links with conventions of practice.* Infrastructure both shapes and is shaped by the conventions of a community of practice; e.g., the ways that cycles of day-night work are affected by and affect electrical power rates and needs. Generations of typists have learned the QWERTY keyboard; its limitations are inherited by the computer keyboard and thence by the design of today's computer furniture [...];
- *Embodiment of standards.* Modified by scope and often by conflicting conventions,

infrastructure takes on transparency by plugging into other infrastructures and tools in a standardized fashion;

- *Built on an installed base.* Infrastructure does not grow *de novo*; it wrestles with the "inertia of the installed base" and inherits strengths and limitations from that base [...];
- *Becomes visible upon breakdown.* The normally invisible quality of working infrastructure becomes visible when it breaks; the server is down, the bridge washes out, there is a power blackout. Even when there are back-up mechanisms or procedures, their existence further highlights the now-visible infrastructure. (113)

If we think of the composing infrastructure on our own campus in these terms, we come up with the following list of infrastructural components:

- computer networks
- network configurations
- operating systems, computer programs, interfaces, and their interrelatedness
- network, server, and storage access rights and privileges
- courses and curricula
- the existence and availability of computer classrooms
- decision-making processes and procedures for who gets access to computer classrooms
- the design and arrangement of computer classrooms
- time periods of classes
- availability of faculty, students, and spaces outside of set and scheduled class times
- writing classifications and standards (e.g., what is writing; what is good writing)
- metaphors of computer programs; metaphors people use to describe programs; metaphors people use to describe their composing processes
- purposes and uses of new-media work
- audiences for new-media work, both inside and outside the university

This list is far from exhaustive, but provides a sense, at least, of the sorts of elements and issues an infrastructural framework can make visible. But there is much more to an infrastructure than what is material or technological. Our list includes standards and classifications—most powerfully what counts as writing, what is permissible in a writing class, and what makes for "good" writing. Infrastructure also entails decision-making processes and the values and power relationships enacted by those processes, and infrastructure is thoroughly penetrated by issues of culture and identity (in ways that space limits prevent us from exploring here). *All* writing activities are contextualized by certain infrastructures; our aim here is to argue for the importance of understanding the distinctive infrastructural dynamics that new-media composing creates as well as the ways that such composing is dependent on infrastructural dynamics that may not be configured to accommodate traditional writing activities.

As an analytical tool, Star and Ruhleder's characteristics of infrastructure have significant scope and heuristic value. However, we don't want the focus of this discussion merely to settle on issues of defining an infrastructure. The most useful question, as Star and Ruhleder assert, may not be *what* an infrastructure is but rather *when* it is. Working from a piece by Yrjö Engeström that asks "When is a tool?" Star and Ruhleder argue that "infrastructure is something that emerges for people in practice, connected to activities and structures" (112). In other words, a tool is not an artifact with "pre-given attributes frozen in time," but rather is given meaning *as* a tool by specific users working on particular problems in specific situations (see also Feenberg; Johnson[Latour]); so too does the meaning and value of an infrastructure emerge. That is, an infrastructure is more than material, is never static, and is always emerging. We want to suggest that writing programs will never adequately come to terms with how to understand and teach new-media composing unless we can come to a productive and activist understanding of infrastructure. For students, understanding infrastructural constraints on new-media composing offers important grounding in the kinds of decisions that influence the possibilities, processes, and final deliverables of their digital writing. Such an understanding will allow students and professors to anticipate and participate in a number of institutional processes that shape infrastructure and so shape how we teach new-media composing.

In what follows, taking Ellen's multimedia writing class as a source of data, we use the notion of infrastructure as a heuristic for reading our local contexts. We focus on when new-media infrastructures emerge and what the dynamics of infrastructure mean for composing in those contexts. Thus, we demonstrate how writing instructors might apply this framework to their classroom and institutional contexts. The material we use here to situate our explanations of an infrastructural approach to writing was collected in a multimedia writing class taught at Michigan State University (MSU). Interested in studying new-media composing processes and the teaching of multimedia writing, Ellen collected student work and also saved the many correspondences to administrators and computing services specialists, the class notes generated on the Blackboard space used for the course, and archives of virtual chats that took place in class.[4] These materials will be excerpted throughout to help us address the larger questions we ponder in this manuscript: What material, technical, discursive, institutional, and cultural conditions prohibit and enable writing with multiple media?[5] How does an infrastructural approach offer a lens through which we can better interpret and understand the multiple conditions at play in our writing classrooms? How can an infrastructural interpretation support and enable new-media writing?

File Management and Standards: Thinking About Products Before Processes

Ellen's multimedia writing class allows us to see the structures, technologies, and decisions that teachers and writers navigate. Questions at the forefront of writing with multiple media emerge as soon as the software launches and the interface expands, questions that force writers to consider the material and rhetorical realities in which they will compose and through which their final products will be produced and viewed. For example, before digital video software opens to an interface for composing, a window prompts composers for their project settings. As with writing, the composer must know something about what the final product will be *before* beginning the process. However, in the case of composing a multimedia video product, the writer must also know what kinds of files will be needed and created to meet the demands of the final product—including types of files and media (e.g., chunks of text, images) and specific forms of files and media (e.g., a voice file saved as a .wav, images saved as .jpgs).

The writer, in the case of fairly robust video software like Adobe Premiere, must also have a sense of how the software is installed and runs on the computer and on the networks within which the user composes. Questions the composer must address include: What should the final product look like on screen (e.g., size of viewers' monitors and viewing windows)? What level of sound quality is expected (e.g., mono, stereo, 8 or 16 bits)? How is this product to be delivered (e.g., VHS, CD, online)? How much memory is available and where in the classroom? How much memory is available on the audience's computers? How will the audience members access this project? These questions—and this is but a very short list of the initial considerations a composer of new media must address—work at both the material and the rhetorical level in ways quite different than traditional writing classrooms might (that is, those that rely primarily on text and paper). Addressing these questions before composing even begins not only affects the writing processes of students, but also deeply affects the set-up and delivery of instruction.

In the case of Ellen's multimedia writing class, answers to these questions began with the file-management system on our campus. File-management issues arose before students even entered the class on the first day, and brought to the forefront institutional limitations that influenced the type, quality, and extent of learning that could take place in the class. The general structure of instructional computing on campus works somewhat like this: The campus computing protocol is to load all software from a main server when a user logs on to a campus computer; the rationale for this is related mainly to security and virus-protection measures. Thus little software is installed on and loaded from the local drives of computers—each time students launch a software application, they do so from a remote server. Writing with multiple media and writing within robust multimedia applications like Premiere or Macromedia Director violates this common network structure in various ways. First, because digital video software does not work well when virtual memory is engaged—and virtual memory is always engaged at MSU because individual users do not have the access required to change the control panel settings on the computers—the software will crash. Also, when a student logs off of a machine—or if a machine happens to crash and then reboot while the student is working—all of the student's preview files are lost because the files are stored in a folder on the local disk, which is erased from the computer each time a user logs off or the machine restarts. Although the student is relying upon a remotely networked software application, the work students create is actually stored locally (and thus wiped out—deleted—upon restart).

Long before the semester began, Ellen realized that this network structure would influence the work for her class. She thus requested a meeting with the staff member who acts as liaison between instructors and the centralized campus computing facilities. During the meeting, Ellen described her needs for the class and the types of projects students would be composing during the semester (three in all, becoming sequentially more complex, with a final product of a digital portfolio on CD). She described the kinds of files associated with student projects: the project file (command file); the tracked files (e.g., images, voiceovers, music); the preview files (compressed motion and audio files created when the command file is executed and stored locally); and the final project, typically a 200- to 300-megabyte .mov file. The immediate response of the liaison upon hearing these file types, sizes, and needs was that students absolutely could not write to the local drive of campus machines. She followed up this statement by noting that Ellen would simply have to require fewer assignments and have students produce smaller, nonvideo, projects. She made suggestions that included students working with still rather than motion images. When Ellen balked at having a computer specialist demand certain teaching methods of her, the liaison argued that MSU computing policy clearly states that students cannot write to the local hard drives because there would be no security—anyone could erase their work. It was at this point in the conversation that Ellen realized that the issue wasn't a memory problem at all, but a *policy* problem. The equipment was available for use, but the computers were to be kept clean and safe from the apparently untrustworthy students. At the end of the meeting, Ellen was told that students would absolutely have to save their work to the campus server, that under no circumstances would students be able to save their work to the local computers, and that Ellen would be lucky to get an additional gigabyte of storage space for student projects.

In Ellen's class, the standards for file management established by the university and standards for system operation within the software itself were at odds. The university's standard operating procedure prohibited allowing students to save to local hard disks, but the software standards demanded that files be saved to local hard disks to facilitate the retrieval and compression process among the project file, dependent files, and preview files.

We approach standards from two directions: First, standards can be thought of as the typical approaches that people take as they perform a task; there are "standard" or conventional ways of accessing a network, launching software, and saving files. Second, standards can be thought of as Bowker and Star do: as procedures for how do to things (234). Although these two definitions might seem much the same, and although they do orbit around each other, they are, in fact, quite different. For example, a procedure might dictate an acceptable or appropriate use (e.g., via an "acceptable-use policy" that regulates a particular network); however, the conventions of practice that emerge among users as they work within the system might differ from and even work against established procedures. Users, in this case writers, invent standards as much as they follow them. Clearly, networks—technological and otherwise—are complex systems of interconnected human beings and machines, and because of the complexity of networks, normally transparent issues (e.g., file management, the operation of programs, and so on) become visible when different standards of operation compete.

On our campus, acting through/with/against standards means attending to the local standards of the centralized computer system and its multiple paths of decision-making power and practices, and paying attention to the larger network standards of state-based bodies (i.e., Michnet, the statewide network service upon which MSU's networks are built) and national organizations (the CCCC Position Statement on Teaching, Learning, and Assessing Writing in Digital Environments). Too often, because of institutional and disciplinary trends, writing teachers are absent from the histories and development of standards. On campuses where technology budgets are limited, writing is still often seen as a low-technology subject, and writing classes as low-technology spaces. Although few administrators would argue with the fact that most composing takes place on computers, writing courses and the concerns of writing teachers may not be seen as high-priority items during discussions of standards and policies, and during other decision-making processes. Standards—scripted as policies or regulations—often emerge from technology committees and information-system offices.

Participating in and perhaps rescripting standards to support new-media writing is an ongoing process.

Encountering and Rupturing Policies

We will return to this conversation on standards and its infrastructural implications, but first we want to continue to follow the file management pathway—in reality a conflict between local network and more general software standards—to trace how these pathways overdetermine composing practices.

After a writer has addressed the questions we mentioned above related to the production and delivery of a composition, the writer translates the answers to these questions into project settings fixed within the software application being used to compose (see Figure 12.2 for an example from Premiere). The application is then launched, with a menu bar across the top; a project bin in the upper left; monitors next to the project bin; transition, navigator, and history tools on the right; and a timeline across the bottom of the screen (see Figure 12.3, again from Premiere). Although each window merits its own summary, the project bin and the timeline windows are perhaps most dependent on careful file management. These two components of the software are powerful meaning-making tools—the project bin is akin to a file cabinet from which the pieces of the project are drawn as needed; the timeline is akin to a command file (although its graphical interface hides the command language underneath) in which each file from the bin is tracked. The MSU computing policy—an

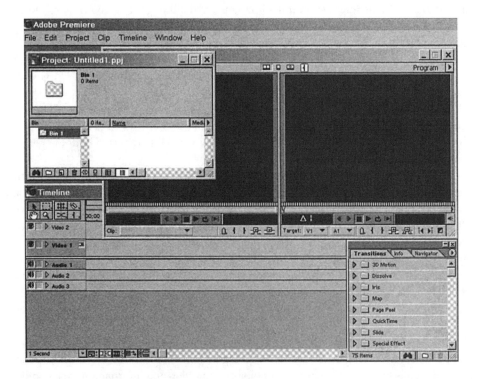

Figure 12.2 Screen Capture of Adobe Premiere Interface.

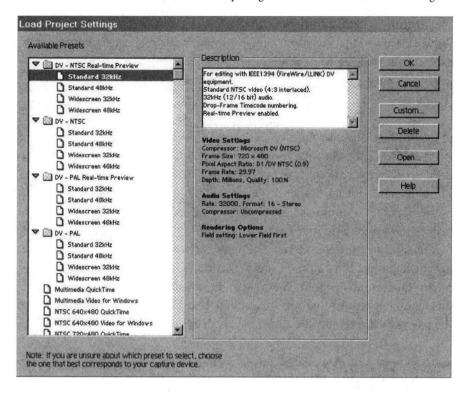

Figure 12.3 Screen Capture of Adobe Premiere Project Settings Interface.

assemblage of classifications, preferences, long-ago-established practices, and standards—hindered not only student access to this composing interface, but the writing they could do within it.

In her conversation with the computing services liaison, Ellen had been told to use specific network space for her class's work; one gig of memory was allocated to this space, for Ellen and for all of the students to share. Ellen's class notes from very early in the semester—January 15, 2002 (the second week of class)—are revealing of the complex routes necessary to access the shared space into which files could be saved:

Locating your server spaces. The icons on your Mac desktop include your own network space, as well as the "root" space for courses. We'll be using both of these spaces to save files this semester. I want you to visualize where you will be saving your files, so that you can better understand the "save as" windows:

1. Click twice on the root-space icon to open the folders there.
2. Go to MSU or MSU.edu (make sure that you consistently stick with one or the other, although I was told that they're essentially the same thing).
3. Go to Course, click twice to open,
4. Go to Eng, click twice to open,

5. Go to 391, click twice to open. Here we will have one gig of space into which we can save. Each of you will create a folder with your last name on it. We will then save all of our project and preview files here in your respective folders.

Although server space for all of the courses offered at the university can be found by following the process detailed above, the courses—hundreds of them offered each semester—do not exist in one space (as the visual folder metaphor suggests). Instead, the memory devoted to a given course is an articulation of parcels of memory distributed across many pieces of hardware across the campus. From a systems perspective, this is efficient. However, the use to which the one gig of space allotted to the multimedia writing class was put by students pushed not only on the technical structure itself, but also on the assumptions and established standards regulating the use of the technical structure.

Once Ellen was made aware of and began to work through the policies and the technological systems in place—which *are* typically highly functional and efficient—and students began using the systems, the software, and the networks in new ways, they broke down. For example, some students were able to create their folders; five students, however, for reasons never explained or understood by the system administrators, were only able to save to their folders sporadically. Other students were not able to save their work at all on the server space. Further, according to the way in which the systems on campus are set up, once the project files were saved to the server space the actual composing could take place. But this didn't prove to be the case. In some sense, our narrative of what Ellen and her students experienced is a commonplace story of writing teachers and technological breakdown. The impression we wish to avoid, however, is that the case we are presenting is *yet another* story of writing teachers struggling with technology. Yes, this is a story of writing teachers struggling with technology, but that is but one thread of a much larger story.

The types of issues commonplace to new-media writing spaces aren't merely issues to be solved by teachers and administrators before classes begin. They are certainly that, but they are also issues that continue to have an impact on the composing practices of writers as a class begins and unfolds, *and* they are our discipline's attempts to negotiate, adopt, and script writing with multiple media into its practices. Note the various ways that the writers in Ellen's class had to make a number of "nonwriting" decisions related to audience and the technological and rhetorical needs of that audience (e.g., bandwidth, screen size, media form and function). All of these decisions entered them into different orders of discourse, different grammars and conventions of practice, and different areas of knowledge than would typically be entertained in a writing classroom. Note, too, that the discussions Ellen had with campus computing officials made visible the need for writers to negotiate what is—and what isn't—infrastructurally possible.

Networks dictate how and in what ways certain technological resources are available within any infrastructure; in our case, the networks within which Ellen and the students in her course were composing were split across computer classrooms and across buildings. How fast software downloaded from central servers, where students could save their files, and how quickly students could upload material for rendering and previewing often dictated the shape of composing, and the pace of the course itself. In fact, in work and conversations with central computing, it became clear that we understand networks themselves very differently than they do (not merely technically but socially and ideologically as well).

Networks—locally and universally—are core to new-media writing, enacting the old marketing cliché that the network *is* the computer. In fact, as more writing instruction moves to digital spaces and as the majority of students' writing activity takes place in online environments (e.g., instant messaging, blogging), the paths of the transparent streams of bits and bytes merit attention as part of the *when* of infrastructure. This *when* is acutely felt when students are seen as potential threats to the networks as opposed to users; it's felt when course content, file size, and location are prescribed by networking policies and physical structures that support these. Tracing and understanding network paths through wires, cards, ports, and servers and across the policies and standards that shape the design and use of such spaces is often necessary to understand complexities and to negotiate new-media writing.

Structures Become Visible upon Breakdown: Locating Points for Institutional Change

Let's return again to the process of composing new media to show one other way that the infrastructural framework helps reveal places to leverage institutional change: Digital video is composed using timelines. When complete, the timeline is essentially a command file that writes "code" based on the icons of the media tracked and on the project settings. The timeline compiles all the separate media files together into preview files typically housed within the software application's local folder on a computer. Preview files are memory-hungry audio and video files that represent a compilation of just a few seconds of the timeline. Preview files are typically created by keying ENTER after every few seconds of timeline tracked, so that composers can, in effect, replay what they've composed, seeing and hearing the rough cut in the monitor window. When compiled along the way, these files are then collected into one large movie project that itself becomes a file saved with the rest of the media files.

Three weeks into Ellen's multimedia writing course, students were expected to have tracked the basic media components of their project timelines. Students had written and revised their papers, collected the other media they were to integrate and choreograph with their texts, and learned the basics of tracking with the software. As they worked, students began running out of memory to store their files; their computers were crashing frequently due to "type 2" errors. Data transfer was stymied or disallowed completely for files over 10 megabytes—very tiny files in multimedia terms. When students tried to compile their projects, their computers froze, and sometimes crashed completely and wouldn't reboot. More often than not, the freezing and crashing corrupted command files, and hours of work were lost. Tensions in class—and after class, as the constraints of time were felt quite acutely when compiling times were long and class time was relatively short—were high. The class came to a complete stop when the first project was due. For whatever reason, Rebecca Leibing's project was the only one the class was able to preview. Like any other writing project, her work required some revision—in this instance, the music she embedded drowned out her voice in places and she needed more motion across the stills to better provide a sense of flow. Rebecca was able to revise her rough cut to create the project from which we've excerpted (see Figure 12.1). Two other students eventually completed their files as well, but the rest were not able to complete their projects at all. Because the archive files were completely erased when the computers crashed, students lost their command files—and thus most of their work. Rebecca's project is interesting because it marks the when of infrastructural meltdown: *when* class came to a standstill, *when* her project was anomalously the only one produced, and *when* the typically invisible policy, cultural, and computer system structures became visible upon breakdown.

At this still-early point in the semester, the composing practices of Ellen's students had once again exceeded the technological space of the classroom. Ellen wrote a letter to the vice provost of libraries, computing, and technology (essentially the head of the centralized campus computing systems and the information services director), making a case for additional server/network space for her class and her students' work. She argued for a specific upgrade (from one gig to two gigs), and noted that the class was at an impasse, and that students were prohibited from writing and producing their digital compositions because of the memory limits of the campus network. Ellen implored the vice provost to bend current university policy and to consider allowing students to have continuous access to the hard drives in a folder saved even after a machine crashes and reboots or a student logs off. If students were able to save directly to a fixed local space, they would be able to save their tracking, project, preview, and final movie files. A key portion of the letter Ellen constructed conveyed her awareness of the fact that her course, new to the College of Arts and Letters and unique in the university, would soon no longer be unique—she emphasized the growing importance of writing in digital environments and writing with multiple media.

In response, the vice provost granted nine gigs of additional storage space. Soon afterwards (approximately six weeks into the class), two system managers visited the class to see firsthand the problems students were experiencing. They walked around the room reading error messages, watching students stall the system with file-transfer bottlenecks, and hearing from students about the problems they were experiencing. The students asked questions of the system managers that began to reveal how they were understanding the when of new media. For instance, when one student wondered why users had differential access to server space, she was told that this had to do with an outdated networking hub that bottlenecked when they tried to save. Another student asked how a type 2 error could occur when, upon checking the information on the computer, it appeared to have ample memory capacity for the work. Finally, another student asked where the archives were located when they were creating these pieces. The entire class session the day the two system managers visited consisted of students making apparent their learning about what should have been transparent: the ways in which the system and policies for its use were incompatible with their needs as composers and incompatible with the software's requirements. To their credit, the system managers listened and worked to solve the problems; over the following weekend, they carried out some changes that made the environment more friendly and more usable.

The first change that took place soon after the visit included installing some software applications locally on the computers. As we mentioned earlier, university policy prohibited software from being stored locally, but in the case of the multimedia writing course it was imperative that software be locally accessible. With this installation, software freezes abated. Together Ellen and the students walked through the instructions from the system managers that explained how to copy software off the university's server and onto the local computers. In this case, we—Ellen as instructor, Jeff and Dànielle as program faculty, and students in the course—all gained insight as to how a system might be opened in ways that facilitate local use. Students were also allowed to read and write from their local computers, yet another manipulation of university computing policy. These two changes allowed students to compile their second projects with fewer bottlenecks, freezes, and crashes. In addition, the system administrators turned off virtual memory for all of the computers, so that the video software would work much more smoothly, with fewer type 2 errors. One of the system managers who had visited the class emphasized that Ellen needed to warn students that their folders were not secure—that they would be working on the "honor system" as they wrote to the hard disk.[6] This itself was a significant shift in policy, albeit a temporary and local one. The campus computers were set up so that all student work was erased upon their logout, in part to protect against the spread of viruses, in part so that students could not access one another's files, and in part to protect against the local drives of computers quickly filling with work students stored and never erased. Allowing students to save permanently and locally required that the students adopt conventions regarding privacy and politeness that the campus policy previously restricted students from dealing with and actively participating in.

After these key changes, the technological spaces of the classroom and of student production worked much more smoothly. In the end, Adrienne Broch finished her second project (see Figure 12.4), as did all the other students. The course activities were truncated—because of the need to negotiate and renegotiate and then eventually change the systems in place and the policies governing those systems—so that students produced only two projects. Adrienne's project was in response to a prompt that asked students to select a piece of creative writing and interpret it through a digital composition. Students were asked to show rather than tell their interpretation. Because of the enhanced performance of the software and the new file-management capabilities students had access to, Adrienne was able to take advantage of a variety of media, and a variety of effects.

In her piece, text files—at times multiply layered and scrolling across the screen—appear simultaneously as an image pan moves the view across the still in the opposite direction. Adrienne's piece, "Der Panther," is a gruesomely beautiful interpretation of a German poem in light of *The Dreaded Comparison,* a book that traces similarities between the ideologies implicit in animal cruelty and slavery. Her composition suggests the possibilities of new-media composing when the infrastructure enables them.

The *When* of Infrastructure

Infrastructures can be transparent in that they do in some sense both preexist *and* work, and so even though infrastructures are always already the conditions in and through which we interact, compose, and think, we often *don't* need to think about them. In a sense, however, infrastructure needs to be reinvented each time or assembled for each task. Again, the issue is not what an infrastructure is but *when* it is. When the tasks of composing—including the tasks of thinking, of imagining, of creating—are not consistent with existing standards, practices, and values, infrastructure breaks down, revealing the need to meet the demands of new meaning-making practices. The rupture points, as we've seen from this case, became teachable moments for both the students and Ellen. Both had to learn enough about the interrelations of networks, software, and file management to be able to simply complete assignments. In Ellen's case, a class that had never before been taught at this university introduced new conventions of practice and new forms of meaning making that stressed—in productive ways—the existing infrastructure. The spaces required and composing processes involved *created* a new infrastructure for multimedia writing. It is this time-space-place nexus—the *when* of infrastructure emergence/construction—that we will now explore a bit further.

An infrastructural analysis has helped us understand the composing and learning that took place in Ellen's class and imagine appropriate responses as we rethink courses, writing, and compositions. As Christine Borgman writes, all information infrastructures are "built upon an installed base of telecommunications lines, electrical power grids, and computing technology" (20), and certainly we can read the material aspects of infrastructure in the examples above. Infrastructures are also built upon available "information resources, organizational arrangements, and people's practices in using all these aspects" (20). We also see these elements unfold—and collide—in the writing enabled within Ellen's class. Johndan Johnson-Eilola notes that we live, are composed, and compose "at the nexus connecting an apparently infinite number of social and technological forces of varying weights, strengths, and directions" ("Negative" 17), and certainly the infrastructural dynamics described here create such a nexus.

Within this nexus, students are presented with infrastructural questions as soon as applications like Adobe Premiere are launched. The first few interfaces, shown earlier, demand an understanding of invisible institutional structures and policies, such as those related to permissions to save on networks, file management and architecture, and file size and compression. Before new-media composing can even begin, the software demands that students negotiate an understanding of the deliverables to be produced. These understandings must take into consideration the audiences' system and platform requirements for file formats, memory allocation, and hardware. These infrastructural concerns permeate most networked composing environments including the organizations, workplaces, and institutions where students are likely to find employment. The *when* of new media, in other words, can and should be taught to students as part of and integral to new-media composing.

For teachers and administrators, the question of when an infrastructure for multimedia writing emerges has been answered (i.e., *now*) and will always be delayed (i.e., it continues to emerge). Ellen began her first interventions by breaking existing systems and drawing upon personal, rhetorical, and departmental tactics to save her class and to afford merit—technological and intellectual—to her students' work. We continue to work within emerging infrastructures by tailoring our curriculum, designing our requirements, and adopting different practices and assignments. We also continue this work by building

Figure 12.4 From "Dear Panther," by Adrienne Broch; Excerpt of Digital Composition Available at http://www.wide.msu.edu/ccc.

new physical spaces (classrooms), arguing for new virtual spaces (new file-management practices), and pushing for changes in both policies and standards. Some infrastructural interventions require seemingly simple revisions to policies or machines that shape the use of a room, a lab, or a network—revisions that alter who can work there, and when, and produce what. We are attracted to these mundane interventions and will assert, despite the ways in which these assertions often bore our colleagues, that these interventions are powerful and important micropolitical acts of institutional critique, agency, and change (Porter, Sullivan, Blythe, Grabill, and Miles). Infrastructural issues have an impact, literally, on the space of the writing classroom and what happens there—and they do so in ways both visible and invisible.

What this brief discussion reveals to us is how situated new-media composing is—how infrastructures of composing both rupture and create possibilities. Rebecca's piece, being the only successful initial project in a classroom of fifteen students, points to the rupture of an infrastructure. Adrienne's piece suggests the possibilities of new-media writing when an infrastructure works: Her piece grew out of multiple revisions and deeper, fuller uses of the technology made available to her as a result of micropolitical changes in network policy and system use. Our own work with exploring and teaching new-media writing has revealed to us the cultural, political, and institutional contexts of composing—so much so that it is no longer possible for us to look at a product of new media without wondering what kinds of material and social realities made it possible. We also have become aware of the need to reach beyond the frameworks that we typically rely upon to understand composing processes and spaces of composing.

To understand the contexts that make possible and limit, shape and constrain, and facilitate and prevent new-media composing, new-media teachers and students need to be able to account for the complex interrelationships of material, technical, discursive, institutional, and cultural systems. An infrastructural approach reveals the layers and patterns behind the products of new-media composing—patterns that directly affect contemporary writing, writing pedagogy, and writing classrooms. Our claim is that in order to teach and understand new media composing, some understanding of new-media infrastructure is necessary. Without such an understanding, writing teachers and students will fail to anticipate and actively participate in the emergence of such infrastructures, thereby limiting—rhetorically, technically, and institutionally—what is possible for our students to write and learn.

We argued earlier that our field has produced rich work that analyzes the currents of online writing, digital spaces, and media convergence. We also argued, however, that few scholars offer frameworks for understanding the spaces within which such compositions are produced. Here we see that the processes of new media are very much mediated by the dynamics of infrastructures and also that infrastructures might be best thought of as a "when" and not a "what." An infrastructural framework, we hope, creates a tool for composers to navigate the systems within and across which they work, creates a moment for reflection and change within institutional structures and networks, and creates a framework for understanding writing that moves forward our understandings of how composing and compositions change shape within the complex dynamics of networks.

Notes

1. This work describes how "writing" has changed to weaving what we might call "traditional" (certainly older) media (like text, graphics, and audio) with and for computer interfaces. Characterizing new media as hybrid, for example, Mary E. Hocks and Michelle R. Kendrick (following the work of Bruno Latour) ask us to move beyond static binaries that separate visual/textual and image/word and to instead create spaces where we can focus on the "complex, interpenetrating relationships between words and images" (5), relationships that are not new but instead remediated with/in today's technologies (see also Bolter and Grusin).

2. We might argue that new media aren't necessarily new: images, motion, sound, video, and other media have existed for decades. What is new, however, are the spaces and interfaces in which and through which these media are woven. What is new is how writing is transformed into composing, requiring the ability to weave together what we might call "traditional" (certainly older) media (like text, graphics, and audio) with and for computer interfaces. What is also new is the access to these media and technologies in our writing classrooms.

3. Consider a traditional writing classroom: Word-processing software is crucial, and a Web browser and Internet access are probably a must. Presentation software might also be used. Students produce primarily text-based documents, which are relatively small in size and can be easily stored, saved, and distributed; these documents are typically designed for print. Compare this classroom to a new-media writing classroom, where robust video-editing and multimedia-production software is in use, where Internet access is necessary to share and stream files, and where files themselves are gigantic—easily filling gigs of hard drives and network space. This is just a thin comparison, but a thick example of the ways in which new-media writing pushes on our established technological systems. From another direction: Consider, also, the assumptions made of writing instruction ten or fifteen years ago. We have each often heard the question, "Why do writing classrooms need computers?" The practices and needs of new-media writing explode this question in multiple directions.

4. Ellen distributed consent forms early in the semester. Most students signed them, thus granting her permission to include their compositions in her research and writing.

5. Although we have taught new-media classes here and at other universities where the courses have run according to plan, this class was chosen for use as a model here because it made visible to us the infrastructural dynamics upon which new-media composing relies. This course also allowed us, because of this visibility, to both critique and alter these infrastructural dynamics.

6. The students knew that they were able to open one another's folders. We agreed to a policy of respecting the privacy of one another's space and of only ever accessing this space with permission. In fact, this "security problem" became an important moment for the class. Students were creating a culture of technology in which they agreed upon practices for use and set a premium on respecting one another's space and work. Students were creating a hospitable environment for learning, an environment that depended upon their shared respect for one another and a shared honoring of an agreement beneficial to everyone. Interestingly, they created this environment inside an infrastructure that doubted their abilities to do so: The computing policy of the classroom that demanded we use remote space as opposed to the local disk space was premised on a belief that students were not honorable—that they would in fact erase the contents of one another's folders if given the chance to do so. What enabled new-media composing here was mutual trust, shared respect, agreement about access, and a culture of technology that ran contrary to the larger computing policy that continued to cripple the progress of the class.

Works Cited

Allen, Nancy, ed. *Working with Words and Images: New Steps in an Old Dance*. Stamford, CT: Ablex, 2002.

Anson, Chris M. "Distant Voices: Teaching Writing in a Culture of Technology." *College English* 61.3 (1999): 261–80.

Bernhardt, Stephen A. "Designing a Microcomputer Classroom for Teaching Composition." *Computers and Composition* 7.1 (1989): 93–110.

——. "The Shape of Text to Come: The Texture of Print on Screens." *CCC* 44.2 (1993): 151–75.

Bolter, Jay David. *The Writing Space: The Computer, Hypertext, and the History of Writing*. Hillsdale, NJ: Erlbaum, 1991.

Bolter, Jay David and Richard Grusin. *Remediation: Understanding New Media*. Cambridge: MIT P, 2000.

Borgman, Christine L. *From Gutenberg to the Global Information Infrastructure: Access to Information in the Networked World*. Cambridge: MIT P, 2000.

Bowker, Geoffrey C. and Susan Leigh Star. *Sorting Things Out: Classification and its Consequences*. Cambridge: MIT P, 1999.

Brady Aschauer, Ann. "Tinkering with Technological Skill: An Examination of the Gendered Uses of Technologies." *Computers and Composition* 16.1 (1999): 7–23.

Britton, Bruce K. and Shawn M. Glynn. *Computer Writing Environments: Theory, Research, and Design*. Hillsdale, NJ: Erlbaum, 1989.

Buckley, Joanne. "The Invisible Audience and the Disembodied Voice: Online Teaching and the Loss of Body Image." *Computers and Composition* 14.2 (1997): 179–87.

Burbules, Nicholas C. "Rhetorics of the Web: Hyperreading and Critical Literacy Practices." Snyder 102–22.

Condon, William. "Selecting Computer Software for Writing Instruction: Some Considerations." *Computers and Composition* 10.1 (1992): 53–56.

Conference on College Composition and Communication (CCCC). "Position Statement on Teaching, Learning, and Assessing Writing in Digital Environments." 2004. 14 June 2005 http://www.ncte.org/groups/cccc/positions/115775.htm.

Conference on College Composition and Communication (CCCC) Committee on Computers and Composition. "Promotion and Tenure Guidelines for Work with Technology." N.d. 14 June 2005 http://www.ncte.org/about/over/positions/level/coll/107658.htm.

Cooper, Marilyn. "Postmodern Pedagogy in Electronic Conversations." Hawisher and Selfe 140–60.

Cooper, Marilyn and Cynthia L. Selfe. "Computer Conferences and Learning: Authority, Resistance, and Internally Persuasive Discourse." *College English* 52.8 (1990): 847–69.

Curtis, Marcia S. "Windows on Composing: Teaching Revision on Word Processors." *CCC* 39.3 (1988): 337–344.

DeWitt, Scott Lloyd. *Writing Inventions: Identities, Technologies, Pedagogies.* Albany: SUNY P, 2001.

Dinan, John S., Rebecca Gagnon, and Jennifer Taylor. "Integrating Computers into the Writing Classroom: Some Guidelines." *Computers and Composition* 3.2 (1986): 33–39.

Faigley, Lester. "Beyond Imagination: The Internet and Global Digital Literacy." Hawisher and Selfe 129–39.

Feenberg, Andrew. *Critical Theory of Technology.* New York: Oxford UP, 1991.

"Forum: A Conversation about Software, Technology, and Composition Studies." *Computers and Composition* 10.1 (1992): 151–68.

George, Diana. "From Analysis to Design: Visual Communication in the Teaching of Writing." *CCC* 54.1 (2002): 11–39.

Grabill, Jeffrey T. "Community Computing and Citizen Productivity." *Computers and Composition* 20.2 (2003): 131–50.

——. "On Divides and Interfaces: Access, Class, and Computers." *Computers and Composition* 20.4 (2003): 455–72.

——. "Utopic Visions, the Technopoor, and Public Access: Writing Technologies in a Community Literacy Program." *Computers and Composition* 15.3 (1998): 297–315.

Grigar, Dene. "Over the Line, Online, Gender Lines: E-mail and Women in the Classroom." *Feminist Cyberscapes: Mapping Gendered Academic Spaces.* Ed. Kristine Blair and Pamela Takayoshi. Stamford, CT: Ablex, 1999, 257–81.

Gruber, Sibylle. "Re: Ways We Contribute: Students, Instructors, and Pedagogies in the Computer-Mediated Writing Classroom." *Computers and Composition* 12.1 (1995): 61–78.

Gurak, Laura J. and Johndan Johnson-Eilola, eds. *Intellectual Property.* Spec. issue of *Computers and Composition* 15.2 (1998).

Haas, Christina. *Writing Technology: Studies on the Materiality of Literacy.* Mahwah, NJ: Erlbaum, 1996.

Handa, Carolyn, ed. *Digital Rhetoric, Digital Literacy, Computers, and Composition.* Spec. issues *of Computers and Composition* 18.1 and 18.2 (2001).

Harris, Leslie D., and Cynthia A. Wambeam. "The Internet-Based Composition Classroom: A Study in Pedagogy." *Computers and Composition* 13.3 (1996): 353–71.

Hawisher, Gail E., and Cynthia L. Selfe, eds. *Passions, Pedagogies and 21st Century Technologies.* Logan: Utah State UP, 1999.

Heba, Gary, "HyperRhetoric: Multimedia, Literacy, and the Future of Composition." *Computers and Composition* 14.1 (1997): 19–44.

Hocks, Mary E. "Feminist Interventions in Electronic Environments." *Computers and Composition* 16.1 (1999): 107–19.

——. "Understanding Visual Rhetoric in Digital Writing Environments." *CCC* 54.4 (2003): 629–56.

Hocks, Mary E., and Michelle R. Kendrick. "Eloquent Images." Introduction. *Eloquent Images: Word and Image in the Age of New Media.* Ed. Hocks and Kendricks. Cambridge: MIT P, 2003.1–18.

Holdstein, Deborah H. "Interchanges: Power, Genre, and Technology." *CCC* 47.2 (1996): 279–84.

Holdstein, Deborah H., and Cynthia L. Selfe, eds. *Computers and Writing: Theory, Research, Practice.* New York: MLA, 1990.

Howard, Tharon W. *A Rhetoric of Electronic Communities.* Greenwich, CT: Ablex, 1997.

Janangelo, Joseph. "Technopower and Technoppression: Some Abuses of Power and Control in Computer-Assisted Writing Environments." *Computers and Composition* 9.1 (1991): 47–64.

Johnson, Jim [Bruno Latour]. "Mixing Humans and Non-humans Together: The Sociology of a Door-Closer." *Social Problems* 35.3 (1988): 298–310.

Johnson-Eilola, Johndan. "Living on the Surface: Learning in the Age of Global Communication Networks." Snyder 185–210.

——. "Negative Spaces: From Production to Connection in Composition." *Literacy Theory in the Age of the Internet.* Ed. Todd Taylor and Irene Ward. New York: Columbia UP, 1998.17–33.

Joyce, Michael. "New Stories for New Readers: Contour, Coherence, and Constructive Hypertext." Snyder 163–83.

Kalmbach, James Robert. *The Computer and the Page: The Theory, History and Pedagogy of Publishing, Technology and the Classroom.* Norwood, NJ: Ablex, 1997.

Kent-Drury, Roxanne. "Finding a Place to Stand: Negotiating the Spatial Configuration of the Networked Computer Classroom." *Computers and Composition* 15.3 (1998): 387–407.

Kinkead, Joyce. "Computer Conversations: E-Mail and Writing Instruction." *CCC* 38.3 (1987): 335–41.

Knadler, Stephen. "E-Racing Difference in E-Space: Black Female Subjectivity and the Web-Based Portfolio." *Computers and Composition* 18.3 (2001): 235–55.

Kress, Gunther. "'English' at the Crossroads: Rethinking Curricula of Communication in the Context of the Turn to the Visual." Hawisher and Selfe 66–88.

——. "Visual and Verbal Modes of Representation in Electronically Mediated Communication: The Potentials of New Forms of Text." Snyder 53–79.

Lang, Susan, Janice R. Walker, and Keith Dorwick, eds. *Tenure 2000.* Spec. issue of *Computers and Composition* 17.1 (2000).

Lave, Jean, and Etienne Wenger. *Situated Learning: Legitimate Peripheral Participation.* Cambridge: Cambridge UP, 1991.

LeBlanc, Paul. *Writing Teachers Writing Software: Creating Our Place in the Electronic Age.* Urbana, IL: NCTE, 1993.

LeCourt, Donna. "Writing (without) the Body: Gender and Power in Networked Discussion Groups." *Feminist Cyberscapes: Mapping Gendered Academic Spaces.* Ed. Kristine Blair and Pamela Takayoshi. Stamford, CT: Ablex, 1999. 153–76.

Markel, Mike. "What Students See: Word Processing and the Perception of Visual Design." *Computers and Composition* 15.3 (1998): 373–86.

McGee, Tim and Patricia Ericsson. "The Politics of the Program: MS Word as the Invisible Grammarian." *Computers and Composition* 19.4 (2002): 453–70.

McKee, Heidi. "'YOUR VIEWS SHOWED TRUE IGNORANCE!!!': (Mis)Communication in an Online Interracial Discussion Forum." *Computers and Composition* 19.4 (2002): 411–34.

Monteiro, Eric and Ole Hanseth. "Social Shaping of Information Infrastructure: On Being Specific about the Technology." *Information Technology and Organizational Work.* Ed. W. J. Orlikowski, G. Walsham, M. R. Jones, and J. I. DeGross. London: Chapman, 1996.

Moran, Charles. "Access: The A-Word in Technology Studies." Hawisher and Selfe 205–20.

——. "From a High-Tech to a Low-Tech Writing Classroom: 'You Can't Go Home Again.'" *Computers and Composition* 15.1 (1998): 1–10.

Moran, Charles and Gail E. Hawisher. "The Rhetorics and Languages of Electronic Mail," Snyder 80–101.

Pagnucci, Gian S. and Nicholas Mauriello. "The Masquerade: Gender, Identity, and Writing for the Web." *Computers and Composition* 16.1 (1999): 141–51.

Palmquist, Michael E. "Network-Supported Interaction in Two Writing Classrooms." *Computers and Composition* 10.4 (1993): 25–58.

Palmquist, Mike, Kate Kiefer, James Hartvigsen, and Barbara Godlew. *Transitions: Teaching Writing in Computer-Supported and Traditional Classrooms.* Stamford, CT: Ablex, 1998.

Porter, James E. "Liberal Individualism and Internet Policy: A Communitarian Critique." Hawisher and Selfe 231–48.

——. *Rhetorical Ethics and Internetworked Writing.* Greenwich, CT: Ablex, 1998.

Porter, James E., Patricia Sullivan, Stuart Blythe, Jeffrey T. Grabill, and Libby Miles. "Institutional Critique: A Rhetorical Methodology for Change." *CCC* 51.4 (2000): 610–42.

Redd, Teresa M. "'Tryin to Make a Dolla outa Fifteen Cent': Teaching Composition with the Internet at an HBCU." *Computers and Composition* 20.4 (2003): 359–73.

Regan, Alison E. and John D. Zuern. "Community-Service Learning and Computer-Mediated Advanced Composition: The Going to Class, Getting Online, and Giving Back Project." *Computers and Composition* 17.2 (2000): 177–95.

Richardson, Elaine B. "African American Women Instructors: In a Net" *Computers and Composition* 14.2 (1997): 279–87.

Rickly, Rebecca. "The Gender Gap in Computers and Composition Research: Must Boys Be Boys?" *Computers and Composition* 16.1 (1999): 121–40.

Rouzie, Albert. "Conversation and Carrying-On: Play, Conflict, and Serio-Ludic Discourse in Synchronous Computer Conferencing." *CCC* 53.2 (2001): 251–99.

Ruszkiewicz, John. "Word and Image: The Next Revolution." *Computers and Composition* 5.3 (1988): 9–16.

Sanchez, Raul. "Our Bodies? Our Selves? Questions about Teaching in the MUD." *Literacy Theory in the Age of the Internet.* Ed. Todd Taylor and Irene Ward. New York: Columbia UP, 1998, 93–108.

Selfe, Cynthia L. *Creating a Computer-Supported Writing Facility: A Blueprint for Action.* Advances in Computers and Composition Studies. Houghton, MI: Computers and Composition P, 1989.

——. "Creating a Computer-Supported Writing Lab: Sharing Stories and Creating Vision." *Computers and Composition* 4.2 (1987): 44–65.

——. "Technology and Literacy: A Story about the Perils of Not Paying Attention." *CCC* 50.3 (1998): 411–36.

Selfe, Cynthia L. and Richard J. Selfe, Jr. "The Politics of the Interface: Power and Its Exercise in Electronic Contact Zones." *CCC* 45.4 (1994): 480–504.

Sirc, Geoffrey. "'What is Composition …?' After Duchamp (Notes toward a General Teleintertext)." Hawisher and Selfe 178–204.

Snyder, Ilana, ed. *Page to Screen: Taking Literacy into the Electronic Era.* London: Routledge, 1998.

Spooner, Michael and Kathleen Yancey. "Postings on a Genre of Email." *CCC* 47.2 (1996): 252–78.

Star, Susan Leigh, and Karen Ruhleder. "Steps toward an Ecology Infrastructure: Design and Access for Large Information Spaces." *Information Systems Research* 7.1 (1996): 111–34.

Sullivan, Laura L. "Wired Women Writing: Toward a Feminist Theorization of Hypertext." *Computers and Composition* 16.1 (1999): 25–54.

Sullivan, Patricia. "Desktop Publishing: A Powerful Tool for Advanced Composition Courses." *CCC* 39.3 (1988): 344–47.

Takayoshi, Pamela. "Building New Networks from the Old: Women's Experiences with Electronic Communications." *Computers and Composition* 11.1 (1994): 21–35.

——. "Complicated Women: Examining Methodologies for Understanding the Uses of Technology." *Computers and Composition* 17.2 (2000): 123–38.

Takayoshi, Pamela, Emily Huot, and Meghan Huot. "No Boys Allowed: The World Wide Web as a Clubhouse for Girls." *Computers and Composition* 16.1 (1999): 89–106.

Taylor, Todd. "The Persistence of Difference in Networked Classrooms: Non-negotiable Difference and the African American Student Body." *Computers and Composition* 14.2 (1997): 169–78.

Thompson, Diane. "Electronic Bulletin Boards: A Timeless Place for Collaborative Writing Projects." *Computers and Composition* 7.2 (1990): 43–53.

Tuman, Myron C., ed. *Literacy Online: The Promise (and Peril) of Reading and Writing with Computers.* Pittsburgh: U of Pittsburgh P, 1992.

Ulmer, Gregory L. *Heuristics: The Logic of Invention.* Baltimore: Johns Hopkins UP, 1994.

Vernon, Alex. "Computerized Grammar Checkers 2000: Capabilities, Limitations, and Pedagogical Possibilities." *Computers and Composition* 17.3 (2000): 329–49.

Webb, Patricia. "Technologies of Difference: Reading the Virtual Age through Sexual (In)Difference." *Computers and Composition* 20.2 (2003): 151–67.

Webb Peterson, Patricia, and Wilhelmina Savenye. *Distance Education* . Spec. issue of *Computers and Composition* 18.4 (2001).

Wolfe, Joanna L. "Why Do Women Feel Ignored? Gender Differences in Computer-Mediated Classroom Interactions." *Computers and Composition* 16.1 (1999): 153–66.

Wysocki, Anne F. "Impossibly Distinct: On Form/Content and Word/Image in Two Pieces of Computer-Based Interactive Multimedia." *Computers and Composition* 18.2 (2001): 137–62.

——. "Monitoring Order: Visual Desire, the Organization of Web Pages, and Teaching the Rules of Design." *Kairos* 3.2 (1998). 14 June 2005 http://english.ttu.edu/kairos/3.2.

Wysocki, Anne F., and Johndan Johnson-Eilola. "Blinded by the Letter: Why Are We Using Literacy as a Metaphor for Everything Else?" Hawisher and Selfe 349–68.

Wysocki, Anne F. and Julia I. Jasken. "What Should Be an Unforgettable Face … "*Computers and Composition* 21.1 (2004): 29–48.

13
RW, Revived

Lawrence Lessig

One of my closest (if most complicated) friends at college was an English major. He was also a brilliant writer. Indeed, in every class in which writing was the measure, he did as well as one possibly could. In every other class, he, well, didn't.

Ben's writing had a certain style. Were it music, we'd call it sampling. Were it painting, it would be called collage. Were it digital, we'd call it remix. Every paragraph was constructed through quotes. The essay might be about Hemingway or Proust. But he built the argument by clipping quotes from the authors he was discussing. Their words made his argument.

And he was rewarded for it. Indeed, in the circles for which he was writing, the talent and care that his style evinced were a measure of his understanding. He succeeded not simply by stringing quotes together. He succeeded because the salience of the quotes, in context, made a point that his words alone would not. And his selection demonstrated knowledge beyond the message of the text. Only the most careful reader could construct from the text he read another text that explained it. Ben's writing showed he was an insanely careful reader. His intensely careful reading made him a beautiful writer.

Ben's style is rewarded not just in English seminars. It is the essence of good writing in the law. A great brief seems to say nothing on its own. Everything is drawn from cases that went before, presented as if the argument now presented is in fact nothing new. Here again, the words of others are used to make a point the others didn't directly make. Old cases are remixed. The remix is meant to do something new. (Appropriately enough, Ben is now a lawyer.)

In both instances, of course, citation is required. But the cite is always sufficient payment. And no one who writes for a living actually believes that any permission beyond that simple payment should ever be required. Had Ben written the estate of Ernest Hemingway to ask for permission to quote *For Whom the Bell Tolls* in his college essays, lawyers at the estate would have been annoyed more than anything else. What weirdo, they would have wondered, thinks you need permission to quote in an essay?

So here's the question I want you to focus on as we begin this chapter: Why is it "weird" to think that you need permission to quote? Why would (or should) we be "outraged" if the law required us to ask Al Gore for permission when we wanted to include a quote from his book

The Assault on Reason in an essay? Why is an author annoyed (rather than honored) when a high school student calls to ask for permission to quote?

The answer, I suggest, has lots to do with the "nature" of writing. Writing, in the traditional sense of words placed on paper, is the ultimate form of democratic creativity, where, again, "democratic" doesn't mean people vote, but instead means that everyone within a society has access to the means to write. We teach everyone to write—in theory, if not in practice. We understand quoting is an essential part of that writing. It would be impossible to construct and support that practice if permission were required every time a quote was made. The freedom to quote, and to build upon, the words of others is taken for granted by everyone who writes. Or put differently, the freedom that Ben took for granted is perfectly natural in a world where everyone can write.

Writing Beyond Words

Words, obviously, are not the only form of expression that can be remixed in Ben's way. If we can quote text from Hemingway's *For Whom the Bell Tolls* in an essay, we can quote a section from Sam Wood's film of Hemingway's *For Whom the Bell Tolls* in a film. Or if we can quote lyrics from a Bob Dylan song in a piece about Vietnam, we can quote a recording of Bob Dylan singing those lyrics in a video about that war. The act is the same; only the source is different. And the measures of fairness could also be the same: Is it really just a quote? Is it properly attributed? And so on.

Yet, however similar these acts of quoting may be, the norms governing them today are very different. Though I've not yet found anyone who can quite express why, any qualified Hollywood lawyer would tell you there's a fundamental difference between quoting Hemingway and quoting Sam Wood's version of Hemingway. The same with music: in an opinion by perhaps one of the twentieth century's worst federal judges, Judge Kevin Thomas Duffy, the court issued "stern" sanctions against rap artists who had sampled another musical recording. Wrote the judge,

> "Thou shalt not steal" has been an admonition followed since the dawn of civilization. Unfortunately, in the modern world of business this admonition is not always followed. Indeed, the defendants in this action for copyright infringement would have this court believe that stealing is rampant in the music business and, for that reason, their conduct here should be excused. The conduct of the defendants herein, however, violates not only the Seventh Commandment, but also the copyright laws of this country.[1]

Whether justified or not, the norms governing these forms of expression are far more restrictive than the norms governing text. They admit none of the freedoms that any writer takes for granted when writing a college essay, or even an essay for the *New Yorker*.

Why?

A complete answer to that question is beyond me, and therefore us, here. But we can make a start. There are obvious differences in these forms of expression. The most salient for our purposes is the democratic difference, historically, in these kinds of "writing." While writing with text is the stuff that everyone is taught to do, filmmaking and record making were, for most of the twentieth century, the stuff that professionals did. That meant it was easier to imagine a regime that required permission to quote with film and music. Such a regime was at least feasible, even if inefficient.

But what happens when writing with film (or music, or images, or every other form of "professional speech" from the twentieth century) becomes as democratic as writing with text? As Negativland's Don Joyce described to me, what happens when technology "democratiz[es] the technique and the attitude and the method [of creating] in a way that we haven't known before. … [I]n terms of collage, [what happens when] anybody can now be an artist"?[2]

What norms (and then law) will govern this kind of creativity? Should the norms we all take for granted from writing be applied to video? And music? Or should the norms from film be applied to text? Put differently: Should the "ask permission" norms be extended from film and music to text? Or should the norms of "quote freely, with attribution" spread from text to music and film?

At this point, some will resist the way I've carved up the choices. They will insist that the distinction is not between text on the one hand and film/music/images on the other. Instead, the distinction is between commercial or public presentations of text/film/music/images on the one hand, and private or noncommercial use of text/film/music/images on the other. No one expects my friend Ben to ask the Hemingway estate for permission to quote in a college essay, because no one is publishing (yet, at least) Ben's college essays. And in the same way, no one would expect Disney, for example, to have any problem with a father taking a clip from *Superman* and including it in a home movie, or with kids at a kindergarten painting Mickey Mouse on a wall.

Yet however sensible that distinction might seem, it is in fact not how the rules are being enforced just now. Again, Ben's freedom with text is the same whether it is a college essay or an article in the *New Yorker* (save perhaps if he's writing about poetry). And in fact, Disney has complained about kids at a kindergarten painting Mickey on a wall.[3] And in a setup by J. D. Lasica, every major studio except one insisted that a father has no right to include a clip of a major film in a home movie—even if that movie is never shown to anyone except the family—without paying thousands of dollars to do so.[4]

However sensible, the freedom to quote is not universal in the noncommercial sphere. Instead, those in thousand-dollar suits typically insist that "permission is vital, legally."

Nor do I believe the freedom to quote should reach universally only in the noncommercial sphere. In my view, it should reach much broader than that. But before I can hope to make that normative argument stick, we should think more carefully about why this right to quote—or as I will call it, to remix—is a critical expression of creative freedom that in a broad range of contexts, no free society should restrict.

Remix is an essential act of RW creativity. It is the expression of a freedom to take "the songs of the day or the old songs" and create with them. In Sousa's time, the creativity was performance. The selection and arrangement expressed the creative ability of the singers. In our time, the creativity reaches far beyond performance alone. But in both contexts, the critical point to recognize is that the RW creativity does not compete with or weaken the market for the creative work that gets remixed. These markets are complementary, not competitive.

That fact alone, of course, does not show that both markets shouldn't be regulated (that is, governed by rules of copyright). But as we'll see in the next part of the book, there are important reasons why we should limit the regulation of copyright in the contexts in which RW creativity is likely to flourish most. These reasons reflect more than the profit of one, albeit important, industry; instead, they reflect upon a capacity for a generation to speak.

I start with a form of RW culture that is closest to our tradition of remixing texts. From that beginning, I will build to the more significant forms of remix now emerging. In the end, my aim is to draw all these forms together to point to a kind of speech that will seem natural and familiar. And a kind of freedom that will feel inevitable.

Remixed: Text

There is a thriving RW culture for texts on the Net just now. Its scope and reach and, most important, sophistication are far beyond what anyone imagined at the Internet's birth. Through technologies not even conceived of when this system began, this RW culture for texts has built an ecology of content and an economy of reputation. There is a system now that makes an extraordinary range of initially unfiltered content understandable, and that helps the reader recognize what he should trust, and what he should question.

We can describe this system in three layers. The first is the writing itself. This has evolved through two different lives. The first of these is obscure to many; the second is the ubiquitous "blog."

The first was something called Usenet. In 1979, two computer scientists at Duke, Tom Truscott and Jim Ellis, invented a distributed messaging system that enabled messages to be passed cheaply among thousands of computers worldwide. This was Usenet. Sometimes these messages were announcementy; sometimes they were simply informational. But soon they became the location of increasingly interactive RW culture. As individuals realized they could simply hit a single button and post a comment or reply to thousands of computers worldwide, the temptation to speak could not be resisted. Usenet grew quickly, and passion around it grew quickly as well.

In 1994, a couple of lawyers changed all this. The firm Canter & Siegel posted the first cross-group commercial message—aka spam—advertising its services. Thousands responded in anger, flaming the lawyers to get them to stop. But many others quickly copied Canter & Siegel. Other such scum quickly followed. Usenet became less and less a place where conversation could happen, and more and more a ghetto for gambling ads and other such scams (see also your e-mail in-box).[5]

Just about the time that Usenet was fading, the World Wide Web was rising. The Web's inventor, Tim Berners-Lee, was keen that the Web be a RW medium—what Benkler calls "the writable Web."[6] He pushed people developing tools to implement Web protocols to design their tools in a way that would encourage both reading and writing.[7] At first, this effort failed. The real drive for the Web, its developers thought, would be businesses and other organizations that would want to publish content to the world. RO, not RW.

But as tools to simplify HTML coding matured, Berners-Lee's idea of a RW Internet became a reality. Web-logs, or blogs, soon started to proliferate at an explosive rate. In March 2003, the best-known service for tracking blogs, Technorati, found just 100,000 blogs. Six months later, that number had grown to 1 million. A year later, more than 4 million were listed.[8] Today there are more than 100 million blogs worldwide, with more than 15 added in the time it took you to read this sentence. According to Technorati, Japanese is now the number one blogging language. And Farsi has just entered the top ten.[9]

When blogs began (and you can still see these early blogs using Brewster Kahle's "Wayback machine" at archive.org), while they expressed RW creativity (since the norm for this form of writing encouraged heavy linking and citation), their RW character was limited.

Many were little more than a public diary: people (and some very weird people) posting their thoughts into an apparently empty void. Most were commentary on other public events. So the writing itself was RW, but the writing was experienced by an audience as RO.

Soon, however, in what Benkler calls the "second critical innovation of the writable Web,"[10] bloggers added a way for their audience to talk back. Comments became an integral part of blogging. Some of these comments were insightful, some were silly, some were designed simply to incite. But by adding a way to talk back, blogs changed how they were read.

This was the first layer of the Net's RW culture for text. Alone, however, this layer would be worth very little. How could you find anything of interest in this vast, undifferentiated sea of content? If you knew someone you trusted, maybe you'd read her blog. But why would you waste your time reading some random person's thoughts about anything at all?

The next two layers helped solve this problem. The first added some order to the blogosphere. It did so by adding not a taxonomy but, as Thomas Vander Wal puts it, a "folksonomy to this RW culture."[11] Tags and ranking systems, such as delicious, Reddit, and Digg, enabled readers of a blog or news article to mark it for others to find or ignore. These marks added meaning to the post or story. They would help it get organized among the millions of others that were out there. Together these tools added a metalayer to the blogosphere, by providing, as *Wired* cofounder Kevin Kelly puts it, "a public annotation—like a keyword or category name that you hang on a file, Web page or picture."[12] And as readers explore the Web, users leave marks that help others understand or find the same stuff.

So, for example, if you read an article about Barack Obama, you can tag it with a short description: "Obama" or "Obama_environment." As millions of readers do the same, the system of tagging begins to impose order on the stuff tagged—even though no one has drafted a table of tags, and no one imposes any rules about the tags. You could just as well tag the Obama article "petunias," and some few petunia lovers will be disappointed as they follow the sign to this nonpetunia site. But as more and more users push the arrows in other ways, more and more follow more faithful taggers.

Tagging thus added a layer of meaning to RW content. The more tags, the more useful and significant they become. Importantly, this significance is created directly by the viewers or consumers of that culture—not by advertisers, or by any other intentional efforts at commercial promotion. This reputation and word-of-mouth technology create a competing set of meanings that get associated with any content. The tools become "powerful forces that marketers must harness," though as Don Tapscott and Anthony Williams point out, this is a force that can "just as easily spin out of control in unpredictable ways."[13]

As they add meaning to content, these tools also enable collaboration. Significance and salience are a self-conscious community activity.[14] Sites such as delicious reinforce this community power by allowing users to share bookmarks, enabling "links [to] become ... the basis for learning new things and making connections to new people."[15] They also change the relative power of the reader. As the reader "writes" with tags or votes, the importance of the original writing changes. A major national newspaper could have the highest-paid technology writer in the world. But what happens to that writer when it turns out that the columns read by more, and recommended by most, are written by eighteen-year-old bloggers? The *New York Times* used to have the power to say who was the most significant. A much more democratic force does that now.

The third layer of this RW culture for text is much less direct. These are tools that try to measure the significance of a conversation by counting the links that others make to the conversations. Technorati is the leader in this area so far. Its (ro)bots crawl the world of blogs, counting who links to whom or what. The company then publishes up-to-the-minute rankings and link reports, so you can post a blog entry and, minutes later, begin watching everyone who links back to that entry. Technorati says it updates its index every ten minutes.[16] With over 100 million blogs indexed, that's a very fast update.

Indices like this show the revealed preferences of the blogosphere. In almost real time, we can see who is wielding influence. And as the space matures, most interestingly, we can see that the influence of blogs is increasingly outstripping mainstream media. In the Q4 report for 2006, Technorati reported that in the 51–100 range of most popular sites on the Web, 25 percent were blogs.[17] Ten years before, 0 percent of nonprofessional content would have been among the most popular of any popular media.

These three layers, then, work together. There would be nothing without the content. But there would be too much to be useful were there only the content. So, in addition to content, content about content—tags, and recommendations—combined with tools to measure the influence of content. The whole becomes an ecosystem of reputation. Those trying to interact with culture now recognize this space as critical to delivering or understanding a message.

Many worry about this blogosphere. Some worry it is just a fad—but what fad has ever caught 100 million users before? Charlene Li reports that 33 percent of teenagers make a blog entry weekly, and 41 percent visit a social networking site daily.[18] And absolutely every major publication devotes a substantial amount of resources to making this presence as important as any.

Others worry about quality; how can bloggers match the *New York Times?* What bloggers will spend the effort necessary to get their stories right?

If the question is asked about blogs on average, then no doubt the skepticism is merited. But if the same question were asked of newspapers *on average*, then great skepticism about newspapers would be merited as well. The point with both is that we have effective tools for assessing quality. And more important, we have increasingly famous examples of blogs outdoing traditional media in delivering both quality and truth. Yochai Benkler catalogs a host of cases where bloggers did better than mainstream media in ferreting out the truth, such as uncovering the truth about Trent Lott's affection for racist statements, or the lack of veracity in Diebold's claims about its voting machines."[19] And even a cursory review of key political blogs—Instapundit or Michelle Malkin on the Right, the Daily Kos or the Huffington Post on the Left—reveals a depth and an understanding that are rare in even the best of mainstream media. The point is there's good and bad on both sides. But perhaps in the blogosphere, there are better mechanisms for determining what is good and what is bad.

The point was driven home to me in the 2004 election. That election, of course, had created public awareness about blogs, since the early front-runner, Vermont governor Howard Dean, had been created by blog culture. But as I watched the returns from that election on national television, I began to feel sorry for the "correspondents" who had to report on this pivotal election on television. In one example, one of our nation's most prominent correspondents was asked to give, as the segment was advertised, an "in-depth analysis of" voters in one particular state. When the segment began, the national desk switched to this correspondent, and he began with a question to three "average voters" from the state. He then had about thirty seconds to add his own witty insight on top of their totally inane blather about why they had voted as they did. And that was it. One minute, and zero substance, broadcast to millions across the country.

It so happened that at the same time, I was reading an "in-depth analysis" of the same state, posted on a blog. The post had been written within the previous three hours. It was chock-full of substance and insight. Timely, smart, and comprehensive—much better than the "human angle" news that is national news today, and much more reflective of the talent of a great journalist. The television reporter no doubt thought he was a journalist. But with TV tuned to the attention span of an increasingly ADD public, who can afford to be a journalist?

There's one more important dimension to the RW culture of text on the Internet: the power of advertising. In this realm, the *editorial* power of advertisers is radically smaller than in traditional media. An advertiser can choose whether and where to advertise. But advertising is still a small part of the economy of blogging, and where it is relevant, many different content sources compete, so the ability of an advertiser indirectly to control content is radically diminished.[20]

The RW Internet is an ecosystem.

Many will remain skeptical. If the quality of the average blog is so bad, what good could this RW creativity be doing? But here we need to focus upon a second aspect of RW creativity—not so much the quality of the speech it produces, but the effect it has upon the person producing the speech.

I've felt one aspect of this effect personally. I'm a law professor. For the first decade of my law professor life, I wrote with the blissful understanding that no one was reading what I wrote. That knowledge gave me great freedom. More important, whatever the three readers of my writing thought remained their own private thoughts. Law professors write for law journals. Law journals don't attach comments to the articles they publish.

Blog space is different. You can see people read your writing; if you allow, you can see their comments. The consequence of both is something you can't quite understand until you've endured it. Like eating spinach or working out, I force myself to suffer it because I know it's good for me. I've written a blog since 2002. Each entry has a link for comments. I don't screen or filter comments (save for spam). I don't require people to give their real name. The forum is open for anyone to say whatever he or she wants. And people do. Some of the comments are quite brilliant. Many add important facts I've omitted or clarify what I've misunderstood. Some commentators become regulars. One character, "Three Blind Mice," has been a regular for a long time, rarely agreeing with anything I say.

But many of the comments are as rude and abusive as language allows. There are figures—they're called "trolls"—who live for the fights they can gin up in these spaces. They behave awfully. Their arguments are (in the main) ridiculous, and they generally make comment spaces deeply unpleasant.

Other commentators find ways around these trolls. Norms like "don't feed the troll" are invoked whenever anyone takes a troll on. But there's only so much that can be done, at least so long as the forum owner (me) doesn't block certain people or force everyone to use his or her real name.

I find it insanely difficult to read these comments. Not because they're bad or mistaken, but mainly because I have very thin skin. There's a direct correlation between what I read and pain in my gut. Even unfair and mistaken criticism cuts me in ways that are just silly. If I read a bad comment before bed, I don't sleep. If I trip upon one when I'm trying to write, I can be distracted for hours. I fantasize about creating an alter ego who responds on my behalf. But I don't have the courage for even that deception. So instead, my weakness manifests itself through the practice (extraordinarily unfair to the comment writer) of sometimes not reading what others have said.

So then why do I blog all? Well, much of the time, I have no idea why I do it. But when I do, it has something to do with an ethic I believe that we all should live by. I first learned it from a judge I clerked for, Judge Richard Posner. Posner is without a doubt the most significant legal academic and federal judge of our time, and perhaps of the last hundred years. He was also the perfect judge to clerk for. Unlike the vast majority of appeals court judges, Posner writes his own opinions. The job of the clerk was simply to argue. He would give us a draft opinion, and we'd write a long memo in critique. He'd use that to redraft the opinion.

I gave Posner comments on much more than his opinions. In particular, soon after I began teaching he sent me a draft of a book, which would eventually become *Sex and Reason*. Much of the book was brilliant. But there was one part I thought ridiculous. And in a series of faxes (I was teaching in Budapest, and this was long before e-mail was generally available), I sent him increasingly outrageous comments, arguing about this section of the book.

The morning after I sent one such missive, I reread it, and was shocked by its abusive tone. I wrote a sheepish follow-up, apologizing, and saying that of course, I had endless respect for Posner, blah, blah, and blah. All that was true. So too was it true that I thought my comments were unfair. But Posner responded not by accepting my apology, but by scolding me. And not by scolding me for my abusive fax, but for my apology. "I'm surrounded by sycophants," he wrote. "The last tiling in the world I need is you to filter your comments by reference to my feelings."

I was astonished by the rebuke. But from that moment on, I divided the world into those who would follow (or even recommend) Posner's practice, and those who wouldn't. And however attractive the anti-Posner pose was, I wanted to believe I could follow his ethic: Never allow, or encourage, the sycophants. Reward the critics. Not because I'd ever become a judge, or a public figure as important as Posner. But because in following his example, I would avoid the worst effects of the protected life (as a tenured professor) that I would lead.

Until the Internet, there was no good way to do this, at least if you were as insignificant as I. It's not like I could go to my local Starbucks and hold a public forum. There are people who do that in my neighborhood. Most of them have not showered for weeks. Famous people could do this, in principle. But the ethic of public appearances today, at least for Americans, militates against this sort of directness. It's rude to be critical. Indeed, if you're too critical, you're likely to be removed from the forum by men with badges.

This is not the way it is everywhere. In perhaps the most dramatic experience of democracy I've witnessed, I watched Brazil's minister of culture, Gilberto Gil, argue with a loving but critical crowd (loving his music and most of his policies, except the part that protected incumbent radio stations).[21] The forum was packed. There was no stage that separated Gii from the hundreds who huddled around to hear him. People argued directly with him. He argued back, equal to equal. The exchange was so honest that it even embarrassed John Perry Barlow, Gil's friend and fan, who stood to defend Gil against the critics.

But Gil loved the exchange. He was not embarrassed by the harshness of the criticism. His manner encouraged it. He was a democratic leader in a real (as opposed to hierarchical) democracy. He was Posner in Brazil.

For those of us who are not Posner and not Gil, the Internet is the one context that encourages the ethic of democracy that they exemplify. It is the place where all writing gets to be

RW. To write in this medium is to know that anything one writes is open to debate. I used to love the conceit of a law review article—presenting its arguments as if they were proven, with little or no space provided for disagreement. I now feel guilty about participating in such a form.

All this openness is the produce of a kind of democracy made real with writing. If trends continue, we're about to see this democracy made real with all writing. The publishers are going to fight the Googlezation of books. But as authors see that the most significant writing is that which is RW, they'll begin to insist that their publishers relax. In ten years, everything written that is read will be accessible on the Net—meaning not that people will be able to download copies to read on their DRM-encumbered reader but accessible in an open-access way, so that others will be able to comment on, and rate, and criticize the writing they read. This write/read is the essence of RW.

Text is just a small part of the RW culture that the Internet is. Consider now its big, and ultimately much more significant, sister.

Remixed: Media

For most of the Middle Ages in Europe, the elite spoke and wrote in Latin. The masses did not. They spoke local, or vernacular, languages—what we now call French, German, and English. What was important to the elites was thus inaccessible to the masses. The most "important" texts were understood by only a few.

Text is today's Latin. It is through text that we elites communicate (look at you, reading this book). For the masses, however, most information is gathered through other forms of media: TV, film, music, and music video. These forms of "writing" are the vernacular of today. They are the kinds of "writing" that matters most to most. Nielsen Media Research, for example, reports that the average TV is left on for 8.25 hours a day, "more than an hour longer than a decade ago."[22] The average American watches that average TV about 4.5 hours a day.[23] If you count other forms of media—including radio, the Web, and cell phones—the number doubles.[24] In 2006, the U.S. Bureau of the Census estimated that "American adults and teens will spend nearly five months" in 2007 consuming media.[25] These statistics compare with falling numbers for text. Everything is captured in this snapshot of generations:

> Individuals age 75 and over averaged 1.4 hours of reading per weekend day and 0.2 hour (12 minutes) playing games or using a computer for leisure. Conversely, individuals ages 15 to 19 read for an average of 0.1 hour (7 minutes) per weekend day and spent 1.0 hour playing games or using a computer for leisure.[26]

It is no surprise, then, that these other forms of "creating" are becoming an increasingly dominant form of "writing." The Internet didn't make these other forms of "writing" (what I will call simply "media") significant. But the Internet and digital technologies opened these media to the masses. Using the tools of digital technology—even the simplest tools, bundled into the most innovative modern operating systems—anyone can begin to "write" using images, or music, or video. And using the facilities of a free digital network, anyone can share that writing with anyone else. As with RW text, an ecology of RW media is developing. It is younger than the ecology of RW texts. But it is growing more quickly, and its appeal is much broader.[27]

These RW media look very much like Ben's writing with text. They remix, or quote, a wide range of "texts" to produce something new. These quotes, however, happen at different layers. Unlike text, where the quotes follow in a single line—such as here, where the sentence explains, "and then a quote gets added"—remixed media may quote sounds over images, or video over text, or text over sounds. The quotes thus get mixed together. The mix produces the new creative work—the "remix."

These remixes can be simple or they can be insanely complex. At one end, think about a home movie, splicing a scene from *Superman* into the middle. At the other end, there are new forms of art being generated by virtuosic remixing of images and video with found and remade audio. Think again about Girl Talk, remixing between 200 and 250 samples from 167 artists in a single CD. This is not simply copying. Sounds are being used like paint on a palette. But all the paint has been scratched off of other paintings.

So how should we think about it? What does it mean, exactly?

However complex, in its essence remix is, as Negativland's Don Joyce described to me, "just collage." Collage, as he explained,

[e]merged with the invention of photography. Very shortly after it was invented … you started seeing these sort of joking postcards that were photo composites. There would be a horse-drawn wagon with a cucumber in the back the size of a house. Things like that. Just little joking composite photograph things. That impressed painters at the time right away.

But collage with physical objects is difficult to do well and expensive to spread broadly. Those barriers either kept many away from this form of expression, or channeled collage into media that could be remixed cheaply. As Mark Hosier of Negativland described to me, explaining his choice to work with audio,

I realized that you could get a hold of some four-track reel-to-reel for not that much money and have it at home and actually play around with it and experiment and try out stuff. But with film, you couldn't do that. It was too expensive . … So that … drove me … to pick a medium where we could actually control what we were doing with a small number of people, to pull something off and make some finished thing to get it out diere.[28]

With digital objects, however, the opportunity for wide-scale collage is very different. "Now," as filmmaker Johan Söderberg explained, "you can do [video remix] almost for free on your own computer."[29] This means more people can create in this way, which means that many more do. The images or sounds are taken from the tokens of culture, whether digital or analog. The tokens are "blaring at us all the time," as Don Joyce put it to me: "We are barraged" by expression intended originally as simply RO. Negativland's Mark Hosier:

When you turn around 360 degrees; how many different ads or logos will you see somewhere in your space? [O]n your car, on your wrist-watch, on a billboard. If you walk into any grocery store or restaurant or anywhere to shop, there's always a soundtrack playing. There's always … media. There's ads. There's magazines everywhere. … [I]t's the world we live in. It's the landscape around us.

This "barrage" thus becomes a source.[30] As Johan Söderberg says, "To me, it is just like cooking. In your cupboard in your kitchen you have lots of different things and you try to connect different tastes together to create something interesting."

The remix artist does the same thing with bits of culture found in his digital cupboard.

My favorites among the remixes I've seen are all cases in which the mix delivers a message more powerfully than any original alone could, and certainly more than words alone could.

For example, a remix by Jonathan McIntosh begins with a scene from *The Matrix*, in which Agent Smith asks, "Do you ever get the feeling you're living in a virtual reality dream world? Fabricated to enslave your mind?" The scene then fades to a series of unbelievable war images from the Fox News Channel—a news organization that arguably makes people less aware of the facts than they were before watching it.[31] Toward the end, the standard announcer voice says, "But there is another sound: the sound of good will." On the screen is an image of Geraldo Rivera, somewhere in Afghanistan. For about four seconds, he stands there silently, with the wind rushing in the background. (I can always measure the quickness of my audience by how long it takes for people to get the joke: "the sound of good will" = silence). The clip closes with a fast series of cuts to more Fox images, and then a final clip from an ad for the film that opened McIntosh's remix: "The Matrix Has You."

Or consider the work of Sim Sadler, video artist and filmmaker. My Favorite of his is called "Hard Working George." It builds exclusively from a video of George Bush in one of his 2004 debates with John Kerry. Again and again, Sadler clips places where Bush says, essentially, "it's hard work." Here's the transcript:

Sir, in answer to your question I just know how this world works. I see on TV screens how hard it is. We're making progress; it is hard work. You know, it's hard work. It's hard work. A lot of really great people working hard, they can do the hard work. That's what distinguishes us from the enemy. And it's hard work, but it's necessary work and that's essential, but again I want to tell the American people it's hard work. It is hard work. It's hard work. There is no doubt in my mind that it is necessary work. I understand how hard it is, that's my job. No doubt about it, it's tough. It's hard work which I really want to do, but I would hope I never have to—nothing wrong with that. But again I repeat to my fellow citizens, we're making progress. We're making progress there. I reject this notion. It's ludicrous. It is hard work. It's hard work. That's the plan for victory and that is the best way. What I said was it's hard work and I made that very clear.

Usually, the audience breaks into uncontrolled laughter at "I would hope I never have to—nothing wrong with that," so people don't hear the rest of the clip. But by the end, the filter Sadler has imposed lets us understand Bush's message better.

Some look at this clip and say, "See, this shows anything can be remixed to make a false impression of the target." But in fact, the "not working hard" works as well as it does precisely because it is well known that at least before 9/11, Bush was an extremely remote president, on vacation 42 percent of his first eight months in office.[32] The success of the clip thus comes from building upon what we already know. It is powerful because it makes Bush himself say what we know is true about him. The same line wouldn't have worked with Clinton, or Bill Gates. Whatever you want to say about them, no one thinks they don't work hard.

My favorite of all these favorites, however, is still a clip in a series called "Read My Lips," created by Söderberg. Söderberg is an artist, director, and professional video editor. He has edited music videos for Robbie Williams and Madonna and, as he put it, "all kinds of pop stars." He also has an Internet TV site—soderberg.tv—that carries all his own work. That work stretches back almost twenty years.

"Read My Lips" is a series Söderberg made for a Swedish company called Atmo, in which famous people are lip-synched with music or other people's words. They all are extraordinarily funny (though you can't see all of them anymore because one, which mixed Hitler with the song "Born to Be Alive," resulted in a lawsuit).

The best of these (in my view at least) is a love song with Tony Blair and George Bush. The sound track for the video is Lionel Richie's "Endless Love." Remember the words "My love, there's only you in my life." The visuals are images of Bush and Blair. Through careful editing, Söderberg lip-synchs Bush singing the male part and Blair singing the female part. The execution is almost perfect. The message couldn't be more powerful: an emasculated Britain, as captured in the puppy love of its leader for Bush.

The obvious point is that a remix like this can't help but make its argument, at least in our culture, far more effectively than could words. (By "effectively," I mean that it delivers its message successfully to a wide range of viewers.) For anyone who has lived in our era, a mix of images and sounds makes its point far more powerfully than any eight-hundred-word essay in the *New York Times* could. No one can deny the power of this clip, even Bush and Blair supporters, again in part because it trades upon a truth we all—including Bush and Blair supporters—recognize as true. It doesn't assert the truth. It shows it. And once it is shown, no one can escape its mimetic effect. This video is a virus; once it enters your brain, you can't think about Bush and Blair in the same way again.

But why, as I'm asked over and over again, can't the remixer simply make his own content? Why is it important to select a drumbeat from a certain Beatles recording? Or a Warhol image? Why not simply record your own drumbeat? Or paint your own painting?

The answer to these questions is not hard if we focus again upon why these tokens have meaning. Their meaning comes not from the content of what they say; it comes from the reference, which is expressible only if it is the original that gets used. Images or sounds collected from real-world examples become "paint on a palette." And it is this "cultural reference," as coder and remix artist Victor Stone explained, that "has emotional meaning to people. ... When you hear four notes of the Beatles' 'Revolution,' it means something."[33] When you "mix these symbolic things together" with something new, you create, as Söderberg put it, "something new that didn't exist before."

The band Negativland has been making remixes using "found culture"—collected recordings of RO culture—for more than twenty-five years. As I described at the start, they first became (in)famous when they were the target of legal action brought by Casey Kasern and the band U2 after Negativland released a mash-up of Casey Kaserns introduction of U2 on his Top 40 show. So why couldn't Negativland simply have used something original? Why couldn't they rerecord the clip with an actor? Hosier explained:

> We could have taken these tapes we got of Casey Kasem and hired someone who imitated Casey Kasem, you know, and had him do a dramatic re-creation. Why did we have to use the actual original … the actual thing? Well, it's because the actual thing has a power about it. It has an aura. It has a magic to it. And that's what inspires the work.

Likewise with their remarkable, if remarkably irreverent, film, *The Mashin' of the Christ.*

This five-minute movie is made from remixing the scores of movies made throughout history about Jesus' crucifixion. The audio behind these images is a revivalist preacher who repeatedly says (during the first minute), "Christianity is stupid." The film then transitions at about a minute and a half when the preacher says, "Communism is good." The first quote aligns Christians, at least, against the film. But the second then reverses that feeling, as the film might also be seen as a criticism of Communism. As Hosier explained the work:

> *The Mashin' of the Christ* just came our of an idle thought that crossed my mind one day when I was flipping around on Amazon.com. I thought, "How many movies have been made about the life of Jesus, anyway?" I came up with thirty or forty of them and I started thinking about [how] every one of those films has similar sequences of Jesus being beaten, flogged, whipped, abused. There's always a shot where he's carrying the cross and he stumbles and he falls. And it just occurred to me ... I thought that would make an interesting montage of stuff.

This montage's point could not have been made by simply shooting crucifixion film number forty-one.

The Significance of Remix

I've described what I mean by remix by describing a bit of its practice. Whether text or beyond text, remix is collage; it comes from combining elements of RO culture; it succeeds by leveraging the meaning created by the reference to build something new.

But why should anyone care about whether remix flourishes, or even exists? What does anyone gain, beyond a cheap laugh? What does a society gain, beyond angry famous people?

There are two goods that remix creates, at least for us, or for our kids, at least now. One is the good of community. The other is education.

Community

Remixes happen within a community of remixers. In the digital age, that community can be spread around the world. Members of that community create in part for one another. They are showing one another how they can create, as kids on a skateboard are showing their friends how they can create. That showing is valuable, even when the stuff produced is not.

Consider, for example, the community creating anime music videos (AMV). Anime are the Japanese cartoons that swept America a few years ago. AMVs are (typically) created by remixing images from these cartoons with a music track or the track from a movie trailer. Each video can take between fifty and four hundred hours to create. There are literally thousands that are shared noncommercially at the leading site, animemusicvideos.org.

The aim of these creators is in part to learn. It is in part to show off. It is in part to create works that are strikingly beautiful. The work is extremely difficult to do well. Anyone who does it well also has the talent to do well in the creative industries. This fact has not been lost on industry, or universities training kids for industry. After I described AMVs at one talk, a father approached me with tears in his eyes. "You don't know how important this stuff is," he told me. "My kid couldn't get into any university. He then showed them his AMVs, and now he's at one of the best design schools in America."

AMVs are peculiarly American—or, though they build upon Japanese anime, they are not particularly Japanese. This is not because Japanese kids are not remixers. To the contrary, Japanese culture encourages this remixing from a much younger age, and much more broadly. According to cultural anthropologist Mimi Ito,

> Japanese media have really been at the forefront of pushing recombinant and user-driven content starting with very young children. If you consider things like *pokémon* and *Yu-Gi-Oh!* as examples of these kinds of more fannish forms of media engagement, the base of it is very broad in Japan, probably much broader than in the U.S. Something like *Pokémon* or *Yu-Gi-Oh!* reached a saturation point of nearly 100 percent within kids' cultures in Japan.[34]

But the difference between cultures is not just about saturation. Henry Jenkins quotes education professors David Buckingham and Julia Sefton-Green, "*Pokémon* is something you do, not just something you read or watch or consume," and continues:

> There are several hundred different *Pokémon*, each with multiple evolutionary forms and a complex set of rivalries and attachments. There is no one text where one can go to get the information about these various species; rather, the child assembles what they know about the *Pokémon* from various media with the result that each child knows something his or her friends do not and thus has a chance to share this expertise with others.[35]

"Every person," Ito explains, thus "has a personalized set of *Pokémon*. That is very different from [American media, which are] asking kids to identify with a single character."

Pokémon is just a single example of a common practice in Japan. This more common practice pushes "kids to develop more persona lives, and remix-oriented pathways to the content." Kids in the second and third grades, for example, will all

> carry around just a little sketchbook … with drawings of manga [cartoon] characters in them. That's what [Japanese] kids do. Then by fourth or fifth grade there are certain kids that get known to be good at drawing and then they actually start making their original stories. Then at some point there needs to be an induction into the whole *doujinshi* scene, which is its own subculture. That usually happens through knowing an older kid who's involved in that.

American kids have it different. The focus is not: "Here's something, do something with it." The focus is instead: "Here's something, buy it," "The U.S. has a stronger cultural investment in the idea of childhood innocence," Ito explains, "and it also has a more protectionist view with respect to media content." And this "protectionism" extends into schooling as well. "Entertainment" is separate from "education." So any skill learned in this "remix culture" is "constructed oppositionally to academic achievement." Thus, while "remix culture" flourishes with adult-oriented media in the United States, "there's still a lot of resistance to media that are coded as children's media being really fully [integrated] into that space."

Yet the passion for remix is growing in American kids, and AMVs are one important example. Ito has been studying these AMV creators, getting a "sense of their trajectories" as creators. At what moment, she is trying to understand, does "a fan see [himself] as a media producer and not just a consumer"? And what was the experience (given it was certainly not formal education) that led them to this form of expression?

Ito's results are not complete, but certain patterns are clear. "A very high proportion of kids who engage in remix culture," for example, "have had experience with interactive gaming formats." "The AMV scene is dominated by middle-class white men"—in contrast to the most famous remixers in recent Japanese history, the "working-class girls" who produced *doujinshi*. Most "have a day job or are full-time students but … have an incredibly active amateur life. … [They] see themselves as producers and participants in a culture and not just recipients of it." That participation happens with others. They form the community. That community supports itself.

Education

A second value in remix extends beyond the value of a community. Remix is also and often, as Mimi Ito describes, a strategy to excite "interest-based learning." As the name suggests, interest-based learning is the learning driven by found interests. When kids get to do work that they feel passionate about, kids (and, for that matter, adults) learn more and learn more effectively.

I wrote about this in an earlier book, *Free Culture*. There I described the work of Elizabeth Daley and Stephanie Barish, both of whom were working with kids in inner-city schools. By giving these kids basic media literacy, they saw classes of students who before could not retain their focus for a single period now spending every free moment of every hour the school was open editing and perfecting video about their lives, or about stories they wanted to tell.

Others have seen the same success grow from using remix media to teach. At the University of Houston—a school where a high percentage of the students don't speak English as their first language—the Digital Storytelling project has produced an extraordinary range of historical videos, created by students who research the story carefully, and select from archives of images and sounds the mix that best conveys the argument they want their video to make.

As Henry Jenkins notes, "[M]any adults worry that these kids are 'copying' preexisting media content rather than creating their own original works."[36] But as Jenkins rightly responds, "More and more literacy experts are recognizing that enacting, reciting, and appropriating elements from preexisting stories is a valuable and organic part of the process by which children develop cultural literacy."[37] Parents should instead, Jenkins argues, "think about their [kids'] appropriations as a kind of apprenticeship."[38] They learn by remixing. Indeed, they learn more about the form of expression they remix than if they simply made that expression directly.

This is not to say, of course, that however they do this remix, they're doing something good. There's good and bad remix, as there's good and bad writing. But just as bad writing is not an argument against writing, bad remix is not an argument against remix. Instead, in both cases, poor work is an argument for better education. As Hosier put it to me:

> Every high school in America needs to have a course in media literacy. We're buried in this stuff. We're breathing it. We're drinking it constantly. It's 24/7 news and information and pop culture. … If you're trying to educate kids to think critically about history and society and culture, you've got to be encouraging them to be thoughtful and critical about media and information and advertising. Doing something with the culture, remixing it, is one way to learn.

The Old in the New

To many, my description of remix will sound like something very new. In one sense it is. But in a different, perhaps more fundamental sense, we also need to see that there's nothing essentially new in remix. Or put differently, the interesting part of remix isn't something new. All that's new is the technique and the ease with which the product of that technique can be shared. That ease invites a wider community to participate; it makes participation more compelling. But the creative act that is being engaged in is not significantly different from the act Sousa described when he recalled the "young people together singing the songs of the day or the old songs."

For as I've argued, remix with "media" is just the same sort of stuff that we've always done with words. It is how Ben wrote. It is how lawyers argue. It is how we all talk all the time. We don't notice it as such, because this text-based remix, whether in writing or conversation, is as common as dust. We take its freedoms for granted. We all expect that we can quote, or incorporate, other people's words into what we write or say. And so we do quote, or incorporate, or remix what others have said.

The same with "media." Remixed media succeed when they show others something new; they fail when they are trite or derivative. Like a great essay or a funny joke, a remix draws upon the work of others in order to do new work. It is great writing without words. It is creativity supported by a new technology.

Yet though this remix is not new, for most of our history it was silenced. Not by a censor, or by evil capitalists, or even by good capitalists. It was silenced because the economics of speaking in this different way made this speaking impossible, at least for most. If in 1968 you wanted to capture the latest Walter Cronkite news program and remix it with the Beatles, and then share it with your ten thousand best friends, what blocked you was not the law. What blocked you was that the production costs alone would have been in the tens of thousands of dollars.

Digital technologies have now removed that economic censor. The ways and reach of speech are now greater. More people can use a wider set of tools to express ideas and emotions differently. More can, and so more will, at least until the law effectively blocks it.

Notes

1. *Grand Uprights Music Ltd. v, Warner Bros. Records Inc.*, 780 F. Supp. 182 (S.D.N.Y. 1991). MLA Ref.
2. All quotes from Don Joyce taken from an interview conducted March 20, 2007, by telephone.
3. David Bollier. *Brand Name Bullies* (Hoboken, N. J., Wiley, 2005), 69.
4. J. D. Lasica. *Darknet: Hollywood', War Against the Digital Generation* (Hoboken, N.J., Wiley, 2005), 72–73.
5. Heidi Anderson, "Plugged In," Smars Computing (November 2000): 90–92.
6. Yochai Benkler, *The Wealth of Networks: How Social Production Transforms Markets and Freedom* (New Haven: Yale UP, 2006), 217.
7. Mark Lawson, "Berners Lee on the Read/Write Web," *BBC News*, August 9, 2005, available at link #22 (last visited July 31, 2007).
8. Niall Kennedy, "Technorati Two Years Later," Niall Kennedy;s Weblog, November 26, 2004, available at link #23; David Sifry, "Technorati," Sifry's Alerts, November 27, 2002, available at link #24, David Sifry, "Over 100,000 Blogs Served," Sifry's Alerts, March 5, 2003, available at link #25, David Sifry, "One Million Weblogs Tracked," Sifry's Alerts, September 27, 2003, available at link #26; David Sifry, "State of the Blogosphere." Sifry's Alerts, October 10, 2004, available at link #27, "About Us," Technorati available at link #28 (last visited July 30, 2007).
9. David Sifry, "The State of the Live Web," Sifry's Alerts, April 5, 2007, available at link #29 (last visited July 23, 2007); David Sifry, "State of the Blogosphere, October 2006, Technorati, available at link #30 (last visited July 23, 2007).
10. Benkler, *Wealth of Networks*, 217

11. Thomas Vander Wal, "Off the Top: Folksonomy Entries," Vanderwal.net, October 3, 2004, available at link #31.
12. Don Tapscott and Anthony D. Williams, *Wilrinomics. How Mass Collaboration Changes Everything* (New York: Portfolio, 2006), 41
13. Ibid., 52.
14. Ibid., 144–45.
15. Ibid., 42.
16. "Blogging Basics-" Technorati, available at link #32 (last visited July 23, 2007)
17. David Sifry, "The State of the Live Web. April 2007," Sifry's Alerts, available at link #33 (last visited August 16, 2007).
18. Charlene Li. *Social Technographers* (Cambridge, Mass.:Forrester, 2007), 2.
19. Benkler, *Wealth of Networks*, 225–33.
20. The blog Corporate Influence in the Media tries to document examples of advertisers pressuring publishers and broadcasters. See Anup Shah, Corporate Influence in the Media, available at link #34 (last visited August 16, 2007). In 2006 the Center for Media and Democracy released a report detailing a large number of instances in which news organizations broadcast "video news releases" as news without revealing to their audiences that the video was provided by a public relations firm. See Diane Farsetta and Daniel Price, "Fake TV News: Widespread and Undisclosed," Center for Media and Democracy, April 6, 2006, available at link #35.
21. Lawrence Lessig, "The People Own Ideas," *Technology Review* (June 2005); 46–48.
22. "To the Point: Trends & Innovations," *Investor's Business Daily*, September 26, 2006.
23. Ibid.
24. Gail Koch, "'$00-Pound Gorilla' Still Rules for Most," *Star Press* (Muncie, Ind.), September 28, 2005.
25. Xinhua News Agency, "Census Bureau: Americans to Spend More Time on Media Next Year," December 15, 2006.
26. U.S. Fed News, "American Time Use Survey-2006 Results," *U.S. Fed News*, June 28, 2007.
27. This is not to say that before the Internet, there was nothing like this RW-media culture. Indeed, for almost a half century, beginning with the *Star Trek* series, there has been a rich "fan fiction" culture, in which fans take popular culture and remix it. Rebecca Tushnet, "Legal Fictions: Copyright, Fan Fiction, and a New Common Law," *Loyola of Los Angeles Entertainment Law Journal* 17 (1997); 655, citing Henry Jenkins and John Tulloch, eds., '*At other Times, Like Females'- Gender and Star Trek Fan Fiction, in Science Fiction Audiences: Watching Dr. Whu and* Star Trek (London: Routledge, 1995), 196. Some trace the history of fan fiction back even earlier, to "metanovels" written in response to classic works of fiction such as *Pride and Prejudice* (Sharon Cumberland, "Private Uses of Cyberspace: Women, Desire and Fan Culture," in *Rethinking Media Change: The Aesthetics of Transition*, ed, David Thorburn and Henry Jenkins (Cambridge, Mass.: MIT Press, 2003), 261. An Internet commentator known as Super Cat argues that the first fan fiction was John Lydgate's *The Siege of Thebes*, a continuation of *The Canterbury Tales* circa 1421: Super Cat, "A (Very) Brief History of Fanfic," Fanfic Symposium, available at link #36 (last visited August 11, 2007). Many believe that the contemporary online fan fiction community is predominantly composed of women, and the genre addresses topics traditionally marginalized in the commercial media, including "The status of women in society, women's ability to express desire, [and] the blurring of stereotyped gender lines" (Cumberland, "Private Uses," 265). In addition to traditional textual fan fiction, cyberspace has spawned an active culture of fan filmmaking. See Henry Jenkins, "Quentin Tarantino's Star Wars? Digital Cinema. Media Convergence, and Participatory Culture," in *Rethinking Media Change: The Aesthetics of Transition*, ed. David Thorburn and Henry Jenkins (Cambridge, Mass.: MIT Press, 2003), 281–84 (Offering a case study of *Star Wars* fan fiction, which began in textual form with the first official film, and developed into digital film distributed on independent creators' Web sites). There is a comprehensive study of fan fiction in chapters 5–8 of Henry Jenkins, *Textual Poachers: Televisions Fans and Participatory Culture* (New York: Routledge, 1992).
28. All quotes from Mark Hosler taken from an interview conducted May 1, 2007, by telephone.
29. All quotes from Johan Söderberg taken from an interview conducted February 15, 2007, by telephone.
30. Telephone interview with Don Joyce, March 20, 2007.
31. "Misperceptions, the Media, and the Iraq War," Program on International Policy Attitudes and Knowledge Networks, available at link #37 (last visited January 18, 2008).
32. Charles Krauthammer, "A Vacation Bush Deserves," *Washington Post*, August 10, 2001.
33. All quotes from Victor Stone taken from an interview conducted February 15, 2007, by telephone.
34. All quotes from Mimi Ito taken from an interview conducted January 24, 2007, by telephone. For more, see Mimi Ito, "Japanese Media Mixes and Amateur Cultural Exchange," in *Digital Generations*, ed. David Buckingham and Rchckah Willets (Mahwah, N.J.: Lawrence Erlbaum, 2006), 49–66.
35. Henry Jenkins, *Convergence Culture: Where Old and New Media Collide* (New York: NYUP, 2006), 128.
36. Ibid., 182.
37. Ibid., 177.
38. Ibid., 182.

14
Writing Center Dynamics
Coordinating Multimodal Consultations

Russell Carpenter

Steven Johnson sees the machine not as an attachment to our bodies, but as an environment, a space to be explored (24). Likewise, the spaces that our writing centers now inhabit need exploration and explanation. Although as writing center practitioners and scholars we understand that we cannot necessarily replicate face-to-face (f2f) consultations in virtual writing spaces or even over the phone, our goal at the University of Central Florida (UCF) was to integrate these types of consultations into our existing system without compromising our mission statement and consulting philosophies. The synchronous nature of phone and online consultations supports the University Writing Center's (UWC) mission of helping to "foster the community of scholarship and shared leadership at UCF through peer consulting, a form of collaborative learning which involves students in each other's intellectual and academic development." The University Writing Center is a nonremedial peer consultant service for undergraduate and graduate students at UCF. Consultants work with writers at every stage of the writing process—from the prewriting stage to finalizing revisions.

In addition to our large main campus in Orlando, FL, UCF also has multiple regional campuses and several specialty campuses, including a hospitality management campus, film and digital media campus, and a health sciences campus, which will also include the new College of Medicine. As we added, complexity to our busy face-to-face consultation services, it became necessary that we expand the UWC to keep up with UCF's growing student population of more than 48,000, as I discussed in "Using RoCs to Inform New Training Methods," a preliminary discourse analysis based on our pilot online writing lab, KnightOWL ("Using RoCs" 10).

In informal conversations around campus and in the UWC, students expressed their need for more accessible resources, including consultations. To address students' needs, we explored options for an online and phone consultation program. Regardless of campus or research travel, students would have access to this resource. In building our online and phone services into the UWC, we established "modes" of consultation, "resources which allow the simultaneous realization of discourses and types of (inter)action," as Gunther Kress and Theo van Leeuwen help explain (21). Thus, the consultations at our UWC are highly multimodal, which also made the UWC a more dynamic place to coordinate. At times, consultants are online, but sometimes they work with students over the phone or f2f. For instance, a consultant might first consult f2f and the next hour over the phone, and the third hour online. Consultants and consultations are constantly changing and fluctuating. We wanted to appeal to students who were more comfortable having their consultations over the phone and others who would prefer an online chat. In both modes, the student and consultant work with the same document on the computer screen while discussing the writing over the phone or in our online chat space. We offer the phone and online consultations through our service that we have named "KnightOWL."

KnightOWL's History

We began piloting KnightOWL during the fall 2005 semester with graduate thesis and dissertation writers. During the piloting stages, we offered online and phone consultations on a space-available basis when there were openings in our f2f schedule. During 2005–2006, KnightOWL helped 42 writers in 81 consultations. After the year-long pilot, we opened our KnightOWL consultations up to all students. During the fall 2006 semester, our first full semester with KnightOWL, we offered 61 hours of online and phone consultations in addition to 163 f2f hours per week, a substantial increase. Our UWC is largely run by students for students, and we wanted KnightOWL to be no different. The transition to a consultant-run system, as opposed to a system managed by UWC administrators, was one that we put a great deal of thought into before implementing. Our goal was to create a program that would expand and complement our current f2f consultation options, making the UWC a more dynamic space to coordinate. The process required us to integrate technology into the UWC in such a way as to create harmony among consultants and administrators, establishing a new virtual space that follows the same policies and philosophies as our physical space. Integrating this new practice into the UWC would not be an easy task. If it was going to happen, it was up to UWC administrators to ensure a smooth transition, or to creale "harmony." staying in tune with Beth Boquet's theme of "noise," among our writing consultants (xiv), the kind that comes front f2f constitutions within the walls of our center. Technology is a powerful resource. "The very presence of a certain technique or technology can alter the goals and aims of a society as well as the way people think in articulating their ideas," Thomas J. Misa explains (265). KnightOWL consultations not only affected the way students visited the UWC. They also affected the culture of the UWC, changing the way consultants interacted with each other and students.

The Challenge: Integrate KnightOWL Consultations into the Existing System

When we began offering KnightOWL consultations, students contacted me directly, and I scheduled them manually. We were dealing with a limited number of students—thesis and dissertation writers. The challenge we faced was to integrate KnightOWL consultations into our system. For face-to-face consultations, we use what we call our "Online Scheduler." The Scheduler allows students to book appointments online from any computer, and students can schedule appointments as they see fit. Consultants can also check their appointments through the Online Scheduler. From an administrative standpoint, we found it important that both students and consultants were able to schedule, view, and manage all appointment modes—f2f, online, and phone. We felt that this would help consultants embrace the new system and have an active voice in the transition process.

The Solution: Create a More Dynamic Virtual Space

Using the existing Online Scheduler, we had to create a more dynamic virtual space where we could schedule KnightOWL appointments for both phone and online consultations. It's important to mention scheduling first before we discuss integrating KnightOWL consultations into the system. The consultants submit schedule requests at the beginning of the semester, blocking out times when they're in class and time for other commitments. I then build the schedule for internal use, using seven consultation modes, according to the level of the consultants. Graduate consultants work with graduate students, and undergraduate consultants with undergraduate students. Consultants are scheduled to work each mode during the day; the modes are face-to-face (at the graduate or undergraduate level), phone, and online. A basic schedule would include graduate, undergraduate, and desk consultants. We schedule KnightOWL consultations during popular times of the day (i.e., afternoon and early evening) or as we have the staff available. Here's a description of each of the seven consultation modes:

Graduate: Graduate f2f consultation
Undergraduate: Undergraduate f2f consultation
Desk: Manages the flow of traffic in the UWC, answers phones, helps students sign in, and makes KnightOWL or f2f appointments
KnightOWL Online Undergraduate: Undergraduate synchronous online consultation
KnightOWL Phone Undergraduate: Undergraduate phone consultation
KnightOWL Online Graduate: Graduate synchronous online consultation
KnightOWL Phone Graduate: Graduate phone consultation

In a given hour, we might have a Graduate consultant for f2f an undergraduate for f2f, a desk consultant, and both phone and online KnightOWL consultants working concurrently in the UWC. Internally, the consultants are scheduled from 9 a.m.–8 p.m., with a maximum shift of five hours for a consultant. Using this schedule, consultants know exactly what mode they're consulting in and for how long. They can also help one another retrieve papers, transfer phone calls within the UWC (for KnightOWL phone consultations), and answer student questions. On the public, student side, all hours are entered into the Online Scheduler so that students can book appointments on their own. The electronic schedule mirrors the internal schedule but is publicly accessible. Once the schedule is set, it is set for the semester. Students can see whether there are f2f, online, or phone consultations available during any hour, day, or week.

When we opened KnightOWL consultations to all students, we built generic KnightOWL consultants by modality and status. A KnightOWL consultant might be scheduled as "KnightOWL Phone Graduate" in the system. The corresponding consultant on our internal schedule would take the consultations, and the student would know, through scheduling on the Online Scheduler, that the consultation would be over the phone or online. That is, f2f appointments are made with named consultants, but KnightOWL appointments are made based on the student's modal preference (online or phone) and consultant availability. We also had to arrange a system for phone and online writers—one where we could assure reliable service.

Phone

Students who schedule phone consultations via the Online Scheduler call the UWC's main line just before their scheduled consultation. The desk consultant answers the phone at the front desk and transfers the call to the KnightOWL station, which is in a separate part of the UWC. The consultant takes the phone consultation from there. Important to the process is the reliability of the desk consultant. We needed the third party to field the phone call and make sure that the KnightOWL phone consultant is prepared to take the call. The desk person is responsible for transferring the writer and ensuring that the writer's call does not disconnect, which would be frustrating for the student.

Online

KnightOWL online consultations take place in a secure chatroom hosted by LivePerson (www.LivePerson.com). To sign in, a student goes to our home page (www.uwc.ucf.edu), clicks on "Scheduler," and then looks for the "Click Here to Chat With Us Live!" portal that takes the student to the chat area where the consultant is waiting. When students sign in, they go into a virtual waiting room, and the consultant then accepts the student. Different from WebCT's chat feature, LivePerson offers a secure area where consultants and writers can work without fear of interruption. Consultants are still working from the UWC, but UCF students can have their appointments from anywhere in the world, even Afghanistan (Carpenter, "Enhancing Diversity Initiatives"). Students sign into the chat area, complete a brief pre-chat survey, which includes identification information, and the online consultation begins.

Student Submissions, Consulting Philosophies, and KnightOWL

It was important that our KnightOWL online consultations were synchronous. Our fear with asynchronous consultations was that they would not encourage a peer-to-peer dialogue about the student's writing. Joanna Castner also articulates this concern with asynchronous consultations in that a "lack of dialogue between consultant and client promotes the wrong idea about the goal of writing centers and the nature of the writing process itself" (120). The ongoing dialogue is what Stephen North simply calls "talking," the essence of writing center methods (443). We feared that the asynchronous consultation, although used successfully at other writing centers throughout the country, would have promoted more directive discourse than the supportive, peer-to-peer discourse that consultants employ on a regular basis.

For all KnightOWL consultations, student writers submit their papers to a designated e-mail address. All consultants have access to the papers there and can pull them at any time. Consultants will typically pull a paper at the beginning of the consultation, not before. This process is similar to our f2f policies in that consultants do not review papers before the scheduled appointment time. The student and consultant work through the paper together, synchronously.

How Our Consultants have Responded

Initially, consultants were hesitant about the new consultation modes. Weekly UWC seminars and online training discussions revealed that some consultants were reluctant to embrace the online mode especially. For example, one consultant mentioned that she felt disconnected from the student when consulting online. To encourage an open dialogue, consultants are free to make suggestions for the system and offer to help revise existing resources. We've also integrated new KnightOWL training methods into our consultant training sessions, weekly Friday seminars, and professional development projects that mirror our f2f training. This way, consultants can draw parallels and discuss differences between KnightOWL and f2f consulting, which has become an important part of our training program. As with any transition, we have experienced some technological glitches, overlap, and miscommunicution. This is to be expected with any new program; however, as a writing center, we know that we must quickly learn from these experiences and adapt our practices.

Helpful policies, procedures, and documents have come from consultant suggestions. For instance, we now have detailed websites for KnightOWL phone and online consultations. Based on consultant feedback, we also have standard protocols for student e-mails and paper attachments. Students put their names and appointment times in the subject lines when they e-mail their papers. We also developed a series of KnightOWL-specific handouts for students, which consultants refer to and distribute when students have questions. A graduate student in a technical writing course also revised our website based on her personal research and KnightOWL's needs. With the help of UCF's Digital Image Processing Lab, we were able to develop a logo for KnightOWL as well, and the image has become a mascot for the UWC at UCE.

As students continue to use the services and praise our efforts, consultants are increasingly able to see the value in having a program that supports all students regardless of location. In fact, consultants work with UCF students in other parts of the country as well. Relocated students often book a series of KnightOWL appointments throughout the semester. One UCF student had a phone consultation from her houseboat on the coast of Florida. Other UCF students have used KnightOWL from Michigan and Georgia. Without KnightOWL, these students, as well as many others, would not have writing support available. It is critical, with a growing campus and traveling researchers, that we continue to build KnightOWL and other programs like it so students, regardless of location and distance, will have the same access to writing support as those students living in our city and on our campus. Currently, UCF houses approximately 8,100 students on campus or in campus-affiliated housing. UCF also boasts a large graduate population, at 7,100 students. To meet students' needs, in a given year we will employ approximately 40 consultants.

Additional consultation "modes" undoubtedly added complexity to the coordination of an already busy UWC. In some ways, adding these modes even changed the language of our center and the way we think about our work. Consultants transition quickly from mode to mode; that is, from f2f to phone to online. They also discuss strategies from consulting students in these different modes during our weekly seminars and online discussions. I attribute these developments not only to our capable staff but also to the time we put into developing (and experimenting with) our system.

Our UWC has undergone significant changes since the pilot stages of KnightOWL. With the addition of online and phone consultations, we plan to implement even more new scheduling software into our center, which will allow consultants and students to have more control over their searching and scheduling options. The new system will allow for multiple "centers," as they are called in the new system (TutorTrac). Students will be able to search for online and phone availabilities specifically, without sorting through f2f options.

Our center is now more reliant on technology, but it is technology that allowed us to grow beyond our four walls and into an active and more dynamic virtual space. When talking about building a more dynamic UWC, we're not only making the "joyful noise" that Boquet describes. We also create what Don DeLillo might consider "white noise," the chatter generated through media and technology (310). However, this noise can also be joyful if we embrace forms of technology for the advantages they afford us. Technology allows us to expand and intertwine our services in ways we never thought possible, enmeshing f2f, phone, and online services seamlessly. Students once limited to f2f consultations now have a dynamic array of consultation options, facilitated on a daily basis primarily through their peer consultants. Students benefit from the more dynamic UWC, one with choices that fit the student's preferred mode and schedule. The dynamic UWC is a more challenging place and space to coordinate, but the rewards are well worth it. Consultants have embraced the dynamics of the UWC, and students have come to rely upon and expect multimodal consultations. Writing center practitioners exploring options for online or even phone consultations should consider the dynamics involved as they build or expand their own resources. The structure offered here may be widely applicable beyond our UWC to other expanding centers around the country.

Works Cited

Boquet, Beth. *Noise from the Writing Center*. Logan: Utah State UP, 2002.

Carpenter, Rusty. "Enhancing Diversity Initiatives through Technology: Writing Center Access from Dallas to Afghanistan." *Praxis: A Writing Center Journal* 5.1 (2007). 24 January 2008 <http://project.uwc.utexas.edu/praxis/?q=node/170>.

——. "Using RoCs to Inform New Training Methods for a 'Growing' OWL" *Writing Lab Newsletter* 32.3 (2007): 10–14.

Castner, Joanna. "The Asynchronous, Online Session: A Two-Way Stab in the Dark?" *Taking Flight with OWLS: Examining Electronic Writing Center Work*. Ed. James A. Inman and Donna N. Swell. Mahwah: Lawrence Earlbaum, 2000, 119–28.

DeLillo, Don. *White Noise*. New York: Penguin, 1986.

Johnson, Steven, *Interface Culture: How New Technology Transforms the Way We Create & Communicate*. San Francisco: Basic, 1997.

Kress, Gunther, and Theo van Leeuwen. *Multimodal Discourse: The Modes and Media of Contemporary Discourse*. New York: Arnold, 2001.

LivePerson. 2 February 2007. LivePerson, Inc. 3 February 2007 <http://www.liveperson.com/>.

Misa, Thomas J. *Leonardo to the Internet: Technology and Culture from the Renaissance to the Present.* Baltimore: Johns Hopkins UP, 2004.

North, Stephen. "The Idea of a Writing Center." *College English* 46.5 (1984): 433–46.

TutorTrac. 24 January 2008 <https://uwc-trac.cah.ucf.edu/TutorTrac/default.html> *UWC Mission.* 24 January 2008 <http://www.uwc.ncf.edu/About_the_UWC/about_home.htm>.

15

Among the Audience

On Audience in an Age of New Literacies

Andrea A. Lunsford and Lisa Ede

With participatory media, the boundaries between audiences and creators become blurred and often invisible. In the words of David Sifry, the founder of Technorati, a search engine for blogs, one-to-many "lectures" (i.e., from media companies to their audiences) are transformed into "conversations" among "the people formerly known as the audience."
> —Andrew Kluth, "Among the Audience:
> A Survey of New Media." *The Economist* (4)

Critics argue that privacy does not matter to children who were raised in a wired celebrity culture that promises a niche audience for everyone. Why hide when you can perform? But even if young people are performing, many are clueless about the size of their audience.
> —Ari Melber, "About Facebook." *The Nation* (23)

When we wrote "Audience Addressed/Audience Invoked: The Role of Audience in Composition Theory and Pedagogy" (hereafter AA/AI), which was published in *College Composition and Communication* in 1984, we little realized the life that it would have. Much has changed in the teaching of writing—and in the technologies of communication—since then. Much has changed, as well, in our culture and cultural awareness. So much so, in fact, that we saw the need in 1996 to critique our earlier essay, calling attention to several unexamined assumptions that we wished to expose and challenge. In "Representing Audience: Successful Discourse and Disciplinary Critique," published in *College Composition and Communication* in 1996, we observed, for instance, that although we intended our essay "to invoke and address a broad range of audiences, it speaks most strongly to those whose identifications and experiences mirror our own, while turning away from the potential difficulties and costs often inherent in the effort to achieve the kind of academic 'success' that our essay takes for granted as well as from those who would wish to subvert such 'success'" (175).

A dozen years later still, we see the need to reflect yet again on the role of audience in composition theory and pedagogy. In this regard, we are particularly interested in the role that new literacies are playing in expanding the possibilities of agency, while at the same time challenging older notions of both authorship and audience. In addition, observations of and talks with students—as well as changes in our own reading, writing, and researching practices—have alerted us to new understandings and enactments of textual production and ownership. As a result, our goal in this chapter is both theoretical and pedagogical. We wish to subject the concept of audience to renewed inquiry, attempting to account for the way texts develop and work in the world in the twenty-first century. We hope, as well, that the resulting analysis will be useful in our classrooms. As we conduct this exploration, we will address the following questions:

- In a world of participatory media—of Facebook, MySpace, Wikipedia, Twitter, and Del.icio.us—what relevance does the term *audience* hold?
- How can we best understand the relationships between text, author, medium, context, and audience today? How can we usefully describe the dynamic of this relationship?
- To what extent do the invoked and addressed audiences that we describe in our 1984 essay need to be revised and expanded? What other terms, metaphors, or images might prove productive? What difference might answers to these questions make to twenty-first-century teachers and students?

On New Media and New Literacies

Before turning to these questions, we would like to situate our discussion in the context of recent research on new media and new literacies, for how we view their relationship matters a good deal to our understanding of both audience and authorship. Are new literacies "new" simply because they rely upon new media, or is the relationship more complex? This is a question that Michele Knobel and Colin Lankshear raise in the introduction to their collection, *A New Literacies Sampler*. Knobel and Lankshear argue that the latter is the case. While acknowledging that new media have certainly played an important role in the development of new literacies, they argue that what they term *paradigm cases* of new literacies have, as they put it, both "new 'technical stuff'" and "new 'ethos' stuff" (7). Central to the development of new literacies, in other words, is the mobilization of "very different kinds of values and priorities and sensibilities than the literacies we are familiar with" (7). New literacies, they argue, are "more 'participatory,' 'collaborative,' and 'distributed' in nature than conventional literacies. That is, they are less 'published,' 'individuated,' and 'author-centric' than conventional literacies." They are also "less 'expert-dominated' than conventional literacies" (9).

New literacies involve, in other words, a different kind of mindset than literacies traditionally associated with print media. In their introduction to *A New Literacies Sampler*, Knobel and Lankshear contrast what they refer to as a "physical-industrial" mindset—the mindset that the two of us certainly grew up with throughout our schooling and a good deal of our working lives—with a "cyberspatial-postindustrial mindset" (10). According to Knobel and Lankshear, those whose experience grounds them primarily in a physical-industrial mindset tend to see the individual person as "the unit of production, competence, intelligence." They also identify expertise and authority as "located in individuals and institutions" (11). Those who inhabit a "cyberspatial-postindustrial mindset," in contrast, increasingly focus on "collectives as the unit of production, competence, intelligence" and tend to view expertise, authority, and agency as "distributed and collective" (11). In a "cyberspatial-postindustrial mindset," in other words, the distinction between author and audience is much less clear than in that of the physical-industrial mindset of print literacy.

Those familiar with research in our field on new media and new literacies—research undertaken by scholars such as Cynthia Selfe, Gail Hawisher, Anne Wysocki, Johndan Johnson-Eilola, the New London Group, and others—will recognize that the distinction that Knobel and Lankshear draw has been made before. (They will recognize, as well, the value of complicating this binary, helpful as it is in a general sense.) The insights these and other scholars in our field have generated have been enriched by research in such related areas as literacy, cultural, and Internet studies. In works ranging from Gunther Kress's *Literacy in the New Media Age* to Howard Rheingold's *Smart Mobs: The Next Social Revolution*, Henry Jenkins's *Convergence Culture; Where Old and New Media Collide*, Lisa Nakamura's *Digitizing Race: Visual Cultures of the Internet*, Keith Sawyer's *Group Genius*, and Clay Shirky's *Here Comes Everybody*, those studying online and digital literacies—particularly Web 2.0 literacies—are challenging conventional understandings of both authorship and audience.[1]

As we have engaged this literature and have attempted to better understand what it means to be a reader and writer in the twenty-first century, we have come to see that what we thought of as two separate strands of our scholarly work—one on collaboration, the other on audience—have in fact become one. As writers and audience merge and shift places in online environments, participating in both brief and extended collaborations, it is more obvious than ever that writers seldom, if ever, write alone.

The End of Audience?

In our contemporary world of digital and online literacies, it seems important to question the status and usefulness of the concept of *audience*. Are the changes brought about by new media and new literacies so substantial that it is more accurate to refer to those who participate in Web 2.0 as "the people formerly known as the audience," as David Sifry suggests in the first epigraph to this chapter?

Even before the explosion of such social networking sites as blogs, Facebook, and YouTube, some scholars in the field of rhetoric and writing argued that the term *audience* may have outlived its usefulness. Some suggested, for instance, that the term *discourse community* better reflects social constructionist understandings of communication. This is the position that James Porter espouses in his 1992 *Audience and Rhetoric: An Archaeological Composition of the Discourse Community*. Others have wondered whether the term *public*, as articulated and developed by Jürgen Habermas and explored and extended in Michael Warner's *Publics and Counterpublics*, might not be just as useful as (or more useful than) the term *audience*, In *Citizen Critics: Literary Public Spheres*, for instance, Rosa Eberly argues that the term *public* is more helpful than the terms *reader* or *audience* for her study of letters to the editor about four controversial literary texts—two published early in the twentieth century and two published later.

These and other efforts to reexamine and problematize the concept of audience reflect developments in the field over the last several decades. In the early 1980s when we were talking, thinking, and writing about audience, the need for such problematization was anything but apparent to us. Our context was different. At that time, we were immersed in research on the contemporary relevance of the classical rhetorical tradition, as our 1984 essay "On Distinctions between Classical and Modern Rhetoric" attests. That same year saw the publication of our coedited *Essays on Classical Rhetoric and Modern Discourse.*

In the years since we published AA/AI, we have come to recognize the limitations, as well as the strengths, of the classical (and more broadly Western) rhetorical tradition. In our 1996 reflection on AA/AI, "Representing Audience," for example, we acknowledge the individualism inherent in this tradition. We also point out that the rhetorical tradition's commitment to *successful* communication has exacted a high hidden price, particularly in terms of efforts to address the ethics of diversity: "For how better to avoid misunderstanding and failure (and to make 'successful' communication more likely) than to exclude, to disenfranchise those who by their very presence in the arena of discourse raise increased possibilities for communicative failures" (174). The rhetorical tradition, as a consequence, risks indifference or hostility to issues of difference, to "audiences ignored, rejected, excluded, or denied" (174).

Does this mean that we wish to reject the term *audience*? No, it does not. We believe that *audience*, like such other terms as *discourse community* or *public*, is inevitably overdetermined, but is still (as is the case with these other terms) in many contexts both helpful and productive. Finally, terms such as *audience, reader, discourse community*, and *public* gesture toward and evoke differing concerns, traditions, and interests. The emphasis on the reader in reader response criticism, for instance, was clearly a salutary response to the emphasis on the text in formalist new criticism.[2]

We continue to believe, then, that the concept of audience provides a helpful theoretical and practical grounding for efforts to understand how texts (and writers and readers) work in today's world. We also believe, as we stated in AA/AI, that a productive way to conceive of audience "is as an overdetermined or unusually rich concept, one which may perhaps be best specified through the analysis of precise, concrete situations" (168). Indeed, in rereading AA/AI we are struck by the powerful role that the analysis of such situations plays in our own essay. As readers may already realize, in remaining committed to the term *audience* we remain committed to rhetoric and to the rhetorical tradition. Our understanding of the rhetorical tradition has changed since we first wrote AA/AI, but we continue to find rhetoric's emphasis on the rhetorical situation to be theoretically and pedagogically enabling.

The "Rhetorical Triangle" Revisited

In AA/AI we described our own experiences with varying audiences, arguing that "the elements [of invoked and addressed audience roles] shift and merge, depending on the particular rhetorical situation, the writer's aim, and the genre chosen" (168). Thus we embedded our discussion of audience in the classical conception of the "rhetorical triangle," the set of relationships between text, author, and audience out of which meaning grows. Twenty-five years ago, while our work attempted to complicate these sets of relationships, this basic understanding served us simply and well. Today, however, we need a more flexible and robust way of understanding these traditional elements of discourse and the dynamic at work among them.

As a result, we now use the following figure (Figure 15.1) to portray the basic elements of the rhetorical situation.

This figure not only specifies medium as an element of the rhetorical situation but also includes context. This element of the rhetorical situation calls attention to the diverse and

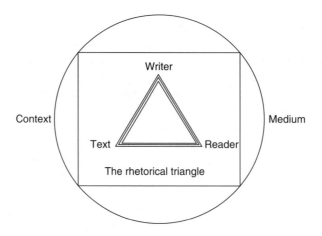

Figure 15.1 The Rhetorical Triangle.

multiple factors that writers must consider when they compose—from generic or situational constraints to ideologies that make some writerly choices seem obvious and "natural," while others are "unnatural" or entirely hidden from view.

As this figure suggests, the relationship between writer and message and medium (or media) is complex and full of reciprocity. In a digital world, and especially in the world of Web 2.0, speakers and audiences communicate in multiple ways and across multiple channels, often reciprocally. And this momentous shift has challenged not only traditional models of communication but also the relationship between "creators" of messages and those who receive them. Today, as we have pointed out, the roles of writers and audiences often conflate, merge, and shift.

The deeply participatory nature of electronic forms of communication provides new opportunities for writerly agency, even as it challenges notions of intellectual property that have held sway now for more than three hundred years, leading—as we have been at pains to point out in our research on collaboration and collaborative writing—both to diverse forms of multiple authorship and to the kind of mass authorship that characterizes sites such as Wikipedia and Google News. To say that the music and film industries, along with some print-based companies, are resisting such shifts in authorship and its embeddedness in traditional intellectual property regimes is an understatement. While these entities will continue to cling to regimes of the past, it seems clear that new ways of managing the relationship between texts, "authors," media, contexts, and audiences are emerging. In this regard, consider the alternative rock group Radiohead's decision to release its seventh album, *In Rainbows*, as a digital download on the Internet. Fans of this group could purchase the DVD on the Web—and they were completely free to pay whatever price they wished for the alburn.[3]

In *The Economics of Attention*, Richard Lanham argues that we have moved from what he calls a "stuff economy" (one based on material goods) to a "fluff economy" (one based on immaterial information). With his typical humor and verve, Lanham shows that while in a "stuff" economy scarcity is the major economic principle at work, that principle utterly fails in a "fluff" economy, where information is anything but scarce. In fact, as Lanham points out, we are drowning in it. In such an economy, what is needed, according to Lanham, is *attention*—that is, a way of attending sensibly to the information pouring in:

> In an attention economy, the center of gravity for property shifts from real property to intellectual property. This shift has plunged us into confusions about the ownership of such property ... that it will take some time to sort out. ... Information, unlike stuff, can be both kept and given away at the same time. As long as the means of notation were fixed in physicality as books, reported, painted images, we could gloss over this major obstacle: that "possession" means something different from a private property in stuff. Now, with information expressed on a digital screen, with its new means of dissemination, we can no longer continue this gloss. Hence the current agonies in the music and film business. They have been caught in a vise, squeezed between the macro and the micro economics of attention.
>
> (259)

We too are caught between the macro and micro economies of attention, since we cannot ignore the world of "stuff." But we are clearly in what Lanham calls a "revisionist" way of thinking. "Our locus of reality has shifted," he argues. "We have not left the physical world behind and become creatures of pure attention. Neither has wealth become totally disembodied. Our view is now bi-stable. We must always be ready to move from one view of the world to another. They are always competing with each other. We are learning to live in two worlds at once" (258). In a time of transition, some workers are differentially advantaged or disadvantaged—a fact which reminds us that in an attention economy we also need to be aware of possible inequities and of differing degrees of access to that economy.

As Lanham's discussion suggests, writers who want and need to shift among worlds must be able to hold flexible views of the real and potential relationships between text, context, author, medium, and audience. They must be able to negotiate distinctions between writing and reading, between author and audience that refuse to remain stable; they must also be able to sort out the competing claims of words, images, and sounds in choosing the best medium or media of communication. And they must also become comfortable with new ways of thinking about property, about ownership of the messages that are created amidst the dynamic interaction of writers, audiences, and media.

In many ways, our students are already experienced inhabitors of Lanham's two worlds, and they are increasingly comfortable with new ways of thinking about textual ownership. Such new ways began to emerge in interviews with students conducted during the Stanford Study of Writing (SSW), when researchers asked the students about their views on intellectual property. These interviews, which took place between 2001 and 2006, revealed what at first felt like a hard-to-describe, nebulous change: the best the researchers could say was that something seemed to be happening to the way students thought about intellectual property and ownership. But more recent analyses of the transcripts of some 150 interviews indicate the kind of flexible shifting back and forth described above.

Perhaps one vivid example will serve to limn this shift in understanding and attitude. One participant in the study, Mark Otuteye, wrote a poem during the first weeks of his fresh year. Titled "The Admit Letter," this poem was performed by Mark later that year during Parents' Weekend: it opens with a "so-called friend" saying to Mark, "Oh sure, you got into Stanford: you're Black." What follows is Mark's imagining of what his "so-called friend" thought his admit letter might have said. The two imaginary versions of the admit letter that Mark performs are biting—and very, very funny; together, they not only put the so-called friend in his place but also manage to send up the university as well. On the Stanford campus, news of this poem spread like proverbial wildfire, and Mark was called on to perform it in numerous venues. In one such venue, the poem changed significantly: now it was performed by Mark and a Chicana student, who powerfully wove together versions of their "admit letters."

"The Admit Letter" went through additional permutations during Mark's college career, and during one of the interviews with him SSW researchers asked him, "So is this poem yours? Do you own it?" In a lengthy conversation, Mark said that he considered the poem to be his—but not exclusively his; in fact, he said, his work is usually written and performed collaboratively, and he sees it as part of a large poetic commons. In short, this student was already effectively moving between the information and the attention world, and he was comfortable writing with as well as for others, in a range of media. For Mark, and for many other students in this study, what has seemed at times to us the perplexing fluidity and even tension between writer, text, context, medium, and audience feels to them like home turf. This home turf is not without its potential dangers and challenges, however. As we discuss in a later section of this chapter, problems can arise if students fail to differentiate between the constraints and opportunities inherent in their self-sponsored writing and those of the academic rhetorical situation.

Taxonomizing Audiences

When we wrote AA/AI, we literally could not have imagined the textual and material world we inhabit today. At that time, we were attempting to intervene in a then-contemporary debate over audience. In our effort to understand and give coherence to this debate, we grouped various scholars' work on audience under two constructs, that of audience invoked and audience addressed. (Since AA/AI is included in this collection, we will not summarize these positions here.) If reprintings and references to AA/AI are any indication, others have found the constructs of audience addressed/invoked useful. But we are also aware that the impulse to taxonomize—to create binaries and various other sorts of categories—has disadvantages as well as advantages. Indeed, the felt need to go beyond addressed and invoked audiences to acknowledge audiences that are "ignored, rejected, excluded, or denied" motivated our effort to look again at AA/AI when we wrote "Representing Audience" (174).

A quarter of a century after AA/AI was published, we want to look again at these two constructs to determine what relevance they hold in an age of new media and new literacies.[4] When we look at our earlier work, we continue to value the way that the constructs of audience addressed and audience invoked enable us to call attention to "(1) the fluid, dynamic character of rhetorical situations; and (2) the integrated, interdependent nature of reading and writing" (156). We value as well the extent to which they discourage overly stark binaries—such as those that posit sharp dichotomies between speaking and writing. In AA/AI we point out, for instance, that Walter Ong's representative situations (in "The Writer's Audience Is Always a Fiction") of "the orator addressing a mass audience versus a writer alone in a room" will always "oversimplify the potential range and diversity of both oral and written communication situations" (161).

If this statement was true in 1984, it is even more compelling today with the proliferation of electronic and online media and social networking programs. Increasingly, for instance, students in our writing classes post messages to course blogs and/or contribute to wikis. When they compose academic texts, they may well insert images and sound, or provide tables or spreadsheets with supporting information. When we turn from students' academic writing to their self-sponsored communication, the possibilities explode—including everything from instant messaging and texting to blogging, creating text and images on Facebook and MySpace (and commenting on others' pages) to posting photos on Flickr and sharing tags on del.icio.us.

As we noted earlier in this chapter, these kinds of participatory communications challenge conventional understandings of both authorship and audience, even as they provide an opportunity for anyone and everyone to become both author and audience, writer and reader.[5] But do they invalidate the general constructs of audience addressed and audience invoked that we established in AA/AI? In the most general sense, the kinds of participatory communication that we have just described can, we believe, be encompassed within these two categories—which, we argue in AA/AI, are best understood as a dialogic pair.

Consider, in this regard, our experience writing this chapter. Rather than relying on the technologies of telephone, electric correcting typewriter, and photocopy machines (technologies essential to the composition of AA/AI), we relied on contemporary electronic technologies, particularly email and the Web. Yet our experience composing this text still required us to negotiate both addressed and invoked audiences. In short, we find that the categories of invoked and addressed audiences still inform the much more complex online communicating we do today. As we post to listservs, look for items on YouTube that we can use in our classes, or participate in a wiki devoted to developing an accreditation report for one of our institutions, we are conscious of both addressed and invoked audiences. In the case of the accreditation report, some thirty members of a task force are contributing to this document, which is addressed directly to the accreditation board. In a more indirect way, this document is also addressed to all members of our team and to our upper administrators as well. But to address these audiences, and especially the first one, we must invoke the accreditation board, which we have done very carefully and cautiously: a lot is at stake in our getting this particular invocation right.

Having said this, we need to acknowledge that precisely because the constructs of audience addressed and audience invoked are so broad and encompassing, they can only take us so far in our understanding of audience, including contemporary online and electronic audiences.[6] Thus while we hope that the constructs of audience addressed and audience invoked will continue to prove useful as a means of understanding the rich and overdetermined concept of audience, we find ourselves with many questions about audiences as they are addressed and invoked today. What motivates someone who has read Barbara Kingsolver's *The Poisonwood Bible* to write a review and add it to the 1,398 customer reviews that, at the time we wrote this chapter, were posted on Amazon.com—and what audiences does such a review address and/or invoke? How can we best understand the relationships among the photographers who as of that same day had posted 27,569 photos of black Labs on Flickr, tagging them so that other audiences with a similar passion for this breed of dog can easily find them?[7] What kind of a relationship (if any) might we be forming with a photographer who has contributed photos and tags to Flickr if we click on his or her contacts, profile, or public groups, or if we comment on a photo that we find particularly compelling? How do we envision or invoke this photographer, and how is such an invocation related to a decision to address the photographer directly or not?

How can we best understand what Henry Jenkins in *Fans, Bloggers, and Gamers: Exploring Participatory Culture* refers to as "the interactive audience" (136)? Those communicating with such audiences must necessarily both address and invoke each other. But having said that, what more might we add? How does the technology of gaming or blogging, for example, ignore or exclude certain audiences? What ideological positions may be unspoken in such activities? How can we avoid the utopian/dystopian ways in which audiences and members of new online communities are often framed, both in the popular press and in more serious scholarly work? In attempting to answer this last question, Jenkins observes that "the interactive audience is more than a marketing concept and less than a 'semiotic democracy'" (136). Jenkins's comment suggests that interactive or participatory audiences fail somewhere along a continuum, from those who consume media and content on the Web in fairly traditional ways to the full shared agency characteristic of many online communities.

We have additional issues and questions as well. In an online, participatory culture, the concerns that we articulated in "Representing Audience" about audiences "ignored, rejected, excluded, or denied" become even more salient (174).[8] As we will discuss more fully in the next section, many students easily forget that when they post something on the Web, they may encounter unwanted audiences—such as an employer checking their Facebook or MySpace entries or a researcher checking on their use of his or her scholarly work.

These questions suggest potential limitations of the constructs of audience addressed and audience invoked. We believe that these constructs can usefully remind us of the rich complexity of any form of communication, written or spoken, print or online. But as we have suggested, they are too general to directly address questions such as the ones we have just articulated. These questions require the kind of "analysis of precise, concrete situations" that we call for near the end of AA/AI (168).[9] Such work is currently being done, most often in qualitative studies that require the depth and breadth of ethnography. One powerful example of such work occurs in Angela Thomas's chapter "Blurring and Breaking through the Boundaries of Narrative, Literacy, and Identity in Adolescent Fan Fiction" in Knobel and Lankshear's *New Literacies Sampler*. In this four-year ethnographic study, Thomas explores the experiences of two adolescent females: "Tiana, aged 14 years, and Jandalf, aged 17 years, friends who met online and who have been collaboratively writing fan fiction for over a year" (139). These two young authors prove to be exceptional in a number of ways, including the degree of self-reflexivity and flexibility that they exhibit. In characterizing their writing, both individual and collaborative, Thomas observes that Tiana and Jandalf move successfully "in and out of media type, text type, form, style, and literary device with an ease and poetry of linguistic dexterity that is truly exceptional" (151). In doing so, they assume a range of audience roles for each other, taking turns, for example, at role-playing as they develop the outlines of plots and of characters for their fan fiction. Tiana explains: "when I transcribe over, I sort of become two people—Tiana and a narrator. I make myself see things from a third-person POV [point of view] while still writing as my characters" (144). In describing the many kinds of writing the pair undertakes, Thomas mentions "the role-playing, the out-of-character discussions occurring synchronously within the role-playing, the character journals, the artwork, the careful plotting out of story lines, the forum discussions, the descriptions of worlds and cultures, the invention of language, the playful spoofing, the in-role poetry, the metatextual allusions to sound effects, movie techniques" (145).[10] As this example suggests, understanding the complexity of writing processes, audience awareness, and participation calls for a much more specific, grounded, and nuanced analysis than the binary of addressed and invoked audiences can provide.

Teaching Audience in the Twenty-First Century

Imagine this: A student in a required writing class composes a research-based argument and then presents an oral version of the argument as part of a panel at an in-class "conference" held at the end of the term. The teacher of the class creates a website and posts all of the student arguments on it, inviting response. Two years later, the teacher gets a response from a professor at another university, pointing out that the student's argument drew on the professor's work, citing that work but often failing to enclose directly quoted passages within quotation marks. The professor demands that the student's argument be taken off the website, accusing the student of sloppy habits at best, plagiarism at worst. Notified of this turn of events, the student—now a prospective graduating senior—is completely surprised: he had not meant to plagiarize, and he certainly had not imagined that one of his sources would go to the trouble of accessing his essay.

Like many others, this student experiences the Internet and many of its sites as fairly private, when the reality is that audiences are there all the time, browsing, searching, engaging, responding, sometimes accusing. Many have commented on the breakdown between private and public today and on the somewhat contradictory attitudes students hold: they often say they are comfortable being in public and that a public stance comes with the territory of digital communication. But they also sometimes view sites—especially social networking sites such as Facebook—as relatively private, away from the prying eyes of parents and other unwanted audiences. We had these students in mind when we quoted Ari Melber at the opening of this chapter: "Critics argue that privacy does not matter to children who were raised in a wired celebrity culture that promises a niche audience for everyone. Why hide when you can perform? But even if young people are performing, many are clueless about the size of their audience" (23).

Clearly, even though many of our students are digital natives, they nevertheless need to become more knowledgeable about the nature and complexity of the audiences for whom they perform, particularly as they shift back and forth from self-sponsored online writing to academic writing. The first lesson we draw from grappling with the questions we pose in this chapter, then, is that we have a responsibility to join with our students in rich and detailed explorations of just what "audience" can mean in their writing and in their lives. Such explorations might well begin with unpacking the problematics of viewing the teacher as the audience for student writing. As the real-life example earlier suggests, the teacher remains *an* audience for student texts, but by no means the only audience, especially when student writing is posted on the Web. Even if it is not posted, student writing often invokes and addresses audiences well beyond the teacher (who is also, often, both addressed and invoked).

Beyond unpacking the concept of teacher as audience, teachers can help students understand the contemporary complexities of audience by providing case studies that exemplify various kinds of audiences. The participatory audience of peer review, for instance, can be theorized and interrogated by students in their composition classes: that is, rather than simply responding to one another, they can take time to get to know these real-life audiences, along with the assumptions and values they bring to their fellow students' texts, literally examining where these members of the audience are coming from. Or students can create a genealogy of audiences for a particular social networking site, exploring the many diverse individuals and groups that have access to the site and asking which audiences the site invokes and which it seems to address. Students could examine the many issues raised, for instance, by various Pro

Ana (pro anorexia) sites on the Web. Who are the sponsors of these sites? Just what kind of collaborative relationships are being invoiced and addressed by those who post to and read this site?

As we have noted in this chapter, what began for us as two different strands of research—one on audience, another on collaboration—have all but merged during the last couple of years as we have seen how frequently writers become audiences and vice versa. Yet more often than not, students resist collaboration in their schoolwork even as they collaborate constantly in their out-of-class online writing. There are reasons for this seeming contradiction or tension: school writing is part of a deeply individualistic system that rewards individual students through a system of grades and points and values the individual GPA; working collaboratively runs counter to that system. But while we work to change the hyper-individualistic base of higher education in the United States, we need also to engage students in intense discussions of this issue. As we have been arguing for some time, we know that most of the innovative work that gets done in the world today gets done in collaborative groups (see Sawyer, Tapscott and Williams, Sunstein, Ede and Lunsford)—including, increasingly, teams that work primarily online. And we know that colleges and universities, for reasons mentioned earlier, are doing very little to prepare students to thrive in such an environment (see Bok, Light). We need to do more, then, than *assign* collaborative projects: we need to provide a theoretical rationale for such projects along with data to support it. In addition, we need to craft collaborative projects that will engage every member of the group and guide the group in analyzing their work together from beginning to end. And we need to join with students in exploring the use of free collaborative writing tools such as Google Docs or Writeboard.

We also need to consider the impact that new literacies are having—and should have—in our teaching. Such literacies often call for producing new texts, often referred to as "new media" texts. The question of whether and how to teach such new media writing poses significant challenges to teachers of writing today. Thanks to the work of Anne Wysocki, Johndan Johnson Eilola, Cynthia Selfe, and Geoffrey Sirc, we have excellent examples of the kinds of new media writing students are doing today, both inside and outside of the classroom. In one chapter in the collaborative *Writing New Media*, Cynthia Selfe points out the double-edged sword that comes along with new media texts as she tells the story of David, a young man who teaches himself to produce effective new media texts only to fail his college classes because of his inability to create acceptable traditional print texts. The point Selfe makes is one all teachers of writing need to heed: we must help our students to learn to conceive and produce a repertoire of texts, from the convincing academic argument to the compelling website or memorable radio essay. (Selfe has also recently published a helpful guide for teachers: *Multimodal Composition: Resources for Teachers.*)

It is important to acknowledge the difficulties inherent in taking on such a task. At Stanford, when the Faculty Senate mandated that the Program in Writing and Rhetoric (PWR) develop a new second-level course that would go beyond academic writing to embrace oral presentations with multimedia support, the PWR teaching staff responded with great enthusiasm. By the time they began piloting courses to equally enthusiastic students, the sky seemed to be the limit: students wanted to write and produce hour-long documentaries; to produce NPR-quality audio essays; to design, write, and produce online magazines; not to mention creating texts to be performed in a wide range of settings. By the end of the second quarter of the pilot, however, both teachers and students realized that their reach had clearly exceeded their grasp. Most notably, the writing that students were doing as they worked their way toward new media texts was declining in quality—and everyone saw it. As a result, before the new course was fully implemented, the teaching staff, working in conjunction with the Undergraduate Advisory Board, pulled back from some of their ambitions, focusing the course first on producing a research-based argument and then working the rest of the term to "translate" that argument into various genres and media.

In answer to our question, "What difference might answers to [the three questions we pose at the beginning of this chapter] make to twenty-first-century teachers and students?" we can sum up by saying, "A lot, a whole lot." In this section of our essay, we have explored several important implications for teaching the concept of audience in the twenty-first century, the most important of which is to engage our students in analyzing and theorizing the new literacies themselves, especially as they call for collaboration, for new understandings of audience, and for a robust ethics of communication. But as this discussion has suggested, we are simply not at a point where we can draw absolute conclusions about what writing teachers should do in this age of new literacies.

Ethics and Participatory Literacies

As we have worked on this chapter, we have found ourselves meditating on audiences across the millennia—the audiences who gathered before the ancient Greek rhapsodes, who "read" the scriptures along with literate scribes in the medieval period, who sat among the groundlings at the Globe and other Elizabethan theaters, who waited in rapt anticipation for the next issue of the latest Dickens novel, who gathered at whistle-stops throughout the United States to engage with political hopefuls, who cheered their teams to victory, and who today log on to check in with Facebook friends or read and comment on their favorite blog. In some ways, there has always been a relational or participatory quality to audiences. Yet it seems clear that changes in technology and other material conditions that have brought us to the present moment have opened avenues for audiences to take on agency and to become participants and creators/shapers of discourse in more profound ways than ever before.

In making this comment, we do not intend to join those who characterize the Web and social networking sites in utopian terms. If there is one thing we have learned from our study of the rhetorical tradition, it is that the nature and consequence of any act of communication can never be determined in advance and that inquiry into issues such as these requires a deeply situated, finely tuned analysis. When consumers post reviews to Amazon.com, for instance, are they expanding their possibilities for agency and for collaborations with others or are they serving as unpaid volunteer workers for this ever-expanding company? There are no simple, decontextualized answers to questions such as these.

Our engagement with the rhetorical tradition, as well as our study of the history of communicative technologies, thus reminds us that both utopian and dystopian views of our current moment are likely to oversimplify. They also remind us of how difficult it is to predict how various communication technologies will be employed. The earliest graphic symbols, it is good to remember, were used for accounting, not writing. We might consider in this regard Twitter, a free online social networking program that allows individuals to send brief, frequent messages to each other. Twitter limits these messages to 140 characters and suggests that those employing this software post regularly in response to this question: "What are you doing?" The intended use of Twitter is fairly obvious: those who want to keep in touch can quickly and easily use this program to do so. Who would have expected, then, that some users of Twitter would decide that this program provides the perfect online space to write haiku, much less that the haiku created on Twitter would hail an avid audience? Just how much interest is there in the world today in Twitter haiku? We can't know for sure, but a quick check on Google instantly pulled up 269,000 hits. In searching the Web, we have also found numerous references to Twitter contests. One frequent challenge invites writers to compose micro-essays and micro-stories limited to Twitter's 140 characters. In case you're interested, a search on Google using the term *Twitter contests* generated 554,000 hits. Here's what one Twitter user, Calvin Jones, posted to his website Digital Marketing Success about his fascination with Twitter: "I love the way twitter makes you condense your writing, squeezing the maximum out of every character. Here's my swiftly penned missive: She paused, shivering involuntarily; the wave of adrenalin surged through her, leaving her giddy and disoriented. It was quiet. He was gone!" Twitter was released to the public in October 2006, and we conducted these Google searches in late May 2008. Thus does a software program designed to help friends, coworkers, and family members keep in touch devolve in lightning speed on the Web, making a space for readers to become writers who then become invoked and addressed audience members for still other writer/readers.

What if a friend or family member prefers not to know what someone close (or not so close) to them is doing throughout the day? Twitter.com addresses this at the level of software architecture—one must sign up for Twitter to receive messages—and via its settings feature. But surely ethical issues remain. Twitter can be used to help groups gather quickly, whether for positive purposes (engaging in civic discussion or action) or negative. How can those interested in participating in this social networking site best understand their responsibilities as writers and audiences for others?

At its strongest and most productive moments, the rhetorical tradition has acknowledged the potentially powerful ethical implications inherent in any act of communication. As we conclude this discussion of audience in an age of new literacies, then, we turn to several other ethical questions that seem most compelling to us as teachers and scholars. Perhaps most important, in a world of participatory media, it seems essential for teachers and students to consider the multiple reciprocal responsibilities entailed in writer-audience relationships. What does a student writer posting to Facebook owe to all the potential audiences of that post, from a former partner to a potential employer? And what responsibilities do audiences have toward those whose messages they receive, seek, reject, or encounter? One goal of future research on audience must surely be to explore the ethical dimensions of such relationships.

It seems equally important for scholars, teachers, and students to collaboratively explore the increasingly complex issue of plagiarism/patchwriting in an online world.[11] As the example earlier, about the professor who found his work used without proper attribution in a student essay on a class website, demonstrates, the ease of cutting and pasting and the wide availability of a multitude of sources make holding to traditional norms of scholarly citation increasingly difficult or even problematic. While students we know roundly condemn buying or downloading a paper wholesale from a website as unacceptable cheating, they are much more ambivalent about using a form of sampling in their writing, and they are downright resistant to the need for what they often think of as excessive (or even obsessive) citation: if you go to the Web with a question and get thousands of "hits" in answer to it, they say, shouldn't that answer be considered as common knowledge that doesn't need to be cited? And even if we answer "no" to that question, which one of the thousands of sources should be *the* one to be cited? These questions and the issues they raise suggest that we must not only continue to explore student understandings of intellectual property but also to engage them in a full discussion of where academic citation practices came from, why they have been so deeply valued, and what is at stake in developing alternative practices—such as a much broader definition of "common knowledge" or ways of distributing citation credit across a wide range of contributor/authors.

Another potential ethical problem that contemporary audiences must address has quite diverse origins and implications: what are the consequences for civic discourse of a world in which those interested in a specific topic or audience can easily find sites where they can communicate with like-minded individuals, where our culture seems to promise, as Ari Melbur observes, "a niche audience for everyone" (23)? Is our culture likely to fragment into what legal scholar Cass R. Sunstein refers to as "information cocoons" (9), and how can we best understand and enact an appropriate relationship between privacy and free speech on the Web? One place to turn in exploring this set of ethical issues is the extensive work on public discourse being pursued by many scholars in rhetoric and communication studies.[12] Another strategy is to encourage (even inspire) students to build bridges between the seemingly private voices they inhabit online and the public ones they can establish, to move from the kind of personal opinions found ubiquitously online to a truly public opinion they can help to create and sustain.

In his 2007 "Vision of the Future," Howard Rheingold notes the need for parents and students alike to take responsibility for the ethical and moral choices they make in reading and writing online. Rheingold is primarily interested in how young people can get beyond the small niches of the Web to participate most effectively in online settings. Noting that while students today are "naturals" when it comes to point-and-click explorations yet "there's nothing innate about knowing how to apply their skills to the processes of democracy" (4), Rheingold calls on teachers to help students make connections "between the literacies students pick up simply by being young in the 21st century and those best learned through reading and discussing texts" (5). We can help students make such connections, Rheingold argues, by allowing them to move "from a private to a public voice" that will help them "turn their self-expression into a form of public participation" (5). Public voice, Rheingold insists, is "learnable, a matter of consciously engaging with an active public rather than broadcasting to a passive audience" (5).

Thus, while Rheingold recognizes the potential for fragmentation, for performing only for small niche audiences, and for existing "information cocoons," he also sees the potential for developing participatory public opinion that can "be an essential instrument of democratic self-governance." We believe that Rheingold is right to argue that if we want such public voices to arise, we must teach to and for them. And along with Rheingold, we recognize that teaching to and for new publics and public voices calls for "a whole new way of looking at learning and teaching" (7) that will, we believe, require close attention to the ethical issues raised by new literacies and new media. It will also call for resisting the dichotomy between those who dream utopian dreams of a vast collective and participatory democracy enabled by Web 2.0 and those who bemoan a collapse into fragmentation and solipsism that can come from talking only with those who already think just as you do.

At its strongest moments, the Western rhetorical tradition, however flawed, has encouraged both writers and teachers of writing to take a deeply situated perspective on communication—and thus to challenge the kind of binaries that we have just described. Whenever we write, read, speak, or (as Krista Ratcliffe has so eloquently reminded us) listen, there are no guarantees that either the process or the outcome will be ethical. This is an understanding that we can—and should—bring with us when we enter our classrooms, especially our first-year writing classrooms. For there we have the opportunity to help our students experience the intellectual stimulation and excitement, as well as the responsibility, of engaging and collaborating with multiple audiences from peers to professors, as well as addressed and invoked audiences of all kinds.

Notes

1. We use the term *Web 2.0* here and elsewhere recognizing that some have argued that this term is inaccurate and/or hyperbolic. In an interview posted on IBM's developer Works site, for instance, Tim Berners-Lee argues that Web 2.0 is "a piece of jargon, nobody even knows what it means. If Web 2.0 for you is blogs and wikis, then that is people to people [as opposed to Web 1, which is sometimes described as computer to computer]. … But that was what the Web was supposed to be all along." Berners-Lee prefers to use the term *Semantic Web* rather than Web 2.0.
2. Two recent monographs helpfully remind us of the differing concerns, traditions, and interests that scholars have brought to the concept of audience. The first study, Mary Jo Rieff's 1994 *Approaches to Audience: An Overview of the Major Perspectives*, chronicles the development of research on audience within English studies in general and rhetoric and writing in particular. The second study, Denis McQuail's 1997 monograph *Audience Analysis*, is written from the perspective of communication studies, particularly mass communication and cultural studies.
3. After making their album available on the Web, Radiohead also released their music as a conventional CD.
4. Other scholars have also examined these constructs in helpful ways. We would particularly like to call attention to Robert Johnson's "Audience Involved: Toward a Participatory Model of Writing," Jack Selzer's "More Meanings of Audience," Rosa Eberly's "From Writers, Audiences, and Communities to Publics: Writing Classrooms as Protopublic Spaces," Mary Jo Reiff's "Rereading 'Invoked' and 'Addressed' Readers through a Social Lens: Toward a Recognition of Multiple Audiences," and the essays published in Gesa Kirsch and Duane H. Roen's edited collection *A Sense of Audience in Written Communication*. Though space limitations do not allow us to discuss these studies, we have benefited from these authors' analyses and critiques.
5. In "Agency and Authority in Role-Playing Texts," Jessica Hammer identifies three kinds of authorship in video games: primary, secondary, and tertiary. As Hammer notes, "The primary author develops a world and a set of rules," while "the secondary author takes the work of the primary author and uses it to construct a specific situation or scenario[;]. … the tertiary authors, then, 'write' the text of the game in play" (71).
6. In *Audience Analysis*, for instance, Denis McQuail helpfully identifies the following dimensions of audience: "degree of activity or passivity; degree of interactivity and interchangeability; size and duration; located-ness in space; group character (social/cultural identity); simultaneity of contact with source; heterogeneity of composition; social relations between sender and receiver; message versus social/behavioral definition of situation; degree of 'social presence'; sociability of context of use" (150).
7. Such tagging is, of course, an imprecise art. On the day that we searched Flickr with the term *black labs*, the sixth photo that appeared was of a black Lab cookie. The twenty-third and twenty-fourth photos were titled "Black Phoenix Alchemy Lab" and "Black and White Photo Lab." Neither photo was of a black Labrador retriever. And needless to say, these anomalous photos undoubtedly address and invoke different audiences than do those of real live black Labs.
8. In *Rhetorical Refusals: Defying Audiences' Expectations*, John Schilb examines cases in which speakers and writers intentionally defy audience expectations.
9. Scholars in such areas as media and cultural studies, communication, sociology, and anthropology have undertaken research in media reception and audience ethnography. For an introduction to this interdisciplinary body of work, see Pertti Alasuutari's *Rethinking the Media Audience: The New Agenda*. Representative studies include Virginia Nightingale's *Studying Audiences: The Shock of the Real*, S. Elizabeth Bird's *The Audience in Everyday Life: Living in a Media World*, and Will Brooker and Deborah Jermyn's *The Audience Studies Reader*.
10. Thomas goes on to observe that "[i]n addition to exploring the scope of the narrative worlds of the fan fiction, it is important to note that the girls also produce multimodal texts to enhance their fan fiction, making avatars (images to represent themselves) for role-playing, making visual signatures as can be seen at the side and end of each post on the forum …, finding icons to reflect mood, creating music bytes, making fan fiction posters in the form of an advertisement and teaser, and creating mini movie trailers using their own spliced-together combination of existing movie clips, music, voiceovers, and text. They also draw maps and room plans of their world, draw and paint scenery, and sketch images of their many characters. As well as hand-drawn sketches, they create digital images, digital colorizations or enhancements of their sketches, or purely digitally created images" (150–51).
11. Rebecca Howard has written extensively and compellingly about the developmental nature of what she calls

"patchwriting" as well as about the ways in which students and teachers understand (and often misunderstand) plagiarism.
12. Several essays in Section IV of *The Sage Handbook of Rhetorical Studies* explore such issues; see, especially, Gurak and Antonijevic and Beasley.

Works Cited

Alasuutari, Pertti, Ed. *Rethinking the Media Audience: The Hew Agenda.* London: Sage, 1999.

Ang, Ien. *Livingroom Wars: Rethinking Audiences for a Postmodern World.* New York: Routledge, 1995.

Beasley, Vanessa. "Between Touchstones and Touchscreens: What Counts as Contemporary Political Rhetoric." *The Sage Handbook of Rhetorical Studies.* Ed. Andrea A, Lunsford, Kirt Wilson, and Rosa Eberly. Thousand Oaks, CA: Sage P, 2009.

Bird, S. Elizabeth. *The Audience in Everyday Life: Living in a Media World.* New York: Routledge, 2003.

Bok, Derek. *Our Underachieving Colleges.* Princeton, NJ: Princeton UP, 2006.

Brooker, Will, and Deborah Jermyn, eds. *The Audience Studies Reader.* London: Routledge, 2003.

Eberly, Rosa. *Citizen Critics: Literary Public Spheres.* Urbana, IL: U Illinois P, 2000.

Ede, Lisa, and Andrea A. Lunsford. *Singular Texts / Plural Authors: Perspectives on Collaborative Writing.* Carbondale, IL: Southern Illinois UP, 2000.

Gurak, Laura, and Smiljana Antonijevic. "Digital Rhetoric and Public Discourse." *The Sage Handbook of Rhetorical Studies.* Ed. Andrea A. Lunsford, Kirt Wilson, and Rosa Eberly. Thousand Oaks, CA: Sage P, 2009.

Hammer, Jessica. "Agency and Authority in Role-Playing Texts." *A New Literacies Sampler.* Ed. Michele Knobel and Colin Lankshear. New York: Peter Lang, 2007. 67–94.

Howard, Rebecca Moore. *Standing in the Shadow of Giants: Plagiarists, Authors, Collaborators.* Stamford, CT: Ablex, 1999.

Jones, Calvin. "Twitter Story Competition." Blog entry 23 May 2008. Digital Marketing Success. 5 June 200S <http://www.digitalmarketingsuccess.com/twitter-story-competition/>.

Kluth, Andrew. "Among the Audience: A Survey of New Media." *The Economist* 20 Apr. 2006.

Knobel, Michele, and Colin Lankshear, *A New Literacies Sampler.* New York: Peter Lang, 2007.

Kress, Gunther. *Literacy in the New Media Age.* New York: Routledge, 2003.

Lanham, Richard A. *The Economics of Attention: Style and Substance in the Age of Information.* Chicago: U Chicago P, 2006.

Laningham, Scott. "Interview with Tim Berners-Lee." 22 August 2006. Podcast. 5 June 2008 developer Works Interviews. <http://www.ibm.com/deveioperworks/podcast/all.html>.

Light, Richard J. *Making the Most of College.* Cambridge: Harvard UP, 2004.

Lunsford, Andrea A. and Lisa Ede. "On Distinctions between Classical and Modern Rhetoric." *Essays on Classical Rhetoric and Modern Discourse.* Carbondale, IL: Southern Illinois UP, 1984: 37–49.

McLuhan, Marshall, and Quentin Fiore. *The Medium Is the Massage.* New York: Bantam, 1967

McQuail, Dennis. *Audience Analysis.* Thousand Oaks, CA: Sage P, 1997.

Melber, Ari. "About Facebook." *The Nation* 20 Dec. 2007: 23.

Nightingale, Virginia, *Studying Audiences: The Shock of the Real.* London: Routledge, 1996.

Porter, James. *Audience and Rhetoric: An Archaeological Composition of the Discourse Community.* Englewood Cliffs, NJ: Prentice Hall, 1992.

Ratcliffe, Krista, *Rhetorical Listening: Identification, Gender, Whiteness.* Carbondale, IL: Southern Illinois UP, 2005.

Reiff, Mary Jo. *Approaches to Audience: An Overview of the Major Perspectives.* Superior, WI: Parlay P, 2004.

Rheingold, Howard. "Vision of the Future." *Education.au Seminar.* Melbourne, Australia, October 2, 2007. <http://www.educationau.Edu/au/jahia/webdav/site/myjahiasite/shared/seminars/Rheingold_Melbourne_Speech.pdf>.

Sawyer, Keith. *Group Genius: The Creative Power of Collaboration.* New York: Basic Books, 2007.

Schilb, John. *Rhetorical Refusals: Defying Audiences' Expectations.* Carbondale, IL: Southern Illinois UP, 2007.

Selfe, Cynthia. *Multimodal Composition: Resources for Teachers.* Cresskill, NJ: Hampton P, 2007.

Sunstein, Cass R. *Infotopia: How Many Minds Produce Knowledge.* Oxford: Oxford UP, 2006.

Tapscott, Don, and Anthony D. Williams. *Wikinomics: How Mass Collaboration Changes Everything.* New York: Penguin, 2006.

Warner, Michael. *Publics and Coanterpublics.* New York: Zone Books, 2005.

Wysocki, Anne, Johndan Johnson Eilola, Cynthia Selfe, and Geoffrey Sirc. *Writing New Media: Theory and Applications for Expanding the Teaching of Composition.* Logan, UT: Utah State UP, 2004.

16

The Movement of Air, the Breath of Meaning

Aurality and Multimodal Composing

Cynthia L. Selfe

Rhetoric and composition's increasing attention to multimodal composing involves challenges that go beyond issues of access to digital technologies and electronic composing environments. As a specific case study, this article explores the history of aural composing modalities (speech, music, sound) and examines how they have been understood and used within English and composition classrooms and generally subsumed by the written word in such settings. I argue that the relationship between aurality (and visual modalities) and writing has limited our understanding of composing as a multimodal rhetorical activity and has thus, deprived students of valuable semiotic resources for making meaning. Further, in light of scholarship on the importance of aurality to different communities and cultures, I argue that our contemporary adherence to alphabetic-only composition constrains the semiotic efforts of individuals and groups who value multiple modalities of expression. I encourage teachers and scholars of composition, and other disciplines, to adopt an increasingly thoughtful understanding of aurality and the role it—and other modalities—can play in contemporary communication tasks.

> *Participation means being able to speak in one' own voice, and thereby simultaneously to construct and express one' s cultural identity through idiom and style.*
> —Nancy Fraser, "Rethinking the Public Sphere"

> *… perhaps we can hear things we cannot see.*
> —Krista Ratcliffe, "Rhetorical Listening"

> *A turn to the auditory dimension is … more than a simple changing of variables. It begins as a deliberate decentering of a dominant tradition in order to discover what may be missing as a result of the traditional double reduction of vision as the main variable and metaphor.*
> —Don Ihde, Listening and Voice

Anyone who has spent time on a college or university campus over the past few decades knows how fundamentally important students consider their sonic environments—the songs, music, and podcasts they produce and listen to; the cell phone conversations in which they immerse themselves; the headphones and Nanos that accompany them wherever they go; the thumper cars they use to turn the streets into concert stages; the audio blogs, video soundtracks, and mixes they compose and exchange with each other and share with anyone else who will listen.

Indeed, students' general penchant for listening to and producing sound can be eloquently ironic for English composition teachers faced with the deafening silence of a class invited to engage in an oral discussion about a written text. This phenomenon, however, may reveal as much about our professions attitudes toward aurality and writing[1]—or the related history of these expressive modalities within our discipline—as it does about students' literacy values and practices. Sound, although it remains of central importance both to students and to the population at large, is often undervalued as a compositional mode.

My argument in this article is that the history of writing in U.S. composition instruction, as well as its contemporary legacy, functions to limit our professional understanding of composing as a multimodal rhetorical activity and deprive students of valuable semiotic resources for making meaning.[2] As print assumed an increasingly privileged position in composition classrooms during the late nineteenth century and throughout the twentieth century, aurality was both subsumed by, and defined in opposition to, writing (Russell, "Institutionalizing" and *Writing*; Halbritter; B. McCorkle, "Harbingers"; Elbow, "What"), thus establishing and perpetuating a false binary between the two modalities of expression (Biber, "Spoken" and *Variation*; Tannen, "Oral" and *Spoken*), encouraging an overly narrow understanding of language and literacy (Kress, "English"), and allowing collegiate teachers of English composition to lose sight of the integrated nature of language arts. Further, I argue that a single-minded focus on print in composition classrooms ignores the importance of aurality and other composing modalities for making meaning and understanding the world. Finally, I suggest that the almost exclusive dominance of print literacy works against the interests of individuals whose cultures and communities have managed to maintain a value on multiple modalities of expression, multiple and hybrid ways of knowing, communicating, and establishing identity (Gilyard; Dunn, *Learning* and *Talking*; Royster, *Traces* and "First Voice"; Hibbitts; Powell; Lyons).

My ultimate goal in exploring aurality as a case in point is *not* to make an either/or argument—*not* to suggest that we pay attention to aurality *rather than* to writing. Instead, I suggest we need to pay attention to *both* writing *and* aurality, *and* other composing modalities, as well. I hope to encourage teachers to develop an increasingly thoughtful understanding of a whole range of modalities and semiotic resources in their assignments and then to provide students the opportunities of developing expertise with *all available means* of persuasion and expression, so that they can function as literate citizens in a world where communications cross geopolitical, cultural, and linguistic borders and are enriched rather than diminished by semiotic dimensionality.

What is at stake in this endeavor seems significant—both for teachers of English composition and for students. When teachers of composition limit the bandwidth of composing modalities in our classrooms and assignments, when we privilege print as *the only* acceptable way to make or exchange meaning, we not only ignore the history of rhetoric and its intellectual inheritance, but we also limit, unnecessarily, our scholarly understanding of semiotic systems (Kress, "English") and the effectiveness of our instruction for many students.

The stakes for students are no less significant—they involve fundamental issues of rhetorical sovereignty[3]: the rights and responsibilities that students have to identify their own communicative needs and to represent their own identities, to select the right tools for the communicative contexts within which they operate, and to think critically and carefully about the meaning that they and others compose. When we insist on print as *the* primary, and most formally acceptable, modality for composing knowledge, we usurp these rights and responsibilities on several important intellectual and social dimensions, and, unwittingly, limit students' sense of rhetorical agency to the bandwidth of our own interests and imaginations.[4]

By way of making this argument, I begin by recounting a very brief, and necessarily selective, history of aurality, focusing on the role it came to assume in college composition classrooms from the mid-nineteenth century onward. I then discuss some of the ways in which aurality has *persisted* in English composition classrooms in the midst of a culture saturated by the written word. Finally, I suggest how digital communication environments and digital multimodal texts have encouraged some teachers of composition to rediscover aurality as a valuable modality of expression.

The irony of making an argument about aurality in print is not lost on me, nor, I suspect, will it be on most other readers of this article. Indeed, it is very much the point of what I try to say in the following pages. Thus, throughout this article I have included references to four sound essays composed by students at Michigan Tech, the University of Louisville, and The Ohio State University. I consider these pieces a crucial part of my argument about valuing aurality as a composing modality. Hence, I encourage readers to go to <http://people. cohums.ohio-state.edu/selfe2/ccc/>, listen to these sound essays, read what their authors have said about composing them.

Aural Composing: Sample 1, Sonya Borton's *Legacy of Music*

At this point, I ask readers to leave this printed text and go to <http://people.cohums.ohio-state.edu/selfe2/ccc/>, where they can listen to Sonya Borton's autobiographical essay, *Legacy of Music*, in which she tells listeners about the musical talents of various members of her Kentucky family. In relating her narrative, Borton weaves a richly textured fabric of interviews, commentary, instrumental music, and song to support her thesis that a love of music represents an important legacy passed down from parents to children within her family.

A Short History of Aurality in College Composition Classrooms

Theorizing the role of aurality in composition classrooms is not a task that comes easily to most composition teachers. Since the late nineteenth century, writing has assumed such a dominant and central position in our professional thinking that its role as the major instructional focus goes virtually uncontested, accepted as common sense. As Patricia Dunn (*Talking*) writes, it seems absurd even to

> question an over-emphasis on writing in a discipline whose raison d'etre is, like no other discipline, for and about writing. That common-sense assumption, however, may be what makes it so difficult for us in Composition to see word-based pedagogies in any way other than supportive of learning.
>
> (150)

Composition teachers, she concludes, have come to believe "writing is not simply *one* way of knowing; it is *the* way" (15). *Doxa*, or common belief, however, always maintains its strongest hold in the absence of multiple historical and cultural perspectives. Although writing has come to occupy a privileged position in composition classrooms—and in the minds of many compositionists—historical accounts by such scholars as David Russell ("institutionalizing" and *Writing*), James Berlin, Nan Johnson, and Michael Halloran confirm this situation as both relatively recent and contested.

In the first half of the eighteenth century, for example, collegiate education in America was fundamentally shaped by Western classical traditions and was oral in its focus. As Michael Halloran notes, within this curriculum students learned to read, speak, and write both classical language and English through recitation—the standard pedagogical approach for all subjects—as well as through a wide range of oratorical performances, debates, orations, and declamations, both inside formal classes and in extracurricular settings such as literary societies. The goal of these activities was to build students' general skill in public speaking, rather than encouraging specialized inquiry as mediated by the written word.

This old model of oratorical education, David Russell notes ("Institutionalizing" and *Writing*), was linked to the cultural values, power, and practices of privileged families in the colonies who considered facility in oral, face-to-face encounters to be the hallmark of an educated class. The male children of these families were expected to help lead the nation in the role of statesmen, enter the judicial and legal arena, or become ministers. For heirs of these families, as Susan Miller has added, little instruction in writing was needed other than practice in penmanship. Their lives were imbricated with oral communication practices—speeches, debates, sermons— and such individuals had to be able to speak, as gentlemen, in contexts of power. Universities were charged with preparing these future leaders to assume their roles and responsibilities.

During the latter half of the nineteenth century, however, universities began to change in response to the rapid rise of industrial manufacturing, the explosion of scientific discoveries, and the expansion of the new country's international trade. These converging trends accumulated with increasing tendential force and resulted in profound cultural transformations that placed an increasing value on specialization and professionalization, especially within the emerging middle class. Such changes required both new approaches to education and a new kind of secular university, one designed to meet the needs of individuals involved in science, commerce, and manufacturing. It was within this new collegiate context that the first departments of English were able to form, primarily by forging identities for themselves as units that educated a range of citizens occupied with business and professional affairs.[5] In response to these cultural trends, Russell has observed, "the modern project of purification, the drive toward specialization, made old rhetoric impossible" ("Institutionalizing" 40).[6]

Instead, departments of English focused on preparing professionals whose work, after graduation, would increasingly rely on writing, as Russell explains—articles, reports, memoranda and communications, "texts as objects to be silently studied, critiqued, compared, appreciated, and evaluated" (*Writing* 4–5). Supporting this work were technological innovations—improved printing presses, typewriters, and pens, among others—that combined with innovations in business operations, efficient manufacturing techniques, and science to lend added importance to writing as a cultural code, both within the new university and outside it (Russell, "institutionalizing").

As they emerged in this context, departments of English sought increasingly modern approaches to changing communication practices and values—hoping to distance themselves from the old-school education in oratory, which was considered increasingly less valuable as a preparation for the world of manufacturing, business, and science, and to link their curricula to more pragmatic concerns of professionalism in the modern university. The new departments of English taught their studies in the vernacular—rather than in Greek or Latin—and separated themselves from a continued focus on oratory, religion, and the classics, which became devalued as historical or narrowly defined studies. These newly emergent departments of English focused primarily on their ability to provide instruction in written composition. During this brief period in the latter third of the nineteenth century, writing became one of a very few subjects required for a university course of study (Berlin; Russell, *Writing*).[7] Charles William Eliot, who became president of Harvard in 1869, noted that instruction in writing—distinguished by a natural, uninflated style—was not only desirable for students at the new university but also necessary for the success of a national culture based on economic development, modern industrial processes, and trade (359).[8]

Scholars have described, in various ways, the historic shift that occurred during the last half of the nineteenth century, from an older style of education based on declamation, oratory, forensics, and delivery[9] to a new style of education based primarily on the study and analysis of written texts, both classical and contemporary[10]—and the production of such texts. Perhaps the most succinct statement, however, and the one most directly to the point for this history of aurality in college composition classrooms is Ronald Reid's (1959) comment:

> The most significant change was rhetorics abandonment of oratory. The advanced courses, commonly known during this period as "themes and forensics," consisted almost exclusively of written work. … The beginning course, too, gave much practice in writing, none in public speaking.
>
> (253)

Although attention to aurality persisted in various ways into the twentieth century, it was clearly on the wane in English studies.[11] By 1913, one year before teachers of speech seceded from the National Council of Teachers of English, John Clapp was moved to ask in an article published by the *English Journal,*

> Is there a place in College English classes for exercises in reading, or talking, or both? The question has been raised now and then in the past, almost always to receive a negative answer, particularly from English departments.
>
> (21)

The general response of the profession to these questions, Clapp noted, was that "for the purposes of the intellectual life, which college graduates are to lead, talking is of little important, and writing of very great importance" (23).

This brief history of composition as a discipline can be productively viewed within a larger historical frame as well—specifically that of the rise of science (and its progeny, technology) in the West before, during, and immediately after the Enlightenment, from the seventeenth to the nineteenth centuries. At the heart of science as a rational project was the belief that humans could unlock the secrets of nature using systematic observations and precisely recorded written measurements. In a world attuned to the systematic methodologies of science, the recorded word, the visual trace of evidence, provided proof, and observations rendered in the visual medium of print revealed truth—Newton's notes on mathematical proofs, Franklin's written descriptions of experiments, Darwins Beagle diaries. If the scientific revolution rested on the understanding that seeing was believing, it also depended on writing—and after the mid-fifteenth century—on printing as a primary means of recording, storing, and retrieving important information and discoveries. Later, with the application of scientific methods to a wide range of legal, military, industrial, and manufacturing practices, the complex network of cultural formations that reinforced the privileged role of visual and print information.

From the seventeenth to the nineteenth centuries, then, as the power of vision and print gradually waxed in the context of a university education, the power of aurality gradually waned, although this trend was, at different times and places, far from even or immediate in its effects. U.S. colleges and universities, for instance, lagged slightly behind those in Europe for a time in this regard, but education within the two cultures followed the same general trajectory. As Hibbitts notes, it was during this period that "the social and intellectual status of vision gradually undermined the position still occupied by the other forms of sensory experience in the Western tradition" (2.25).

In educational institutions and, later, departments of English and programs of English composition, the effects of this shift were far reaching. Writing and reading, for example, became separated from speech in educational contexts and became largely silent practices for students in classroom settings. Written literature, although including artifacts of earlier aural forms (Platonic dialogues, Shakespearean monologues, and poetry, for instance), was studied through silent reading and subjected to written analysis, consumed by the eye rather than the ear.[12] The disciplined practices of silent writing, reading, and observation that characterized collegiate education became normalized and, importantly, linked to both class and race. In educational contexts, Hibbitts observes, "[t]he most important meta-lesson became, as it today remains, how to sit, write, and read in contented quiet" (2.25). It was through such changes that writing became the focus of a specialized academic education delivered primarily to, and by, privileged white males.

If print became increasingly important within the new U.S. universities in the nineteenth and early twentieth centuries, however, aurality retained some of its power and reach in other locations, where individuals and groups were forced to acquire both written and aural literacies by a range of informal means or through an educational system that retained a fundamental integration of the language arts. Many women during this period, for instance, were discouraged from pursuing a university education or had less time and money for such a luxury. Blacks, Hispanics and Latinos/as, and American Indians, in addition, were, for prolonged periods, persecuted for learning to read and write (Gere; Royster, *Traces*; Richardson), educated outside the schools that males attended, and denied access to the white colleges and universities.[13] Although individuals from these groups learned—through various means and, often, with great sacrifice—to deploy writing skillfully and in ways that resisted the violence of oppression, many also managed to retain a deep and nuanced appreciation for aural traditions as well: in churches and sacred ceremonies, in storytelling and performance contexts, in poetry and song.

The history of slavery in the United States, for example, shaped the educational opportunities of black citizens, many of whom survived and resisted the violence and oppression in their lives by developing literacy values and practices—often, but certainly not exclusively, aural in nature—that remained invisible to whites and that were, often because of this fact, highly effective. Although many of the legal prohibitions against teaching blacks to read and write were lifted after the Civil War, de facto barriers of racism continued to function. Many black citizens were denied access to schools with adequate resources and others had to abandon their own formal education to help their families survive the economic hardships that continued to characterize the lives of blacks in both the North and the South (Hibbitts). And although black citizens, under adverse conditions, found their own routes for acquiring written literacy—in historically black colleges and universities, in churches, literary societies, homes, segregated public schools—artifacts of this historical period persisted in black communities in verbal games, music, vocal performance, storytelling, and other "vernacular expressive arts" (Richardson 680). These aural traces identify communities of people who have survived and thrived, not only by deploying but also by resisting the literacy practices of a dominant culture that continued to link the printed word and silent reading, so closely to formal education, racism, and the exercise power by whites (Banks; Smitherman, "CCCC"; Richardson; Royster, "First Voice" Mahiri). "[T]he written word," notes Ashraf Rushdy, in part "represents the processes used by racist white American institutions to proscribe and prescribe African American subjectivity."[14]

Hispanic/Latino communities, too, while valuing a wide range of literacy practices in their cultural, familial, and intellectual lives (Guerra; Guerra and Farr; Kells, Balester, and Villanueva; Gutierrez, Baquedano-Lopez, and Alvarez; Cintron; Villanueva; Trejo; Limon; and Ruiz) also managed to retain, to varying extents and in a range of different ways, an investment in collective storytelling, cuentos, corridos, and other aural practices developed within a long—and continuing—history of linguistic, educational, economic, and cultural discrimination. Contributing to the persistence of these traditions has been the history of U.S. imperialism and discrimination in Texas, California, and other border states; the troubled history of bilingual education in this country; the devaluing of Latin American, Puerto Rican, and Mexican Spanish speakers; and the persistence of the English-Only movements in public education. Given this history of discrimination, as Hibbitts points out, Hispanic citizens often find themselves "drawn and sometimes forced back into the soundscapes of their own ethnic communities" (2.43), while simultaneously deploying a wide range of written discourses—skillfully and, sometimes, in ways that productively resist mainstream discourses (Kells, Balester, and Villanueva; Reyes and Halcon; Cintran).

Many American Indians, too, have managed to sustain a value on aurality—as well as on writing and a range of other modalities of expression—as means of preserving their heritage and identities: in public speaking, ceremonial contexts, shared stories, poetry, and song (Clements; Blaeser; Keeling; Evers and Toelken), although as both Scott Lyons and Malea Powell point out, the diversity of tribal histories and the "discursive intricacies" and complexity of Native American's literacy practices and values remain misunderstood, under-examined in published scholarship, and prone to painful and simplistic stereotypes. The aural literacy practices that many tribal members have valued and continue to value—along with the skillful and critical use of other modalities—serve as complex cultural and community-based responses to the imperialism of the "Euroamerican mainstream" (Powell 398). Such practices form part of the story of survival and resistance that American Indians have composed for themselves during the occupation of their homeland and the continuing denigration of their culture as their battles for sovereignty continue.

In sum, the increasingly limited role of aurality within U.S. English and composition programs during the last half of the nineteenth and the twentieth centuries was intimately tied to the emerging influence of writing as the primary mode of formal academic work, of commercial exchange and recordkeeping, and of public and professional expression. This trend, influenced by the rise of manufacturing and science, as well as the growing cultural value on professionalism, was instantiated in various ways and to varying extents in courses and universities around the country and enacted variously by groups and individuals according to their different cultures, literacy values, and practices. The trend was, nevertheless, consistent in its general direction and tendential force. In formal educational contexts, writing and reading increasingly became separated from speech and were understood as activities to be enacted, for the most part, in silence.

In this discussion, I take an important lesson from colleagues like Jacqueline Royster ("First Voice"), Geneva Smitherman (*Talkin'*), Adam Banks, Scott Lyons, and Malea Powell, who point out the serious risks, when discussing the oral traditions and practices of people of color, to cede written English as "somehow the exclusive domain of Whites" (Banks 70). The work of these scholars reminds us in persuasive and powerful terms that people of color have historically deployed a wide range of written discourses in masterful and often powerfully oppositional ways while retaining a value on traditional oral discourses and practices. My goal in this article, then, is not to suggest that teachers focus on *either* writing *or* aurality, but rather that they respect and encourage students to deploy *multiple* modalities in skillful ways—written, aural, visual—and that they model a respect for and understanding of the various roles each modality can play in human expression, the formation of individual and group identity, and meaning making. In this work, the efforts of the scholars such as those cited above as well as attention to historical and contemporary discursive practices of blacks, Native Americans, Hispanics, and other peoples of color can help direct our thinking and lead our profession forward in productive ways.

Audio Composing: Sample 2: Elisa Norris's "Literacy = Identity: Can You See Me?"

At this point, please go to <http://people.cohums.ohio-state.edu/selfe2/ccc/> and listen to Elisa Norris's audio poem, "Literacy = Identity: Can You See Me?" which opens with a school bell, a teacher reading a classroom roll, and her own personal call and response, "Elisa Norris, Elisa Norris … is she absent today? No. Do you see her? No." In this poetic text, an aural variation on a conventional writing assignment, Norris layers music, voice, and poetic images to create a composition that asks listeners to acknowledge her presence and the complex dimensions of her cultural identity. Through the sonic materiality of her own voice, Norris invites listeners to enter her life, and with her to resist the cultural erasure and racial stereotypes that shape her experience.

Artifacts of Aurality

Tracing how aurality became subsumed by print within composition classrooms in the United States during the nineteenth century, however, provides us only one part of a complex historical picture. Another, and perhaps as important, part of the picture involves investigating how and why aurality has *persisted* in English composition classrooms, in the midst of a culture saturated by print.

From one perspective, this process can be understood as a kind of cultural and intellectual *remediation*.[15] Within the specialized cultural location of the college classroom in the United States, aural practices became gradually, but increasingly, subsumed by academic writing, which was presented as the improved medium of formal communication characterizing new

U.S. universities. At the same time, academic writing often made its case for superiority by referring backwards to characteristics of aurality, which was never entirely erased. By the end of the nineteenth century, for instance, as scholars such as Ben McCorkle ("Harbingers") has noted, the academic focus on the production and delivery of *aural texts* was increasingly to be mediated by *written textbooks* on delivery and elocution. English studies faculty still lectured and students still engaged in some oral activities, but within the context of the new university, instruction was increasingly mediated by writing and printed materials—published textbooks, in written assignments, collected and printed lectures, written examinations for students.

Throughout the twentieth century, too, English composition faculty continued to talk about oral language, but primarily in comparison with written language. They continued to make reference to the oral qualities of language, but often metaphorically and in the service of writing instruction and in the study of written texts (the *voice* of the writer, the *tone* of an essay, and the *rhythm* of sentences) (Yancey; Elbow, "What"). Similarly, although students continued to have opportunities for oral performance, they were carefully circumscribed and limited to conferences, presentations, and class discussions focused on writing.[16] And although writing assignments in the twentieth century sometimes focused on topics that touched on aurality and oral performances—popular music, for example—students were expected to *write* their analyses of songs, to focus on *written* lyrics, or to use music as a prompt for *written* composition. In scholarly arenas, scholars studied the history of rhetoric but considered orality and the canon of delivery (McCorkle, "Harbingers") to be of interest primarily as a historical artifact. Even rhetoric scholars whose work was designed to focus attention on the discursive practices and "voices" of long-ignored groups—blacks, Latinos/as, Native Americans, women—*wrote* about these oral practices.[17] The majority of English composition scholars who spoke about their work at professional conferences delivered written papers that they wrote first and, only then, read. By the end of the twentieth century, the ideological privileging of writing was so firmly established that it had become almost fully naturalized. The program of the 1998 Watson Conference, for example, included Beverly Moss as a featured speaker. Moss, who had fractured the elbow of her right arm, delivered a talk about oral language practices in black churches. She introduced her presentation by mentioning her own struggle to prepare a talk without being able to write her text first. Moss's presentation and delivery were superb—cogent and insightful—but her framing comments highlighted how difficult and unusual it was for her, and many other scholars, to deliver an oral presentation without a written text.

Writing as Not-Speech

A brief examination of some aural artifacts in English composition classrooms during the twentieth century can be instructive in helping readers understand the ways in which attention to orality has persisted in U.S. composition classrooms.

By the time the Conference on College Composition and Communication was formed in 1949, attention to students' writing in English departments, with a few brief exceptions, had almost completely eclipsed attention to aural composition. Although the professional focus on speech was revived somewhat after scholars like Lev Vygotsky published his ground-breaking work on the developmental relationship between speech and writing in 1962, many composition scholars—concerned with staking out the territory of the new field and identifying the intellectual and professional boundaries of the nascent discipline—chose to focus on the differences between writing and speech, to define the work of composition classrooms (i.e., writing and the teaching of writing) in opposition to talking, speech, and aurality.[18] This scholarly effort continued throughout the 1960s, 1970s, and early 1980s, until informed by the work of linguists like Douglas Biber ("Spoken" and *Variation*) and Deborah Tannen ("Oral" and *Spoken*), many in the profession came to recognize that writing and speaking actually shared many of the same characteristics and did not exist in the essentialized, dichotomous relationship that had been constructed by scholars.

During the 1960s and 1970s, however, many compositionists defined writing primarily in terms of how it differed from speech. Motivating some of this activity, at least in part, were two converging trends. The first, well underway at this point, was the movement away from current-traditional rhetoric (which posited knowledge as pre-existing language, as external, as discoverable, and as verifiable) and toward a social-epistemic understanding of rhetoric (which posited knowledge as socially constructed and created in, and through, the social uses of language) (Berlin). During roughly the same period, teachers of composition were also attempting to digest poststructuralist theories of language, which occasionally proved less than directly accessible. In his 1976 work *Of Grammatology*, for example, Jacques Derrida pointed out the fallacy of immediacy and questioned the notion of coherent, self-presentation of meaning in *spoken* discourse, and he urged close attention to *writing* as the ground for understanding the active play of difference in language and the shifting nature of signification. Although Derrida's aim was *not* to reverse the historical hierarchy of speech over writing, but rather to call into question logocentricity itself, many composition scholars connected his focus to the field's emerging understanding of writing as both social and epistemic. Influenced not only by these scholarly streams of thought, but by the overdetermined forces of specialization that continued to shape the field within the modern university, compositionists turned their scholarly attention and pedagogical efforts, increasingly, away from speech and toward writing, defining the figure of writing against the ground of speech.[19]

In 1984, for instance, Sarah Liggett annotated fifty-one articles on "the relationship between speaking and writing" (354) and suggested another nineteen pieces for "related reading." The majority of these works, not surprisingly, concluded that the aural language practices of talking and speaking were related to writing in various ways and at various levels, but also that they differed significantly from writing in terms of important features (Emig; Barritt and Kroll; Connors, "Differences"; Farrell; Halpern; Hirsch). Further, in a number of cases, scholars claimed that writing posed more intellectual challenges to students than speech or oral composing, that writing was more sophisticated or complex than speech (Sawyer). Many of these works associated speaking and talking with less reflective, more "haphazard" communication (Snipes) and with popular culture, while writing was considered "inherently more self-reliant" (Emig 353), a "more deliberate mode of expression" and "inherently more intellectual" (Newman and Horowitz 160). In their 1965 article in *College Composition and Communication*, John Newman and Milton Horowitz concluded:

> Writing and speaking clearly represent different strata of the person. Although both functions funnel thought processes, speaking evidences more feeling, more emotive expression and more "first thoughts that come to mind." While writing is more indicative of the intellectualized, rational, and deliberative aspects of the person.
>
> (164)

Other scholars (Dyson; Bereiter and Scardemalia; Carroll; Furner; Lopate; Snipes; Zoellner) explored speech and talking as auxiliary activities that could help students during the process of writing. The ultimate goal of these activities, however, was always a written composition or a literate writer. The profession's bias against aural forms of expression was also evident in the work of scholars who implied that students' reliance on the conventions of oral discourse resulted in the presence of problematic features in their written work (Cayer and Sacks; Collins and Williamson; Robinson, 1982; Snipes; Shaughnessy). In 1973, for example, Wilson Snipes investigated the hypothesis that "orientation to an oral culture has helped cause a gradual decrease in student ability to handle written English in traditionally acceptable ways" (156), citing "haphazard punctuation," "loose rambling style," and "diminutive vocabulary" (159), writing that is "superficial, devoid of subtle distinctions," and thought that remains "fixed in a larval state" (160).

Despite the scholarly work of linguists (Biber, "Spoken" and *Variation*; Tannen, "Oral" and *Spoken*) who identified a broad range of overlapping elements that writing and speaking shared as composing modalities, the bias toward writing continued to grow in composition studies throughout the twentieth century. By 1994, Peter Elbow sounded a wondering note at the professions continued efforts to separate voice from writing:

> What interests me is how ... most of us are unconscious of how deeply our culture's version of literacy has involved as decision to keep voice out of writing, to maximize the difference between speaking and writing—to prevent writers from even using those few crude markers that could capture more of the subtle and not so subtle semiotics of speech. Our version of literacy requires people to distance their writing behavior further from their speaking behavior than the actual modalities require.
>
> ("What" 8)

The Silence of Voice

Another persistent artifact of aurality in the composition classroom has been the reliance on metaphors of *voice* in writing. In Kathleen Yancey's germinal collection *Voices on Voice*, for instance, the bibliography annotates 102 sources that inform professional thinking about voice. Yet Yancey and Elbow, the authors of this bibliography, describe it as "incomplete" because "'voice' leads to everything" (315). The treatment of voice in *College Composition and Communication* and *College English* attests to that statement: between 1962 and 1997, in articles or citations to other scholarly works, voice was explored in connection with feminist theory (Finke), rhetorical theory (Shuster); personal expression, identity, and character (Gibson; Faigley, "Judging"; Stoehr); the writing process (Winchester); style and mimesis (P. Brooks); academic writing (Bartholomae); race, gender, and power (Royster, "First Voice"; Smitherman, "CCCC's Role"; Wiget, Hennig); technology (Eldred), political dissent (Murray), advertisements (Sharpe), public and private discourses (Robson), and authenticity and multiplicity (Fulwiler), and evangelical discourse (Hashimoto), among many other subjects. Between 1972 and 1998, ten books with *voice* in their titles were reviewed in *CCC*.[20]

What these works on composition had in common, however, was less an understanding of embodied, physical human *voice* than a persistent use of the metaphorical language that remediated voice *as a characteristic of written prose.*

As Kathleen Yancey outlined the scope of work on voice in 1994,

[W]e use the metaphor of voice to talk generally around issues in writing: about both the act of writing and its agent, the writer, and even about the reader, and occasionally about the presence in the text of the writer. ... Sometimes we use voice to talk specifically about what and how a writer knows, about the capacity of a writer through "voice" to reveal (and yet be dictated by) the epistemology of a specific culture. Sometimes we use voice to talk in neo-Romantic terms about the writer discovering an authentic self and then deploying it in text.

(vii)

Aurality in Popular Culture

Although aurality continued to take a back seat to writing throughout the twentieth century in collegiate composition classrooms—especially in terms of the texts that students were asked to produce—teachers continued to recognize its importance in the lived experience of young people. In 1968, for instance, Jerry Walker wrote of his concern that English majors were asked to focus almost exclusively on printed works of "literary heritage" (634) that provided youths little help in dealing with the problems of the Cold War era. Given students' concerns about "alienation, war, racial strife, automation, work, and civil disobedience" (635), Walker noted, they often found the texts of television and radio, which involved the aural presentation of information, to resonate more forcefully than the written texts of historical eras. Walker pointed to the successes of teachers who focused on popular culture and who used aural texts and popular music as foci for classroom assignments. Similar suggestions for assignments were put forward in subsequent years—with assignments that examined the music of the Beatles (Carter) and Billie Holiday (Zaluda); popular music in general (Kroeger); and the writing associated with popular music (Lutz)—for instance, the liner notes that accompany albums and CDs.

In general, however, the aural text was not the focus of these scholars. Music and communication in mass media (especially radio, film, newspapers) was considered part of popular culture, and teachers of English composition—influenced by the biases of the belletristic tradition (Trimbur; Paine) that shaped composition as a discipline—distinguished such texts from academic discourse, dismissing them as part of the "philistine culture" outside the walls of the university (George and Trimbur 694).[21] Although most composition teachers in the twentieth century were willing to accept the draw of popular culture, the goal of the composition classroom remained, at some level, as Adams Sherman Hill had described it in the nineteenth century: to "arm" students (Hill, qtd. in Paine 292), to "inoculate" (Paine 282) them against the infectious effects of popular culture and various forms of mass communication, to encourage them to turn to the written texts of geniuses from the past as a means of discovering their "real selves" (Hill, qtd. in Paine, p. 282) and *resisting* mass culture" (Paine 283). Although it was permissible to lure students into English classes with the promise of focusing on popular culture or music, most composition teachers agreed it was best to approach such texts as objects of study, analysis, interpretation, and, perhaps most importantly, critique (Sirc).

As representative pieces of popular—or low—culture, aural texts were not generally recognized as appropriately intellectual vehicles for composing meaning in composition classrooms. Only writing held that sinecure, and the goal of composition teachers' assignments continued to be excellence in reading and writing. Robert Heilman summarized this view succinctly in 1970, within the context of a discussion about the use of electronic media in composition classrooms:

> the substitution of electronic experience [music, film, radio] in the classroom, for the study of the printed page is open to question. It tends to reduce the amount of reading by creating a thirst for the greater immediate excitement of sound and light. The classroom is for criticism; the critical experience is valuable; and it cannot be wise to attenuate it by the substitution of sensory experience which the age already supplies in excess.
>
> (242–43)

Despite this common characterization, some pioneering teachers during the 1960s, 1970s, and 1980s continued to experiment with more contemporary texts and assignments that involved aural components. Lisa Ede and John Lofty, for instance, suggested incorporating oral histories into composition classrooms. Both authors, however, also considered the goal and the final step of such assignments to be written essays that quoted from conversations with interview subjects. Although aurality was acknowledged and deployed as a way of engaging students and even a way of investigating various phenomena, it was generally ignored as a compositional modality.

Aurality and Pedagogy

A value on aurality—in limited and constrained situations—also persisted in the context of certain classroom practices throughout the twentieth century. One strikingly persistent thread of work, for instance, focused on teachers and using audio recordings to convey their responses to student papers (G. Olson; Sommers; Mellen and Sommers; Anson; Sipple). In such articles, faculty talked about the fact that their taped oral responses to students' written work allowed for a clearer acknowledgment of the "rhetorical nature" of response to a piece of writing, because remarks could be "more detailed and expansive" (Mellen and Sommers 11–12) and unfold across time. As Jeff Sommers noted, the sound of an instructor's voice seemed at once more immediate and more personal; the aural nature of the comments were able to give students a "'walking tour'" through their texts, as if a reader were conversing with them (186). Interestingly, however, none of these authors mentioned some of the more basic affordances of aural feedback—that speech conveys a great deal of meaning through pace, volume, rhythm, emphasis, and tone of voice as well as through words themselves.[22]

Teachers continued to provide other aspects of their instruction orally, as well. Diana George, for example, explored the use of audio taping in the composition classroom as a way of recording the texts of small-group interactions and responding to these texts with her own suggestions, observations, and remarks. George noted that this approach provided her insight about the problems that such groups encountered when discussing each other's written papers, as well as the work that small groups accomplished when a teacher was not present. This scholarship deserves attention because it is one of the relatively rare instances in which students' oral exchanges were considered *as semiotic texts* that were composed and could be studied for the meaning they contained.

As much of this scholarship suggests, however, while students were expected to engage in discussion and oral group work in many composition classrooms, their speaking was located within specific contexts and occasions and was expected, generally, to happen on cue. Such occasions were limited in many classrooms and often were not wholly satisfying to teachers. In 1974, for instance, Gerald Pierre noted that well-meaning teachers who depended on lecturing to convey information often short-circuited their own attempts to generate class discussions, turning them into "oral quizzes, guess-my-conclusion games, or bristling silences" (306).

In an attempt to address such concerns, some teachers turned to oral presentations as venues for student talk within the classroom. Mary Saunders, in a 1985 article in *College Composition and Communication*, described a sequence of assignments in which students were asked to make short oral presentations abstracted from drafts of their written research papers and then to revise their papers based on the feedback they received from classmates. The primary goal of these presentations, of course, was to improve students' *written* work, to help them "write better papers" (358). Similarly the aural work accomplished within teacher-student conferences (Schiff; North; Arbur; A. Rose; Memering) and writing-center appointments (North; Clark) was subordinated almost wholly to the end goal of writing. For students, the primary reason for speaking and listening in composition classrooms was identified as improved writing.

In this context, it is interesting to note that aurality also continued as a key form of *faculty* teaching and testing practices.[23] Lecturing, for instance, remained a relatively popular form of teaching in many composition classrooms through the end of the century and beyond—despite a growing agreement that classrooms should be centered around students' opportunities to practice composing strategies rather than teachers' chances to talk about such strategies (Finkel; Dawe and Dornan; Pierre; Lindemann).[24]

The continued use of the lecture as one method of conducting instruction foregrounds some of the complications and contradictions of the profession's stance toward aurality and writing: although students have been encouraged to focus on the production of *written* texts and such texts have increasingly become the standard of production for composition classes, many teachers have continued to impart information through *oral* lectures, often expending a great deal of time to craft and deliver effective oral texts. In this respect, as every teacher and student understands, power and aurality are closely linked. Indeed, the enactment of authority, power, and status in composition classes is expressed, in part, *through* aurality: how much one is allowed to talk and under what conditions. This phenomenon has been mapped as well in teachers' aural evaluations of both undergraduate and graduate students, which, although not generally considered as important as the evaluation of *written* work, has remained nonetheless persistent. For undergraduates, for instance, such evaluations have continued to be conducted in highly ritualized one-on-one conferences in which students are expected to explain the purposes, audiences, and approaches taken in their written projects (Schiff; North; Arbur; Rose; Memering). For graduate students, oral questioning and disputation has persisted in candidacy exams, as well as in more public defenses of theses and dissertations. To pass such exams, graduate students are expected to succeed both in producing a written text and defending their ideas in disputational aural exchanges, forms rooted historically in verbal argument and display (Ong, *Fighting*; Connors, "Teaching").

Aurality and Silenced Voices

It is important to note that attention to aurality has also persisted in the work of scholars who focused on the rhetorical contributions and histories of marginalized or underrepresented groups. Individual scholars such as Jacqueline Jones Royster (*Traces* and "First Voice") and Beverly Moss, Scott Lyons and Malea Powell, Anne Ruggles Gere and Geneva Smitherman ("CCCC's Role"), among others, for example, brought to bear an understanding of aurality—and its complex relationship to written literacy—informed by the historical richness of their own families, communities, and experiences, and trained it on the complex problems associated with race, class, and gender inequities, and the exercise of power in education and English composition.

This richly textured scholarship—which holds great value for the profession and our larger culture—contributes, in particular, to resisting simplistic binary splits between writing and aurality that have informed instruction in mainstream college composition classrooms during much of the twentieth century, despite linguistic evidence suggesting the erroneous nature of such a division. At the same time, this work acknowledges aurality as an important way of knowing and making meaning for many people in this country—especially those for whom, historically, higher education has often been part of a system of continued domination and oppression. Royster, for example, in her 1996 *College Composition and Communication* article "When the First Voice You Hear Is Not Your Own" and in her later book *Traces in the Stream: Literacy and Social Change among African American Women*, explored the cumulative and multiplied power of her own authentic voice and those of other African American women—and the responses of a racist culture to these voices. In doing this work, Royster outlines a powerful argument for aural discourses (as well as, and in combination with, written discourses and hybrid forms of communication) that take up the challenge of border crossing and political action to confront the insidious "cross-cultural misconduct" (32) so frequently characterizing racism, especially in educational contexts.

The work of Malea Powell and Scott Lyons, too, has helped compositionists complicate the profession's "uncritical acceptance of the oral/literate split" (Powell 397) which helps mask the complexity, range, and depth of Native American texts and discourses, and perpetuate the stereotypes that continue to sustain racism. Native Americans, these authors point out, have employed both oral and written discourses as tactics of "survivance" (Powell 428), while acknowledging the many problems associated with communicating in discursive systems—academic writing, legal writing, treaties, legislative venues—that have been "compromised" (Lyons) as part of a racist, colonial mainstream culture. As Lyons reminds us, because writing for many Native American people is bound so intimately to the project of white colonization and domination, and oral discourse so often supports uncritical and racist stereotyping, "rhetorical sovereignty" (449) is a centrally important feature of Native American self-determination.

Aural Composing, Sample 3: Wendy Wolters Hinshaw's *Yelling Boy*

At this point, please go to <http://people.cohums.ohio-state.edu/selfe2/ccc/> and listen to Wendy Wolters Hinshaws *Yelling Boy*, a reflective examination of her interaction with an undergraduate student in a section of first-year composition. The reflection, a painfully frank and honest look at Wolters Hinshaw's own teaching is rendered in stark terms—no music and no soundmarks of the classroom,[25] no chalk sounds on a blackboard, no scraping of chairs as a class session ends, no rustling of papers or announcements of assignments due. This piece, a memory of what took place in a "dirty grey office," is focused on a single exchange that happened across a "small teacher's desk" and takes three minutes for Wolters Hinshaw to recount in its entirety.

Aurality and Digital Environments for Composing

As many contemporary scholars have pointed out—among them Graff, Gee, Brandt ("Accumulating" and *Literacy*), Barton and Hamilton, Powell, Royster ("First Voice"), Hawisher and Selfe—we cannot hope to fully understand literacy practices or the values associated with such practices unless, and until, we can also understand the complex cultural ecology that serves as their context. Such ecologies both shape peoples' literacy practices and values and are shaped by them in an ongoing duality of structuration (Giddens). In the United States, then—especially at the end of the twentieth century and the beginning of the twenty-first century—we cannot hope to fully understand aural or written literacy practices and values without also understanding something about digital and networked contexts for communication, among many other factors.

Although digital environments have had many different effects at local, regional, national, and international levels (Castells, *End*; *Power*; *Rise*), some of the most profound and far-reaching changes have involved communication forms, practices, values, and patterns. Although the relationship between digital technologies and literacy remains complexly articulated with existing social and cultural formations, and digital environments continue to be unevenly distributed along axes of power, class, and race, it is clear that the speed and extended reach of networked communications have directly affected literacy efforts around the globe (*Human Development Report*). Digital networks, for example, have provided routes for the increasing numbers of communications that now cross geopolitical, cultural, and linguistic borders, and because of this situation, the texts exchanged within such networks often assume hybrid forms that take advantage of multiple semiotic channels. The international versions of the Aljazeera, *Japan Times*, BBC, and the *International Herald Tribune* websites, for example, offer not only traditional alphabetic journalism, but also video and audio interviews. Similarly, the United Nations, Human Rights Watch, and the International Olympic Movement, among many other international organizations, all maintain richly textured websites that offer not only print reports and white papers, but audio, video, and photographic essays as well. These communications—which consist of not only words, but also audio and video transmissions, images, sounds, music, animations, and multimedia presentations—are used by organizations, nongovernmental agencies, multinational corporations, international financial institutions, governments, affinity groups, and individual citizens who form around common interests and projects, and who compose, exchange, and interpret information, and through these efforts and others, these communications help establish the cultural codes of communication in the twenty-first century.

At the same time, new software and hardware applications—video and audio editing systems and conferencing software, electronic white boards, digital video cameras, multimodal composing environments, and digital audio recorders, among many, many more—have provided increasing numbers of people the means of producing and distributing communications that take advantage of multiple expressive modalities.

These two converging trends have had many effects,[26] among them an increasing interest in aurality and modalities of expression other than the printed word—not only in linguistics, literacy, and language studies (Ong, *Orality*; Kleine and Gale; McCorkle, "Harbingers"; Halbritter; Hawisher and Selfe; DeVoss, Hawisher, Jackson, Johansen, Moraski, and Selfe; Tannen, "Oral," and *Spoken*) but also in medicine (Sterne; Sykes), legal studies (Hibbitts; Gilkerson; Hespanha), cultural studies (Bull and Back), geography (Sui; J. Olson; Carney), architecture (Labelle, Roden, and Migo; C. N. Brooks, *Architectural*; Kahn), film (Altman; O'Brien; Chion), and history (B. Smith; Yow; Richie) among many other areas and disciplines. As Hibbitts sketches the connection:

> The history of Western culture over the past 125 years suggests that the recent turn toward the aural is largely a product of new aural technologies. In essence, cultural aurality has tended to become more pronounced as aural technologies have multiplied and spread. At every stage in this process, the existence of these technologies has radically extended the power and range of aurally communicated information. As technologically transmitted and amplified sound has become able to assume more of the cultural burden, culture itself has turned towards sound for information.
>
> (3.12)

In composition studies, then, it is not surprising that some of the impetus for a new turn toward aurality has been contributed by technology scholars focusing on electronic, multimedia, and multimodal composing. This early thread of scholarship resisted, for the most part, simplistic distinctions between orality and writing, and connected digital writing to aurality in *metaphorical* terms. Such work became increasingly important throughout the last decade of the twentieth century as computer systems developed to accommodate new forms of communicative exchanges: online conferences (Bruce, Peyton, and Bertram; Faigley, *Fragments*); listservs (Cubbison; Selfe and Myer); MOOs and MUDs (Haefner; Haynes and Holmevik), and email (Yancey and Spooner), for example.[27]

By the end of the decade and the century, low-cost and portable technologies of digital audio recording, such as minidisc recorders, and simplified open-source audio editing software, such as Audacity, put the material means of digital audio production into the hands of both students and English composition teachers.[28] Many of these teachers were already experimenting with digital video, using Apples iMovie or Microsoft's Movie Maker,[29] both which contained an audio track and limited audio-editing capabilities, but digital audio-editing programs made it possible for teachers and students to *compose with audio* in ways that they could not do previously: recording and layering environmental and artificial sounds to create a textured sonic context and collection of detail, weaving vocal interview and commentary sources together to provide multiple perspectives on a subject; adding music, silence, and audio effects to ways of changing emphasis, tone, pace, delivery, and content.

Although new software environments expanded the opportunities for experimentation with audio compositions in English classrooms, the intellectual basis of such work was also fueled by the germinal scholarship of the New London Group, Gunther Kress and Theo van Leeuwen, and Cope and Kalantzis—who identified the aural as *one modality among many* on which individuals should be able to call as a rhetorical and creative resource in composing messages and making meaning. These scholars argued for an increasingly robust theory of semiosis that acknowledged the practices of human sign makers who selected from a range of modalities for expression (including sound, image, and animation, for example) depending on rhetorical and material contexts within which the communication was being designed and distributed. They also noted that no one expressive modality, including print, was capable of carrying the full range of meaning in a text, and pointed out that the texts sign makers created both shaped and were shaped by the universe of semiotic resources they accessed.

This expanded semiotic theory brought into sharp relief the hegemony of print as an expressive mode in English composition classrooms—especially for scholars studying emerging forms of communication in digital environments. Many of these scholars had observed the professions love-hate relationship with these new forms of expression during the last decade of the twentieth century—blogs,[30] home-made digital videos,[31] multimedia sites like MySpace[32] and Facebook,[33] digital audio and podcasting.[34] Although such texts had begun to dominate digital environments and self-sponsored literacy venues, print continued to prevail as *"the* way" of knowing (Dunn, *Talking* 15), *the* primary means of learning and communicating in composition classrooms. Although email, websites, and multimedia texts were accepted as objects for study, critique, and analysis—and while many students were already engaging in the self-sponsored literacy practices of creating digital video and audio texts—composition assignments, for the large part, continued to resemble those of the past hundred years (Takayoshi and Selfe).

In a 1999 chapter, "English at the Crossroads," in *Passions, Pedagogies, and 21st Century Technologies*, for instance, Kress described the cultural changes he saw literacy practices undergoing in an increasingly technological world and compared these to the continued privileging of print by teachers of English. The exclusive focus on print and written language, he noted,

> has meant a neglect, an overlooking, even suppression of the potentials of representation and communicational modes in particular cultures, an often repressive and always systematic neglect of human potentials in many ... areas; and a neglect equally, as a consequence of the development of theoretical understandings of such modes—Or, to put it provocatively: the single, exclusive and intensive focus on written language has dampened the full development of all kinds of human potential, through all the sensorial possibilities of human bodies, in all kinds of respects, cognitively and affectively.
>
> (85)

With the development of the Internet and digital audio and video applications, new depth and scope were added to scholarship around aurality. In 2004, for example, Scott Halbritter, of the University of North Carolina at Chapel Hill, wrote a dissertation that explored sound as a rhetorical resource in multimedia compositions. In 2005, Tara Shankar, in her MIT dissertation, described a project in which young students composed using a "spriting" software that she had developed to take advantage of their oral exchanges; and in a 2005 dissertation completed at Ohio State University, Warren Benson (Ben) McCorkle explored the remediation of aurality by print and writing, as well as the subsequent diminishment of professional attention to the canon of delivery in nineteenth century collegiate instruction.

By 2006, *Computers and Composition: An International Journal* published a special issue on sound, edited by Cheryl Ball and Byron Hawk. In tandem with this collection of print articles, Ball and Hawk also published a related set of online essays and resources in *Computers and Composition Online*, an online version of the journal edited by Kristine Blair. The collection contained not only print essays but also video and audio texts that offered key arguments, illustrations, and examples that could not be rendered in a print environment.

As such scholarly works have emerged during the last decades, compositionists have continued to experiment with assignments that encouraged students to create meaning in and through audio compositions, focusing assignments on podcasting,[35] mashups, voice-mail compositions and sound poems,[36] radio essays,[37] audio documentaries and interviews,[38] audio ethnographies,[39] as well as video, multimedia, and other forms of multimodal composition. Other rhetoric and composition scholars, taking their cue from increasingly visible projects in history, folklore, and anthropology, began to involve students in recording and collecting the oral histories of two-year college composition teachers,[40] key figures in rhetoric and composition studies,[41] and pioneers in the writing center movement.[42]

Aural Composing Sample 4: Daniel Keller's *Lord of the Machines: Reading the Human Computer Relationship*

At this point, please go to <http://people.cohums.ohio-state.edu/selfe2/ccc/> and listen to Daniel Keller's audio essay, *Lord of the Machines: Reading the Human Computer Relationship.* This richly textured composition explores the complex relationship that humans have established with computers through their daily interaction and through media representations.

By Way of Concluding, But Not Ending …

In this essay, I offer some perspective about the way in which U.S. composition studies has subsumed, remediated, and rediscovered aurality during the past 150 years. This story, however, is far from complete, and far from as tidy as I have suggested. The recent attention to, and rethinking of, sound as a composing modality—and the understanding and use of other composing modalities such as video, images, and photographs—remain fragmented and uneven, far from a broadly defined professional trend. Although many teachers who work with digital media in this country recognize the efforts I describe here and have participated in them or helped sustain them, for other teachers the bandwidth of composing resources remains limited to words on a printed page.

Sustaining this situation is a constellation of factors—not all of them technological. Chief among them, for instance, is the profession's continuing bias toward print and ongoing investment in specialization, understandable as historically and culturally informed methods of ensuring our own status and continuity. Given this context, many English composition programs and departments maintain a scholarly culture in which, nonprint forms, genres, and modalities of communication are considered objects of study and critique, but not a set of resources for student authors to deploy themselves. As Gunther Kress observes, "Control over communication and over the means of representation is, as always, a field in which power is exercised" ("English" 67).

It is also true that recording and editing sound—or images or video—in digital environments is still far from a transparent or inexpensive activity, and many composition teachers lack the technology, the professional development training, and the technical support needed to experiment with assignments such as those I have described. Although most schools now have access to computers, and most departments of English and writing programs can count on some kind of computer facility, work with sound and video still requires computers specially equipped for such projects, access to mass storage for student projects, support for teachers who want to learn to work with audio, and sympathetic and knowledgeable technical staff members who understand the importance of such work These resources are unevenly distributed in small state- and privately-funded schools, historically black colleges and universities, and reservation schools, rural schools, and schools that have been hit by devastating events such as Hurricane Katrina. None of this, of course, is helped by the reduction of support for education in the wake of our country's massive expenditures on national security and the wars in Afghanistan and Iraq.

I should be as clear as possible here about exactly what I am advocating, and why. My argument is not *either/or*, but *both/and*. I am *not* arguing against writing, the value we place on writing, or an understanding of what writing—and print—contribute to the human condition that is vitally important. Indeed, it is evident to me that the ability to express oneself in writing will continue to be a hallmark of educated citizens in the United States for some time to come. Nor do I want to contribute to re-inscribing the simplistic terms of a writing/aurality divide, a division that is as limiting as it is false.

I *do* want to argue that teachers of composition need to pay attention to, and come to value, the *multiple* ways in which students compose and communicate meaning, the exciting hybrid, multimodal texts they create—in both nondigital and digital environments—to meet their own needs in a changing world. We need to better understand the importance that students attach to composing, exchanging, and interpreting new and different kinds of texts that help them make sense of their experiences and lives—songs and lyrics, videos, written essays illustrated with images, personal Web pages that include sound clips. We need to learn from their motivated efforts to communicate with each other, for themselves and for others, often in resistance to the world we have created for them. We need to respect the rhetorical sovereignty of young people from different backgrounds, communities, colors, and cultures, to observe and understand the rhetorical choices they are making, and to offer them new ways of making meaning, new choices, new ways of accomplishing their goals.

I *do* want to convince compositionists how crucial it is to acknowledge, value, and draw on a range of composing modalities—among them, images (moving and still), animations, sound, and color—which are *in the process of becoming increasingly important to communicators*, especially within digital networks, now globally extended in their reach and scope. The identities that individuals are forging through such hybrid communicative practices, as Manual Castells (*Power* 360) points out, are key factors in composing the cultural and communicative codes that will characterize coming decades. Students are intuitively aware of these related phenomena, being immersed in them, but they need help understanding the implications of such cultural trends as well as managing their own communicative efforts in ways that are rhetorically effective, critically aware, morally responsible, and personally satisfying. Responsible educators, critically aware scholars of semiotic theory and practice, will not want to ignore these world-order changes or the opportunities they offer.

To understand how literacy practices change, especially in times of rapid transformation, Deborah Brandt ("Accumulating") maintains that both teachers and students need to understand how literacy forms emerge and contend and to study those contexts within which "latent forms of older, residual literacies … are at play alongside emerging ones" (665). To undertake such work in classrooms, Brandt suggests, we can talk to students about how both "'school based' and 'home-based' literacies form and function within larger historical currents" (666). Composition classrooms can provide a context not only for *talking about* different literacies, but also for *practicing* different literacies, learning to create texts that combine a range of modalities as communicative resources: exploring their affordances, the special capabilities they offer to authors; identifying what audiences expect of texts that deploy different modalities and how they respond to such texts.

Within such a classroom, teaching students to make informed, rhetorically based uses of sound as a composing modality—and other expressive modalities such as video, still images, and animation—could help them better understand the particular affordances of written language, and vice versa. Pam Takayoshi and I have outlined this case elsewhere in the following pragmatic terms:

> [T]eaching students how to compose and focus a thirty-second public service announcement (PSA) for radio—and select the right details for inclusion in this audio composition—*also helps teach* them specific strategies for focusing a written essay more tightly and effectively, choosing those details most likely to convey meaning in effective ways to a particular audience, for a particular purpose. In addition, as students engage in composing a script for the audio PSA, they are motivated to engage in meaningful, rhetorically-based writing practice. Further, as students work within the rhetorical constraints of such an audio assignment, they learn more about the particular affordances of sound (the ability to convey accent, emotion, music, ambient sounds that characterize a particular location or event) and the constraints of sound (the difficulty of going back to review complex or difficult passages, to convey change not marked by sound, to communicate some organizational markers like paragraphs). Importantly, students also gain the chance to compare the affordances and constraints of audio with those of alphabetic writing—and, thus, improve their ability to make *informed and conscious choices* about the most effective modality for communicating in particular rhetorical contexts.
>
> (3)

The challenges and difficulties of such work cannot be underestimated. The time that students spend in composition classrooms is altogether too short—especially during the first two years of college. Indeed, many teachers will argue that they do not have enough instructional time to teach students what they need to know about writing and rhetoric, let alone about composing digital audio texts (or digital videos or photo essays, for instance). A variation of this argument will be familiar to any compositionist who has offered a writing-across-the-curricuium workshop to colleagues who understand their job as involving coverage of a set amount of disciplinary material rather than the task of teaching students how to think through problems using writing. Frequently, these colleagues—who design instruction around the mastery of facts, procedures, or series of historical events—consider writing instruction to be add-on content, material that detracts from the real focus of disciplinary mastery. Like most writing-across-the-curriculum specialists, however, I would argue that the primary work of *any* classroom is to help students use semiotic resources to think critically, to explore, and to solve problems. In composition classes, this means helping students work through communicative problems—analyzing a range of rhetorical tasks and contexts (online, in print contexts, and face to face); deploying a range of assets (both digital and nondigital) effectively and responsibly; and making meaning for a range of purposes, audiences, and information sets.

It is an understandable, if unfortunate, fact, as Patricia Dunn ("Talking" 150) argues, that our profession has come to equate *writing* with *intelligence*. Even more important, she adds, we have allowed ourselves to ignore the "back story" implications of this equation, the unspoken belief that those who *do not privilege writing above all other forms of expression*—those individuals and groups who have "other ways of knowing," learning, and expressing themselves—may somehow lack intelligence. This unacknowledged and often unconscious episteme has particular salience for contemporary literacy practices that are not focused solely on print or alphabetic writing. As teachers of rhetoric and composition, our responsibility is to teach students effective, rhetorically based strategies for taking advantage of *all available means* of communicating effectively and productively as literate citizens.

And so back to what's at stake. As faculty, when we limit our understanding of composing and our teaching of composition to a single modality, when we focus on print alone as the communicative venue for our assignments and for students' responses to those assignments, we ensure that instruction is less accessible to a wide range of learners, and we constrain students' ability to succeed by offering them an unnecessarily narrow choice of semiotic and rhetorical resources. By broadening the choice of composing modalities, I argue, we expand the field of play for students with different learning styles and differing ways of reflecting on the world; we provide the opportunity for them to study, think critically about, and work with new communicative modes. Such a move not only offers us a chance to make instruction increasingly effective for those students from different cultural and linguistic backgrounds, but it also provides an opportunity to make our work increasingly relevant to a changing set of communicative needs in a globalized world. As Gunther Kress ("English") has suggested, it may also make us better scholars of semiotic systems by providing us with additional chances to observe, systematically and at close quarters, how people make meaning in contemporary communication environments when they have a full palette of rhetorical and semiotic resources on which to draw, new opportunities to theorize about emerging representational practices within such environments, and additional chances to study the communicative possibilities and potentials of various modes of expression. It gives us another reason to pay attention to language and to learn.

For students, the stakes are even more significant. Young people need to know that their role as rhetorical agents is open, not artificially foreclosed by the limits of their teachers' imaginations. They need a full quiver of semiotic modes from which to select, role models who can teach them to think critically about a range of communication tools, and multiple ways of reaching their audience. They do not need teachers who insist on *one* tool or *one* way.

Students, in sum, need opportunities to realize that different compositional modalities carry with them different possibilities for representing multiple and shifting patterns of identity, additional potential for expression and resistance, expanded ways of engaging with a changing world—as the four audio essays I reference in this article indicate. As student Elisa Norris put it, "If we can imagine using these types of projects in our writing studios, we can open up that learning space so that *all* students have room to express themselves."

Students need these things because they will join us as part of an increasingly challenging and difficult world—one plagued by destructive wars and great ill will, marked by poverty and disease, scarred by racism and ecological degradation. In this world, we face some wickedly complex communicative tasks. To make our collective way with any hope for success, to create a different set of global and local relations than currently exists, we will need *all available means* of persuasion, all available dimensions, all available approaches, not simply those limited to the two dimensional space of a printed page.

Acknowledgments

I am deeply grateful to Diana George whose work on the visual (CCC54.1) inspired this piece, as well as to all the generous friends and colleagues who helped me think about aurality as I wrote this article: Dickie Selfe, Gail Hawisher, Randy Freisinger, Marilyn Cooper, Erin Smith, Gary Bays, Michael Moore, Dennis Lynch, Scott De Witt, Debra Journet, Ben McCorkle, Michael Harker, Jason Palmeri, Beverly Moss, and Peter Elbow, among others. I am also most grateful for the valuable revision suggestions provided by the CCC reviewers. All of these individuals have contributed to making this a better, more insightful, and more thoughtful text.

Notes

1. With the term *aurality*, I refer to a complexly related web of communicative practices that are received or perceived by the ear, including speech, sound, and music. In exploring aurality, I focus on both the *reception* and the *production* of aural communications. I also focus on the purposeful composition of aural texts. One of my goals in exploring the role of aural communication in composition classrooms is to suggest that the written word is not the only way of composing and communicating meaning or understanding, nor should it be *the* sole focus of composition instruction in a world where people make meaning and extend their understanding through the use of multiple semiotic modalities in combination—sound, printed words, spoken words, still and moving images, graphical elements.

   In using the term *aurality*, rather than the more common *orality*, I hope to resist models of an oral/literate divide and simplistic characterizations of cultures or groups as either oral or literate in their communicative practices. Humans make and communicate meaning through a combination of modalities—sound, still and moving images, words, among them—and using a variety of media. And they read and interpret texts that combine modalities as well.

2. The term *multimodal* is used by the New London Group to indicate the range of modalities—printed words, still and moving images, sound, speech, and music, color—that authors combine as they design texts.

3. I borrow the term *rhetorical sovereignty* from Scott Lyons (2000), but extend it, advisedly, and in ways that I recognize might not remain faithful to his use of the term. Lyons uses the term to describe the right of indigenous peoples to have "some say about the nature of their textual representations," to determine their own representational needs and identities, their own accounts of the past and present. For Lyons, rhetorical sovereignty is intimately connected to the land; to the history, the present, and the future of native peoples; to culture and community. I use *rhetorical sovereignty* to refer to the rights of students to have "some say" about their own representational needs, identities, and modalities of expression. In making this statement, however, I do *not* want to suggest that all college students are subject to the same systems of domination and cultural violence as native peoples. They are not. Nor do I want to diminish, in any way or to any degree, the importance of Lyons's insights or our professional responsibility for supporting the sovereignty efforts that native peoples have undertaken. I stand in solidarity and support of these efforts.

4. As I suggest throughout this article, aurality remains a relatively small but valued part of the composition classroom—only, however, in limited and constrained circumstances: in the occasional oral presentation, in classroom discussions, or in one-on-one conferences, for example. In these situations, aurality is valued and even prized. In the vast majority of compositions classrooms, however, the formal expression of knowledge is reserved for writing, and written papers are the product toward which students are taught to work.

5. In 1873, Harvard formed its Department of English. The mission of this unit was to teach written English within the new secular, specialized university. For extended and informative discussions of how rhetorical education was conducted during this period, see Russell ("Institutionalizing"); Halloran; Wright and Halloran; Johnson; Berlin; and Congleton.

6. Within this context, David Russell (*Writing*) notes, writing

   > was now embedded in a whole array of complex and highly differentiated social practices carried on without face-to-face communication. The new professions ... increasingly wrote ... for specialized audiences of colleagues who were united not primarily by ties of class but by the shared activities, the goals, ... the unique conventions of a profession or discipline.
   >
   > (4–5)

7. James A. Berlin notes that "Charles William Eliot, Harvard's president from 1869 to 1909 ... considered writing so central to the new elective curriculum he was shaping that in 1874 the Freshman English course at Harvard was established, by 1894 was the only requirement except for a modern language, and by 1897, was the only required course in the curriculum, consisting of a two-semester sequence" (20). Influenced variously by the belles lettristic tradition, the pressures of increasing collegiate enrollments, the influential move toward graduate education on the German model, and continued moves toward specialized study in the new university, however, writing gave way, in fairly short order, to a focus on the reading and analysis of contemporary and classical literary texts. And by the first part of the twentieth century, the efforts of most departments of English were focused primarily on literary works. For an extended discussion of this trend, see Halloran; Berlin; and Russell.

8. In the *Atlantic Monthly* of March 1869, Eliot wrote

   No men have greater need of the power of expressing their ideas with clearness, conciseness, and vigor than those whose avocation require them to describe and discuss material resources, industrial processes, public works, mining enterprises, and the complicated problems of trade and finance. In such writings, embellishment maybe dispensed with, but the chief merits of style—precision, simplicity, perspicuity, and force are never more necessary.

   (359)

9. See Ben McCorkle's article "Harbingers of the Printed Page" for an extended explanation of how the canon of delivery fared in nineteenth-century composition classes and how orality became subsumed to, and remediated by, writing in composition classrooms.

10. Ronald Reid describes these changes in terms of the Boyleston Professorship at Harvard—and the occupants of this position—as cases in point.

    In 1806, rhetoric was concerned primarily with persuasive oratory and sunk its roots deeply in the classical tradition. By the time of Hill's retirement [in 1904], what was called "rhetoric" was concerned not with oratory, but with written composition, expository and literary as well as persuasive and made little direct reference to classical authors. And not even these new concerns were those of the Boyleston professorship, which abandoned rhetoric for literature, oratory for poetry. Such a dramatic shift took place not only at Harvard, but in higher education generally.

    (239)

    The Boyleston Professorship of Rhetoric and Oratory, was held by the following individuals from 1806 to 1904: John Quincy Adams (statesman, 1806–1809), Joseph McKean (former minister, mathematician, 1809–1818), Edward T. Channing (attorney, editor of *North American Review*, 1819–1851), Francis James Child (who studied at Gottingen University in Germany and applied many German practices to the revision of U.S. curricula, 1851–1876), and Adams Sherman Hill (1876–1904). For an extended discussion of this professorship and the changes it underwent at the end of the nineteenth century, see Ronald Reid's article "The Boyleston Professorship of Rhetoric and Oratory, 1806–1904."

11. Although oral composition—both scripted and nonscripted—waned relatively rapidly in English composition classrooms during the last half of the nineteenth century, it persisted in other locations. One of these was the extracurricular literary and debate societies that gained popularity in the eighteenth century and persisted throughout the nineteenth century in various collegiate and noncollegiate forms (Gere; Halloran; Royster, *Traces*; Berlin). In colleges, this movement was often initiated and carried on by students, often with little help from faculty, to support practice in public speaking and debating topics of interest. Many such clubs engaged in intercollegiate contests.

    Attention to aurality was also sustained by the popular Elocutionary Movement, which began its rise to prominence in the late eighteenth century and continued throughout the nineteenth century. This movement, too, was built on the general interest in systematic and scientific knowledge, identifying elaborately prescriptive texts with "highly encoded notational systems to precisely regulate vocal inflection, gestures of the arms, hands, and legs, and even facial countenances as a means of directly manipulating different faculties in the minds of listeners." (B. McCorkle, "Harbingers" 35). In this movement, oral delivery figured centrally and prescriptively.

12. As Hibbitts (2.25) describes this shift,

    Within the white community, public speech became more dependent on visual, written scripts; old-fashioned oratory was increasingly dismissed as "mere rhetoric." Storytelling survived, but it was largely, if not altogether accurately, associated with children, members of less literate lower classes, and inhabitants of backward rural areas. Most white American authors jettisoned the more obvious aural mannerisms and formats that had characterized so much American literature in the antebellum era. At the same time, white Americans gradually embraced silence as both a social norm and a primary means of social discipline. Increasingly used to sitting quietly in front of texts, white American theater- and concert-goers who had formerly been inclined to spontaneously talk to each other and interact with stage performers became more willing to sit in silent (or at least suspended) judgment on the musicians and actors who appeared before them. In the schoolroom where white American teachers had once taught their students to read by recitation, the most important meta-lesson became, as it today remains, how to sit, write, and read in contented quiet.

13. I write about the complexly articulated effects of race, class, and gender from my subject position as a white female academic. As Marilyn Cooper reminds me, this position limits my work: I can write *about* people of color, but never *as* a person of color. I also recognize the great danger, especially in such a brief article, of glossing over the important differences, cultural complexities, and rich histories of different groups, ignoring

the specific ways in which individuals and communities have figured in the history of the United States, the distinctive kinds of oppression and discrimination they have experienced, the ways in which they have been treated within educational, judicial, and legislative arenas. I encourage readers to refer to more extended works by the notable scholars cited in this section who write *as* people of color, as well as *about* people of color.

14. For a rich and insightful discussion of how African Americans have both retained a value on historical oral forms and skillfully deployed written discourses in resistant ways, see Adam Banks's *Race, Rhetoric, and Technology: Searching for Higher Ground*. In this book, Banks notes how black online discourse and spaces such as Black Planet have served as nonmainstream sites for keeping "self-determination, of resistance, of keeping oppositional identities and worldviews alive, refusing to allow melting pot ideologies of language and identity" (70) to prevail.

15. Bolter and Gruisin's term *remediation*—explored in their 1999 book of the same name—refers to the processes by which new media and media forms (for instance, flat-screen television) take up and transform prior media (conventional televisions)—promising to fulfill a particular unmet need or improve on some performance standard. Bolter and Grusin note, however, that new media *never completely supplant or erase prior media* because they must refer to these forms in making the case for their own superiority (54). Their discussion of remediation extends far beyond the simple, limited, and metaphorical use of the term I make in this article.

16. Technical, professional, and business communication courses offer an important exception to the diminishing role of aurality. In these courses, the oral presentation has consistently retained its currency as an important part of the curriculum. In 1994, Heather A. Howard reported that every single one of the authors of the ten leading textbooks in business and professional communication considered "oral communication and public speaking as worthwhile topics" for inclusion in their books, and 70 percent of these authors specifically mentioned "informative and persuasive" speeches (5). And, in 2003, Kelli Cargile Cook noted that oral presentations were the most frequently assigned tasks in 197 technical communication courses identified in a random sampling of ATTW listserv members (54). It is possible that this situation persists because such courses are so responsive to the needs of employers. In 1995, for example, Karen K. Waner noted that "oral communication skills" such as "using appropriate techniques in making oral presentations"; using "appropriate body action in interpersonal and oral communication"; "analyzing the audience before, during, and after an oral report"; and "objectively" presenting information in oral reports" were considered "important" or "very important" by both business faculty and business professionals (55).

17. Contributing to these practices, of course, was the cultural value that the academy placed—and continues to place—on written scholarship published in print journals. This value has been instantiated at numerous levels of university culture and through articulated systems of salaries, raises, hirings, and promotion and tenure guidelines. These related formations have shaped the professional culture of composition studies and continue to do so in fundamental ways.

18. One of the notable exceptions to this trend can be found in the work of Peter Elbow, who has, for years, reminded readers that writing and speech, far from being absolutely distinct activities, are complexly connected through a constellation of cognitive, linguistic, and social relationships. See Elbow's "The Shifting Relationships between Speech and Writing" and "What Do We Mean When We Talk about Voice."

19. I thank Debra Journet, of the University of Louisville, for this insight and for many others.

20. The books with "voice" in their title included: Frank O'Connor's *The Lonely Voice: A Study of the Short Story*, Donald Stewart's *The Authentic Voice: A Pre-Writing Approach to Student Writing*; Otis Winchesters *The Sound of Your Own Voice*; Jill Wilson Cohn's *Writing: The Personal Voice*; Martin Medhurst's *Voice and Writing*; Jim W. Corder's *Finding a Voice*; Kathleen Yancey's *Voices on Voice*; Johnny Payne's *Voice and Style*; Michael Huspek and Gary P. Radford's *Transgressing Discourses: Communication and the Voice of the Other*; and Albert Guerard, Maclin Guerard, John Hawkes, and Claire Rosenfield's *The Personal Voice: A Contemporary Prose Reader*.

21. In this article, and elsewhere, George and Trimbur argue persuasively against this conception, as well as English studies' adherence to the historical distinction between high and low culture.

22. For further explanation of this technique and a bibliography see Susan Sipple's and Jeff Sommers's "A Heterotopic Space: Digitized Audio Commentary and Student Revisions."

23. My thanks to Peter Elbow for pointing out the persistence of aurality and lecturing in both composition classroom settings and testing contexts for graduate students.

24. Increasingly throughout the 1960s to 1990s, lecturing in composition classrooms became supplanted by peer-group and project-based work and the one-on-one conferencing approaches that characterized student-centered pedagogies. This process, however, was slow, often uneven, and certainly never complete.

In a 1965 Conference on College Composition and Communication workshop session ("New Approaches in Teaching Composition") that was attended by James Moffett, for example, William Holmes reported on using "televised lectures" developed by Ohio University as a "solution to teaching ever more freshman with ever more graduate students" (207), W. Grayson Lappert described lecture sessions at Balwin Wallace (208); and Eric Zale described using lectures used to teach composition at Eastern Michigan University (208).

In 1972, James R. Sturdevant—defending lectures as one effective method for teaching large groups of students, especially when such methods were combined with other approaches—described a pilot program at Ohio Wesleyan University. This program was developed to teach large groups of students effectively and efficiently: "Students were exposed to the study of composition through assigned readings in a rhetoric text and an essay anthology," large group lectures, short diagnostic exercises, small group meetings, and coordinating writing assignments" (420).

And even later, in 1997, Martha Sammons, providing readers advice on using PowerPoint, noted:

> Electronic presentations tend to make you lecture more quickly than usual, so remember to move slowly from slide to slide. To maintain suspense, you can use the feature of hiding bullets until you are ready. Use traditional lecturing techniques to elaborate on key points. Most important, don't lose your normal teaching style.

Indeed lecturing has never entirely disappeared from college-level writing classrooms, although it has certainly become less popular. In 2000, Donald Finkel wrote in his book *Teaching with Your Mouth Shut*:

> Most people have a set of ready-made assumptions about what a teacher does. A teacher talks, tells, explains, lectures, instructs, professes. Teaching is something you do with your mouth open, your voice intoning. … After hearing their stirring lectures, we left their classrooms inspired, moved. But did we learn anything? What was left of this experience five years later? These questions usually don't get asked.
>
> (1)

25. *Soundmark* is R. Murray Schafer's (1977) term, derived from the word *landmarks*, to refer to sounds that characterize the life of a particular place, time, or group, sonic markers that "make the acoustic life of a community unique" (10).

26. I do not mean to suggest that digital technologies are the *only* reason for a renewed interest in orality. The cultural ecology of literacy is a complexly rendered landscape and comprises a large number of related factors.

27. It is important to note that one of the very earliest online conferencing systems—ENFI (Electronic Networks for Interaction)—was used as a communicative environment for deaf students. As my colleague Brenda Brueggeman has reminded me, innovations in communicative technologies often begin in communities of people who have different abilities and forms of making and exchanging information, of composing meaning. For more about ENFI, see Bruce, Peyton, and Batson. For more about technology and disability, see Brueggemann and Snyder, Brueggemann, and Garland-Thomson.

28. The minidisc recorder was developed by Sony in 1991–1992 ("Hardware and Software"), providing consumers with a low-cost and highly portable digital audio recording device that is still used today. Audacity, a widely used open-source audio editor, was invented in 1999 by Dominic Mazzoni. As the Audacity manual describes the project's development, Mazzoni was a "graduate student at Carnegie Mellon University in Pittsburgh, PA, USA. He was working on a research project with his advisor, Professor Roger Dannenberg, and they needed a tool that would let them visualize audio analysis algorithms. Over time, this program developed into a general audio editor, and other people started helping out" (Oetzmann). This combination put digital audio recording, editing, and production within the reach of teachers and students in English composition, much like the personal computer put word processing within the reach of such classes in the early 1980s.

29. Apple's iMovie was first released to consumers in 1999 ("Apple Computer"). Microsoft's MovieMaker was released on 14 September 2000 as part of the Windows Millennium Edition ("Windows ME").

30. According to Technorati, by January of 2006, over 75,000 new blogs were being created each day, an average of one new blog every second of every day. In addition, 13.7 million bloggers are still posting three months after their blogs were created. At this point, Technorati tracked 1.2 million new blog posts a day, about 50,000 per hour. For further statistics, see the Technorati website at <http://www.technorati.com/>.

31. In August of 2006, YouTube.com reported more than 100 million video views every day with 65,000 new videos uploaded daily and approximately 20 million unique users per month (<http://www.youtube.com/t/fact_sheet>). Grouper.com, another site that allows users to upload their homemade videos, reported 8 million unique visitors (<http://www.grouper.com/about/press.aspx>).

32. Kevin Poulson reported in 2006 that MySpace has "gathered over 57 million registered users (counting some duplicates and fake profiles). As of last November, it enjoyed a 752-percent growth in web traffic over one year, according to Nielsen//NetRatings."

33. Facebook, the "second most-trafficked PHP site in the world," reports "175 million active (users who have returned to the site in the last 30 days)."

34. The Arbitron/Edison Media Research report, *Internet and Multimedia 2006*, notes that the ownership of MP3 players increased from 14 percent to 22 percent among all age groups in the United States and from 27 percent to 42 percent among 12- to 17-year-olds in 2005–2006 (32), and that more than 27 million people in the United States have listened to audio podcasts (Rose and Lenski 29).

35. See Daniel Anderson, Erin Branch, and Stephanie Morgans website, *Casting about with Sound: A Podcast Workshop*, offered at the 2006 Computers and Writing conference <http://www.siteslab.org/workshops/podcast/>.

36. See Daniel Andersons blog, *I am Dan: A Writing Pusher in the Media Age* at <http://www.thoughtpress.org/daniel/> for innovative uses of sound in the composition classroom.

37. See Jeff Porter's course "Radio Essays" at the University of Iowa at <http://isis5.uiowa.edu/isis/courses/details.page?ddd=08N&cccc=145&sss=001&session=20063> and Jonah Willihnganz's course "The Art of the Audio Essay" at Stanford University at <http://www.stanford.edu/~jonahw/PWR2-W06/Radio-Home.html>.

38. See Lisa Spiro's course "The Documentary Across Media" at Rice University at <http://www.owlnet.rice.edu/~hans320/syllabus.html>.
39. See Katherine Braun's course "Documenting Community Culture" at Ohio State University at <http://people.cohums.ohio-state.edu/Braun43/teaching/10901Au05/index.htm>.
40. See "Oral History Project" (24 March 2005) on the Community College English website at <http://twoyearcomp.blogspot.com/2005/03/oral-history-project.html>.
41. See The Rhetoric and Composition Sound Archives (18 Feb. 2006) at Texas Christian University at <http://www.rcsa.tcu.edu/collection.htm>.
42. See the "Oral History Archive" on the Writing Centers Research Project website at <http://coldfusion.louisville.edu/webs/a-s/wcrp/oral.cfm>.

Works Cited

Aljazeera.net news website. 17 Feb. 2007 <http://engIish.aljazeera.net/News/>.

Altman, Rick. *Silent Film Sound.* New York: Columbia UP, 2004.

Anderson, Daniel. "Mostly Partially Occasional Words." *I am Dan: A Writing Pusher in the Media Age* (blog). 29 March 2009 <http://thoughtpress.org/daniel/>.

Anson, Chris. "Talking about Text: The Use of Recorded Commentary in Response to Student Writing." *A Sourcebook for Responding to Student Writing.* Ed. Richard Straub. Cresskill, NJ: Hampton P, 1999. 165–74.

"Apple Computer: 1998–2005 New Beginnings." *Wikipedia* website. 13 Oct. 2006 <http://en.wikipedia.org/wiki/Apple_Computers>.

Arbur, Rosemarie. "The Student-Teacher Conference." *College Composition and Communication* 28.4 (Dec. 1977): 338–42.

Ball, Cheryl, and Byron Hawk. "Special Issue: Sound in/as Compositional Space: A Next Step in Multiliteracies." *Computers and Composition* 23.3 (2006): 263–65. Online version: *Computers and Composition Online.* 28 Sept. 2008 <http://www.bgsu.edu/cconline/sound/>.

Banks, Adam. *Race, Rhetoric, and Technology: Searching for Higher Ground.* Mahwah, NJ: Laurence Erlbaum, 2006.

Barritt, Loren S., and Barry Kroll. "Some Implications of Cognitive-Developmental Psychology for Research in Composing." *Research on Composing: Points of Departure.* Ed. Charles R. Cooper and Lee O'Dell. Urbana, IL: National Council of Teachers of English, 1978.49–57.

Bartholomae, David. "Inventing the University." *When a Writer Can't Write: Research on Writer's Block and other Writing Problems.* Ed. M. Rose. New York: Guilford, 1986.134–66.

Barton, David, and Mary Hamilton. *Local Literacies: Reading and Writing in One Community.* London: Routledge, 1998.

BBC: International Version. News website. 17 Feb. 2009 <http://www.bbc.co.uk/home/i/index.shtml>.

Berlin, James A. *Rhetoric and Reality: Writing Instruction in American Colleges, 1900–1985.* Carbondale: Southern Illinois UP, 1987.

Bereiter, Carol, and Marlene Scardamalia. "From Conversation to Composition: The Role of Instruction in Developmental Process." *Advances in Instructional Psychology.* Ed. R. Glaser. Hillsdale, NJ: Lawrence Erlbaum, 1982, 1–64.

Biber, Douglas. "Spoken and written textual dimensions in English: Resolving the Contradictory Findings." *Language* 62 (1986): 384–414.

——. *Variation across Speech and Writing.* Cambridge: Cambridge UP, 1988.

Blaeser, Kimberly (Ojibwa). *Gerald Vizenor: Writing in the Oral Tradition.* Norman: U of Oklahoma P, 1996.

Bolter, J. David, and Richard Grusin. *Remediation: Understanding New Media.* Cambridge, MA: MIT, 1999.

Borton, Sonya. "Self-Analysis: A Call for Multimodality in Personal Narrative Composition." *Computers and Composition Online* (Spring 2005). 26 Aug. 2006 <http://www.bgsu.edu/cconline/home.htm>.

Brandt, Deborah. "Accumulating Literacy: Writing and Learning to Write in the Twentieth Century." *College English* 57.6 (1995): 649–68.

——. *Literacy in American Lives.* Cambridge: Cambridge UP, 2001.

Brooks, Christopher N. *Architectural Acoustics.* Jefferson, NC: McFarland, 2002.

Brooks, Phyllis. "Mimesis: Grammar and the Echoing Voice." *College English* 35.2 (Nov. 1973): 161–68.

Bruce, Bertram, Joy Kreeft Peyton, and Trent Batson, eds. *Network-Based Classrooms: Promises and Realities.* New York: Cambridge UP, 1993.

Brueggemann, Brenda Jo. *Lend Me Your Ear: Rhetorical Constructions of Deafness.* Washington DC: Gallaudet UP, 1999.

Bull, Michael, and Les Back, eds. *The Auditory Culture Reader.* Oxford, UK: Berg, 2003.

Carney, George O., ed. *The Sounds of People and Places: A Geography of American Music from Country to Classical and Blues to Bop.* 4th ed. Lanham, MD: Roman & Littlefield, 2003.

Carroll, Joyce Armstrong. "Talking through the Writing Process." *English Journal* 70 (Nov. 1981): 100–102.

Carter, Steven. "The Beatles and Freshman English." *College Composition and Communication* 20 (1969): 228–32.

Castells, Manuel. *End of the Millennium.* Vol. 3 in *The Information Age: Economy, Society, and Culture.* Malden, MA: Blackwell, 1998.

——. *The Power of Identity.* Vol. 2 in *The Information Age: Economy Society, and Culture.* Malden, MA: Blackwell, 1997.

——. *The Rise of the Network Society.* Vol. 1 in *The Information Age: Economy, Society, and Culture.* Malden, MA: Blackwell.

Cayer, Roger L., and Renee Sacks. "Oral and Written Discourse of Basic Writers: Similarities and Differences." *Research in the Teaching of English* 13 (May 1979): 121–28.

Chion, Michel. *The Voice in Cinema.* Trans. Claudia Gorbman. New York: Columbia UP, 1999.

Cintron, Ralph. *Angels' Town.* Boston: Beacon, 1997.

Clapp, John M. *English Journal* 2.1 (Jan. 1913): 18–33.

Clark, Beverly Lyon. "Tutoring, within Limits." *College Composition and Communication* 35.2 (May 1984): 238–40.

Clements, William M. *Native American Verbal Art: Texts and Contexts.* Tucson: U of Arizona P, 1996.

Cohn, Jill Wilson. *Writing: The Personal Voice.* New York: Harcourt Brace Jovonavich, 1975.

Collins, James L., and Michael M. Williamson. "Spoken Language and Semantic Abbreviations in Writing." *Research in the Teaching of English* 15 (Feb. 1981): 23–35.

Conference of College Composition and Communication. "New Approaches in Teaching Composition: Further toward a New Rhetoric." *College Composition and Communication* 16.3 (Oct. 1965): 207–8.

Congleton, J. E. "Historical Development of the Concept of Rhetorical Perspective." *College Composition and Communication* 5 (1954): 140–49.

Connors, Robert J. "The Differences between Speech and Writing: Ethos, Pathos, and Logos." *College Composition and Communication* 30 (Oct. 1979): 285–90.

——. "Teaching and Learning as a Man." *College English* 58.2 (Feb. 1996): 137–57.

Cook, Kelli Cargile. "How Much Is Enough? The Assessment of Student Work in Technical Communication Courses." *Technical Communication Quarterly* 12.1 (2003): 47–65.

Cope, Bill, and Mary Kalantzis, eds. *Multiliteracies: Literacy Learning and the Design of Social Futures.* London: Routledge, 2000.

Corder, Jim W. *Finding a Voice.* Glenview, IL: Scott Foresman, 1973.

Cubbison, Laurie. Configuring Lisbserv, Configuring Discourse. *Computers and Composition* 16.3 (1999): 371–82.

Dawe, Charles W., and Edward A. Dornan. *One to One: Resources for Conference-Centered Writing.* Boston: Little, Brown, 1981.

Derrida, Jacques. *Of Grammatology.* Trans. Gayatri Chakravorty Spivak. Baltimore: Johns Hopkins UP, 1976.

DeVoss, Danielle, Gail Hawisher, Charles Jackson, Joseph Johansen, Brittney Moraska, and Cynthia L. Selfe. "The Future of Literacy." *Literate Lives in the Information Age: Stories from the United States.* Ed. Gail E. Hawisher and Cynthia L. Selfe. Mahwah, NJ: Lawrence Erlbaum, 2004. 183–210.

Dunn, Patricia A. *Learning Re-Abled: The Learning Disability Controversy and Composition Studies.* Portsmouth, NH: Boynton/Cook, 1995.

——. *Talking, Sketching, Moving: Multiple Literacies in the Teaching of Writing.* Portsmouth, NH: Boynton/Cook, 2001.

Dyson, Anne Hass. "The Role of Oral Language in Early Writing Processes." *Research in the Teaching of English* 17 (Feb. 1983): 1–30.

Ede, Lisa. "Oral History: One Way out of the Slough of Despond." *College Composition and Communication* 28.4 (Dec. 1977): 380–82.

Elbow, Peter. "The Shifting Relationships between Speech and Writing." *College Composition and Communication* 36.3 (Oct. 1986): 283–303.

——. "What Do We Mean When We Talk about Voice in Texts? *Voices on Voice: Perspectives, Definitions, Inquiry.* Ed. Kathleen Blake Yancey. Urbana, IL: National Council of Teachers of English, 1994, 1–35.

Eldred, Janet C. "The Technology of Voice." *College Composition and Communication* 48.3 (Oct. 1997): 334–47.

Eliot, Charles William. "The New Education, Its Organization—II." *Atlantic Monthly* 23 (March 1869): 359.

Emig, Janet. "Writing as a Mode of Learning." *College Composition and Communication* 28 (May 1977): 322–28.

Evers, Larry, and Barre Toelken, eds. *Native American Oral Traditions: Collaboration and Interpretation.* Logan: Utah State UP, 2001. Originally published as a special issue of *Oral Tradition* 13 (1998).

"Facebook Factsheet." Facebook website. 8 March 2009 <http.www.facebook.com/press/info.php?factsheet>.

Faigley, Lester. *Fragments of Rationality: Postmodernity and the Subject of Composition.* Pittsburgh: U of Pittsburgh P, 1992.

——. "Judging Writing, judging Selves." *College Composition and Communication* 40.4 (Dec. 1989): 395–412.

Farrell, Thomas, J. "Differentiating Writing from Talking." *College Composition and Communication* 29 (Dec. 1978): 346–50.

Finke, Laurie. "Knowledge as Bait: Feminism, Voice, and the Pedagogical Unconscious." *College English* 55.1 (Jan. 1993): 7–27.

Finkel, Donald. *Teaching with Your Mouth Shut.* Portsmouth, NH: Heinemann Boynton Cook, 2000.

Fraser, Nancy. "Rethinking the Public Sphere: A Contribution to the Critique of Actually Existing Democracy." *Habermas and the Public Sphere.* Ed. Craig Calhoun. Cambridge, MA: MIT Press. 1992. 109–42.

Fulwiler, Toby. "Looking and Listening for My Voice." *College Composition and Communication* 41.2 (1990): 214–20.

Furner, Beatrice A. "An Oral Base for Teaching Letter Writing." *Elementary English* 51 (April 1974): 589–94, 600.

Gee, James Paul. *Social Linguistics and Literacies: Ideology in Discourses*, 2nd ed. London: Taylor and Francis, 1996.

Gere, Anne Ruggles. "Kitchen Tables and Rented Rooms: The Extracurriculum of Composition." *College Composition and Communication* 45.1 (Feb. 1994): 75–92.

George, Diana. "Working with Peer Groups in the Composition Classroom." *College Composition and Communication* 35.3 (Oct. 1984): 320–26.

George, Diana, and John Trimbur. "The 'Communication Battle,' or Whatever Happened to the 4th C?" *College Composition and Communication* 50.4 (June 1999): 682–98.

Gibson, Walker. "The Voice of the Writer." *College Composition and Communication* 13.3 (1962): 10–13.

Giddens, Anthony. *Central Problems in Social Theory: Action, Structure and Contradiction in Social Analysis.* Berkeley: U of California P, 1979.

Gilkerson, Christopher. "Poverty Law Narratives: The Critical Practice and Theory of Receiving and Translating Client Stories." *Hastings Law Journal* 43 (1992): 861.

Gilyard, Keith. "Literacy, Identity, Imagination, Flight." *College Composition and Communication* 52.2 (Dec. 2000): 260–72.

Graff, Harvey J. "The Legacies of Literacy: Continuities and Contradictions in Western Culture and Society," Bloomington: Indiana UP, 1987.

Guerard, Albert J., Maclin B. Guerard, John Hawkes, and Claire Rosenfield. *The Personal Voice: A Contemporary Prose Reader.* Philadelphia: J. B. Lippincott, 1964.

Guerra, Juan C. "Emerging Representations, Situated Literacies, and the Practice of Transcultural Repositioning." *Lantino/a Discourses: On Language, Identity, and Literacy Education.* Ed. Michelle Hall Kells, Valerie Balester, and Victor Villanueava. Portsmouth, NH: Boynton/Cook, 2004. 7–23.

Guerra, Juan C., and Marcia Farr. "Writing on the Margins: The Spiritual and Autobiographical Discourse of Two Mexicanas in Chicago." *School's Out: Bridging Out-of-School Literacies with Classroom Practice.* Ed. Glynda A. Hull and Katherine Shultz. New York: Teachers College P, 2002. 96–123.

Gutierrez, Kris D., Patricia Baquedano-Lopez, and Hector H. Alvarez. "Literacy as Hybridity: Moving beyond Bilingualism in Urban Classrooms." *The Best for Our Children: Critical Perspectives on Literacy for Latino Students.* Ed. Maria de la Luz Reyes and John J. Halcon. New York: Teachers College P, 2000, 122–41.

Haefner, Joel. "The Politics of the Code." *Computers and Composition* 16.3 (1999): 319–24.

Halbritter, Scott K. "Sound Arguments: Aural Rhetoric in Multimedia Composition." Diss. U of North Carolina at Chapel Hill, 2004. Ann Arbor, MI: UMI 3140325.

Halloran, Michael. "Rhetoric in the American College Curriculum: The Decline of Public Discourse" *Pre/Text: The First Decade.* Ed. Victor J. Vitanza. Pittsburgh: U of Pittsburgh P, 1993. 93–116.

Halpern, Jeanne W. "Differences between Speaking and Writing and Their Implications for Teaching." *College Composition and Communication* 35.3 (1984): 345–57.

"Hardware and Software Get an Early Start." Sony Corporation website. 21 Feb. 2009 <http://www.sony.net/Fun/SH/1-21/h5.html>.

Hashimoto, I. "Voice as Juice: Some Reservations about Evangelic Composition." *College Composition and Communication* 38.1 (Feb. 1987): 70–80.

Hawisher, Gail E., and Cynthia L. Selfe, eds. *Literate Lives in the Information Age: Stories from the United States.* Mahwah, NJ: Lawrence Erlbaum, 2004.

Haynes, Cynthia, and Jan Rune Holmevik, eds. *High Wired: On the Design, Use, and Theory of Educational MOOs.* Ann Arbor: U of Michigan P, 1998.

Heilman, Robert B. "The Full Men and the Fullness Thereof." *College Composition and Communication* 21.3 (1970): 239–44.

Hennig, Barbara. "The World Was Stone Cold: Basic Writing in an Urban University." *College English* 53.6 (Oct. 1991): 674–85.

Hespanha, Antonio Manuel. "The Everlasting Return of Orality." Paper presented to Readings of Past Legal Texts. International Symposium in Legal History in Tromsø, Norway, 13–14 June 2002. 17 Aug. 2005 <www.hespanha.net/papers/2003_the-everlasting-retum-of-orality.pdf>.

Hibbitts, Bernard. "Making Sense of Metaphors: Visuality, Aurality and the Reconfiguration of American Legal Discourse." *Cardozo Law Review* 16 (1994): 229. 24 Sept. 2008 <http://www.law.pitt.edu/hibbitts/meta_int.htm>.

Hinshaw, Wendy Wolters. "Re. CCC Article." Email message to the author. 17 Feb. 2007.

Hirsch, E. D., Jr. "Distinctive Features of Written Speech." *The Philosophy of Composition*, Chicago, IL: U of Chicago P, 1977.14–32.

Howard, Heather A. "Communication Practices of Yesteryear: A Qualitative Analysis of Business and Professional Communication Textbooks in the Last Ten Years." Paper presented at the Annual Meeting of the Speech Communication Association, New Orleans, Nov. 1994, ED 381820. 16 Feb. 2006 <http://edres.org/eric/ED381820.htm>.

Human Development. Report 2001: Making New Technologies Work for Human Development. United Nations Development Programme. New York: Oxford UP, 2001.

Human Rights Watch website. 17 Feb. 2007 <http://www.hrw.org/>.

Huspek, Michael, and Gary P. Radford, eds. *Transgressing Discourses: Communication and the Voice of the Other.* Albany: State U of New York P, 1997.

Ihde, Don. *Listening and Voice: A Phenomenology of Sound.* Athens: Ohio UP, 1976.

International Herald Tribune website. 17 Feb. 2007 <http://www.iht.com/>.

Japan Times. Website. 17 Feb. 2007 <http://www.japantimes.co.jp/>.

Johnson, Nan. *Nineteenth-Century Rhetoric in North America.* Carbondale: Southern Illinois UP, 1991.

Kahn, Douglas. *Noise, Water, Meat: A History of Voice, Sound, and Aurality in the Arts.* Cambridge, MA: MIT, 1999.

Keeling, Richard. *Cry for Luck: Sacred Song and Speech among the Yurok, Hupa, and Karok Indians of Northwestern California.* Berkeley: U of California P, 1992.

Keller, Daniel. "Re. CCC Article." Email to author. 17 Feb. 2007.

Kells, Michelle Hall, Valerie Balester, and Victor Villanueva, eds. *Latino/a Discourses: On Language, Identity, and Literacy Education.* Portsmouth, NH: Boynton/Cook, 2004.

Kleine, Michael, and Fredric G. Gale. "The Elusive Presence of the Word: An Interview with Walter Ong." *Composition FORUM* 7.2 (1996): 65–86.

Kress, Gunther. "Design and Transformation: New Theories of Meaning." *Multiliteracies: Literacy Learning and the Design of Social Futures.* Ed. Bill Cope and Mary Kalantzis. London: Routledge. 2000.153–61.

——. "'English' at the Crossroads: Rethinking Curricula of Communication in the Context of the Turn to the Visual." *Passions, Pedagogies, and 21st Century Technologies.* Ed. Gail E. Hawisher and Cynthia L. Selfe. Logan: Utah State UP, 1999. 66–88.

——. "Multimodality." *Multiliteracies: Literacy Learning and the Design of Social Futures.* Ed. Bill Cope and Mary Kalantzis. London: Routledge, 2000. 182–202.

Kress, Gunther, and Theo van Leeuwen. *Reading Images: The Grammar of Visual Design.* London: Routledge, 1996.

Kroeger, Fred. "A Freshman Paper Based on the Words of Popular Songs." *College Composition and Communication* 19.5 (1968): 337–40.

Labelle, Brandon, Steve Roden, and Christof Migo. *Site of Sound: Of Architecture and the Ear.* Copenhagen: Errant Bodies P, 2000.

Liggett, Sarah. "The Relationship between Speaking and Writing: An Annotated Bibliography." *College Composition and Communication* 35.3 (1984): 334–44.

Limon, Jose E. "Oral Tradition and Poetic Influence: Two Poets from Greater Mexico. *Redefining American Literary History.* Ed. A. Lavonne Brown Ruoff and Jerry Washington Ward. New York, Modern Language Association, 1990. 124–41.

Lindemann, Erika. *A Rhetoric for Writing Teachers.* New York: Oxford UP, 1995.

Lofty, John. "From Sound to Sign: Using Oral History in the College Composition Class." *College Composition and Communication* 36.3 (Oct. 1985): 349–53.

Lopate, Phillip. "Helping Students Start to Write." *Research on Composing: Points of Departure.* Ed. Charles R. Cooper and Lee O'Dell. Urbana, IL: National Council of Teachers of English, 1978. 135–49.

Lutz, William D. "Making Freshman English a Happening," *College Composition and Communication* 22.1 (Feb. 1971): 35–38.

Lyons, Scott. "Rhetorical Sovereignty: What Do American Indians Want from Writing?" *College Composition and Communication* 51.3 (Feb. 2000): 447–68.

Mahiri, Jabari. *Shooting for Excellence: African American and Youth Culture in New Century Schools.* Urbana, IL: National Council of Teachers of English; New York: Teachers College P, 1998.

McCorkle, Ben. "Harbingers of the Printed Page: Nineteenth Century Theories of Delivery as Remediation." *Rhetoric Society Quarterly* 35.4 (2005): 25–49.

McCorkle, Warren Benson, Jr. "Tongue, Nib, Block, Bit: Rhetorical Delivery and Technologies of Writing." Diss. Ohio State University, 2005.

Medhurst, Martin. *Voice and Writing.* Davis, CA: Hermagoras P, 1994.

Mellen, Cheryl, and Jeff Sommers. "Audio-Taped Response and the Two-Year Campus Writing Classroom: The Two-Sided Desk, the 'Guy with the Ax,' and the Chirping Birds." *Teaching English in the Two-Year College* 31.1 (Sept. 2003): 25–39.

Memering, W. Dean. "Talking to Students: Group Conferences." *College Composition and Communication* 24.3 (Oct. 1973): 306–7.

Miller, Susan. *Rescuing the Subject: A Critical Introduction to Rhetoric and the Writer.* Carbondale: Southern Illinois UP, 1989.

Moss, Beverly J. "Creating a Community: Literacy Events in African-American Churches." *Literacy across Communities.* Ed. Beverly J. Moss. Creskill, NJ: Hampton P, 1994.

Murray, Donald, M. "Finding Your Own Voice: Teaching Composition in an Age of Dissent." *College Composition and Communication* 20.2 (May 1969): 118–23.

New London Group. "A Pedagogy of Multiliteracies: Designing Social Futures." *Harvard Education Review* 66.1 (1996): 60–92.

Newman, John B., and Milton W. Horowitz. "Writing and Speaking." *College Composition and Communication* 16.2 (Oct. 1965): 160–64.

North, Stephen M. "Training Tutors to Talk about Writing." *College Composition and Communication* 33.4 (Dec. 1982): 434–41.

O'Brien, Charles. *Cinema' s Conversion to Sound*: *Technology and Film Style in France and the US*. Bloomington: Indiana UP, 2005.

O'Connor, Frank. *The Lonely Voice*: *A Study of the Short Story*. Cleveland, OH: World, 1963.

Oetzmann, Anthony. "Who Developed Audacity?" Manual on the Audacity software website. 17 Aug. 2006 <http://audacity.sourceforge.net/manual-1.2/index.html>.

Olson, Gary A. "Beyond Evaluation: The Recorded Response to Essays." *Teaching English in the Two-Year College* 8.2 (Winter 1982): 321–23.

Olson, Judy M. "Multimedia in Geography: Good, Bad, Ugly, or Cool." *Annals of the Association of American Geographers* 87.4 (1997): 571–78.

Olympic Movement website. 2007. 17 Feb. 2007 <http://www.oiympic.org/uk/index_uk.asp>.

Ong, Walter, J. *Fighting for Life*: *Contest, Sexuality, and Consciousness*. Ithaca, NY: Cornell UP, 1981.

——. *Orality and Literacy*: *The Technologizing of the Word*. London: Methuen, 1982.

Paine, Charles. "The Composition Course and Public Discourse: The Case of Adams Sherman Hill, Popular Culture, and Cultural Inoculation," *Rhetoric Review* 15.2 (Spring 1997): 282–99.

Payne, Johnny. *Voice and Style*. Cincinnati: Writer's Digest Books, 1996.

Pierre, Gerald J. "Generating Discussion: The First Ten Minutes." *College Composition and Communication* 25.4 (Oct. 1974): 305–7.

Poulson, Kevin. "Scenes from the MySpace Backlash," *Wired News*, 27 Feb. 2006. 8 March 2008 <http://www.wired.com/politics/law/news/2006/02/70254>.

Powell, Malea. "Rhetorics of Survivance: How American Indians Use Writing." *College Composition and Communication* 53.3 (Feb. 2002): 396–434.

Ratcliffe, Krista. "Rhetorical Listening: A Trope for Interpretive Invention and a 'Code of Cross-Cultural Conduct.'" *College Composition and Communication* 51.2 (Dec. 1999): 195–224.

Reid, Ronald F. "The Boyleston Professorship of Rhetoric and Oratory, 1806–1904: A Case Study in Changing Concepts of Rhetoric and Pedagogy." *Quarterly Journal of Speech* 45.3 (Oct. 1959): 239–57.

Reyes, Maria de la Luz, and John J. Halcon. *The Best for Our Children*: *Critical Perspectives on Literacy for Latino Students*. New York: Teachers College P, 2001.

Richardson, Elaine. "'To Protect and Serve': African American Female Literacies." *College Composition and Communication* 54.4 (2002): 675–704.

Richie, Donald A. *Doing Oral History*. Oxford: Oxford UP, 2003.

Robinson, Jay L. "Basic Writing and Its Basis in Talk: The influence of Speech on Writing." *Forum* 4 (Fall 1982): 73–83.

Robson, John. "Mill's 'Autobiography': The Public and the Private Voice." *College Composition and Communication* 16.2 (May 1965): 97–101.

Rose, Alan. "Spoken versus Written Criticism of Student Writing: Some Advantages of the Conference Method." *College Composition and Communication* 33.3 (Oct. 1982): 326–330.

Rose, Bill, and Joe Lenski, presenters. *Internet and Multimedia 2006*: *On-Demand Media Explodes*. Arbitron/Edison Media Research report. 16 Aug. 2006 <http://www.arbitron.com/downloads/im-2006study.pdf>.

Royster, Jacqueline Jones. *Traces of a Stream*: *Literacy and Social Change among African American Women*. Pittsburgh: U of Pittsburgh P, 2000.

——. "When the First Voice You Hear Is Not Your Own." *College Composition and Communication* 47.1 (1996): 29–40.

Ruiz, Reynaldo. "The Corrido as a Medium for Cultural Identification." *Imagination, Emblems, and Expressions*: *Essays on Latin American, Caribbean, and Continental Culture and Identity*. Ed. Helen Ryan-Ranson. Bowling Green, OH: Popular, 1993. 53–64.

Rushdy, Ashraf H. A. "Reading Mammy: The Subject of Relation in Sherley Anne Williams' Dessa Rose." *African American Review* 27 (1993): 365–66.

Russell, David R. "Institutionalizing English: Rhetoric on the Boundaries." *Disciplining English Alternative Histories, Critical Perspectives*. Ed. David R. Shumway and Craig Dionne. Albany: State U of New York P, 2002. 39–58.

——. *Writing in the Academic Disciplines, 1870–1990*: *A Canicular History*. Carbondale: Southern Illinois UP, 1991.

Sammons, Martha C. "Using PowerPoint Presentations in Writing Classes." Aug. 1997. Technology Source Archives at the University of North Carolina. 14 Feb. 2007 <http://technologysource.org/article/using_powerpoint_presentations_in_writing_classes/>.

Saunders, Mary. "Oral Presentations in the Composition Classrooms." *College Composition and Communication* 36.3 (Oct. 1985): 357–60.

Sawyer, Thomas M. "Why Speech Will Not Totally Replace Writing." *College Composition and Communication* 28.1 (Feb. 1977): 43–48.

Schafer, R. Murray. *The Soundscape*: *Our Sonic Environment and the Tuning of the World*. Rochester, VT: Destiny Books, 1977.

Schiff, Peter M. "Revising the Writing Conference." *College Composition and Communication* 29.3 (Oct. 1978): 294–96.

Selfe, Cynthia L., and Paul R. Meyer "Gender and Electronic Conferences." *Written Communication* 8.2 (1991): 163–92.

Shankar, Tara M. Rosenberger. "Speaking on the Record." Diss. Media Laboratory, MIT, Cambridge, MA, 2005.

Sharpe, Susan G. "The Ad Voice in Student Writing," *College Composition and Communication* 36.4 (Dec. 1985): 488–90.

Shaughnessy, Mina P. *Errors and Expectations: A Guide for the Teacher of Basic Writing.* New York: Oxford UP, 1977.

Shuster, Charles. "Mikhail Bakhtin as Rhetorical Theorist." *College English* 47.6 (Oct. 1985): 594–607.

Sipple, Susan. "Digitized Audio Commentary in First Year Writing Classes." 16 Aug. 2006. Academic Commons website. 25 Aug. 2006 <http://www.academic-commons.org/ctfl/vignette/digitized-audio-commentary-first-year-writing-classes>.

Sipple, Sue, and Jeff Sommers. "A Heterotopic Space: Digitized Audio Commentary and Student Revisions." 16 Nov. 2005. Academic Commons website. 21 Feb. 2009 <http://www.users.muohio.edu/sommerjd/>.

Sirc, Geoffrey. "Never Mind the Tagmemics, Where's the Sex Pistols?" *College Composition and Communication* 48.1 (Feb. 1971): 9–29.

Smith, Bruce R. "Tuning in London c. 1600." *The Auditory Culture Reader.* Ed. Michael Bull and Les Back. Oxford, UK: Berg, 2003. 127–35.

Smitherman, Geneva. "CCCC's Role in the Struggle for Language Rights." *College Composition and Communication* 50.3 (Feb. 1999): 349–76.

——. *Talkin' That Talk: Language, Culture, and Education in African America.* New York: Routledge, 2000.

Snipes, Wilson Currin. "Oral Composing as an Approach to Writing." *College Composition and Communication"* 24.2 (May 1973): 200–205.

Snyder, Sharon L., Brenda Jo Brueggemann, and Rosemarie Garland-Thomson, eds. *Disability Studies: Enabling the Humanities.* New York: Modern Language Association, 2002.

Sommers, Jeff. "Spoken Response: Space, Time, and Movies of the Mind." *Writing with Elbow.* Ed. Pat Belanoff, Marcia Dickson, Sheryl I. Fontaine, and Charles Moran. Logan: Utah State P, 2002.

Sterne, Jonathan. "Medicine's Acoustic Culture: Mediate Auscultation, the Stethoscope and the 'Autopsy of the Living.'" *The Auditory Culture Reader.* Ed. Michael Bull and Les Back. Oxford, UK: Berg, 2003. 191–217.

Stewart, Donald. *The Authentic Voice: A Pre-Writing Approach to Student Writing.* Dubuque, IA: Wm. C. Brown, 1972.

Stoehr, Taylor. "Tone and Voice." *College English* 30.2 (Nov. 1968): 150–61.

Sturdevant, James R. "'Large Group' Doesn't Have to Be a Dirty Word." *College Composition and Communication* 23.5 (1972): 419–21.

Sui, Daniel Z. "Visuality, Aurality, and Shifting Metaphors of Geographical Thought to the Late Twentieth Century." *Annals of the Association of American Geographers* 90.2 (2000): 322–43.

Takayoshi, Pamela, and Cynthia L. Selfe. "Thinking about Multimodality." *Multimodal Composition: Resources for Teachers.* Ed. Cynthia L. Selfe. Cresskill, NJ: Hampton P, 2007. 1–12.

Tannen, Deborah. "Oral and Literate Strategies in Spoken and Written Narratives." *Language* 58 (1982): 1–21.

——. ed. *Spoken and Written Language: Exploring Orality and Literacy.* Norwood, NJ: Ablex, 1982.

Trejo, Arnulfo D. "Of Books and Libraries." *The Chicanos: As We See Ourselves.* Ed. Arnulfo Trejo. Tucson: U of Arizona P, 1979. 167, 172–74.

Trimbur, John. "Taking the Social Turn: Teaching Writing Post Process." *College Composition and Communication* 45.1 (1994): 108–18.

United Nations website. 2007. 17 Feb. 2007 <http://www.un.org>.

Villanueva, Victor. *Bootstraps: From an American Academic of Color.* Urbana, IL: National Council of Teachers of English, 1993.

Vygotsky, Lev. *Thought and Language.* Cambridge, MA: MIT P, 1962.

Walker, Jerry L. "Bach, Rembrandt, Milton, and Those Other Cats." *English Journal* 57 (1968): 631–36.

Waner, Karen K. "Business Communication Competencies Needed by Employees as Perceived by Business Faculty and Business Professionals." *Business Communication Quarterly* 58.4 (Dec. 1995): 51–56.

Wiget, Andrew. "Sending a Voice: The Emergence of Contemporary Native American Poetry. *College English* 46.6 (Oct. 1984): 598–608.

Winchester, Otis. *The Sound of Your Own Voice.* Boston: Allyn and Bacon, 1972.

"Windows ME." 14 Oct. 2006. *Wikipedia.* 14 Oct. 2006 <http://en.wikipedia.org/wiki/Windows_Me>.

Wright, Elizabethada A., and S. Michael Halloran. "From Rhetoric to Composition: The Teaching of Writing in America to 1900." *Writing Instructor* Dec. 2001. 8 March 2009 <http://www.writinginstractor.com/haloran-wright.html>.

Yancey, Kathleen B., ed. *Voices on Voice: Perspectives, Definitions, Inquiry.* Urbana, IL: National Council of Teachers of English, 1994.

Yancey, Kathleen, and Michael Spooner. "Postings on a Genre of Email." *College Composition and Communication* 47.2 (May 1996): 252–78.

Yow, Valerie R. *Recording Oral History: A Guide for the Humanities and Social Sciences.* 2nd ed. Lanham, MD: AltaMira P, 2005.

Zaluda, Scott. "Sophisticated Essay: Billie Holiday and the Generation of Form and Idea." *College Composition and Communication* 42.4 (Dec. 1991): 470–83.

Zoellner, Robert. "Talk-Write: A Behavioral Pedagogy for Composition." *College English* 30 (Jan. 1969): 267–320.

17

New Media Matters

Tutoring in the Late Age of Print

Jackie Grutsch McKinney

At the turn of the century, John Trimbur predicted that writing centers would become "Multiliteracy Centers," drawing on the terminology of the New London Group (30). These re-envisioned centers, he suggested, would provide help for students working on a variety of projects: essays, reports, PowerPoint presentations, web pages, and posters. His prediction has proved true to some degree—most notably in the state of Michigan. The University of Michigan's Sweetland Writing Center opened a Multiliteracy Center in 2000 within its writing center, a place where students "could receive one-to-one support as they worked on digital projects such as websites, PowerPoint presentations, and other forms of communication that depend on multiliteracies" (Sheridan, "Sweetland" 4). Additionally, at Michigan State, digital writing consultants worked with students on digital texts as early as 1996 (see Sheridan, "Words" and DeVoss). Institutions outside of Michigan have responded to new media writing also. The Worcester Polytechnic Institute—where Trimbur works renamed its writing center the Center for Communication Across the Curriculum, with "workshops" in writing, oral presentation, and visual design (Trimbur 29), and the Center for Collaborative Learning and Communication was created at Furman University (Inman). Many other centers have not changed names but have begun tutoring students on a variety of texts.

However, in one of the few published articles on writing centers and new media, entitled "Planning for Hypertexts in the Writing Center ... or Not," Michael Pemberton asks if writing centers should open their doors to students working on hypertexts. Although he answers "maybe"—he believes directors should decide based on their local needs and constraints—the bulk of his argument seems to say "no" more loudly than "yes" as seen here:

> Ultimately, we have to ask ourselves whether it is really the writing center's responsibility to be all things to all people. There will always be more to learn. There will always be new groups making demands on our time and our resources in ways we haven't yet

planned for. And there will never be enough time or enough money or enough tutors to meet all those demands all of the time. If we diversify too widely and spread ourselves too thinly in an attempt to encompass too many different literacies, we may not be able to address any set of literate practices particularly well.

(21)

Now—twenty years after Stephen Bernhardt urged us to *see* student texts: after Craig Stroupe, more recently, argued for the visualization of English studies; after Diana George showed us how visual literacy has been a part of writing instruction since the 1940s; and after Gunther Kress argued convincingly that the revolution in writing dominated by the image is not coming, if is already here—the writing center community seems divided on whether writing centers should work with new media.

Though at first blush I thought that Pemberton's argument was shortsighted, upon reflection. I think this sort of response actually speaks to an understandable uncertainly. We are fairly sure that we do good work with paper essays, pencils, and round tables. We are just not sure that we can do good work when those things change into new media texts, computer screens and speakers, mice and keyboards, and computer desks. The argument follows that if we are not certain we can do good work, then we should not do it at all.

I agree with Pemberton that we shouldn't take on work that we are not prepared for. But our agreement only goes so far, because I *do* think it is our job to work with all types of writing in the writing center—including new media. In this article, then, I suggest that writing centers need to offer tutoring in new media texts, but not the same tutoring we've always done. I begin by briefly defining *what* new media are (or really, how I will use the term) and outlining *why* I think writing center tutors should work with new media texts. The bulk of this essay is devoted to *how* to tutor new media, since I see that as the crux of the issue, so in the last part, I describe the ways that writing center directors and staffs wanting to work with new media can evolve their practices to do so.

What Is New Media?

Scholars use the term "new media" in a handful of ways that both overlap and diverge, which can make matters complicated. Are new media texts digital? Can they be print? Are they the same as multimodal texts? Or are they employing a different rhetoric? Cynthia Selfe, Anne Wysocki and Cheryl Ball each offer definitions of new media that I find helpful, not because they agree with one another, but rather because I can see from the sum of their individual definitions the exciting range of new media texts.

For Cynthia Selfe, new media texts are digital. She defines new media texts as "texts created primarily in digital environments, composed in multiple media, and designed for presentation and exchange in digital venues" ("Students" 43). Although such texts contain alphabetic features, she claims that "they also typically resist containment by alphabetic systems, demanding multiple literacies of seeing and listening and manipulating, as well as those of writing and reading" ("Students" 43). She would use "new media" to describe a web portfolio or another text viewed on screen that would contain alphabetic texts and other modes, too.

Anne Wysocki, though, sees new media as any text that in its production calls attention to its own materiality:

> I think we should call "new media texts" those that have been made by composers who are aware of the range of materialities of texts and who then highlight the materiality: such composers design texts that help readers/consumers/viewers stay alert to how any text–like its composers and readers–doesn't function independently of how it is made and in what contexts.
>
> ("Openings" 15)

This attention to materiality means the text might or might not be digital. As Wysocki writes, "new media texts do not have to be digital; instead, any text that has been designed so that its materiality is not effaced can count as new media" (15). An example of a new media text that isn't digital is Wysocki et al.'s *Writing New Media* itself. Design choices in this text, such as the horizontal orientation of the page numbers, make readers "stay alert" to how the writers are playing with the usual conventions of a book. The key term for Wysocki's conception of new media, then, is materiality.

A third definition of new media comes from Cheryl Ball in "Show, Not Tell: The Value of New Media Scholarship." She writes that new media are "texts that juxtapose semiotic modes in new and aesthetically pleasing ways and, in doing so, break away from print traditions so that written text is not the primary rhetorical means" (405). For Ball, then, like Selfe, new media is multimodal and digital. Unique to Ball's definition, however, is that what's "new" in new media is the way in which these texts make arguments—the primacy of non-textual modes. New media texts make fundamentally different types of arguments. She illustrates this difference in her article through analysis of two web texts. One relies on print conventions to make its linear argument: the other radically departs from print conventions as it asks readers to compose the argument by dragging and dropping audio, still images, and text to play together in an order determined by the viewer/reader.

Combined, the three definitions show a range of texts that are "new" in significant ways: 1) their digital-ness; 2) their conscious materiality or form; 3) their multimodality; and/or 4) their rhetorical means. Of course, texts that fall under the category of *new* media by one or more of these definitions have existed for some time, but it is only recently that students, especially in writing classrooms, have been regularly asked to read or compose new media texts. The norm in colleges and universities for decades has been typed, double-spaced, thesis-driven texts on $8^1/_2$-by-11-inch, stapled, white paper. Thus, in this article, when I say that we should train tutors to work with new media. I mean the sorts of texts that would fit any of the three (Wysocki's, Selfe's, or Ball's) definitions outlined above. Practically speaking, this would mean that tutors would also be trained to work with texts that are not traditional, paper, alphabetic, text-only, academic print essays or assignments. Increasingly common, new media assignments in first-year composition (FYC) include PowerPoint presentations or slidecasts; video essays and documentaries; audio essays or podcast series; posters, collages, and other visual arguments; websites or hypertexts; and comic books, animations, or graphic novels. These are the sorts of texts we must be prepared to work with in the writing center in the twenty-first century in addition to the more traditional texts that have been the norm.

Why Tutor New Media?

Pemberton suggests four ways of dealing with new texts in writing centers: 1) ignore them since they will rarely appear; 2) use specialist tutors; 3) treat new media texts like other texts; or 4) train all tutors to work with them.[1] The last of these is the approach I will argue for; I believe the writing center is the place to tutor students with their new media texts. I think all tutors should be trained to work with these texts and that these texts have unique features, which means some of our traditional tutoring practices will not work (more on this later). Here, I will briefly defend my belief that we should take on the task of tutoring new media. Many readers, I imagine, will not need convincing, as writing centers around the country already work with new media writing. For these readers, this section might help them articulate this new work to colleagues or administrators who question the evolution of their writing centers. Other readers might find themselves more resistant to offering what they perceive as yet another service when demands on their resources and time are already too high. I can empathize with this position but do my best to articulate how I do not think tutoring new media is something we can or should opt out of. It is not another thing—it is *the* thing we have always done, just in new forms, genres, and media.

Reason #1: New Media Is Writing

Writing has irrevocably changed from the early days of writing centers. Early writing centers in the 1960s and 1970s developed peer tutoring techniques when student texts were written by hand or with typewriters. Adding another mode—even a simple image—to paper texts was difficult and usually avoided. The 1980s and 1990s brought us personal computers with word processing, but for the earlier part of this period, the texts writing centers worked with did not radically change. Word processors made texts that looked like they came from typewriters; texts were composed on screen but printed and distributed on paper.

Fast forward to the 2000s. Student texts now are nearly always composed on screen. Most students have their own computers—laptops are popular. Many texts that students compose, even for FYC, never leave the screen. Students write reading responses in a course management system, like Black Board. They post the response to the course discussion board where the instructor and other students respond. Likewise, longer writing assignments—essays and web pages—can be "turned in" and "turned back" without ever being printed out. In fact, when Microsoft Word 2007 was released, it sported a new default typeface created for onscreen viewing, replacing the long-reigning Times New Roman, because of the frequency with which texts—even word-processed texts—were viewed on screen.

In these ways, we have witnessed a fundamental change in the textual climate. Before, putting a text on paper—and writing for that linear, left-to-right, top-to-bottom, page-to-page form was *the* way to write. That has changed. Now, there are many ways to communicate through writing: consequently, putting a text to paper is now a rhetorical choice that one should not make hastily. We ought to really think through whether a paper essay, say, is the best way to reach our audience or purpose. If we decide to compose paper essays knowing we have the wide range of available textual choices, we are deeming the paper essay the best way to meet our rhetorical ends. Many of us, perhaps, have spent our lifetimes writing paper essays because that was how arguments were made—academically if not otherwise. The paper essay was the default. This is no longer the case even in academic circles. Many academic conference presentations are not paper essays read to the audience but arguments presented with PowerPoint slideshows, videos, animations, and print or digital posters, suggesting that many academic writers, upon weighing their rhetorical choices, are no longer choosing paper essays.

I think it is unreasonable to grant that writers have a wide range of options for meeting their rhetorical ends—even academically—yet to insist that we will only help with those texts that writing centers have historically worked with, namely, paper essays and assignments. New media is "new," as the earlier definitions show, yet it is still writing. More than that, it is a type of writing that academia and the greater public value more and more.

Sending students with new media texts to another center or a specific tutor, as some centers have done, could give the message that new media is not writing, that it is not something the writing center values. Some universities might be in the position, as the University of Michigan was, to create a separate center for new media texts. But many of us struggle, annually, to keep one center open. Many of us also struggle to run one center, and most of us would not find additional compensation for willingly increasing our workload, I imagine. However, preparing all tutors to work with new media texts requires no second space or additional staffing. It does not necessarily require great investments in new technology or technology training. Most writing centers are likely adequately outfitted with at least one, if not several, computers on which to view digital texts. We might very well want to acquire large monitors or projectors to enable viewing of certain texts (e.g., slidecasts, video essays, or PowerPoint presentations), but these texts can be viewed on small screens for the purpose of tutor response.

Reason #2: The Line Between New Media and Old Media Is Blurry

Though I attempted a clear-cut definition of new media texts in the previous section, it is often the case that a text straddles the old media/new media line. A writing center that officially works with only essays, reports, and other such alphabetic texts will increasingly, if not already, find multimodality and digitality a part of such texts. Pemberton's question about hypertexts is a good example. He meant, I think, to question whether writing centers ought to work with digital texts composed in HTML and viewed in web-browsers, otherwise known as web pages. Yet many programs now, including Microsoft Word and PowerPoint, allow for hypertext links (not to mention color, images, charts, sound, animation, and videos), so traditional essays are quickly becoming less, well, traditional. If we say we do not work with hypertexts, would we then not work with essays that contain links? Or what of a webpage that contained an essay with no links? When is it an essay and when is it hypertext?

I think a writing center that sets out to determine when a traditional essay becomes a new media text in order to say "yes" we work with these or "no" we don't work with those—will find this an increasingly difficult task. Likewise, a writing center that asserts that it can only help with the "writing" part of a new media text is also on shaky ground. The alphabetic text in a new media text is subsumed into the whole and must be read in context of the whole composition.

Reason #3: If We Don't Claim It for Writing, Others Will Subsume It as Technology

If we surrender the composition of web texts or other new media texts to computer science or another department on campus, we allow new media composition to be lost to the technology As Dànielle DeVoss writes, "Writing center theory and practice must … evolve so we can situate ourselves as crucial stakeholders, working towards more complex and critical use of computing technologies and computer-related literacies" (167). If composing new media texts are just about mastering the technology, then we can be convinced (or others will try to convince us) that new media is better left to those on campus who know the most about technology. For example, if creating a website is only about learning HTML or CSS, then we could let the computer science department teach it. Yet, if we consider new media as texts composed consciously in multiple modes, we would have to acknowledge that we are responsible for and good at teaching composing.[2] We ought to speak up about how creating digital texts involves more than mastering a software program just as loudly as we speak up about how writing in general is more than mastering MLA format or rules for comma usage.

New media texts are texts—written for particular occasions, purposes and audiences. As such, writers of new media still need human feedback. Related to this, the "CCCC Position Statement on Teaching, Learning, and Assessing Writing in Digital Environments," a guide for classroom instruction of digital writing, advises, "Because digital environments make sharing work especially convenient, we would expect to find considerable human interaction around texts: through such interaction, students learn that humans write to other humans for specific purposes." The statement reminds us that digital texts are rhetorical and therefore need rhetorical feedback—of the ilk a writing center typically provides—not just technical troubleshooting. The evolved writing center secures a spot for humans to meet other humans over texts, digital or not. Working with students on their new media texts asserts our stake as composing professionals in the new media age.

How to Tutor New Media

In the previous two sections I argued, perhaps paradoxically, that there is something new and different about new media writing, yet that it is writing and therefore we should tutor writers working on it. For me, there is enough that is "new" about new media that I had to ask myself how well our traditional tutoring practices address it. Trimbur is clear, too, that the change in types of projects we see in the center will change our tutoring. He writes,

> The new digital literacies will increasingly be incorporated into writing centers not just as sources of information or delivery systems for tutoring but as productive arts in their own right, and writing center work will, if anything, become more rhetorical in paying attention to the practices and effects of design in written and visual communication—more product-oriented and perhaps less like the composing conferences of the process movement.
>
> (30)

I have to agree with Trimbur that it would be foolish not to prepare my tutors to work with these texts. What I have come to believe is that accepting new media texts necessitates rethinking our dominant writing center ideas and revising our common practices. Practices vary from center to center, from tutor to tutor. Still, there are some practices espoused repeatedly in the literature of the field and tutor training manuals that seem to compose our general tenets. Many of these practices will have to change. Although such radical re-imaginings of writing center work may seem daunting, we could see this as an occasion to reconsider how well we are responding to all texts, to all writers—an occasion to improve the work we do.

Up to this point, I have been concerned with arguing that we ought to work with new media: now I complicate that. I think it would be irresponsible not to think through (and follow through with) consequent changes to our practices. In what follows, I look at the often-espoused practices for tutoring writing, particularly the ways we read student texts and the ways we respond.

How We Read Student Texts

Ever since Stephen North published his writing center manifesto, "The Idea of a Writing Center," writing center scholars and practitioners have been guided by this statement: "in a writing center the object is to make sure that writers, and not necessarily their texts, are what get changed by instruction. In axiom form it goes like this: our job is to produce better writers, not better writing" (37). What follows this writing center mantra is important; he writes, "In the center, we look *beyond* or *through* that particular project, that particular text, and see it as an occasion for addressing our primary concern, the process by which it is produced" (38, emphasis added). This idea has been translated into practice in various ways. For one, Christina Murphy and Steve Sherwood, in *The St. Martin's Sourcebook for Writing Tutors*, describe tutoring in terms of "pre-textual," "textual," and "post-textual," where the goal of tutoring is, indeed, to get beyond the text. In these three stages, the tutor is to first talk about the paper with the client, then read the paper with the client, and finish by moving from the paper and dealing with the client's issues in writing in general.

Another way to "look beyond" particular projects is to not physically look at them. This comes in the form of a hands-off policy in relation to student texts. We train our tutors to leave the text in front of the client or between tutor and client. As Leigh Ryan and Lisa Zimmerelli suggest in *The Bedford Guide for Writing Tutors*, "Give the student control of the paper. Keep the paper in front of the student as much as possible. If you are working at a computer, let the writer sit in front of the screen as well as control the keyboard" (19). When a student hands a tutor a paper, the tutor often quickly puts it down on the table. Irene Clark and Dave Healy note that this practice, which they call the pedagogy of noninterventionalism, exists because of an ethical concern in some centers. If tutors hold the paper, write on the paper, or otherwise "own" the paper, they may be unwillingly helping the student too much, i.e., plagiarizing or editing. Linda Shamoon and Deborah Burns, in turn, call this hands-off practice "The Bible," an orthodoxy that has attained the force of an ethical or moral code within writing center studies (175).

Likewise, tutors are encouraged to use a read-aloud method for tutoring. Tutors read the student text aloud to the client or request the client to do so. However, this common approach of reading texts in writing centers might not be helpful for students with new media texts. The intertwining of multiple modes may be lost if the tutor looks *through* the text or does not look *at* the paper or *at* the screen. Furthermore, there is no way to "read aloud" visual elements or sounds. Consequently, the tutor may just skip over these elements thereby privileging the verbal, perhaps to the detriment of the student.

For example, several years ago one of my composition students. "Amy," took her final project to the writing center for help. She was working on her "book," a type of portfolio project that asked students to rethink their semester's work in terms of a consistent theme and design. She had decided to use divider pages featuring Winnie the Pooh throughout her book. It was an odd choice as a design feature that became downright inappropriate when one of her "chapters" was an essay on Hitler. The baffling juxtaposition of Pooh and Piglet and the horrific details in her essay surely did not escape her tutor: however, the tutor did not say anything to Amy about this choice quite possibly because the tutor was working under the typical assumption that the alphabetic text was her domain, or because the tutor never even saw this visual element since Amy held the book and read aloud to the tutor. Amy might have received a similar silence had she used certain types of online tutoring which ask writers to cut and paste their text into email forms or whiteboards, allowing tutors to see only the alphabetic text.

How we read texts in writing centers is especially problematic for certain new media texts, such as digital texts, which offer the reader a choice in navigation—where to start, when to go back, where to go next. A tutor must look at a hypertext and interact with it to read it, which begs the question: how would one—or why would one—read aloud a website? The first step in evolving writing center practice, then, is insisting that tutors look at texts to *see* student writing. Stephen Bernhardt's suggestion to composition teachers that they ought to look *at* student texts instead of *through* them seems just as important for writing centers now. If we don't, Bernhardt warns that we are ensuring our own irrelevance as the gap widens between the literacies we have traditionally taught and the ones students need: "Classroom practice which ignores the increasingly visual, localized qualities of information exchange can only become increasingly irrelevant" (77). Doing so, we ask tutors to consider the materiality of texts from the resolution of images to the quality of paper for a resume.

Secondly, instead of asking tutors to read aloud, we can ask tutors to talk aloud as they negotiate a text—a subtle yet important change. In reading aloud, the tutor may be tempted to skip over nonverbal elements since the elements are, well, not verbal. In fact, in my own tutoring experience. I have worked with students who quickly turn the page past charts or graphs as if they are inconsequential to the text at hand. However, if the tutor talked through the text, he or she would instead render a reading of it, showing the student how it could be read in its entirety. For instance, imagine Amy taking her book to a talk-aloud session. The tutor right away would begin with the materiality of the text. "Wow; this is quite a big document. I see it has lots of pages. This, here, seems to be a title. Is this a collection of writings of sorts?" And then. "I'm noticing as we go through this that you've used Winnie the Pooh on each divider page. Why is that?³"

This tactic would be immensely helpful for hypertexts, too. The tutor could talk through the links and her expectations for how to negotiate the pages. "OK, we've read through this page on Senator Clinton. I'd like to go back to the page on Moveon.org, but I don't see how I'd do that." Or, "The first thing I notice is these images changing—fading into one another. They all seem connected by their subject—all protesters of sorts? This makes me think this website is about protesting even though the title says, 'Citizens of America.'" This sort of talking aloud would let students see how a reader makes meaning by reading the various modes in the text: images, text, layout, color, movement, and so forth.

How We Talk About Student Writing

In a typical writing center session, tutors are trained to read through the student's text and then to set an agenda on what issues to tackle during the remainder of the session. Many tutors are trained to focus the tutorial on higher order concerns (HOCs) first. These are defined as "the features of the paper that exist beyond the sentence-level; they include clarity of thesis or focus, adequate development and information, effective structure or organization, and appropriate voice and tone" (McAndrew and Reigstad 42). Only after working through the "higher order" issues does the tutor turn to lower order concerns (LOCs), which primarily manifest on the sentence level. All in all, this practice makes sense. It is only logical to work students through revisions that might necessitate substantial changes first, before tackling what is happening on a micro-level.

Nonetheless, there may be a problem with this practice for new media texts since tutors are not trained to see other modes, such as visual elements, as contributing to the overall meaning of the text. That is, they are not trained to see that visual elements can be and often are a higher order concern and should be attended to as such. For instance, a tutor, Bryan, told me last year of a student he worked with who was composing a scholarship essay. The student had selected an apple clip art border for his text that he felt was fitting for the type of scholarship—a scholarship for future teachers. These apples, which Bryan felt inappropriate for the genre, were really the only thing he remembered about the essay, yet were not something he discussed with the student since he said he wanted to discuss "the more important issues" first. Clearly, this is just one example, but I believe it does speak to the way we set agendas—what we decide to talk about with writers.

Tutors do not typically broach the subject of formatting without direct questioning from the student because issues of formatting, if they are seen at all, are seen as LOCs or because tutors usually work with drafts and may assume the students will know how to "fix" such elements by the final copy. The visual aspects of a text may not even be on the tutor's radar, let alone other modes such as sound, color, or motion. In numerous tutoring manuals, there is little acknowledgement that visual elements or document design are important for tutors to read and discuss with students. The closest are Ryan and Zimmerelli's *Bedford Guide*, which states that lab reports should have headings, includes a page on PowerPoint presentations, and asks tutors to consider if resumes are "pleasing to the eye" (87), and Bertie Fearing and W. Keats Sparrow's "Tutoring Business and Technical Writing Students," which focuses mainly on issues of voice, diction, economy, emphasis, and parallelism, but also devotes one paragraph to typography, headings, and lists. Beyond this, there is little about the multimodality of academic essays and more often than not nothing about considering the multimodality of any other type of assignment. Even when telling tutors how to work with typically visually-heavy forms manuals, instructions, memos, proposals, progress and feasibility reports—McAndrew and Reigstad do not show tutors how to give feedback on the non-verbal elements. Obviously, if writing centers are going to work with new media texts—those texts which purposely employ various modes to make meaning—tutors will have to be trained to know when and how the interaction of various modes are HOCs.

Furthermore, unless trained otherwise, tutors might not suggest the use of non-textual modes in revision planning with the student. There are moments as readers when the use of a diagram, illustration, or image could help with our comprehension of ideas, and there are times when the use of a bulleted list, graph, or chart allows a writer to present ideas succinctly. Tutors, as readers of and responders to texts, need to be able to describe to clients their expectations in terms of verbal and other elements and plot out the tutoring sessions to reflect that. Tutors need to be able to talk about new media texts, which requires both a broader understanding of rhetoric (of how new media texts are rhetorical) and a new set of terms about the interactivity between modes and the effects of that interactivity.

Several composition scholars have theorized how we might respond to or assess classroom-assigned new media writing. Several of them emphasize the rhetorical nature of new media, thereby arguing that we can respond to new media in ways similar to how we respond to other texts, as they are all rhetorical. For example, in "Looking for Sources of Coherence in a Fragmented World," Kathleen Blake Yancey argues that we need new ways of talking about digital writing: "Without a new language, we will be held hostage to the values informing print, values worth preserving for that medium, to be sure, but values incongruent with those informing the digital" (89–90). To that end, she offers a heuristic for readers to ask of digital texts: What arrangements are possible? Who arranges? What is the intent? What is the fit between intent and effect? (96) Though she sees digital composition as different, she sees rhetoric as "being at the heart" of all the writing composition teachers assign and assess (90).

Likewise, Madeleine Sorapure's "Between Modes: Assessing Student New Media Compositions" suggests teachers look for the use of the rhetorical tropes of metaphor and metonymy when assessing students new media compositions, thereby focusing on the relationship of modes. She writes,

> Focusing assessment on the relations of modes might alleviate part of what Yancey described as the "discomfort" of assessment: that part that comes from our sense that we are not the most qualified people on campus to judge the effectiveness of the individual modes of image, audio, or video in a multimodal composition. But I think we are indeed qualified to look at the relations between modes and to assess how effectively students have combined different resources in their compositions.
>
> (4)

I think Sorapure's idea is on the right track. We don't need to be, say filmmakers to respond to video in new media compositions. However, we do need to be able, at a minimum, to respond to how the video relates to the whole of the text. As Yancey, Sorapure, and others suggest, new media texts are rhetorical. We can talk about how the text is motivated, how it is purposeful, how it is written to a particular audience. These conversations can be similar to the conversations we have about old media texts.[4] Yet if we do read rhetorically to determine how well a text meets its ends, our tutors need to be able to explain how a text has or has not done so. I do not think our language for talking about texts is adequate in and of itself for this task.

Instead, I have increasingly drawn on other fields to give tutors ways to talk about the interactivity of modes and their sense of the gestalt in students' new media texts. Teaching tutors these terms will give them a vocabulary to describe the relationships between modes; without such an understanding, many times students and tutors assume that images, graphics, animation, or other modes are decoration or supplementation (although they probably won't use that term) for the real mode of writing: the words. I've tutored more than one student who assumed that visuals always make sense to readers, that other modes don't need interpretation like words do.

As a start, I think it is appropriate to teach tutors Karen Schriver's terms for the relationships between modes. Robin Williams's principles of good design, and Cynthia Selfe's criteria for visual assessment. Each of these, I believe, gives more concrete language for tutors or teachers responding to new media. The space of this article will not permit me to draw out extended examples of each of the terms; I hope that readers interested in these ideas will look to the primary texts. However, I will briefly look at a sample new media text to see how this terminology as a whole might help a tutor respond to such a text.

Relationships Between Modes: Karen Schriver

Schriver's terms were intended to describe how visuals work with alphabetic text, though they easily translate to the relationships between different modes, too, such as sound, video, and color.

Redundant:	"substantially identical content appearing visually and verbally in which each mode tells the same story, providing a repetition of key ideas" (412)
Complementary:	"different content visually and verbally, in which both modes are needed in order to understand the key ideas" (412)
Supplementary:	"different content in words and pictures, in which one mode dominates the other, providing the main ideas, while the other reinforces, elaborates, or instantiates the points made in the dominant mode (or explains how to interpret the other)" (413)
Juxtapositional:	"different content in words and pictures, in which the key ideas are created by a clash or semantic tension between the ideas in each mode: the idea cannot be inferred without both modes being present simultaneously" (414)
Stage-setting:	"different content in words and pictures, in which one mode (often the visual) forecasts the content, underlying theme, or ideas presented in the other mode" (414)

Principles of Design: Robin Williams Williams's four basic design principles come from her work *The Non-Designer's Design Book*, where she tries to simplify design concepts for those who must design on paper or screen but do not do so as their primary occupation. Using this sort of text draws on the field of graphic design, which has multimodal composition at its heart.

Contrast:	Difference created between elements for emphasis; elements must be made quite different or else the elements simply *conflict* with one another (63)
Repetition:	How consistently elements (e.g., typeface, color, pattern, transition) are used; repetition unifies (49)
Alignment:	How elements line up on a page, the visual connection between elements; "every item should have a visual connection with something else on the page" (31)
Proximity:	How closely elements are placed on page or screen: related items should be close to one another, unrelated items should not be (15–17)

Visual Assessment Criteria: Cynthia Selfe

The last set of terms comes from a chapter of *Writing New Media* in which Selfe, drawing on the work of Gunther Kress and Theo van Leeuwen, gives assignments and rubrics for helping writing instructors incorporate new media into their classes. This set of terms is helpful in looking, literally, at the gestalt of a new media text.

Visual impact:	"the overall effect and appeal that a visual composition has on an audience" ("Toward" 85)
Visual coherence:	"the extent to which the various elements of a visual composition are tied together, represent a unified whole" ("Toward" 86)
Visual salience:	"the relative prominence of an element within a visual composition. Salient elements catch viewers' eye [*sic*]; they are conspicuous" ("Toward" 86)

Visual organization: "the pattern of arrangement that relates the elements of the visual essay to one another so that they are easier for readers/viewers to comprehend" ("Toward" 87)

Using the New Terminology to Respond to a New Media Text

Figure 17.1 is a grayscale reproduction of a poster created by the Writing Center staff at Clarion University. They produce these posters collaboratively as a staff and sell customized versions via their website. This one, the "Criminal Justice Poster," is one of my favorites.

Figure 17.1 Clarion "Criminal Justice Poster."

I selected this text to model a new media response because it fits within the very general definition of new media that I have used throughout this article, because it consciously takes advantage of its materiality as a poster, and because it relies on multiple modes to make its argument. It also is exchanged as a digital text first—composed digitally and bought from digital previews before it is printed poster-size. In addition, I wanted to select a text which a reader of this article could see in its entirety (though my response is to the original full-color file which can be viewed at http://www.clarion.edu/80053.jpg).

So, first off, what kind of relationship do we see between the modes here? The composer has used text, photograph, color, and typography to make this text. The image of the hand-cuffed person is in a *complementary* relationship with the text, "Don't let your writing get so out of hand it has to be put behind bars." The image helps give the reader context. Though the text is a threatening command (do this or else), the orange, bright blue, and green colors and typography are more playful than foreboding. Perhaps this *juxtaposition* is purposeful to play up the humor of the poster or perhaps it takes away from the effect. This could be something to discuss with the writer.

We can also look at the principles of design at work here. *Contrast* is evident in the change in typeface. The composer wanted to emphasize the word "Don't," so it appears larger than the other words. The different colors, sizes, and weight of the other words and background signal difference, perhaps of importance. "Don't let your writing" is in one typeface; the rest of the text is in a very similar sans serif typeface, which makes for a *conflict. Repetition* is evident in the color choices; the background colors are also used for the type. The words "Don't" and "writing" are actually repeated and faded into the background. There are varied *alignments* here. Mostly, the text is center-aliened and shares the same base line. However, "Don't" and "let your" don't share a common baseline. The (mostly) center alignment makes the words on the left margin and right margin nearly line up. Further, there is no consistent alignment within the colored blocks; the text sits near the bottom in blue and green squares but floats to the top in orange. There are two sentences here, and the *proximity* is very close between them, signaling to the reader that these ideas are closely related. The image breaking through the first sentence makes the reader understand the picture as part of the message of that first sentence.

Finally, we could look at this as a visual argument. Using Selfe's terms, we would probably acknowledge that the overall *visual impact* is quite striking. This is a poster that stands out because of the image and bright (though not garish) colors. The purpose of a poster is to call attention to itself, and this poster has the potential to do that. The *visual coherence* is also quite strong because of the repetition of colors and type. The poster will be customized in the white box with the purchaser's logo or information. There is a possibility that there will be less coherence when that element is introduced if there are different types or colors. The elements that are *visually salient* are the word "Don't" and the photograph. Both hold key—positions one in the top left corner and one across the center of the poster. The quick in-a-glance message provided by these two elements is, "don't end up in cuffs"—pretty powerful! The placement of the prominent "Don't" at the top invites the reader to start there and move down; thus the *visual organization* of elements tells the reader how to use the text.

At this point, I should mention two things. First, I am not implying that a tutor would or should go through reading/responding to a text as extensively as text during a session. Like other sessions, the tutor and student would discuss what seems most pressing. I, for one, would probably talk to this composer about how color and type relate to text and image and the overall alignment—another tutor might focus on other elements. Which brings me to my second point: not everyone using these terms is going to come to the same reading. The reader's job with new media is still interpretation. Responding to new media requires close interaction with the text and ways to talk about what we read/view/interact with.

Summary and Closing Thoughts

This article has been about reconsidering how we train tutors to read and respond to texts. The subject here has been new media texts. I've asked us to reconsider how we tutor and how we talk to students about their writing. The impetus for these evolved practices is the arrival of increasing numbers of new media texts assigned in university classes. As new media texts consciously and purposefully employ multiple modes to make meaning, they require us to direct our attention to texts differently. Current practices won't suffice, as they limit us to the alphabetic text. Thus, I believe it is imperative to train all tutors in these evolved practices because they will change the ways we respond to all texts, considering more than we have before, perhaps in significant ways. In short, here's the 28-word, visually-arranged version of this article:

Twentieth-Century Tutoring	Twenty-First-Century Tutoring
Read aloud	Talk aloud
Getting beyond the text	Interacting with the text
Zoomed in: talk about words	Zoomed out: talk about whole

It strikes me that writing center studies is at a crossroads, a moment in time where tough decisions regarding the scope of our practices need to be made. Certainly, changes in composing technologies have asked us to push beyond the writing center practices that developed in the 1970s writing center boom. I, for one, do not think this is a time for conservatism, for preserving the tradition for the sake of tradition. Though I understand the impulse as a writing center director to say, "Not one more thing! We do enough!" to me, tutoring new media is not another thing. Writing has evolved with new composing technologies and media, and we must evolve, too, because we are in the writing business. A radical shift in the way that writers communicate both academically and publically necessitates a radical re-imagining and re-understanding of our practices, purposes, and goals.

Finally, I want to address one of the concerns that I discussed earlier: that we are not sure that we can do a good job of tutoring new media, so perhaps we shouldn't try. I think we need to remember that writing centers are largely based on the idea that talk among peers will help. We've never been concerned about expert tutors or perfection, and our feathers get ruffled when others (students or professors) expect this. If we evolve the practices in the ways I suggest, tutors will not be experts in new media composing, but they will be able to offer a response. And that is what we do.

Notes

1. Pemberton focuses exclusively on hypertexts, not all new media.
2. For more on this, see Grutsch McKinney.
3. This could also hold true for tutoring via email or chat. The texts may be copied and pasted into an email and the tutor will not see the text as it will materialize for its intended audience, for example, how it prints out on the page.

4. For example, see JoAnn Griffin's schema in "Making Connections with Writing Centers" for discussing audience, purpose, form, context, organization, unity/focus, detail/support, style, and correctness of alphabetic essays, audio essays, and video essays (155–56).

Works Cited

Ball, Cheryl. "Show, Not Tell: The Value of New Media Scholarship." *Computers and Composition* 21.4 (2004): 403–25. Print.

Bernhardt, Stephen A. "Seeing the Text." *College Composition and Communication* 37.1 (1986): 66–78. Print.

Conference on College Composition and Communication. "CCCC Position Statement on Teaching, Learning, and Assessing Writing in Digital Environments." Adopted 25 Feb. 2004. Web. 15 Dec. 2007.

Clark, Irene and Dave Healy. "Are Writing Centers Ethical?" *WPA: Writing Program Administration* 20.1/2 (1996): 32–48. Print.

DeVoss, Dànielle. "Computer Literacies and the Roles of the Writing Center." *Writing Center Research: Extending the Conversation.* Ed. Paula Gillespie, Alice Gillam, Lady Falls Brown, and Bryon Stay. Mahwah, NJ: Erlbaum, 2002. 171–90. Print.

Fearing, Bertie E. and W. Keats Sparrow. "Tutoring Business and Technical Writing Students in the Writing Center." *Writing Centers: Theory and Administration.* Ed. Gary A. Olson. Urbana, IL: NCTE, 1984. 215–56. Print.

George, Diana. "From Analysis to Design: Visual Communication in the Teaching of Writing." *College Composition and Communication* 54.1 (2002): 11–39. Print.

Griffin, JoAnn. "Making Connections with Writing Centers." *Multimodal Composition: Resources for Teachers.* Ed. Cynthia Selfe. Kresskill, NJ: Hampton P, 2007. 153–66. Print.

Grutsch McKinney, Jackie. "The New Media (R)evolution: Multiple Models for Multiliteracies." *Multiliteracy Centers.* Ed. David Sheridan and James Inman. Cresskill, NJ: Hampton P, Forthcoming. Print.

Hassett, Michael and Rachel W. Lott. "Seeing Student Texts." *Composition Studies* 28.1 (2000): 29–47. Print.

Inman, James. "At First Site: Lessons From Furman University's Center for Collaborative Learning and Communication." *Academic Writing* 2 (2001): n. pag. Web. 15 Dec. 2007.

Kress, Gunther. *Literacy in the New Media Age.* New York: Routledge, 2003. Print.

McAndrew, Donald and Thomas J. Reigstad. *Tutoring Writing: A Practical Guide for Conferences.* Portsmouth, NH: Boyton/Cook, 2001. Print.

Murphy, Christina and Steve Sherwood. *The St. Martin's Sourcebook for Writing Tutors.* 2nd ed. Boston: Bedford/St. Martin's, 2003. Print.

North, Stephen M. "The Idea of a Writing Center." *College English* 46.5 (1984): 433–46. Print.

Pemberton, Michael. "Planning for Hypertexts in the Writing Center … or Not." *Writing Center Journal* 24.1 (2003): 9–24. Print.

Ryan, Leigh and Lisa Zimmerelli. *The Bedford Guide for Writing Tutors.* 4th ed. Boston: Bedford/St. Martin's, 2006. Print.

Schriver, Karen A. *Dynamics in Document Design.* New York: Wiley Computer P, 1997. Print.

Selber, Stuart. *Multiliteracies for a Digital Age.* Carbondale, IL: Southern Illinois UP, 2004. Print.

Selfe, Cynthia. "Students Who Teach Us: A Case Study of A New Media Text Designer." Wysocki et al. 43–66. Print.

——. "Toward New Media Texts: Taking Up the Challenges of Visual Literacy." Wysocki et al. 67–110. Print.

Shamoon, Linda K. and Deborah H. Burns. "A Critique of Pure Tutoring." *Writing Center Journal* 15.2 (1995): 134–51. Rpt. in Murphy and Sherwood. 174–90. Print.

Sheridan, David. "The Sweetland Multi-Literacy Center." *Sweetland Newsletter.* Oct. 2002. Web. 15 Dec. 2007.

——. "Words, Images, Sounds: Writing Centers as Muitiliteracy Centers." *The Writing Center Director's Resource Book.* Ed. Christina Murphy and Byron Stay. Mahwah, NJ: Erlbaum, 2006. 339–50. Print.

Sorapure, Madeleine. "Between Modes: Assessing Student New Media Compositions." *Kairos* 10.2 (Spring 2006): n.pag. Web. 15 Dec. 2007.

Stroupe, Craig. "Visualizing English: Recognizing the Hybrid Literacy of the Visual and Verbal Authorship on the Web," *College English* 62.5 (2005): 607–32. Print.

Trimbur, John, "Multiliteracies, Social Futures, and Writing Centers." *Writing Center Journal* 20.2 (2000): 29–31. Print.

Williams, Robin. *The Non-Designer's Design Book.* Berkeley, CA: Peachpit P, 2003. Print.

Wysocki, Ann Frances. "Opening New Media to Writing: Openings and Justifications." Wysocki et al. 1–42. Print.

Wysocki, Ann Frances, Johndan Johnson-Eilola, Cynthia L. Selfe, and Geoffrey Sirc. *Writing New Media.* Logan, UT: Utah State UP, 2004.

Yancey, Kathleen Blake. "Looking for Sources of Coherence in a Fragmented World." *Computers and Composition* 21.1 (2004): 89–102. Print.

18

Creating a Center for Communication Design

Negotiating Pedagogy, Disciplinarity, and Sustainability in Communities of Practice

Jennifer Sheppard

As our conceptions of writing broaden to include interactive, networked, and multimodal components, many scholars (Gee, 2003; Kress & van Leeuwen, 2001; The New London Group, 2000; Selber, 2004; Yancey, 2004) have theorized about the complex set of literacy and rhetorical practices needed to read and write with new media. These practices require communicators to negotiate a multiplicity of modes and media as meaning-making resources and to shape those meanings in light of the particular audiences, purposes, and contexts to which they are applied.

Although much attention has been given to the responsibilities teachers have far helping students learn how to interact with and create their own new media texts, far less attention has been paid to the infrastructure considerations needed for creating technological environments to support this teaching and learning. As Williams pointed out in a 2002 review of computer classroom (CC) literature, after much interest in the mid-1980s, research on the continued maintenance and development of technology-rich learning spaces decreased dramatically. The few pieces that have been published in the last 10 years have focused primarily on the ongoing sustainability of CCs (e.g., Selfe, 2005), pedagogy in CCs (e.g., Duffelmeyer, 2003), and the integration of wireless technologies into CCs (e.g., Dean, Hochman, Hood, & McEachern, 2004). However, few scholars have addressed the ways in which the specific needs of new media literacies change how such spaces are designed and administered.

Although many institutions are implementing the necessary hardware and software resources for students to read and write with new media (although this is far from universal), technological access alone does no automatically lead to development of purposeful, competent literacy practices. In order to create learning spaces that support reading and composition of new media a number of pedagogical and contextual challenges must be negotiated. In particular, I argue that teachers and scholars can benefit from attention to the concept of *communities of practice*. This model provides a theoretical and practical framework to inform our pedagogical and administrative approaches in setting up and running technology centers, computer labs, and new media studios in ways that support acquisition of digital literacies.

This chapter examines the process of developing a Center for New Media Communication Design (the Design Center) structured on the concept of communities of practice. In 2004, as a newly hired faculty member in rhetoric and professional communication (RPC), one of my first charges was to set up and run the Design Center to enrich graduate student[1] technology learning in a diverse English Department. Although it was intended primarily to support MA and PhD students in RPC, the Design Center also needed to serve as an interdisciplinary, multipurpose space for new media design and communication that could benefit MFA creative writing and MA literature students as well. Building on a key assumption of communities of practice theory—that learning is a situated, social, and interactive endeavor among participants of varying levels of expertise (Lave & Wenger, 1991; Paré, 2002; Wenger, 1999)—I envisioned the Design Center as an environment in which graduate students would engage collaboratively in the practical application of design, development, and usability for coursework, community and industry clients, and personal projects. Through this work, students would not only gain experience creating new media materials for authentic rhetorical situations, they would also collaborate with other learners and have an opportunity to explore how such work might be integrated into their studies, their own teaching of undergraduate writing, and their professional aspirations. Bringing this vision to reality was an exciting opportunity but also one fraught with complications. It was a process that required attention to pedagogical, programmatic, and departmental values to shape the ways in which the Design Center would be integrated into the needs and goals of its many stakeholders. My hope is that the insights gained through this experience will be of value to readers tasked with developing similar learning environments for reading and writing new media.

Background and Context

The development of the Design Center originated from many years of discussion about the need for such a facility and associated resources. Faculty in our RPC program had long realized the importance for students in gaining collaborative, theoretically based, hands-on experience in designing digitally produced materials for a variety of purposes and audiences. In the early 1990s, faculty and students in our graduate program were creating the first Web pages for other departments on campus, as well as doing contract communication work for a local hospital, the regional Forest Service office, and other entities (Stephen Bernhardt, personal communication, April 11, 2006). One faculty member recalled that there was a big demand for these kinds of materials, as there are today, and that graduate students had all kinds of "untapped experience," but the department lacked a physical space and the resources to fully develop these opportunities (Stuart Brown, personal communication, April 11, 2006). As a result, they originally envisioned this Design Center as a kind of consulting studio in which students would engage collaboratively in the practical application of design, development, and usability for community and industry clients. It would be a space that would not only have the appropriate technological resources, but that would also encourage interaction and mutual learning among designers as they developed communication materials and their own practices. Having learned much about new media design through similar kinds of extracurricular projects during my own graduate education, this vision fit well with my pedagogical and disciplinary commitments.

When I came on board, fresh from graduate school and the experience of working in a productive, well run, and well-known computers and writing environment. I knew there were aspects that I wanted to emulate. During my time as a student in Michigan

Technological University's Center for Computer-assisted Language Instruction (CCLI), I had benefited greatly from the informal atmosphere and abundance of fellow learners engaged in new media work who were willing to share their expertise. When working on a Flash project, Web site, or digital video, I would often have questions (as do most learners of new media and technologies) about how to do something, why I was encountering a particular problem, or how well my communicative intentions were being realized. The ability to get immediate help from trained consultants and/or other learners was an invaluable part of my growing competence with new media composition. Being a member of this community of practice not only allowed me to move forward wich my own projects but also gave me opportunities to develop practices in teaching others when I had suggestions to offer.

As I began to pian for the Design Center, I wanted to build on my positive experiences as a student, as well as the scholarship of those early "scouts and trailblazers" who had designed and researched the first CCs in writing studies (Albers & Cargile Cook, 2002, 246). However, since this Design Center was intended more as a studio than as a typical CC or lab space. I needed to make some adaptations. Additionally, I had to attend to the contextual factors specific to my new institution, its programmatic goals, and its student population in order to develop a productive teaching and learning environment. Among the challenges were the absence of an undergraduate program in the discipline (and thus far fewer students pursuing this work and willing to serve as consultants), a department not focused exclusively on composition and technical communication programs (and thus not viewing this space as an essential component of its work), and a centralized technical administration rather than local control (and thus no system administrator within the department to help select, set up, and maintain technologies). Beyond these challenges I also had to negotiate specific issues of pedagogy, departmental disciplinarity, and technological sustainability in order to create a space specifically tailored to support new media literacy development.

A primary pedagogical challenge was that as a result of faculty turnover, the program had not had personnel working at the intersection of technology and writing for several years. Without this kind of academic leadership, there were few students in the RPC program pursuing this work. Simply constructing the Design Center would not automatically lead to an environment that encouraged new media learning. I would need to find ways of attracting students to this area of study and of providing consistent support for their work.

A second major challenge had to do with the departmental context in which the Design Center would be situated. With a department covering such a broad swath of English studies, there was little consensus on what constituted new media, why it was important to studies in rhetoric and professional communication, or how it might connect to a variety of other disciplinary interests. One primary implication of this situation was the conceptions (and misconceptions) of what the Design Center would be able to do. This space was intended (by me and by those who had set development of this Design Center in motion before I was hired) as more than a computer laboratory or classroom, but this identity was vague to many faculty. Expectations about its potential uses included everything from seeing the Design Center as a studio for extracurricular client-based projects, to seeing it as seminar/lab space for coursework connected to classes in document, Web, and multimedia design, to seeing it as a service center where digitally oriented but largely clerical work could be dropped off to be completed by others. Attending to these diverse concepts of the Design Center and providing a theoretically backed justification for the decisions I made about what it would and would not do was a significant challenge to be addressed.

A final concern had to do with planning for technological sustainability. Unlike the lab from my graduate experience, this one was not supported financially by student fees nor by a central technical administration. Once the initial start-up funding was spent, I would have to become what Bernhardt (1989) described as a hustler, "look[ing] everywhere for money" and resources (109). In such a disciplinary diverse department I would need to think hard about how to justify and argue for the proportionally large and ongoing financial costs of maintaining and upgrading the technology. It was especially important to find ways of making the Design Center an asset and resource for all members of the department, not just a single program, as well as to find external funding opportunities to create financial sustainability.

In trying to navigate each of these contextual challenges, I chose to use the concept of communities of practice because it provided support for envisioning the Design Center as a unique learning environment for the development of new media literacies. The concept offered a theoretical touchstone against which I could consider critically the rationales for administrative decisions while still keeping pedagogical concerns at the forefront. It was also in line with my vision of the Design Center as a collaborative setting where participants could explore the communicative and expressive possibilities of various media and technologies.

Communities of Practice and Learning as a Collaborative, Social, and Interactive Endeavor

Based on work within literacy, social cognition, and sociocultural approaches to language, the concept of *communities of practice* emphasizes co-participation and the idea that "learning doesn't happen in the individual mind" (Hanks, 1991, 15). Instead, as Lave and Wenger (1991) argued, this view claims that "learning, thinking, and knowing are relations among people in activity in, with, and arising from the socially and culturally structured world" (50). As they demonstrated through a number of case studies, communities of practice allow newcomers to develop competency in a given practice by engaging with more experienced members in increasingly central parts of a community's activities. Importantly much of the learning occurs not through formal instruction but through informal interaction where newcomers get necessary information in the context of activity as they need it. It is precisely this unstructured interaction among co-participants that allows learners to gradually join in the actual practices of a given field or activity, thus helping them to master those ways of doing over time.

Similarly, reflecting on his years of professional writing consultancy work with social workers, Paré (2002) argued:

> Expertise is, in part, a gradual transformation that occurs in *situ*, under the guidance and direction of experienced members of particular communities of practice. ... Neophytes do not become experts *at* writing; they become experts at *using* writing to perform or participate in something. They learn to write texts of type X in way Y to achieve Z. Without Z, there is no way Y and no text X.
>
> (62)

In other words, practices such as those involved with reading and writing new media cannot be learned in an isolated, artificial context. Instead, the extent of purposeful, hands-on activity and collaboration with others of varying levels of expertise holds important implications for the degree to which learners become competent in the literacies of a given context and medium. To have pedagogical value, new media learning activities must help students to situate the rhetorical purpose of a text, rather than focus solely on the technologies needed to construct it and the product that results.

Furthermore, an engaged community of practice is not just about the activities undertaken, but also about the social participation of the individuals involved. As Wenger (1999) explained, "participation here refers not just to local events of engagement in certain activities with certain people, but to a more encompassing process of being active participants in the *practices* of social communities and constructing *identities* in relation to these communities" (p. 4). Because learning and working with new media is such a diverse and exploratory set of practices, having a community of others engaged in similar work is a critical component for support and mutual development. However, creating a learning space which encourages formation of a community of practitioners, particularly outside of formal class time, does not happen without careful, deliberate planning.

Applying Communities of Practice

In what follows, I use the concept of communities of practice to examine how I addressed the specific pedagogical, departmental/disciplinary, and technological sustainability challenges of setting up and administering the Design Center. My intention was to create a learning space that supported development of new media literacies through hands-on projects, and to do so in a way that attended to the contextual constraints and stakeholder concerns within which the Design Center is situated. Although the local constraints and approaches discussed here were specific to my institution, the decisions made reflect the kinds of theoretical and practical moves that must be made in many academic environments to create and sustain technological learning spaces.

Communities of Practice on a Pedagogical Level

As a number of scholars (Harralson, 1992; Kobulnicky, 1999; R. Selfe, 2005; Williams, 2002) argued, the development and administration of CCs and lab environments must be driven by pedagogical goals, not technology choices. These goals must not only reflect theoretical trends in our discipline(s) and the academic requirements of our programs, but also knowledge of how learning most productively takes place. The concept of communities of practice is especially well suited to the development of environments devoted to new media literacies because it highlights the value of immersive activity done in collaboration with others of varying backgrounds and experience levels. Such a view of learning assumes that "information stored in explicit ways is only a small part of knowing," and that instead, "knowing involves primarily active participation in social communities" (Wenger, 1999, p. 10). Wenger suggested the following:

> What does look promising are the inventive ways of engaging students in meaningful practices, of providing access to resources that enhance their participation, of opening their horizons so they can put themselves on learning trajectories they can identify with, and of involving them in actions, discussions, and reflections that make a difference to the communities that they value.
>
> (p. 10)

These assumptions about learning fit particularly well with development of new media literacies because such practices are often most productive when students can engage with others in genuine projects and contexts. In such situations, as learners work to negotiate their technology and media options to best fit a particular rhetorical situation, interaction with others for discussion, support, and reflection is critical. Also important in this concept is the idea that learning, in part, is self-directed. Learners follow their own interests, developing their practices in relation to what they want and need to know.

One of the biggest pedagogical challenges in helping students to develop new media literacies is that these practices often require far more time, experience, and interaction than is available in a typical 50-minute, 3-day-a-week classroom setting. Although instructors can and do provide theoretical frameworks, instructional support, and inventive assignments to push students' learning, classroom environments often lack the kinds of intense, ongoing interaction with mutually engaged others that technology-rich learning requires, in other words, formal instruction is important, but competency with new media literacies generally requires extensive time for experimentation, trial and error, and multiple iterations.

For these reasons, the Design Center was an exciting opportunity not only to build a formal instructional space but also to create an environment that extended the new media practices students developed through their coursework. The Design Center had to function, in part, as a classroom space, but its more remarkable and productive possibilities laid in opportunities for informal and collaborative learning outside of structured class time. It provided a unique situation for students to develop a community of practice around new media literacies, and to use this to collaborate and build from the expertise of one another.

To begin shaping the Design Center based on these assumptions about learning, I developed two strategies for supporting new media literacies. First, as I worked with my RPC colleagues to revamp or develop courses that integrated theory and practice of communication design and new media, I considered ways to use the Design Center for extending the experience of students beyond the classroom setting. Second, I began soliciting extracurricular projects that would allow students to gain further hands-on experience through internships and consultancy opportunities. My goal was to use these strategies to build a culture of sustained interest and participation in new media design. I wanted to create an environment where students and faculty could engage in design activities for a variety of projects, share ideas, questions, and solutions to technological and rhetorical problems, and generally develop a sense of community for digital media practitioners at all levels of expertise.

As part of a curricular makeover to update our program and to continue its relevance to the profession, my RPC colleagues and I re-envisioned our communication design courses, such as Document Design, and developed additional offerings such as Multimedia Theory and Production and Design for Page and Screen. These courses were a good fit for the new media resources of the Design Center because they also allowed for the introduction of research and theory on new media, as well as direct instruction in and application of design and technological skills. In these courses, our pedagogical goals focused on helping students to develop rhetorical and aesthetic practices for examining and creating a variety of print and digital texts and for analyzing their effects on users/audience members. Students read widely on issues of multiliteracies (e.g., Cope & Kalantzis, 2000; Lankshear & Noble, 2003; The New London Group, 2000; C. Selfe, 2004), rhetorics of multimodality and new media (e.g., Kress, 2003; Kress & van Leeuwen, 2001; Manovich, 2001) and design in technical communication (e.g., Kostelnick & Roberts, 1997; Shriver, 1996). We introduced various technologies as a means for exploring the ideas of these readings in practice and for developing materials to accomplish particular projects' communicative objectives. The resulting student projects, including interactive tutorials, audio documentaries, informational Web sites, and more demonstrated the range of student interests and the pedagogical value of integrating theory and practice in a collaborative environment. Although the courses themselves did not always develop the kinds of communities of practice I envisioned, they provided a foundation of new media knowledge and social relationships among students on which to build.

In planning how the Design Center could support and extend the classroom-based new media learning of our students. I needed to consider issues of access, community-building, and participant investment in the space. With no funding available to pay for staffing, the Design Center was originally opened only when supervised by myself or two graduate assistants (assigned to departmental technology duties for 4 hours per week). One of the ways I addressed this time restriction was to offer open access to any user willing to undergo a short training session and to offer their assistance to other users when they were in the Design Center.[2] This volunteer system not only expanded access for all users but also encouraged participants to develop a sense of responsibility for the Design Center. This sense of investment by students is key from a community of practice perspective because participants need to determine ways of interacting that serve their needs and interests rather than having this imposed externally. During training, I encouraged volunteers to see their interaction with other users as valuable to their own new media competencies, as well as to the: knowledge base of the community as a whole. I also shared my pedagogical vision of the Design Center with them in the hope that they too would help to create a community of people committed to exploring new media from multiple perspectives. Finally, I held regular meetings with graduate assistants, volunteers, and interested Design Center users to seek their Input on technology upgrades, possible workshop topics, and various usage issues. To strengthen students' commitment to the space it was important that they had a voice in how the Design Center was run and what resources were available to them.

What has been an encouraging result of these efforts is evidence of a forming community of practice and of students using their experience to help others accomplish their own new media goals. I have observed current and former students and volunteers teaching Design Center users how to do everything from editing digital images in Photoshop, to creating multimodal podcasts, to developing digital portfolios for job searches. Although some of this work concerned technical issues, a majority of these interactions also included consideration of the rhetorical appropriateness of specific content, the communicative pros and cons of various media options, and considerations of how the materials would be experienced by their intended audiences. In the future I hope to see even more of these informal interactions as they demonstrate the ways in which the Design Center is working to extend the new media learning of students beyond the classroom. It also illustrates how an informal learning community can help participants develop their expertise in direct relation to their needs and interests through collaboration with other practitioners.

As the Design Center began to see expanded use and formation of a community of practice, my next pedagogical strategy was to begin accepting client-based consultancy work. Such projects provide excellent opportunities for engaging students in the situated practice of new media development because they can learn to respond in creative and rhetorically sophisticated ways to the dynamic needs and interests of variable contexts, audiences, and clients. Furthermore, with genuine rhetorical situations for their communication products, development processes of such projects not only offer students occasions for engaged participation in design, but also contexts in which they can collaborate with others as they learn. Communities of practice develop as experienced and novice practitioners participate in both the acts of production and the social relations in which that work is situated. The outcome for all community members is not learning of discrete technology or communication skills, but development of improvisational practices for negotiating the unique demands of each situation (Lave & Wenger, 1991, 97).

Among the first client-based projects the Design Center undertook were a digital video project for a campus-wide alcohol awareness initiative, a series of interactive lessons for emergency medical technicians (EMTs) done in conjunction with the county medicai director, a Web site on research about Native American women leaders, and an audio archive project for *La Sociedad para las Artes'* Southwestern writers readings series. With each of these projects, students (graduate assistants, interns, and volunteers) had to become proficient with all the involved production technologies. They also had to conduct research about the intended audiences and their needs, as well as the ways and contexts in which these materials would be used. With the interactive EMT lessons, for example, students had to learn about the users for these materials (prehospital emergency medical personnel in a semi-rural county) and the setting and technologies with which this material would be used (fire stations throughout the county, often with minimal technology and for the purpose of obtaining continuing medical education credits required for accreditation renewal).

Although each of these projects was challenging to complete outside of traditional semester timelines and without funding to compensate those doing the work, they did provide involved participants with invaluable experience in developing new media for authentic purposes and audiences (and, in some cases, with academic credit for internships). Additionally, because this work was complex and exploratory, it encouraged participants to seek support and input from other practitioners in the community. All students, whether responsible directly for design or those who offer advice from the periphery, benefit from development and discussion of such projects by practitioners.

Communities of Practice on an Interdisciplinary/Intradepartmental Level

Using communities of practice theory was especially helpful in thinking about the Design Center in relation to the academically diverse department within which it is situated. Of particular use is Wenger's (1999) discussion of *negotiation* and his intention with the term "to convey a flavor of continuous interaction, of gradual achievement, of give and take. … Negotiated meaning is at once both historical and dynamic, contextual and unique" (pp. 53–54). This idea works to express the ways in which a disciplinarily diverse departmental community functions over both the short and long term to undertake and construct understandings of new endeavors. As a space intended to support traditional classroom activities, as well as to function on an extracurricular level, the role of the Design Center within the department required (and still requires) negotiation among members of the department about its function and value. Both the reading and the writing of new media differ from the kinds of texts and activities traditionally pursued by English departments and adjusting to the new theoretical and pedagogical approaches of this work takes time to gain acceptance However, critical analytical and composing abilities with new media also share much with work on other kinds of texts and helping colleagues to see this connection is an ongoing and necessary part of integrating media-rich technology environments into departmental contexts. Active negotiation over new media's value, contribution, and connection to disciplinary concerns has to be attended to or there is great risk that such learning is viewed as merely acquiring technical skills.

As part of my attempts to navigate these departmental constraints in setting up the Design Center, I undertook a number of activities aimed specifically at engaging my colleagues. These included writing a policy for the Design Center to outline its function and guidelines for use, holding open houses to introduce the space and its resources to all department members, and conducting informal workshops on software applications that could be of use for pedagogical and scholarly projects. With each of these activities my intention was to help my colleagues understand how the space and resources might contribute to their own scholarly endeavors, as well as to see the academic potential new media work has for students from all disciplines.

Collaborating with other learners as they negotiate the value of multimodal components for a given project as well as engaging in the activities necessary to compose and analyze these texts are major goals for the Design Center. To this end, I wrote a vision and policy statement that was intended to establish priorities and guidelines for use. Directed toward department faculty and graduate student users, the policy begins with the following statement:

> The overarching goal for the Center is to offer multimedia technologies, development resources, and instructional support for English Department graduate students interested in creating multimodal texts for varied audiences. Through coursework and student-run consultancy projects, it immerses learners in authentic communicative, expressive, and creative activities by providing an environment that combines direct instruction and theoretical inquiry with practice-based approaches. It provides opportunities for production and research collaboration across disciplinary, university, community, and industry boundaries. Through this outreach, students work on projects that provide situations for learning to respond in creative and rhetorically sophisticated ways to the dynamic needs and interests of variable contexts and audiences.

Through this policy I wanted to establish an agenda for teaching, learning, and supporting new media literacy that incorporated a situated, community-oriented approach in all activities undertaken there. Additionally, another central goal of this policy was to help my colleagues (and my promotion and tenure committee) understand how approaching the work in this way would encourage learning that was relevant and valuable to our students. As numerous passing conversations and mailroom questions indicate, some of my traditionalist colleagues still have difficulty seeing the Design Center as a learning space (rather than a service center) with numerous possibilities for connections between reading, writing, and the integration of technology and new media. Producing and distributing this policy was an opportunity to demonstrate the potentials of new media literacy and to provide theoretical background on the approaches suggested earlier. This policy was a first step in attempting to shape an environment in which students not only gain collaborative experience creating new media materials for authentic rhetorical situations, but in which other faculty have an opportunity to consider how new media might be integrated into their own teaching and scholarly work.

After drafting this policy, seeking input from RPC colleagues, and revising. I submitted the policy to the faculty for approval and made a short presentation about it at one of our monthly department meetings. Although I would not characterize the short ensuing discussion as especially vigorous, the policy and presentation afforded an opportunity to talk about the pedagogical and disciplinary value of reading and writing new media. The policy and presentation themselves were likely less important than the avenues they opened for future conversations. Writing and presenting this policy statement provided a platform on which to engage in negotiation within my departmental community about the pedagogical value of new media and the role the Design Center could play in our teaching and research practices. What I have come to realize is that this negotiation was (and still is) as much about helping my colleagues to see how new media literacy fits within writing studies as it is about understanding and addressing their concerns and ideas. As Wenger (1999) suggested, "the negotiation of meaning is a productive process, but meaning is not negotiated from scratch. Meaning is not pre-existing, but neither is it simply made up" (p. 54). What this means for building new media learning environments is that while we must attend to the theoretical and pedagogical assumptions of writing studies, we must also make space for a range of alternative disciplinary views and for discussion of how these spaces will function in practice.

A second strategy in drawing on community of practice theory with departmental members was to hold a series of open houses and informal technology workshops. These outreach events invited participation of graduate students and faculty by helping newcomers to new media and the Design Center see possibilities for their own diverse academic and professional interests. Holding open houses, voluntary workshops, and other events provides a low risk way for stakeholders not involved through coursework or scholarly background to consider how new media might benefit them and to gain some basic background in knowing where to start.

In the beginning, these events focused on the set-up of the space, basic familiarity with the equipment (especially for those new to Macs), and software for manipulating images for inclusion in multimodal (though largely print-based) texts. I realized, however, that these events drew largely on existing users rather than functioning to expand the community. As a result, I talked with faculty and students about their needs and interests and tried to develop workshops that reflected these concerns. One resulting shift I made was from providing general demonstrations of graphic design and HTML-editing software to focusing specifically on creating content for online learning. As first-year writing and undergraduate technical communication courses were recently required to have a WebCT component, many instructors were frustrated with their inability to adapt provided templates or to create their own. Although much of the early work in these sessions did not involve the kind of multimodal, new media work I had envisioned for the Design Center, this began to change as participants grew more comfortable with integrating technology with their communicative and pedagogical intentions. Members of this growing community began to experiment with incorporating images, audio, and video into their materials and relying on one another for support in figuring out how to do it. As instructors hear positive feedback from their students about the role this content plays in their learning and course experiences, interest in these workshops has continued to increase. More importantly, these participants have become more frequent Design Center users, contributing their knowledge and drawing on the experience of other community members.

Communities of Practice and Sustainability

A final consideration in designing new media learning environments is planning for sustainability of both the technology and the community that uses it. As R. Selfe (2005) contended,

"Those of us who honestly believe in the computer–literacy linkage must help each group [students, faculty, and administrators] understand the exciting possibilities" (16). After all, he argued, to build a sustainable culture of support requires the active collaboration of many stakeholders, not just a few individuals (33). Similarly, Williams (2002) argued the following:

> Those of us who administer computer classrooms realize very soon after assuming our positions that if we want to be as flexible as possible and meet as many pedagogical needs as possible, we cannot do it all. … We realize, then, that while our job ostensibly is to help students and faculty learn to use the technology as a communication and writing tool, doing that job requires a whole host of dependent technological and management work to maintain and enable the tools.
>
> (344)

What both Selfe and Williams pointed to is the need for ongoing engagement and support of a wide range of stakeholders in order to sustain and extend initial efforts to develop technological learning spaces. Communities of practice theory is applicable to this need because it highlights the ways in which participants decide collaboratively on what matters to their interests and needs. In Wenger's (1999) words, such an approach "value[s] the work of community building and make[s] sure that participants have access to the resources necessary to learn what they need to learn in order to take actions and make decisions that fully engage their knowledgeability" (10). In other words, creating a sustainable environment that supports new media learning requires the necessary technologies as well as a flexibility in structure to accommodate the interests and directions of new and continuing users.

To apply this community-sustaining approach to the Design Center, I wanted to encourage other faculty and students to make connections to these efforts, even if their expertise was not directly tied to new media. It was critical to the long-term sustainability of the Design Center that departmental stakeholders could see collaborative and interdisciplinary opportunities for their involvement. Each of the external projects discussed above is a direct outgrowth of this commitment. For example, the audio archive project was a collaboration between professional communication and creative writing faculty chat served to make a wealth of analog recordings accessible to a larger public. The Web site on Native American women leaders was the result of a graduate student's research interests and collaboration with a faculty member in government. The project provided the student with an opportunity to explore a range of media options for sharing auditory, visual, and textual data in a way that was appealing to a broad audience. And beyond client-based projects, I have talked with other departmental faculty about using the resources of the Design Center for courses in hypertextual literature, book making, and medieval rhetoric and manuscripts. Without providing for these kinds of diverse uses, spaces such as the Design Center run the risk of withering from lack of support. Not only does planning for flexibility pay off for users in the diversity of connections and directions they pursue but it also helps to provide justification for the large financial expenditures required to maintain and update these spaces.

Related to this issue of financial sustainability for technology and new media centers is the need to seek external funding through either consultancy-based work or grants. Such client-based projects provide valuable experience for students as well as offer the potential for revenue and thus technological sustainability. In an ever-changing technological environment, the costs of updating and staying current with new media hardware and software is a constant challenge. While I am not advocating a commoditized approach to education, I am suggesting that by working with campus and community clients to create relevant communicational materials, both students and technology spaces can benefit. Rather than trying to create a for-profit venture, the idea is to undertake pedagogically and educationally suitable projects that have the added incentive of providing minimal financial support for technological maintenance. Although external projects require additional time and planning to manage, they contribute substantially to the development of a productive learning community. They afford students the opportunity to develop their new media practices within the context of real-world constraints and to build the knowledge and experience of the community as a whole.

Conclusion: Looking Toward the Future

The concept of communities of practice provides a number of avenues for shaping pedagogical, departmental, and sustainable approaches to technology learning spaces for reading and writing new media. Although these theories do not dictate specifics for teaching students the literacy practices necessary for working with new media, they do offer guidance on creating an environment conducive to productive learning conditions. As Lave and Wenger (1991) argued, "A learning curriculum consists of situated opportunities ... for the improvisational development of new practice" (97). In other words, creating new media learning centers is not about implementing a discrete set of activities, but rather about developing a context in which students can explore new media literacies in ways appropriate to the unique situation, purpose, and audience of a given project. Additionally, by engaging in this work with other learners at all levels of expertise, students can help to create a community of practitioners who are committed to experimenting with a variety of new media literacies.

There is no doubt that the Design Center is still in its early stages of development. We need to develop more curricula that introduce and support students as they learn new media literacy practices and integrate this into our programmatic requirements. We need to involve a larger portion of the faculty in making use of the Design Center and its resources for their own pedagogical and research interests. We need to continue developing structures that compensate faculty and students for the time and effort required for new media work. We need to continue cultivating relationships with local organizations and industries to contract for materials designed and produced by the Design Center. And lastly, we need to be proactive in searching and applying for grants to create new media communications. Managing the logistics of these goals is demanding in terms of academic scheduling, the flow of students through their programs, the constant need for experienced/interested students, and the tenure and promotion considerations for affiliated faculty.

While the challenges for implementing, sustaining, and growing new media technology environments necessarily entails mediation of pedagogical, programmatic, technological, and institutional factors by faculty directors, the communities of practice approach outlined here provides a starting point for this work. By developing a theoretical and pedagogical framework for structuring such centers, communicating this vision to stakeholders, and actively inviting project-based participation from both faculty and students, new media design spaces offer excellent opportunities for academic, rhetorical, creative, and critical development. Coursework, client-based projects, and interdisciplinary collaboration provide students with invaluable experience in negotiating audience, information, design, and media variables. Additionally, because such work is complex and exploratory, it encourages collaboration and the development of communities of practitioners as a means to support technology learning and project completion. Although the process of realizing the goals outlined here is a challenging one, the educacional potentials that centers far new media design hold for our students make the effort worthwhile.

Notes

1. This space is devoted to graduate student use for several reasons. These include limited physical space in the Design Center, curricular specializations in rhetoric, professional communication, and creative writing at the graduate level only, and original funding sources from the department and college which restrict use to students in our department's programs. Additionally, undergraduate students from other departments and colleges who take courses from us that potentially utilize new media (e.g. technical communication, first-year writing, film studies, etc.) have unrestricted access to departmental and campus-wide computer labs. Although these spaces lack many professional-level new media resources, they do offer software and technology sufficient for undertaking a range of new media projects.
2. This training program is an adaptation based loosely on Richard Selfe's lab consultant program at the Center for Computer-assisted Language Instruction established at Michigan Technological University in which I worked and taught as a graduate student. See his book, *Sustainable Computer Environments: Cultures of Support in English Studies and Language Arts* (2005), for a more detailed account of this approach.

References

Albers, Michael, & Cargile Cook, Kelli. (2002). Scouts, trailblazers, pioneers: Settling the computer classroom [Guest editor's column]. *Technical Communication Quarterly, 11* (3), 245–250.

Bernhardt, Stephen. (1989). Designing a microcomputer classroom for teaching composition. *Computers and Composition. 7*, 93–110.

Cope, Bill, & Kalantzis, Mary. (Eds.). (2000). *Multiliteracies: Literacy learning and the design of social futures.* New York: Routledge.

Dean, Christopher, Hochman, Will, Hood, Carra, & McEachern, Robert. (2004). Fashioning the emperor's new clothes: Emerging pedagogy and practices of turning wireless laptops into classroom literacy stations. *Kairos: Rhetoric, Technology, Pedagogy, 9*(1). Retrieved December 10, 2007, from http://kairos.technorhetoric.net/9.1/binder2.html?coverweb/hochman_et_al/intro.html

Duffelmeyer, Barb Blakely. (2003). Learning to learn: New TA preparation in computer pedagogy. *Computers and Composition, 20*, 295–311.

Gee, James Paul. (2003). *What video games have to teach us about learning and literacy.* New York: Palgrave.

Hanks, William F. (1991). Foreword. In Jean Lave and Etienne Wenger (Eds.), *Situated learning: Legitimate peripheral participation* (pp. 13–24). Cambridge: Cambridge University Press.

Harralson, Dave. (1992). We've barely started—and we've already done it wrong: How not to start a computer-assisted writing classroom. *Computers and Composition, 9*, 71–77.

Kobulnicky, Paul J. (1999). Critical factors in information technology planning for the academy. *Cause/Effect, 22*(2). Retrieved September 15, 2006, from http://www.educause.edu/ir/library/html/cem/cem99/cem9924.html

Kostelnick, Charles, & Roberts, David. (1997). *Designing visual language: Strategies for professional communicators.* Needham Heights, MA: Allyn & Bacon.

Kress, Gunther. (2003). *Literacy in the new media age.* New York: Routledge.

Kress, Gunther, & van Leeuwen, Theo. (2001). *Multimodal discourse: The modes and media of contemporary communication.* London: Arnold.

Lankshear, Colin, & Noble, Michele. (2003). *New literacies: Changing knowledge and classroom learning.* Buckingham, UK: Open University Press.

Lave, Jean, & Wenger, Etienne. (1991). *Situated learning: Legitimate peripheral participation.* Cambridge: Cambridge University Press.

Manovich, Lev. (2001). *The language of new media.* Cambridge, MA: MIT Press.

New London Group. (2000). A pedagogy of multiliteracies: Designing social futures. In Bill Cope & Mary Kalantzis (Eds.), *Multiliteracies: Literacy learning and the design of social futures* (pp. 9–57). New York: Routledge.

Paré, Anthony. (2002). Keeping writing in its place: A participatory action approach to workplace communication. In Barbara Mirel & Rachel Spilka (Eds.), *Reshaping technical communication: New directions and challenges for the 21st century* (pp. 57–73). Mahwah, NJ: Erlbaum.

Selber, Stuart A. (2004). *Multiliteracies for a digital age.* Carbondale: Southern Illinois University Press.

Selfe, Cynthia L. (2004). Students who teach us: A case study of a new media text. In Anne Wysocki, Johndan Johnson-Eilola. Cynthia Selfe. & Geoff Sirc (Eds.), *Writing new media: Theory and applications for expanding the teaching of composition* (pp. 43–66). Logan: Utah State University Press.

Selfe, Richard J. (2005). *Sustainable computer environments: Cultures of support in English studies and language arts.* Cresskill, NJ: Hampton Press.

Shriver, Karen A. (1996). *Dynamics in document design: Creating text for readers.* New York: Wiley.

Wenger, Etienne. (1999). *Communities of practice: Learning, meaning, and identity.* New York: Cambridge University Press.

Williams, Sean. (2002). Why are partnerships necessary for computer classroom administration? *Technical Communication Quarterly, 11,* 339–358.

Yancey, Kathleen Blake. (2004). Made not only in words: Composition in a new key. *College Composition and Communication, 56,* 297–328.

19
All Things to All People
Multiliteracy Consulting and the Materiality of Rhetoric

David M. Sheridan

Although it would be easy to pursue this trail of possible resources further, identifying an assortment of sites and texts that could be used to teach tutors HTML and JavaScript, or how to use Microsoft FrontPage or Netscape Composer, we should stop and think carefully about how far we are really willing to go down this path in our quest to create "better" writing tutors. Ultimately, we have to ask ourselves whether it is really the writing center's responsibility to be all things to all people.

—(Pemberton, 2003, 21)

I Just Want to Scan!

At the MSU Writing Center, we have been, at various times, plagued by a recurring nightmare. The details change, but the basic narrative remains the same. It goes something like this. A client makes an appointment with one of our Digital Writing Consultants (DWCs). When the client arrives, the DWC leads with our usual set of questions meant to generate a rich profile of the rhetorical situation: Tell me a little bit about your project? Who is your audience? What is your purpose? What opportunities are there for using images, sounds, and words to reach your audience and achieve your purpose more effectively? But the client waves his or her hand through the air impatiently, cutting these questions short. He or she pulls out a photograph and hands it to the DWC, saying, "I just need to scan this."[1]

This scenario is scary because it seems to suggest a reductive model for our Writing Center that we daily labor against, a model that reduces us to something even worse than a grammar lab: a tech lab where students come not to engage in critical conversations about communication, but to perform mindless technical procedures. Our skills-drills nightmare has been replaced by a point-and-click one.

There are institutional dimensions of this nightmare as well. If we offer basic how-to technical instruction, we are potentially encroaching on turf staked out by other units on campus. Our claim that tech work is within our mission rests on our belief that technology is inextricably linked to communication. We point out that communication increasingly occurs in spaces different from the 8.5" X 11" sheets of paper used for traditional essays. Increasingly, communication is accomplished through websites, digital slide presentations, digital videos, and desktop-published documents. Communicators are asked to avail themselves of the affordances associated with these media and modes, which means that communication is not limited to written words, but is the result of the "interanimation" (Blakesley, 2004, 112) of semiotic elements: written and spoken words, moving and still images, graphs, diagrams, illustrations, animations, layout elements, and music and other sounds. Even composing in print media increasingly means using sophisticated desktop-publishing applications to create intensely designed, multimodal documents. The sociocognitive processes of composing in and for these "new media" are inextricably linked to technical processes. Supporting the one without the other makes no sense.

But what happens when student composers want to separate out their technical concerns and anxieties? What happens when—impatient with our questions about their rhetorical situations and the messages they hope to communicate—they try to pressure us into providing basic technical tutorials? Surely something is wrong.

Or is it? The field of composition and rhetoric is currently reconfiguring itself in ways that malte this "I just want to scan" nightmare less scary. In this chapter, I would like to locate the preparation and practice of multiliteracy (ML) consultants within the field's newly reinvigorated concern for rhetoric as a material practice. It should be noted from the start, however, that an emphasis on the material and the corporeal is a retreat from neither the cultural nor the symbolic. As John Fiske (1992) observes, "the material, the symbolic, and the historical are not separate categories but interactive lines of force" (155).

In focusing on rhetoric's materiality, I mean to emphasize two fundamental and related considerations. First, I mean to focus on the specific material forms that rhetorical compositions take: black words on a white sheet of paper, black words and color photographs on a glossy sheet of cardstock, a PDF document posted on a website, and so on. The message "Stop the war" can be communicated through a photograph depicting the horrors of war, through a set of bullet points on a PowerPoint slide, or through a research-intensive essay. These differences in material form are not incidental (see e.g., Blair, 1999; Kress & van Leeuwen, 2001).

Second, I wish to emphasize the material processes involved in rhetorical production, reproduction, and distribution. We are used to treating the "composing process" as a sociocognitive activity, but until recently, we have not paid much attention to it as a process that involves technologies, media, and other material resources. Still less have we thought about what happens after the composition is complete. The question of how a given composition will get to its audience is often elided (see Trimbur, 2000; Yancey, 2004).

Multiliteracy Consulting at MSU

Before I begin my proposal for materializing consulting practices, I want to briefly describe the context that facilitated my thinking about these issues. My views have been shaped primarily by my experience at MSU's Writing Center, where I worked as a graduate student (1998–2000) and then as associate director (summer 2003–summer 2006), codirector (fall 2006), and director (spring and summer 2007).[2] MSU's Center has a long history of experimenting with emergent technologies and media (DeVoss, 2002; Thomas, Hara, & DeVoss, 2000). The Center supports a wide range of practices related to technology, new media, and multimodal communication. DWCs provide one-on-one support for composers working on multimodal compositions, including webpages, desktop-published documents, digital animations, and digital videos. We also offer a series of "Communicating Effectively with …" classroom presentations ("Communicating Effectively with Poster Displays," "… with the Web," "… with Designed Print Documents," "… with PowerPoint," "… with Digital Video"). In addition to working with students, we contribute to faculty development through workshops on integrating new media into the writing-intensive classroom and through one-on-one support. Faculty make appointments with DWCs to work on their own websites or PowerPoint presentations, and they meet with administrators to plan assignments and syllabi. To support all of this work, the MSU Writing Center provides a technology-rich space for composers, investing not only in computers, but also scanners, cameras, microphones, and other media-production tools. As laptops have become increasingly powerful, the Center has successfully applied for funding for laptop carts, which has increased our capacity in numerous ways. The perspectives I articulate in this chapter have been thoroughly shaped by this environment.

Materiality and the Labor of Rhetorical Production

When I said a moment ago that the message "Stop the war" can be communicated through a variety of modes and media, I was engaging in a bit of sleight of hand. These various semiotic options have not all historically been treated under the domain of rhetoric, and they have not all been available to nonspecialist composers. Writing and speaking have been considered "general skills," but producing video content or complex print documents have long been relegated to highly trained specialists: cinematographers, photographers, audio engineers, graphic designers, illustrators, typesetters, lithographers, and so on. The "writer," in this system, is only contributing a fraction of the labor that results in effective communication.

But systems for dividing labor are always in a state of flux. This division of labor is not inevitable, but rather the result of complex cultural and technological realities. At one time, those who could afford to do so might have written documents longhand and paid someone else to type them. The ease of word processing, however, has altered this practice. Digital technologies are bringing about radical changes in the way we think about and practice the labor or rhetorical production. As John Trimbur (2004) points out, "distinctions between author, designer, and printer are starting to collapse" (269). Likewise, Kress and van Leeuwen (2001) observe that, although multimodal texts may have previously required multiple composers with different specialties,

> in the age of digitization, the different modes have technically become the same at some level of representation, and they can be operated by one multi-skilled person, using one interface, one mode of physical manipulation, so that he or she can ask, at every point: "Shall I express this with sound or music?", "Shall I say this visually or verbally?", and so on.
>
> (2)

The ensemble of specialists who have historically divided up the tasks of media production in previous eras is converging into a new kind of rhetor, a nonspecialist who controls a dizzying variety of semiotic resources (words, graphs, music, photographs, video clips, colors, interactive components) and who is not just responsible for the production of rhetorical compositions, but who is also responsible for overseeing their circulation, including their *reproduction* and *distribution.*

This reconception of the rhetor, however, runs counter to some of our more entrenched constructions of the academy and the work that goes on there. The academy is populated by scholars and researchers whose job it is to have ideas and write about them. The labor of giving that writing material form, of typesetting and design, as well as the labor of delivering that writing to an audience has historically been viewed as nonacademic labor. Not only does this reconception of the rhetor involve a "collapse" in the division of labor associated with rhetorical production, it also involves a critique of traditional hierarchies that privilege the symbolic expression of ideas in words over the material labor of production. Writing has always had what John Trimbur (2000) calls its "blue-collar side" (189); we have all experienced the work of photocopying, collating, and binding a complicated report for a large group of people; we have all had to deal with paper jams and misfeeds. New media production, however, can involve rather more work of this sort: digitizing video, burning DVDs, managing files on a networked drive—and, yes, scanning photographs.

"For post-process theorizing to rematerialize writing," John Trimbur (2004) writes, "we need to recast the figure of the composer and its essayist legacy—to see writers not just as makers of meaning but as makers of the means of producing meaning out of the available resources of representation (262). Trimbur cites Walter Benjamin's conception of the "author as producer." Benjamin rejects the reliance on academically privileged forms, claiming that

> Significant literary work can only come into being in a strict alternation between action and writing: it must nurture the inconspicuous forms that better fit its influence in active communities than does the pretentious, universal gesture of the book—in leaflets, brochures, articles, and posters. Only this prompt language shows itself actively equal to the moment.
>
> (cited in Trimbur, 2004, 265–266)

Given this embrace of multiple material forms, one suspects that Benjamin would have loved the idea of multiliteracy centers.

Stuart Selber helps us confront the transformation from composer to producer that Trimbur describes. Selber (2004) argues for a "professionally responsible" approach to computer literacy. Conceding that "most approaches to functional literacy are utterly impoverished." Selber sets forth "parameters" that "position functional literacy as essentially a social problem, one that involves values, interpretation, contingency, communication, deliberation, and more" (498). Within this more sophisticated framework, Selber argues that the writing classroom should include opportunities to learn the technical quotidian that many writing instructors—adopting what Haas and Neuwirth (1994) have called a "computers are not our job" attitude (325)—would rather ignore. Noting that "students reach technological impasses when they lack the computer-based expertise needed to solve a writing or communication problem," Selber suggests that "a functionally literate student resolves technological impasses confidently and strategically" (493).

Likewise, DeVoss, Cushman, and Grabill (2005) explore the notion of author as producer in their recent discussion of the relationship between infrastructure and communication. Claiming that "infrastructures are absolutely necessary for writing teachers and their students to understand if we hope to enact the possibilities offered by new-media composing" (16), they offer the following list of infrastructural components:

- computer networks
- network configurations
- operating systems, computer programs, interfaces, and their interrelatedness
- network, server, and storage access rights and privileges
- courses and curricula
- the existence and availability of computer classrooms
- decision-making processes and procedures for who gets access to computer classrooms
- the design and arrangement of computer classrooms
- time periods of classes
- availability of faculty, students, and spaces outside of set and scheduled class times
- writing classifications and standards (e.g., what is writing; what is good writing)
- metaphors of computer programs; metaphors people use to describe programs; metaphors people use to describe their composing processes
- purposes and uses of new-media work
- audiences for new-media work, both inside and outside the university. (21–22)

Embodying the interrelatedness of the material, the cultural, and the historical that Fiske references in the passage quoted earlier, in this list, the technical intermingles with the human, the material with the social and symbolic.

DeVoss, Cushman, and Grabill (2005) observe that new-media composers are asked to make "a number of 'nonwriting' decisions related to audience and the technological and rhetorical needs of that audience (e.g., bandwidth, screen size, media form and function)" (30). Noting that "few scholars offer frameworks for understanding the spaces within which such compositions are produced" (37), they provide an "infrastructural framework," which

> creates a tool for composers to navigate the systems within and across which they work, creates a moment for reflection and change within institutional structures and networks, and creates a framework for understanding writing that moves forward our understandings of how composing and compositions change shape within the complex dynamics of networks.
>
> (37)

A multiliteracy center can be both a part of the infrastructure that supports new media composing and a space where students critically reflect on and learn to exploit the infrastructural resources available to them. It can facilitate a professionally responsible approach to functional computer literacy. In short, it can be a site that welcomes the author as producer. From this perspective, the nightmare of the student who comes to the multiliteracy center to scan is no longer scary. Trimbur (2000, 2004), Selber (2004), and DeVoss, Cushman, and Grabill (2005) recover the importance of supporting the material dimensions of composing as both crucial to the concerns of communicators in a digital age and as legitimate points of focus for those charged with the teaching of writing.

Of course, while the scanner's lamp slides across the photograph, an ML consultant might happen to ask the student composer a few questions, such as, "How do you plan to use this image in your project?" and "What does this image mean to you?" ML consultants know how to be sneaky. More important, as the student looks around the Center and meets consultants, she or he will hopefully see the value of returning for additional support and may be more receptive to these richer conversations.

Multiliteracy Consulting and Expertise

With this orientation toward materiality, we are better able to confront the question of how to prepare ML consultants for their daily work. What do ML consultants need to know if they are to support the material processes of production, reproduction, and distribution that new media rhetors must engage in? What kinds of expertise and skill sets should they possess? How does materiality ask us to transform our models of consulting?

These questions raise the vexed issue of expertise as it relates to the collapse in the division of rhetorical labor. Communicators in the age of new media are able to choose from a broader range of semiotic assets, and they are asked to control a broader range of material processes, including processes of reproduction and distribution. This convergence, however, does not imply that communicating with words is the same as communicating with photographs or that a paper-based essay is no different from a digital video. Different materials require different literacies and different competencies. On any given day, ML consultants might find themselves helping clients lighten and color-correct digital photographs, offering "readings" of video clips that clients have embedded in their websites and manipulating type in complex and precise ways to accommodate a graphical element in a poster. Here is the hard truth of the matter: ML consultants *are* asked to be "all things to all people." They are asked to be photographers, graphic designers, illustrators, web coders, technicians, programmers, as well as teachers and meaning makers.

To confront rhetoric as a material practice, ML consultants need three fundamental literacies: (a) ML consultants need to understand the particular material forms that rhetorical compositions can take, as well as the material contexts in which they circulate: a web page that combines photographs, words, and design elements or a chapbook that combines charts, graphs, and illustrations. ML consultants need to be sensitized to the affordances and constraints of these material forms. This set of literacies allows ML consultants to engage clients in generative conversations about their work, suggesting at times that it might be useful to offer an interpretation of a photograph, while at other times it might be more productive to explore the placement of the photograph within the larger composition. But the clients with whom ML consultants work want to do more than just talk and plan. They will want to produce and publish their compositions. Therefore, (b) ML consultants will need to understand the material processes of production and distribution, which means (in part) helping clients negotiate the technical processes demanded by the specific material forms within which they are working. But a brilliant rhetorician who is also an expert technician will not necessarily be able to create rich learning environments for the clients with whom she or he works. For that, (c) ML consultants will need pedagogical literacies. This means knowing when to offer an interpretarían of a video clip or illustration and when to invite clients to articulate for themselves the messages they are hoping to communicate. It means knowing when to ask a question ("Can you remember the protocol for naming an HTML file?") and when to provide direction ("HTML file names should not contain space characters"). It means knowing when to impose a firm structure on a session and when to invite the client to play freely with the available technologies.

As I describe them here, multiliteracy center workers sound like super-consultants. They possess an amazing array of literacies and capacities related to everything from desktop publishing to video editing. They can provide a sophisticated rhetorical analysis of a photograph or poster as easily as of an academic essay. They know just how to use their knowledge and skills to create the richest possible learning environment for the student composers they serve. Asking for such consultants might seem like asking for the sun, moon, and stars if it were not for the fact that we are all increasingly asked to have these skills in our public, professional, and personal lives—and if it were not for the fact that I have been fortunate enough to have worked at writing centers over the past 10 years alongside many ML consultants who have more than met these expectations and have collectively provided effective support for thousands of clients working on new media projects.

Preparing ML Consultants: the Problem of Reductionism

If I am right, and to some extent ML consultants need to be all things to all people, how does a multiliteracy center develop a cohort of these superconsultants? Clearly, the answer calls for a multifaceted approach. Recruitment strategies are an important piece of the puzzle. In addition to recruiting through long-cultivated connections with language-centered units, we need to develop relationships with folks in graphic design, film and video production, and related units. We need to pay more attention to sections of resumes—like "Technical Skills" or "Computer Experience"—that previously seemed peripheral. Certain experiences that consultants bring to the center—past employment as webmaster, for instance, or serving as layout editor of the high school newspaper—will take on new relevance. Elective classes in web design or video production will become noteworthy (for discussions of recruitment, see Selfe, 2005; Sheridan, 2006).

Most ML consultants I have worked with have entered the writing center with a foundation of relevant literacies developed through professional, academic, and personal experiences. They might be amateur film-makers, for instance, or might have served as web designers for a local nonprofit organization. At MSU, except for a few special cases, our DWCs are generalist consultants as well. They have been prepared alongside their "analog" peers and have extensive experience creating rich learning opportunities for students working on traditional academic writing. They have a deep understanding of the fundamental philosophy of the writing center, including our desire to "produce better writers, not [just] better writing" (North, 1984, 438). Preparing DWCs. then, rarely means starting from ground zero. Instead, the challenge is to supplement the existing experiences and competencies that consultants bring to the project of multiliteracy consulting by creating additional opportunities for guided observation, practice, reading, and dialogue.

Having said this, I want to turn to what I perceive to be one of the key challenges of preparing ML consultants. Faced with the overwhelming task of having to be all things to all people, it is easy to become reductive. Most of us who consider ourselves amateur web designers, for instance, are familiar with the various "rules" or "tips" that proliferate on the web: "avoid clutter," "use a consistent color scheme," and "never use popup windows." I would argue that such tips serve an important function. To find our way in territories of communication that are new to us, we need concrete help that guides us through decisions, especially when those decisions need to be made quickly and expediently.

But there are risks involved here as well. Relying on easy formulas risks communicating to learners an impoverished understanding of multimodal rhetoric. Writing centers and the field of composition have had to fight against a rule-based approach to the teaching of writing. We have labored to help students and the broader public see that writing cannot be distilled into simple forms and formulas or rules for "correctness," but is a complex set of social, cultural, and cognitive practices learned over time through embedded experience. Expanding our work to include multimodality should not be an occasion to reintroduce a skills-drills approach.

Designer Nick Ragouzis (1997) addresses this issue, noting that, "in our concern to help amateur designers to avoid making the worst web design mistakes, we forge and promulgate a body of rules—those familiar lists of Dos and Don'ts that we find in countless texts on 'good' web design." But this "rule-making ... is insidious" because "it encourages the notion that one can do an acceptable design without wrestling with the difficult questions raised by the total context in which a site exists." If we "are really concerned with educating amateur designers to do good design on the web, then we should teach them design ... not give them lists of silly rules." I do not know whether Ragouzis has ever taught writing, but I find the goal of getting communicators to "wrestle with the difficult questions raised by the total context" a nice encapsulation of what I try to do in the writing classroom and what I try to prepare my writing consultants to help their clients do in the Writing Center. The question, then, is how do we preserve the richness and complexity of wrestling with multimodal rhetoric as an embedded practice (as Ragouzis suggests, we should be wary of shortcuts).

I offer four answers to this question: (a) make a point of mapping out the knowledge domains that relate to multimodal rhetoric, (b) seek out heuristic rules rather than algorithmic ones, (c) have conversations about lots of examples of multimodal compositions, and (d) adopt a project-based approach.

1. *Map the Terrain.* Rather than turning hastily to a reductive set of rules and formulas, we might ask ML consultants to be strategic surveyors of relevant knowledge domains and paradigms. They might not have time to add a second major in video production, for instance, but they can map out the broad contours of this field, gaining a broader sense of the possibilities and options available to them and the clients they serve. This became clear to me at a recent presentation by Susan Hilligoss. In her talk at the 2004 CCCC, Hilligoss (2004) handed out a map of visual rhetoric that consists of useful categories, each illustrated by key works. Hilligoss' categories include "Vision research," "Visual culture," "Information graphics and visualization," "Visual rhetoric and visual argument," and "Formalist theory." Although some might find this gesture unremarkable, I would argue that, for those of us new to visual rhetoric, important learning happens as we interrogate this map. We learn, for instance, that visual studies is not just another word for graphic design. We are introduced to different paradigms that approach the problem of visuality from different directions. Hilligoss offers us a taxonomy of possibilities. Without this broader sense of the range of possibilities, we cannot make informed choices about what to focus on at any given moment as we work on our own professional development or as we work with other composers. Our choices will be capricious rather than strategic.

2. *Seek out heuristic rules instead of algorithmic ones.* Mike Rose (1980) makes a distinction between an "algorithmic" rule (which tends to be rigid, authoritative, and

limiting) and a "heuristic" rule (which tends to be flexible, open ended, and genera-tive). We should seek out heuristic rules as we confront multimodality. Many of us, for instance, have found Robin Williams' *Non-Designer's Design Book* useful. Rather than offering a series of tips or formulas, Williams presents four principles of design: contrast, repetition, alignment, and proximity (CRAP). Using simple examples, Wil-liams demonstrates the power and elasticity of these principles, which can be applied to a variety of modes and media: from brochures to web pages. I am sure some pro-fessional graphic designers would object to the simplicity of Williams' presentation, but her principles have a greater heuristic value than the "avoid clutter" variety that composers new to multimodality often turn to in desperation.

3. *Have conversations about lots of examples.* Discussing examples of multimodal rhetoric allows ML consultants to apply diverse approaches to multimodality. For Instance, one of my favorite texts to use in ML consultant preparation is the famous *We Can Do It!* poster that depicts Rosie the Riveter. The goal is to inquire not just into our interpretation of this text, but into the various frameworks that enable the interpretive process. We systemati-cally rotate through different approaches, interrogating what each one reveals and hides.

> *Rhetoric*
> What was the rhetorical context that gave rise to this text?
> What exigencies was it meant to address?
> Who was its intended audience?
> What strategies of persuasion are employed?
> What considerations of the ethics of persuasion need to be considered?
> Is this propaganda?
>
> *Graphic Design and Illustration*
> How are space, typography, and color used in this composition?
> What visual style does this depiction take (e.g., photoistic, pen and ink, watercolor)?
> What tools were used to produce this composition?
>
> *Cultural Studies*
> What do we need to know about the cultural and historical context for this composition in order to approach it productively?
> How are gender, class, race, and national identity evoked?
> What considerations of the ethics of representation need to be accounted for?

We take a similar approach with a wide range of multimodal artifacts: photographs, video clips, websites, and desktop-published documents.

To foreground the challenges that multimodal rhetoric as a set of rhetorical prac-tices introduces into writing center practice, I have developed a set of "thought puz-zles" like the following:

> Max is working on a brochure for a student organization and comes to the writ-ing center for help. The organization values diversity and Max is determined to select a photograph for the cover of the brochure that visually communicates

this. But he's been unable to find a suitable photograph and asks his consultant to show him how to make a composite photo. He hopes to insert a student of color from one photo into another photo that includes only white students. What kind of conversation should the digital writing consultant have with Max? Would it change things if Max possessed a photo similar to the proposed composite, but couldn't use it because it was technically deficient (dark, blurry, small, etc.)?[3]

Narratives like this one help us go beyond issues of design and communication to discuss pedagogical options, providing a chance for ML consultants to generate ideas for shaping the conversation in productive ways.

4. *Take a project-based approach.* The most important learning occurs as ML consultants work individually and collaboratively on their own multimodal projects. Depending on the situation, they identify projects that are relevant to their personal or professional goals, such as a digital portfolio, or identify projects that will contribute to the mission of the Writing Center, such as a new brochure or a new resource for our website. Projects are selected so that consultants can experience and reflect on a wide range of practices related to multimodal rhetoric within an authentic rhetorical context that includes an exigency, purpose, and audience. Again, we systematically name for each other the different frameworks that can be applied to our projects, asking how a graphic designer might critique our layout, how a cultural studies critic might analyze a photograph that we have chosen, or how a usability specialist might test the site's architecture.

As we go about this project-based work in the technology-rich space of the Writing Center, we are working to establish a professional community of collaboration and inquiry. We rely on each other as resources for solving technical and rhetorical problems. We critique each other's compositions and share examples of compositions that make productive comparisons with our own. This working community of what Richard Selfe calls "advanced literacy practitioners," I would argue, more than a set of skills or a body of knowledge, is the basis for our practice.

Multiliteracy Consulting

If kairos refers, as James Kinneavy (1986) says, to "the appropriateness of the discourse to the particular circumstances of the time, place, speaker, and audience involved" (84), our approach to consulting at the Writing Center is fundamentally kairotic. As writing consultants, our job is to facilitate conversations in which students explore the possibilities for rhetorical success that can be realized through a negotiation between themselves as rhetorical agents and the context in which they are writing. This means, among other things, that we do not adapt simplistic notions of "good" writing or "bad" writing. A poem might be wildly successful within the context of a literary journal and its readers, but completely useless as a memo. To make the concept of kairos accessible to writers, we use the acronym Mode/medium/genre. Audience, Purpose, Situation (MAPS). MAPS is an easy way to remind ourselves and our clients of fundamental contextual variables that converge into an opportunity for rhetorical intervention at any given moment in time.[4]

As several writers have observed, a kairotic approach can be productively extended to include not just traditional rhetorical choices about diction, style, and argumentative strategy, but also choices about mode and medium and the technologies associated with them (see Sheridan, Ridolfo, & Michel, 2005; Shipka, 2005; Yancey, 2004). For instance, a composer who hopes to communicate a message to a particular neighborhood might decide that a more traditional paper-based newsletter hand-delivered to residents would be more effective than a beautiful web page in a neighborhood whose residents lacked access to the Internet. Even a client who has been assigned a particular medium (e.g., a PowerPoint to accompany an oral presentation) typically has a number of choices to make about material issues, such as mode: Should the composition include photos, charts, illustrations, music? What color schemes, layout schemes, and fonts should be used? Like choices about diction and argumentative strategy, we feel that such choices should be informed by the audience of and purpose for the rhetorical intervention. One audience might find that strategic integration of music would be engaging, whereas another might feel it distracting (for related discussions, see Griffin 2007; Thomas, Hara, & DeVoss, 2007).

When clients come to the Writing Center seeking help with a web page, digital video, or other multimodal project, we typically begin by developing a rich profile of their rhetorical situations. We initiate conversations away from the computer, which allows us to have a generative discussion without the distraction of keyboards, mice, and urgently flashing cursors Thomas, Hara, & DeVoss, 2000). We tell clients that we will be able to serve them more effectively if we begin by gathering important information about their assignment, their project, and the context in which they are working. We ask to see assignment sheets; we ask clients to identify their target audience and rhetorical purpose.

But with a material understanding of kairos operating, new issues arise. To this end, I have adapted MAPS so that it focuses attention on materiality, expanding the contextual variables to include, for instance, media of delivery and media of distribution (see Table 19.1). Moreover listing these factors along both X and Y axes helps to establish relationships between factors, reminding us that these variables are not isolated and independent, but instead form a network of interconnected concerns. At the intersection of mode and purpose, for instance, we are reminded of concerns about which modes will best address the rhetorical purpose of the project. A student exploring the way the dominant culture reinforces gender stereotypes, for instance, might decide that a visual mode is important because it will allow the student to directly address images found in print and TV advertisements. Looking at the intersection of mode and media of delivery would help remind us to select media that are appropriate for visual modes; for instance, a digital slide presentation might be more effective than paper because it negates the need for color printers. But how will this slide show get to its intended audience? We are reminded of this question at the intersection of audience and media of distribution, which forces us to inquire into whether it is practical to distribute a digital slide show to our intended readers. If our only audience is the teacher, we can burn the slide show on a disk and hand it to him or her during class. But if we need to get the show to 100 end users who are dispersed in space, CDs might not be practical. We might turn to e-mail, but that decision will lead to other decisions about keeping the file size of the presentation small enough. I designed this table not for clients, but for ML consultants, wanting to provide them with a tool for keeping track of the web of relationships that can inform their conversations with the student composers who come to them for support.

	PURPOSE AND EXIGENCY	AUDIENCE	GENRE	MODES
GENERAL	What is this rhetorical intervention meant to accomplish? What problems is this composition meant to address?	Who is (are) the target audience(s) for this composition? what values, attitudes, behaviors and beliefs do I need to take into account as I plan for this rhetorical intervention?	What are the constraints and affordances of available genres? (e.g., argumentative essay, memo, poem, letter, jeremiad, etc.)	What are the constraints and affordances of available modes? (e.g., aural, visual, kinesthetic, multimodal.)
PURPOSE AND EXIGENCY	—	What is the relationship between my target audience and my purpose? what role does my audience play in addressing my exigency? what beliefs, dispositions, and actions should my rhetorical intervention facilitate in order to address my exigency? What audiences does my purpose suggest that I address?	What genres will best address my exigency? (e.g., a personal narrative might be suited to establishing an emotional connectiion with an audience, but might not be suited to communicating more general information necessary for informed action.)	What modes will best address my exigency? (e.g., if I'm trying to address the negative images people associate with the city of Detroit, perhaps a visual mode is appropriate.)
AUDIENCE	See Audience > Purpose	—	What genres will be most effective with my target audience? What genres do they value? Are they familiar with? (e.g., if I try to introduce a neighborhood group I'm helping to start through an academic essay, I might alienate my non-academic audience.)	What modes will be most effective with my target audience? Do they value? (e.g., some audiences might be pre-disposed to appreciate multimodal rhetoric while others might privilege the written word.)
GENRE	See Genre > Purpose	See Genre> Audience	—	What confluence of genre and mode will be most effective in my rhetorical situation? (e.g., if my goal is detailed

Figure 19.1 Maps Heuristic, Reconfigured to Reflect Materiality.

MEDIA OF DELIVERY	MEDIA OF DISTRIBUTION	INFRASTRUCTURAL RESOURCES	RELATION TO OTHER TEXTS
What are the constraints and affordances of available media of delivery? (e.g., website, DVD, paper, etc.)	What are the constraints and affordances of available media of distribution? (e.g., e-mail, WWW, telephone, radio, TV, direct mail, community bulletin boards, etc.)	What infrastructural resources are available to me? What technologies, raw materials? How much time? What knowledge and competencies do I possess? What knowledge and competencies do potential collaborators possess?	How does this composition relate to other texts that I have created or might create? That others have created or might create?
What MoDe of delivery will best adddress the problem that I'm hoping to address? (e.g., if I'm trying to raise initial interest in a neighborhood group, perhaps a tri-fold brochure is appropriate.)	What MoDi will best address my exigency? (e.g., if I want to raise initial interest in a neighborhood group, perhaps walking door-to-door with my brochure is an effective way of getting my message to my audience.)	What do I discover when I assess my infrastructural resources from the perspective of purpose and exigency? (e.g., to produce a photo-intensive website, I might need a camera, computer, web editing application, etc.)	How can an orchestrated use of multiple texts (written by me or by others) help me achieve my purpose? (e.g., my brochure might include a URL to a website that contains more detailed information.)
What MoDe will be most efective with my target audience? What MoDe do they value? What attitudes and dispositions do I need to consider? (e.g., some audiences might value a video while other audiences might privilege the book as a form.)	What MoDi will be most effective with my target audience? What MoDi do they value? (e.g., if the most salient fact about my audience is that they are intensive web users, web-based distribution might be appropriate.)	What infrastructural resources does my audience have access to? (e.g., if my audience doesn't have access to the Internet, a webpage isn't going to be an effective medium.)	What relationship does my audience have with other texts that I and others might create? (e.g., If I put the URL to a website on a brochure, will my audience visit it?)
What confluence of MoDe and genre will be most effective in my rhetorical situation? (e.g., A long analytical	What confluence of MoDe and genre will be most effective in my rhetorical situation?. (e.g., if my goal is to	How to infrastructural resources available to me and my audience support my choice of genre?	What other genres might be placed into service to complement the affordances of my chosen genre?

Figure 19.1 continued

	PURPOSE AND EXIGENCY	AUDIENCE	GENRE	MODES
				deconstruction of negative images associated with the city of Detroit, perhaps an analytical essay combined with visuals like photographs would be appropriate.)
MODE	See Mode > Purpose	See Mode > Audience	See Mode > Genre	—
MEDIUM OF DELIVERY	See MoDe > Purpose	See MoDe > Audience	See MoDe > Genre	See MoDe > Modes
MEDIUM OF DISTRI-BUTION	See MoDi > Purpose	See MoDi > Audience	See MoDi > Genre	See MoDi > Modes
INFRA-STRUC-TURAL RESOURCES	See IR > Purpose	See IR > Audience	See IR > Genre	See IR > Modes
RELATION TO OTHER TEXTS	See Texts > Purpose	See Texts > Audience	See Texts > Genre	See Texts > Modes

Note: For the purposes of this table, *Media of Delivery* refers to the end experience of the reader, whereas *Media of Distribution* refers to the way a composition gets to a reader. I might, for instance, know that my target audience is mostly faculty at research universities who have

Figure 19.1 continued

MEDIA OF DELIVERY	MEDIA OF DISTRIBUTION	INFRASTRUCTURAL RESOURCES	RELATION TO OTHER TEXTS
essay is appropriate might be easier to read on paper than on a computer monitor.)	distribute a detailed written analysis printed on paper, perhaps email-ing a PDF or mailing a hardcopy would be best.)		(e.g., a website might have links to both a white paper and a fact sheet.)
What medium will support the modes that you have identified as appropriate? What modes does your chosen medium lend itself to? (e.g., the Web can support visual and aural modes; at the same time, the Web demands certain attention to the visual in ways that other media might not.)	What medium of distribution will support your preferred modes? What modes does your preferred medium lend itself to? (e.g., a brochure might accommodate photographs and design elements—visual modes —but it might be more difficult to distribute than a website.)	What kinds of modes do the available raw materials, technologies, and skills enable? What kinds of resources do your chosen modes require?	What modes might be enabled by past or future texts that I or others might create? (e.g., a white paper with lots of written information might be coupled with a website that contains more iconic information.)
—	What media of distribution will enable my chosen media of delivery (and vice versa)?	What infrastructural resources are needed to enable my chosen modes? What modes to available resources suggest?	How can other texts that I or others might create complement my chosen mode?
See MoDi > MoDe	—	What MoDi are enabled by available resources? What resources are needed to enable the MoDi I've chosen?	How can various media enable the distribution of other texts that I or others might create?
See IR > MoDe	See IR > MoDi	—	What other texts might available resources enable?
See Texts > MoDe	See Texts > MoDi	See Texts > IR	—

access to free laser printing and high-speed Internet connections. I might distribute an article to them by e-mailing a PDF. The medium of distribution is the Internet and computer, but (if my readers print the PDF and read from hardcopy) the medium of delivery is a paper.

Figure 19.1 continued

In the initial stages of our session, we often ask clients to sketch the layout of their website. We have photocopied on oversized paper the image of an empty web browser—scaled to 800 X 600 pixels (a common monitor resolution)—so that clients can create quick mock-ups of their sites. For digital video projects, we might suggest that clients storyboard their projects. Although analogous to outlining in the sense that it involves the representation of ideas through time, storyboarding is different in the way that maps out the sequence and simultaneity of multiple semiotic resources (visual and aural elements) in a way that does not have a ready analogue in traditional academic essays.

If clients are at the beginning of their composing process when we meet with them, some of the decisions they make during this session will dictate possibilities and limitations that they will have to live with for the remainder of their projects. For instance, most clients, as experienced consumers of web content, can describe the layout and semiotic elements of a website, but many cannot guess the constellation of software applications that might be used to produce such a composition. They see the use of specialized fonts, graphical elements, and animations configured in a precise spatial relationship, but they do not understand the amount of time and the level of expertise that went into creating the page. They rely on us to guide them through this planning process. If, for instance, they follow our recommendation to begin by mocking up their site in Photoshop, they will have to live with the consequences of that decision. One set of the consequences arises from the fact that, although Photoshop can create the graphical elements of a website and is often used as a tool for mocking up a layout, it is not the best application for producing the working HTML version of the page. This means that clients will have to plan for the extra step of converting their mockup to an HTML format in order to complete their project. My point here is not to rehearse the technical details of Photoshop and HTML, but to give a sense of the literacies that ML consultants rely on as they help clients negotiate the material processes of production.

Conclusion

My goal in this chapter has been to locate multiliteracy consulting within the field's evolving understanding of rhetoric as a material practice. This undersanding can provide a coherent basis for a set of practices that at other momenters in history writing centers might not have viewed as writing." To many, it may still feel strange that writing centers even if they are received as multiliteracy centers, should take on the mission of supporting communication that happens through photographs, music: clips, and other media elements, in addition to the written word. It may feel even assume responsibility for providing technical support: scanning photographs, digitizing video, recording voiceovers, and coding CSS style sheets web pages. If we accept, however, that rhetoric is a material practice as well as a sociosymbolic one, these extensions of our work may seem less strange. Indeed, they may seem essential.

Notes

1. The earliest documentation of this problem at MSU that I can find is in an unpublished paper that Mark Hara wrote as an Undergraduate Writing Consultant in MSU's Writing Center in 1997 (see Thomas, Hara & DeVoss, 2000).
2. The current director of the MSU Writing Center is Trixie G. Smith.
3. This scenario was inspired by an actual case in which an African-American student was inserted into a photograph being used for a college recruitment brochure (see Durhams, 2000). (See also Dragga, 1993, 84–85.)
4. Patricia Stock, founding director of the MSU Writing Center, introduced the use of MAPS to our practice. She was introduced to this approach by Bernard, van't Hul, former director of composition at the University of Michigan (Stock, 2001).

References

Blair, Carole. (1999). Contemporary U.S. memorial sites as exemplars of rhetoric's materiality. In Jack Selzer & Sharon Crowley (Eds.), *Rhetorical bodies* (16–57). Madison: University of Wisconsin Press.

Blakesley, David. (2004). Defining film rhetoric: The case of Hitchcock's *Vertigo*. In Charles A. Hill & Marguerite Helmers (Eds.), *Defining visual rhetorics* (111–134). Mahwah, NJ: Erlbaum.

DeVoss, Dànielle. (2002). Computer literacies and the roles of the writing center. In Paula Gillespie (Ed.), *Writing center research: Extending the conversation* (167–185). Mahwah, NJ: Erlbaum.

DeVoss, Dànielle, Cushman, Ellen, & Grabill, Jeff. (2005). Infrastructure and composing: The *when* of new-media writing. *College Composition and Communication. 57* (1), 14–44.

Dragga, Sam. (1993). The ethics of delivery. In John Frederick Reynolds (Ed.), *Rhetorical memory and delivery: Classical concepts for contemporary composition and communication* (79–95). Hillsdale, NJ: Erlbaum.

Durhams, Sharif. (2000, September 20). UW-Madison doctors photo to stress diversity. *Milwaukee Journal Sentinel.* Retrieved May 13, 2008 from http://www2.jsonline.com:80/news/metro/sep00/uw20091900a.asp

Fiske, John. (1992). Cultural studies and the culture of everyday life. In Lawrence Grossberg (Ed.). *Cultural studies* (154–173). New York: Routledge.

Griffin, Jo Ann. (2007). Making connections with writing centers. In Cynthia L. Selfe (Ed.), *Multimodal composition: Resources for teachers* (153–166). Cresskill, NJ: Hampton.

Haas, Christina, & Neuwirth, Christine M. (1994). Writing the technology that writes us: Research on literacy and the shape of technology. In Cynthia L. Selfe & Susan Hilligoss, (Eds.), *Literacy and computers: The complications of teaching and learning with technology* (319–355). New York: MLA.

Hilligoss, Susan. (2004). *Handout for* A matter of course: Toward advanced studies in visual rhetoric San Antonio, TX: CCCC.

Kinneavy, James L. (1986). *Kairos*: A neglected concept in classical rhetoric. In Jean Dietz Moss (Ed.), *Rhetoric and praxis: The contribution of classical rhetoric to practical reasoning* (79–105). Washington, DC: The Catholic University of America Press.

Kress, Gunther R., & van Leeuwen, Theo. (2001). *Multimodal discourse: The modes and media of contemporary communication.* London: Arnold.

North, Stephen M. (1984). The idea of a writing center. *College English, 46* (5), 433–446.

Pemberton, Michael. (2003). Planning for hypertexts in the writing center … or not. *Writing Center Journal. 24* (1), 9–24.

Ragouzis, Nick. (1997). *Misbegotten rules of web design.* Retrieved May 13, 2008, from http://www.enosis.com/resources/misbegot.html

Rose, Mike. (1980). Rigid rules, inflexible plans', and the stifling of language: A cognitivist analysis of writer's black. *College Composition and Communication, 31* (4), 389–401.

Selber, Stuart A. (2004). Reimagining the functional side of computer literacy. *College Composition and Communication, 55* (3), 470–503.

Selfe, Richard J. (2005). *Sustainable computer environments: Cultures of support in English studies and language arts.* Cresskill, NJ: Hampton.

Sheridan, David M. (2006). Words, images, sounds: Writing centers as multiliteracy centers. In Christina Murphy & Byron Stay (Eds.), *The writing center director's resource book* (339–350). Mahwah, NJ: Erlbaum.

Sheridan, D. M., Ridolfo, J., & Michel, A. J. (2005). The available means of persuasion: Mapping a theory and pedagogy of multimodal public rhetoric. *JAC, 24* (5), 803–844.

Shipka, Jody. (2005). A multimodal task-based framework for composing. *College Composition and Communication, 57* (2), 277–306.

Stock, Patricia. (2001). Toward a theory of genre in teacher research: Contributions from a reflective practitioner. *English Education. 33* (2), 100–114.

Thomas, Sharon, Hara, Mark, & DeVoss, Dànielle. (2000). In James A. Inman & Donna N. Sewell (Eds.), *Taking flight with OWLs: Examining electronic writing center work* (65–73). Mahwah, NJ: Erlbaum.

Trimbur, John. (2000). Composition and the circulation of writing. *College Composition and Communication. 52* (2), 188–219.

Trimbur, John. (2004). Delivering the message: Typography and the materiality of writing. In Carolyn Hands (Ed.), *Visual rhetoric in a digital world: A critical sourcebook* (260–271). Boston: Bedford.

Williams, Robin. (1994). *The non-designer's design book.* Berkeley: Peachpit Press.

Yancey, Kathleen Blake. (2004). Made not only in words: Composition in a new key. *College Composition and Communication. 56* (2), 297–328.

Permissions

Chapter 1 was originally published in Lanham, Richard A. (Ed.). *The Electronic Word: Democracy, Technology, and the Arts*. Chicago, IL: University of Chicago Press, 1994. 29–52. Reprinted by permission of University of Chicago Press.

Chapter 2 was originally published in Manovich, Lev. *The Language of New Media*. Cambridge, MA: Massachusetts Institute of Technology, 2001. 21–48. Reprinted by permission of The MIT Press.

Chapter 3 was originally published in *A Pedagogy of Multiliteracies: Designing Social Futures*, 66.1 (1996):60–92. Reprinted by permission of *Harvard Educational Review*.

Chapter 4 was originally published in Bolter, Jay David & Richard Grusin. *Remediation: Understanding New Media*. Cambridge, MA: Massachusetts Institute of Technology, 1998. 53–62. Reprinted by permission of The MIT Press.

Chapter 5 was originally published in Trimbur, John. "Multiliteracies, Social Futures, and Writing Centers." *Writing Center Journal*. 20.2 (2000): 28–32. Print. Reprinted by permission of *Writing Center Journal*.

Chapter 6 was originally published in Kress, Gunther & Theo Van Leeuwen. *Multimodal Discourse: The Modes and Media of Contemporary Communication*. Oxford, UK: Oxford U|niversity Press, 2001. 45–65. Reprinted by permission of Oxford University Press.

Chapter 7 was originally published in Mayer, Richard E. *Multimedia Learning*. New York, NY: Cambridge University Press, 2001. 41–62. Reprinted by permission of Cambridge University Press.

Chapter 8 was originally published in Hayles, Katherine N. *Writing Machines*. Cambridge, MA: Massachusetts Institute of Technology, 2002. 35–45. Reprinted by permission of The MIT Press.

Chapter 9 was originally published in Pemberton, Michael A. "Planning for Hypertexts in the Writing Center . . . or Not." *Writing Center Journal*. 21.1 (2000): 9–24. Print. Reprinted by permission of *Writing Center Journal*.

Chapter 10 was originally published in Hocks, Mary E. & Michelle R. Kendricks (Eds.). *Eloquent Images: Word and Image in the Age of New* Media. Cambridge, MA: Massachusetts Institute of Technology, 2003. 117–136. Reprinted by permission of The MIT Press.

Chapter 11 was originally published in Selber, Stuart A. "Rhetorical Literacy: Computers as Hypertextual Media, Students as Reflective Producers of Technology." *Multiliteracies for Digital Age*. Carbondale, IL: Southern Illinois University Press, 2004. Print. Reprinted by permission of Southern Illinois University Press.

Chapter 12 was originally published in DeVoss, Danielle Nicole, Ellen Cushman, and Jeffrey T. Grabill. "Infrastructure and Composing: The *When* of New-Media Writing." *College Composition and Communication*. 57.1 (2005): 14–44. Print.

Chapter 13 was originally published in Lessig, Lawrence. *Remix: Making Art and Commerce Thrive in the Hybrid Economy*. New York, NY: The Penguin Press. 2008. Print. Reprinted by permission of The Penguin Press, a division of Penguin Group (USA) Inc.

Chapter 14 was originally published in Carpenter, Russell. "Writing Center Dynamics: Coordinating Multimodal Consultations." *Writing Lab Newsletter*. 2009. 11–15. Print. Reprinted by permission of *Writing Lab Newsletter*.

Chapter 15 was originally published in Lunsford, Andrea A. and Lisa Ede. "Among the Audience: On Audience in an Age of New Literacies." *Engaging Audience: Writing in an Age of New Literacies*. Eds. Angela Gonzalez, Elizabeth Weiser, Brian Fehler. NCTE, 2009. 42–72. Print. Reprinted by permission of National Council Teachers of English.

Chapter 16 was originally published in Selfe, Cynthia L. "The Movement of Air, The Breath of Meaning: Aurality and Multimodal Composing." *College Composition and Communication*. 60.4 (2009): 616–663. Print. Reprinted by permission of *College Composition and Communication*.

Chapter 17 was originally published in McKinney, Jackie Grutsch. "New Media Matters: Tutoring in the Late Age of Print." *Writing Center Journal*. 29.2 (2009): 28–51. Print. Reprinted by permission of *Writing Center Journal*.

Chapter 18 was originally published in Sheppard, Jennifer "Creating a Center for Communication Design." *Reading and Writing New Media (RAW)*. 2010. 323–341. Print. Reprinted by permission of Hampton Press, Inc.

Chapter 19 was originally published in Sheridan, David M. "All Things to All People: Multiliteracy Consulting and the Materiality of Rhetoric." *Multiliteracy Centers: Writing Center Work, New Media, and Multimodal Rhetoric*. 2010. 75–107. Print. Reprinted by permission of Hampton Press, Inc.

Index